Christian Promitzer, Klaus-Jürgen Hermanik,
Eduard Staudinger (Eds.)

(Hidden) Minorities

Studies on South East Europe

edited by

Prof. Dr. Karl Kaser

(Graz)

vol. 5

LIT

(HIDDEN) MINORITIES

Language and Ethnic Identity between Central Europe and the Balkans

edited by

Christian Promitzer, Klaus-Jürgen Hermanik,
Eduard Staudinger

LIT

Cover Picture: Michael Wienzek and Bernhard Mühr

Printed with support of
European Science Foundation (ESF)
Alfred Schachner Gedächtnisfonds (ASGF)

Bibliographic information published by the Deutsche Nationalbibliothek
The Deutsche Nationalbibliothek lists this publication in the Deutsche Nationalbibliografie; detailed bibliographic data are available in the Internet at http://dnb.d-nb.de.

ISBN 978-3-643-50096-0

A catalogue record for this book is available from the British Library

Krotenthallergasse 10/8
A-1080 Wien
Tel. +43 (0) 1-409 56 61
Fax +43 (0) 1-409 56 97
e-Mail: wien@lit-verlag.at
http://www.lit-verlag.at

LIT VERLAG Dr. W. Hopf
Berlin 2009
Fresnostr. 2
D-48159 Münster
Tel. +49 (0) 2 51-620 32 22
Fax +49 (0) 2 51-922 60 99
e-Mail: lit@lit-verlag.de
http://www.lit-verlag.de

Distribution:
In Germany: LIT Verlag Fresnostr. 2, D-48159 Münster
Tel. +49 (0) 2 51-620 32 22, Fax +49 (0) 2 51-922 60 99, e-Mail: vertrieb@lit-verlag.de

In Austria: Medienlogistik Pichler-ÖBZ GmbH & Co KG
IZ-NÖ, Süd, Straße 1, Objekt 34, A-2355 Wiener Neudorf
Tel. +43 (0) 22 36-63 53 52 90, Fax +43 (0) 22 36-63 53 52 43, e-Mail: mlo@medien-logistik.at

In Switzerland: B + M Buch- und Medienvertriebs AG
Hochstr. 357, CH-8200 Schaffhausen
Tel. +41 (0) 52-643 54 30, Fax +41 (0) 52-643 54 35, e-Mail: order@buch-medien.ch

In the UK by: Global Book Marketing, 99B Wallis Rd, London, E9 5LN
Phone: +44 (0) 20 8533 5800 – Fax: +44 (0) 1600 775 663
http://www.centralbooks.co.uk/html

In North America by:

Transaction Publishers
New Brunswick (U.S.A.) and London (U.K.)

Transaction Publishers
Rutgers University
35 Berrue Circle
Piscataway, NJ 08854

Phone: +1 (732) 445 - 2280
Fax: + 1 (732) 445 - 3138
for orders (U. S. only):
toll free (888) 999 - 6778
e-mail: orders@transactionpub.com

Preface

This book is based on the papers and discussions at the workshop "(Hidden) Minorities: Language and Ethnic Identities in the Alpine-Adriatic Region" held in Radenci, Slovenia, on 21-23 March, 2002.[1] Both workshop and book could not have been realised without the financial support of the *European Science Foundation* (ESF). The ESF selected the topic as one of eleven workshops in the field of the humanities funded in that year.

The editors also want to thank the *Austrian Science Fund* (FWF) which during 2001-2004 financially supported the research project P15080 "Hidden Minorities between Central Europe and the Balkans" and made it possible to realise and refine the general results of the workshop. The project was headed by Christian Promitzer (Graz) and conducted in collaboration with Klaus-Jürgen Hermanik (Graz), Marijana Jakimova (Graz), Tanja Petrović (Ljubljana), Eduard G. Staudinger (Graz) and Ivica Šarac (Mostar), all of whom are authors in this reader.

We want furthermore to express our special thanks to the *Scientific Research Centre of the Slovene Academy of Sciences and Arts* (ZRC SAZU), to its director Oto Luthar and his staff who have organised technical and intellectual support for the workshop. Luthar himself and scholars of his institution have written contributions in this volume.

Additional funding was granted by the *Austrian Science and Research Liaison Office in Ljubljana*, headed by Miroslav Polzer, whom we want to thank for his openhearted support.

Books such as this one may have a long history. In our case this history has to do with the fact that none the authors is a native English speaker. Furthermore, we had to organise authors from six countries (Austria, Bosnia and Herzegovina, Bulgaria, Italy, Slovenia and Serbia) and get them to write using a common catalogue of terms. This required a great deal of subsequent reworking of the papers. Therefore we are not only grateful for their participation, but also for their unending patience.

The original English texts were then corrected by Andreas Hemming (Halle/Saale) to whom we feel deeply indepted. Bernhard Mühr from the Institute for Meteorology and Climatic Research at the University of Karlsruhe was generous enough to provide us with a meteorological photograph of clouds hiding the area between Central Europe and the Balkans taken by Michael Wienzek; we considered this image appropriate for the cover of the book.

Our special thanks go to a circle of renowned persons, who gave us their useful and critical comments in the process of refining the concept of hidden minori-

[1] Cf. http://www.esf.org/generic/1363/0009HReport.pdf.

ties. These persons are: Ulf Brunnbauer (Regensburg), Wolfgang Gombocz (Graz), Mirko Križman (Maribor), Robert G. Minnich (Bergen), Albert F. Reiterer (Vienna), Sevasti Trubeta (Berlin), Christian Voss (Berlin) and Nikola Živković (Berlin). We would also like to express our thanks to Biljana Sikimić (Belgrade) who was the first to edit a book on hidden minorities in the Balkans.

We finally want to thank the LIT-Verlag for accepting the reader among its publications and Karl Kaser (Graz) as the editor of the book series for his successful mediation.

Graz, August 2009

Christian Promitzer, Klaus-Jürgen Hermanik, Eduard G. Staudinger

Contents

Introduction

Christian Promitzer, Klaus-Jürgen Hermanik, Eduard G. Staudinger

"(Hidden) Minorities: Language and Ethnic Identity between Central Europe and the Balkans" – the title of this book needs some explanation. The usual procedure would be to start with the first term and then to go on to the subtitle. In view of the peculiarity and ambiguity of the subject, however, it seems appropriate to take the opposite route and approach the topic by way of inductive reasoning: We will start with the geographic setting, then we will explain the issue of language and ethnic identity within this framework and, consequently, we will deal with the central issue of *hidden minorities*.

1. Between Central Europe and the Balkans – imagination and construction of an intermediate area

The recent enlargement of the European Union has shown that reinterpretations of European values are underway. Even today, imaginations of Europe are no longer the monopoly of think tanks from the Western part of the continent; and this process will continue, when other new members join the EU in the coming years. Within this process of the crumbling of ideological borders we can also observe that residual memories of a common space of East Central Europe until the First World War are readdressed. We can discern *intermediate areas* (*Zwischenräume* in German) characterised by common elements extending beyond the borders of nation states across the continent.[1] The stimulation of such memories of common spaces and their adaptation to the democratic mind of the 21st century have to do with symbolic geographies; they are furthermore apt to be appropriated and misused by various intellectuals and political thinkers.[2] Such concepts are often hierarchical and have the purpose to incorporate those, who are at least "partly similar with oneself", as can be seen in the use of the term *Mitteleuropa*. At the same time the distinct difference to those, who are treated as being *totally different*, like Russia and the Balkans, is reinforced.[3]

With respect to the relationship and the differences between the Balkans on the one hand and the West and the centre of Europe on the other, we may observe that discussions concentrate on the otherness of the Balkans and its place in

---

[1] Cf. Philipp Ther/Holm Sundhaussen (eds.): Regionale Bewegungen und Regionalismen in europäischen Zwischenräumen seit der Mitte des 19. Jahrhunderts. Marburg 2003 (= Tagungen zur Ostmitteleuropa-Forschung 18).

[2] Cf. Maria Todorova: Imagining the Balkans. New York – Oxford 1997, pp. 140-160.

[3] Cf. e.g. Karl Kaser/Dagmar Gramshammer-Hohl/Robert Pichler (eds.): Europa und die Grenzen im Kopf. Klagenfurt – Vienna – Ljubljana 2003 (= Wieser Enzyklopädie des Europäischen Ostens 11).

Europe.[4] Much will need to be done until the traditional colonial and hierarchical character of this relationship will be overcome. In any case we should avoid to overemphasise and exaggerate differences if we want to grasp what Europe *is* and *could be* in all its richness.[5]

Discussions concentrating explicitly on the commonalties between Central Europe and the Balkans are rather scarce, however. There have been some attempts to constitute an intermediate area between these two parts of Europe. It would include north-eastern Italy, eastern and southern Austria, south-western Hungary, Slovenia, Croatia and maybe the Vojvodina. This regional focus itself, of course, bears the danger of being only a further construction based on a hierarchical and even colonialist scheme. It is dependent on how rigidly or loosely the borders of Central Europe and the Balkans are defined by the *symbolic geographies* of the West. The latter are a concomitant of the respective historical and strategic situation. In the first half of the 1990s, when the Yugoslav wars were raging, the Balkans seemed to be immeasurable; "Central Europe", in the narrower sense of the meaning, had to defend its values and borders. At the time, quite many persons ominously recalled the saying that the Balkans extended even to the outskirts of Vienna. Today, however, with EU-enlargement on the agenda, geographical borders of the Balkans are for the most part clearly to be defined (extending to the banks of the rivers Danube and Sava); at the same time, those of Central Europe are tending to loosen. Thus, for example, Croatia became, and maybe even Bosnia-Herzegovina, Montenegro and Serbia will become candidates for integration.[6] We had that already: During the Third Reich the intermediary space between Central Europe and the Balkans was called South-East Central Europe and had a specific function in the Nazi economy of replenishment ("Ergänzungswirtschaft").[7] After the hiatus of communist rule in this part of

---

[4] Cf. the disscussion between Holm Sundhaussen and Maria Todorova on that topic: Holm Sundhaussen: Südosteuropa und Balkan: Begriffe, Grenzen, Merkmale. In: U. Hinrichs (ed.), Handbuch der Südosteuropa-Linguistik. Wiesbaden 1999, pp. 27-49; Holm Sundhaussen: Europa balcanica. Der Balkan als historischer Raum Europas. *Geschichte und Gesellschaft* 25 (1999), pp. 626-653; Holm Sundhaussen: Der Balkan: Ein Plädoyer für Differenz. *Geschichte und Gesellschaft* 29 (2003), 608-624; Maria Todorova: Der Balkan als Analysekategorie: Grenzen, Raum Zeit. *Geschichte und Gesellschaft* 28 (2002), pp. 470-492; Maria Todorova: Historische Vermächtnisse als Analysekategorie. In: K. Kaser/D. Gramshammer-Hohl/R. Pichler (eds.), Europa und die Grenzen im Kopf, pp. 227-252; Dietmar Müller: Southeastern Europe as a Historical Meso-region: Constructing Space in Twentieth-Century German Historiography. *European Review of History* 10/2 (2003), pp. 393-408.

[5] Cf. Karl Kaser: Freundschaft und Feindschaft auf dem Balkan. Euro-balkanische Herausforderungen. Klagenfurt – Vienna – Ljubljana 2001, pp. 333-353.

[6] Cf. Christopher Lord (ed.): Central Europe: Core or periphery? Copenhagen 2000; Horst Fassel/Christoph Waack (eds.): Regionen im östlichen Europa – Kontinuitäten, Zäsuren und Perspektiven. Tübingen 2000.

[7] Cf. Hugo Hassinger: Lebensraumfragen der Völker des europäischen Südostens. In: K.H. Diezel/O. Schmieder/H.Schmitthenner (eds.), Lebensraumfragen europäischer Völker, vol. 1. Leipzig 1941, pp. 594-612; Hugo Hassinger: Mitteleuropa, Donaueuropa, Südosteuropa. *Volkstum im Südosten* 3 (1941), pp. 173-176.

Europe, another initiative in this direction – this time based on mutual understanding – was created by establishing the *Alps-Adriatic Working Community*. It was formed when Communist rule already was in crisis. As a regional initiative the working community tried to overcome the ideological bipolarity of that period. After the fall of the Iron Curtain and the demise of Yugoslavia, however, it gradually lost its importance. There have also been attempts to explain the Alpine-Adriatic region as a historical region[8]; but in consideration of its attachment to the ideological and hierarchical notion of "Mitteleuropa", this designation has also to be questioned, too.

It is necessary and an issue of political correctness to put the implicit hierarchical background of definitions aside and to approach this intermediate area *between Central Europe and the Balkans*[9] on equal terms. We could furthermore try to describe this geographical setting as a zone of overlapping cultural areas – and not by absolute cultural frontiers.[10] This will not totally mitigate the danger of essentialism; the idea of an *intermediate area between Central Europe and the Balkans* should be only used as a working model. Its possible function is dependent both on the contents with which it is filled and on the respective historical framework.

2. Nation building, ethnicity and borders – the issue of hidden minorities

What could the contents of the phrase "between Central Europe and the Balkans" be? There has been one issue connecting all of Central Europe and the Balkans throughout the last one and a half centuries – the tendency to interpret collective identities mostly in terms of nationality and ethnicity. Within such interpretations we observe a common sense that nations in the Balkans are rather new, i.e. without history, while those in Central Europe are old and with tradition. A simple illustration can repudiate such assumptions. The Austrian nation is also a rather new one, founded at the same time as the Macedonian one, i.e. at the end of the Second World War. Previously, the Austrians had simply *defined themselves* as Germans, while the Macedonians *were being treated* either as Bulgarians or as Southern Serbs.[11]

---

[8] Cf. Andreas Moritsch (ed.): Alpen-Adria. Zur Geschichte einer Region. Klagenfurt – Ljubljana – Vienna 2001.

[9] Even the word order could be a cause for discussion.

[10] On the dangers of drawing "cultural frontiers" cf. Edgar Hösch: Kulturgrenzen in Südosteuropa. *Südosteuropa* 47/12 (1998), pp. 601-623.

[11] For more on the issues of nation building cf. e.g. Andreas Kappeler (ed.): The formation of national elites. Aldershot et al. 1992 (= Comparative studies on governments and non-dominant ethnic groups in Europe [1850 – 1940] 6); Ernest Gellner: Nationalismus. Kultur und Macht. Berlin 1999; Ulrike v. Hirschhausen/Jörn Leonhard (eds.): Nationalismen in Europa. West- und

We could, secondly, continue with the fact that the Balkans and Central Europe are characterised by a variety of ethnic groups, which did not become nations.[12] Much has been written on ethnic minorities, on their respective situations and on their respective histories. The literature on ethnic minorities, however, is always attached to the narrow frame of a given canon of legally recognised ethnic groups; its focus is always on those who in the last two centuries had the chance to develop their own intellectual elite able to put their claims on the agenda. But how shall we treat those ethnic groups, whose legal status is unsolved and who do not have a representation of their own – groups, who furthermore do not possess of a significant intellectual elite and who are not present in the public? It is this kind of groups we have chosen to designate as *hidden minorities*.

The common background for switching national affiliations and of various ethnic and "hidden" minorities has to be sought in the multiethnic legacy of the Habsburg and Ottoman Empires inherited by the two historical Yugoslav states. While the first Yugoslavia in vain tried to establish itself as an integral nation state, the second Yugoslavia proved doomed to fail because of its inconsequent attempt to constitute itself as a multiethnic state.

This background will be a constant companion of the discussion on issues of *language and identity* in this volume. But its focus will be on those small ethnic groups we just before have addressed as hidden minorities. In the Balkans they were called "ethnographic groups" since the end of the 19th century and they consequently became the domain of – ethnographers.[13] Closer to Central Europe, however, research on these phenomena was marginal; it was conducted mainly as "Sprachinselforschung", a linguistically-orientated approach concentrating on various isolated German minorities outside the coherent German language area. During the Third Reich it was even misused as ideological justification for German predominance in East Central Europe.[14] It would take some time before a modern approach to small ethnic groups would be realised. This is also the credit of the American-Norwegian social anthropologist Robert G. Minnich. In the 1980s he conducted fieldwork among a small, in part still

---

Osteuropa im Vergleich. Göttingen 2001; Nancy Wingfield (ed.): Creating the other. Ethnic conflict and nationalism in Habsburg Central Europe. New York – Oxford 2003.

[12] On the discussion between the differences and commonalties of national and ethnic identities cf. Stefan Troebst: Ethnien und Nationalismen in Osteuropa. *Österreichische Zeitschrift für Geschichtswissenschaft* 5:1 (1993), pp. 7-22; Thanasis D. Sfikas/Christopher Williams (eds.): Ethnicity and nationalism in East Central Europe and the Balkans. Aldershot et al. 1999.

[13] Cf. Christian Promitzer in this volume.

[14] Cf. Ingeborg Geyer: Sprachinseln. Anmerkungen zu Definition und Forschungstradition. In: P. Wiesinger/W. Bauer/P. Ernst (eds.), Probleme der oberdeutschen Dialektologie und Namenkunde. Vorträge zum 100. Geburtstag von E. Kranzmayer. Vienna 1999, pp. 150-170; Wilhelm Fielitz: Das Stereotyp des Wolhyniendeutschen Umsiedlers. Popularisierungen zwischen Sprachinselforschung und nationalsozialistischer Propaganda. Marburg/Lahn 2000 (= Schriftenreihe der Kommission für deutsche und osteuropäische Volkskunde in der Deutschen Gesellschaft für Volkskunde e.V. 82).

Slovene-speaking village in north-eastern Italy, close to the borders with Austria and Slovenia. Minnich avoided the nostalgic reminiscences of a "lost and forgotten minority". Instead, he concentrated on the hegemonic discourse of unity of territory, nation and language and its consequences for a local community. His notion of "Speaking Slovene – being Slovene"[15] proved paradigmatically the general parameters of how to define ethnic boundaries – i.e. through self ascription and through ascription by the outer world.[16]

One of the main lessons one can learn from Minnich is to question the appropriateness and scope of the term ethnicity. Is ethnicity, in its common sense meaning, even applicable for those phenomena that we call hidden minorities? We are aware, that "ethnicity, race and nationality are fundamentally ways of perceiving, interpreting, and representing the social world. They are not things in the world, but perspectives on the world." (Rogers Brubaker)[17]

One thing is for sure, hidden minorities are a special case of distinctive identity constructions on a local level. But how did these identity constructions come into being? The evolving nation state tried to sift out who would form the "core of the nation". It confirmed which groups, after having been assimilated, could also be "with us". Finally, it also had the power to define which groups had categorically to be treated as "the other". But we also have to take the surrounding communities into consideration, and last but not least, even from within the group there could develop the perception that "we" are different.

Such clear-cut constructions of the self and the other did not result in the legal recognition of these groups as ethnic or national minorities however. Within the wide spectrum of options there is "the possibility that groupness may not happen, that high levels of groupness may fail to crystallize [...]".[18] This may be the case because they were too weak and too marginalised to impose such an agenda on the nation state or that there was no manifestation of a common will of the persons and groups concerned. And what is more, an outside scholar may even overestimate the impact of the cultural traits, which make hidden minorities different from their surroundings and from the respective nation state they are living in. In everyday life and in contact with neighbouring communities such differences may only play a secondary role. We should furthermore keep in mind that identity constructions are temporary and tend to

---

[15] Robert G. Minnich: Speaking Slovene – Being Slovene. Verbal Codes and Collective Self-images: Some Correlations between Kanalska Dolina and Ziljska Dolina. *Slovene Studies* 10/2 (1988), pp. 125-147.

[16] Cf. Frederic Barth: Introduction. In: F. Barth (ed.), Ethnic groups and Boundaries: The Social Organization of Cultural Difference. Bergen – London 1969, pp. 9-38. On the continuation of this theoretical discussion cf. Hans Vermeulen/Cora Govers (eds.): The Anthropology of ethnicity. Beyond 'Ethnic groups and boundaries'. Amsterdam 1996, second edition; Hans Vermeulen/Cora Govers (eds.): The Politics of Ethnic Consciousness. New York 1997.

[17] Rogers Brubaker: Ethnicity without Groups. Cambridge (MA) – London 2006, p. 17.

[18] Ibidem, p. 12.

switch, are rather complex and versatile; they are not black-and-white.[19] Or as Rogers Brubaker puts it: "Ethnicity, race, and nation should be conceptualized not as substances or things or entities or organisms or collective individuals [...], but rather in relational, processual, dynamic, eventful, and disaggregated terms."[20]

Having downplayed the possible role of ethnic difference, we still cannot deny that hidden minorities, like other ethnic groups, are *transcultural* phenomena: the state they live in has imposed different cultural and linguistic norms than those they perform in their private lives.[21] Hidden minorities are furthermore characterised by a strong feeling of local affiliation. Even when a former hidden minority has become overwhelmingly assimilated, we can observe the differential function of local identity: it tends to be the one of the remaining outlets where the collective memory of being "different" (or having once been "different") continues to work.[22] Hidden minorities often live close to state borders. In these cases the interconnection between ethnicity and territoriality acquires an additional meaning, creating so-called *border identities*[23]. Linguists[24], geographers[25], social and cultural anthropologists[26] and historians[27] have already analysed this issue.

---

[19] Cf. Georg Elwert: Boundaries, Cohesion and Switching. In: B. Brumen/Z. Šmitek (eds.), MESS: Mediterranean Ethnological Summer School, Piran, Slovenia, 1994-1995. Ljubljana 1995 (= Knjižnica Glasnika Slovenskega etnološkega društva 24), pp. 105-121; Heiner Keupp et al.: Identitätskonstruktionen. Das Patchwork der Identitäten in der Spätmoderne. Reinbeck 1999 (= rowohlts enzyklopädie 55634).

[20] Brubaker, Ethnicity without Groups, p. 11.

[21] Cf. Christian Giordano et al. (eds.): Interkulturelle Kommunikation im Nationalstaat. Freiburg 1998 (= Studia Ethnographica Friburgensia. 20).

[22] Cf. Christian Giordano: Ethnizität und Territorialität. Zur sozialen Konstruktion von Differenz in Mittel- und Osteuropa. *Ethnologica Balcanica* 3 (1999), pp. 9-43; Klaus Zeitler: Raumbezogene Identität – ein Entwicklungsfaktor für den ländlichen Raum? Eine soziologische Analyse der Determinanten und Inhalte ländlicher Raumentwicklung. Augsburg 2001 (= Angewandte Sozialgeographie 42); Peter Čede/Dieter Fleck: Die Steirischen Slowenen im Spiegel der amtlichen Volkszählungen. *Razprave in Gradivo – Treatises and Documents* 46 (2005), pp. 167-194.

[23] Cf. Andrea Komlosy et al.: Kulturen an der Grenze. Vienna 1995; T. Wilson/H. Donnan (eds.): Border Identities. Cambridge 1998; Ulrike H. Meinhof (ed.): Living (with) borders. Identity discourses on East-West borders in Europe. Aldershot 2002.

[24] On the Austrian-Slovene border cf. Mirko Križman: Jezikovna razmerja. Jezik pragmatike in estetike v obmejnih predelih ob Muri. Maribor 1997.

[25] On the Slovene minority in Italy cf. Milan Bufon: Minorities, Regional Transformation and Integration in Borderlands: A Case Study. *Annales* 13 (2003), pp. 1-8.

[26] Cf. Robert G. Minnich: Homesteaders and Citizens: An Ecology of Person and Self-realization among Slovene Speaking Villagers on the Austro-Italian Frontier. Bergen 1992.

[27] Cf. Andrea Haberl-Zemljič: Die Sprache im Dorf lassen. Festhalten und Aufgeben der slowenischen Sprache in Radkersburg und Umgebung. Graz 2004 (= Wissenschaftliche Schriftenreihe des Pavelhauses 6); Klaus-Jürgen Hermanik: Eine versteckte Minderheit. Mikrostudie über die Zweisprachigkeit in der steirischen Kleinregion Soboth. Weitra 2007; Christian Promitzer: Verlorene Brüder. Die Geschichte der zweisprachigen Region Leutschach in der südlichen Steiermark (19.-20. Jahrhundert). Graz 1996 (unpublished doctoral dissertation).

Since the early 1990s a variety of studies have been published, which not only touch the issue of ethnic minorities in Central Europe and the Balkans, they also include those small groups which we call hidden minorities.[28] Among these at least three readers can be adopted fully into the context of our agenda. They discuss respectively "Contested Identities" in South-East Europe[29], "Forgotten Minorities" in Eastern Europe[30] and explicitly "Hidden Minorities in the Balkans".[31]

This volume may be considered a continuation of these three works. It wants furthermore to refine the concept of hidden minorities through case studies from the intermediary area between Central Europe and the Balkans.[32] Here we can find the unique possibility of cross cultural comparison with respect to hidden minorities of Central European descent (like hidden Slovene minorities in Austria and Italy, German-speaking groups, or "Old Austrians", in Slovenia), and with respect to those of Balkan heritage (like the Serbs in the southern Slovene region of Bela Krajina, Montenegrin and Albanian colonies in Istria and Dalmatia, the Catholic Serbs of Dalmatia and Bulgarian gardeners in Aus-

---

[28] A selected bibliography of noteworthy handbooks and readers would include Robert Hinderling/Ludwig M. Eichinger (eds.): Handbuch der mitteleuropäischen Sprachminderheiten. Tübingen 1996; Gerhard Seewann: Bibliographisches Handbuch der ethnischen Gruppen Südosteuropas, 2 vol. Munich 1997; Miloš Okuka (ed.): Lexikon der Sprachen des europäischen Ostens. Klagenfurt – Vienna – Ljubljana 2002 (Wieser Enzyklopädie des Europäischen Ostens 10); Valeria Heuberger/Arnold Suppan/Elisabeth Vyslonzil (eds.): Brennpunkt Osteuropa. Minderheiten im Kreuzfeuer des Nationalismus. Vienna – Munich 1996 (= Schriftenreihe des Österreichischen Ost- und Südosteuropa-Instituts XXIV); Michael John/Oto Luthar (eds.): Un-Verständnis der Kulturen. Multikulturalismus in Mitteleuropa in historischer Perspektive. Klagenfurt – Ljubljana – Vienna 1997; Ernst-Peter Brezovsky/Arnold Suppan/Elisabeth Vyslonzil (eds.): Multikulturalität und Multiethnizität in Mittel-, Ost- und Südosteuropa. Frankfurt/M. et al. 1999; Cay Lienau/Ludwig Steindorff (eds.): Ethnizität, Identität und Nationalität in Südosteuropa. Munich 2000 (= Südosteuropa-Studien 64); Heinz-Dietrich Löwe/Günther H. Tontsch/Stefan Troebst (eds.): Minderheiten, Regionalbewußtsein und Zentralismus in Ostmitteleuropa. Cologne-Weimar-Vienna 2000 (= Siebenbürgisches Archiv 3/35); Stefan Wolff (ed.): German minorities in Europe. Ethnic identity and cultural belonging. New York – Oxford 2000; Sevasti Trubeta/Christian Voss (eds.): Minorities in Greece – Historical issues and new perspectives. Munich 2003 (= Jahrbücher für Geschichte und Kultur Südosteuropas 5).

[29] Ulf Brunnbauer (ed.): Umstrittene Identitäten. Ethnizität und Nationalität in Südosteuropa. Frankfurt/M. et al. 2002.

[30] Arno Tanner (ed.): The forgotten minorities of Eastern Europe. The history and today of selected ethnic groups in five countries. Helsinki 2004.

[31] Biljana Sikimić (ed.): Skrivene manjine na Balkana/Hidden Minorities in the Balkans. Belgrade 2004 (= Srpska akademija nauka i umetnosti, Balkanološki institut, posebna izdanja 82). Biljana Sikimić is in close cooperation with the editors of this book.

[32] On recognised national minorities cf. Vladimir Klemenčič: Narodne manjšine kot element politične, prostorske, socialne in ekonomske stvarnosti v Alpsko-Jadransko-Panonskem prostoru. In: Arbeitsgruppe Minderheiten der ARGE Alpen Adria et al. (eds.), Minderheiten im Alpen-Adria-Raum. Konferenzbericht. Ljubljana 1994, pp. 1-8.

tria); we furthermore have to include Roma communities, who do not fit into either of the above mentioned concepts.[33]

3. Hidden minorities and minority laws

When dealing with hidden minorities, we cannot omit the ongoing discussion of minority rights.[34] Here we have nevertheless to apply a different approach than earlier, since the essentialist juridical discourse does not allow for ambiguities or hybrid definitions as they are used in the humanities (ethnology and cultural anthropology, history, linguistics etc.). It can merely state that ethnic groups exist, which are not legally protected. The next few years will show, in how far multilateral endeavours will improve their situation. This refers to the implementation of the "Framework Convention for the Protection of National Minorities" of the Council of Europe, which came into effect in 1998, the "European Charter for Regional or Minority Languages" from 1992 and to the "CEI Instrument for the Protection of Minority Rights", adopted by the Central European Initiative in 1994.[35]

Furthermore, the role of the nation state has to be stressed clearly:

> The state is thus a powerful 'identifier', not because it can create identities in the strong sense – in general it cannot – but because it has the material and symbolic resources to impose the categories, classificatory schemes, and modes of social counting and accounting with which bureaucrats, judges, teachers, and doctors must work and to which nonstate actors must refer.[36] (Rogers Brubaker)

What does this mean for those small ethnic groups, which do not demand legal protection? One thing should be clear: Nobody can be compelled to ask for minority rights, whatever their reasons may be. Legal protection for national

---

[33] Cf. Will Guy (ed.): Between past and future. The Roma of Central and Eastern Europe. Hertfordshire 2001.

[34] cf. Sergij Vilfan (ed.): Ethnic Groups and Language Rights. Comparative Studies on Governments and Non-dominant Ethnic Groups in Europe, 1850-1940. Aldershot 1993; Österreichisches Volksgruppenzentrum (ed.): Internationales und Europäisches Volksgruppenrecht. Klagenfurt 1995 (= Österreichische Volksgruppenhandbücher 8); Joseph Marko: Der Minderheitenschutz in den jugoslawischen Nachfolgestaaten. Slowenien, Kroatien und Mazedonien sowie die Bundesrepublik Jugoslawien mit Serbien und Montenegro. Bonn 1996 (= Minderheitenschutz im östlichen Europa 5); Herbert Küpper: Das neue Minderheitenrecht in Ungarn. Munich 1998 (= Untersuchungen zur Gegenwartskunde Südosteuropas 36); Günther Rautz: Die Sprachenrechte der Minderheiten. Ein Rechtsvergleich zwischen Österreich und Italien. Bozen 1998 (unpublished doctoral dissertation); Peter Hilpold: Modernes Minderheitenrecht. Eine rechtsvergleichende Untersuchung des Minderheitenrechts in Österreich und in Italien unter besonderer Berücksichtigung völkerrechtlicher Aspekte. Vienna et al. 2001; Anna-Mária Bíró/Petra Kovács (eds.): Diversity in action. Local public management of multi-ethnic communities in Central and Eastern Europe. Budapest 2001.

[35] for a survey cf. http://www.coe.int/t/e/human_rights/minorities/2._FRAMEWORK_CONVENTION_%28MONITORING%29/.

[36] Cf. Brubaker, Ethnicity without Groups, p. 43.

and ethnic minorities is not applicable for those who want to be treated as part of the majority population. They are not interested in minority kindergartens or school education, topographic names in their mother language or minority rights in the (mass) media, such as access to newspapers, radio and TV, even if they use their local vernacular in private. It must be questioned, if well-meaning intellectuals from outside should inspire them to stand up for such rights. Their will must be respected, and protection of such groups has much more to do with their full integration into the majority population and its civil society by means directed against discrimination.

Representatives of legally recognised minorities often take a critical stance with respect to censuses asking about the use of minority languages. One of their main fears is that their group will be marginalised, i.e. to be increasingly outnumbered by the majority population in each census. They feel that political pressure and ongoing assimilation will reduce the number of those declaring before the state that they wish to use a minority language. But groups and individuals who refuse legal protection do just this as a rule; they hide and do not want to "out" themselves in censuses. We could even say that censuses are one of the reasons behind the phenomenon of hidden minorities. They develop out of marginal members of the imagined entity of the group, and after a transitional period of reconsideration, these individuals are on their way to join the majority population. Anyway, nations, politicians, and researchers overestimate the importance of censuses in relation with the ethnicity of individuals.[37]

The issue, of course, is different for groups of recent migrant origin generally called *new minorities*. They are mostly urban. Some of them want indeed to become a legally recognised national or ethnic minority, but are hidden by the authorities. With their legal status unresolved, they have likewise to be considered in this subchapter, all the more, since some of them can even look back on a local tradition of their own, which is already in the third generation.

Whatever the origin of the respective group may be, with respect to its relationship to the state we have to deal with two different strategies. Some of them *hide themselves* from the state and the public because they want to be treated as part of the majority population on equal terms; others have to live "undercover", because they do not get the necessary protection from the state. Within the same group we can encounter both strategies, as can be widely demonstrated in the case of Roma communities.

The following survey on the situation in the intermediate area between Central Europe and the Balkans tries to include both issues of *hiding* and *being hidden*. It must necessarily be incomplete as it only deals marginally with the quality of minority legislation and with human rights issues. It does not claim to treat all possible cases of hidden minorities, since many of them remain unseen or are

---

[37] Ibidem, p. 67.

as of yet undiscovered. In any case, the number of ethnic groups enjoying legally granted minority rights is at first sight impressive.

Six ethnic groups are recognised in *Austria* as national minorities (*Volksgruppen*) on the grounds of the law on ethnic groups (*Volksgruppengesetz*) of 1976: Croats, Czechs, Hungarians, Roma, Slovaks and Slovenes. Each of them is organised in a minority advisory board (*Volksgruppenbeirat*). For about a decade, the representatives of the Slovenes in the Federal Province of Styria, a rather small and widely assimilated group, have been looking to organise a *Volksgruppenbeirat* of their own, or at least to acquire regular seats in the existing respective body, which is dominated by the Slovenes in Carinthia. In early 2004 they indeed acquired one seat there. A hidden minority – or, to put it more exactly, its representation – became slightly more visible than before.[38]

According to legal practice, the recognition of an Austrian *Volksgruppe* has three preconditions: a) a continuity of residence in the country for at least three generations or ninety years; b) residence and home ("Beheimatung") in Austria; and c) Austrian citizenship.[39] These preconditions deny minority rights for recent immigrant groups, since they have not been in Austria for such a long period. This was the reason why the Austrian government in 2001 rejected the recognition of a Polish minority. The applicant, the Polish association *Strzecha*, was founded in Vienna in 1894, but the government regarded the "ethnical core" of this group too small to allow for a continuity of ninety years – the majority of the group would consist of recent immigrants from Poland.[40]

Until recently, certain national minorities were listed in the in *Croatian* constitution, while others were not. In the 1990s a gap appeared between minority legislation and its implementation. This was especially valid for Serbs, who lost their status as a constitutive nation and were reduced to a "national minority". Furthermore, their situation deteriorated as a consequence of the war in the first half of the 1990s, when Serbs occupied a considerable part of the country. In 1995 the majority of Serbs fled the country and the nationalist and restrictive policy of the regime of the late Franjo Tuđman did not encourage their return. In that period we could observe severe human rights violations with respect to the remaining Serbs; in places, where they did not live together in compact masses, many of them applied a strategy of staying "undercover". To a minor extent such strategies still can be observed today. The percentage of minorities among the population has been reduced by half between the censuses of 1991 and 2001 (from about 20 to 10 percent).

---

[38] Cf. http://www.coe.int/t/e/human_rights/minorities/2._framework_convention_%28monitoring%29/2._monitoring_mechanism/3._state_reports_and_unmik_kosovo_report/2._second_cycle/PDF_2nd_SR_Austria_en.pdf.

[39] cf. Hilpold, Modernes Minderheitenrecht, p. 375.

[40] Cf. http://www.parlament.gv.at/portal/page?_pageid=908,284981&_dad=portal&_schema=PORTAL and http://members.chello.at/strzecha/.

But the situation for minorities has changed tremendously since Tuđman's death in 1999. In 2002 the Croatian parliament passed a new and exemplary Constitutional Law for the Rights of National Minorities. In its provisions and scope it goes further than regulations in any other country of the region. It provides for the representation of national minorities in parliament and in local self-governing bodies as well as for the election of councils of national minorities on a national and a regional level. Seventeen minorities, irrespective of how long they have been living in Croatia, are represented in the councils: Albanians, Austrians, Bosniaks, Bulgarians, Czechs, Germans, Hungarians, Italians, Jews, Macedonians, Montenegrins, Roma, Ruthenians, Serbs, Slovaks, Slovenes and Ukrainians. These groups as well as the Polish and Russian minorities get state funding for fulfilling their minority issue desires. Only Romanians, Turks and Vlachs[41] are denied these possibilities, as are several other small groups, which can look back on some tradition of their own. Among these are the speakers of three Romance dialects in Istria, a marginal group among the inhabitants of Greek-Catholic villages in the Žumberak mountains close to the border to Slovenia, which during the 1990s were initially declared to be Serbs and, later, Slovenes, the descendants of Catholic Albanians (*Arbanasi*), who formed a community in the Dalmatian city of Zadar, and the Catholic Serbs of Dalmatia. The Montenegrin colony of Peroj in Istria is at least recognised by Montenegrin minority organisations from other parts of Croatia.

The legal provisions for minorities in *Hungary* are one of the best in the region. The Hungarian parliament passed the Minorities Act as a constitutional law in 1993. It increased the number of recognised minorities to thirteen: Bulgarians, Roma, Greeks, Croats, Poles, Germans, Armenians, Romanians, Ruthenians, Serbs, Slovaks, Slovenes and Ukrainians. Like in Austria, however, an ethnic group needs a hundred years of residence in the country in order to be recognised as a national or ethnic minority.

At first sight, the Hungarian society seems to be rather multicultural: Members of smaller ethnic groups live in 1500 out of a total 3200 municipalities. But, being only 3.2 percent of the population (according to the census of 2001), the lack of compact communities will contribute to their gradual assimilation. Most of the traditional minorities have, furthermore, never learned the standard literary languages of their referential nations, since they settled here before they came into being. As a consequence, they tend increasingly to use Hungarian even in mutual private contacts, which is true for the majority of the Roma

[41] In the census of 2001 only twelve Vlachs were counted in the whole country. Another question, which cannot be discussed here, is the actual implementation of regulations on the spot. For the whole issue cf. Report on the implementation of the Framework Convention for the Protection of National Minorities in the Republic of Croatia to be found at cf. http://www.coe.int/t/e/human_rights/minorities/2._framework_convention_%28monitoring%29/2._monitoring_mechanism/3._state_reports_and_unmik_kosovo_report/2._second_cycle/PDF_2nd_SR_Croatia_en.pdf.

community in particular. Although minorities have the legal possibility to learn their language in school, many of them are not interested in doing so.[42]

Minority rights are not fixed by a constitutional law in *Italy*. They are covered by the law 482/1999 on Protection of Historical Linguistic Minorities. It divides minorities into two groups: *Strong* ones (Germans in the province of South Tyrol, Slovenes in the province of Friuli-Venezia Giulia and the Franco-Provençal minority in the Aosta Valley) have a special status in their respective home region; *weak minorities* (Sardinians, Friulians, Occitanians, Albanians, Ladinians, Greeks, Katalans, Croats and Germans outside South Tyrol), however, have fewer rights. The law 38/2001 on the Norms for the Protection of the Slovene Linguistic Minority of the Friuli Venezia Giulia Region broadened the geographical scope of legal application for this community. But as in general, we have to consider that a certain degree of leeway has to be given in the implementation of the respective regulations depending both on the respective policy of the government in power and on the will of the ethnic group concerned.[43]

In *Slovenia,* only the Italian and Hungarian *national minorities* belong to the category of traditional communities. They are protected by article 64 of the constitution. Article 65 defines the Romany community as an *ethnic minority* and stipulates that "the status and special rights of the Romany community living in Slovenia shall be regulated by law."[44] In the 1990s, only the Roma community in the eastern Slovenian municipality of Murska Sobota had the opportunity to vote a representative of their own into local self-government. In 2002, however, in the Act Amending the Law on Local Self-Government foresaw twenty municipalities, where one Romany representative should be elected to the respective municipal council. Today – after intense discussions – this right has been realised in all but one municipality. The constitutionally promised law on the Roma minority, however, still has not been realised.

There are, though, other groups in Slovenia, which do not have a legal status and could be therefore treated as hidden minorities: The small but traditional community of Serbs in the region of Bela Krajina to the south of the country, living in four villages, never asked for such legal treatment. The remaining representatives of the once strong German (speaking) minority, on the other hand, have found an advocate in the Austrian government, which tends to call them "Old Austrians". In 2001 the Austrian and Slovene governments signed an Agreement on Collaboration in the Fields of Culture, Education and Science. It foresees projects for language instruction, the preservation of monu-

---

[42] Cf. Antal Paulik/Judit Solymosi: Language policy in Hungary. *Noves SL. Revista de Sociolingística*, Spring-summer 2004, http://www6.gencat.net/llengcat/noves/hm04primavera-estiu/paulik1_2.htm; Küpper, Das neue Minderheitenrecht.

[43] Cf. http://www.coe.int/t/e/human_rights/minorities/2._framework_convention_%28monitoring%29/2._monitoring_mechanism/3._state_reports_and_unmik_kosovo_report/2._second_cycle/PDF_2nd_SR_Italy_en.pdf.

[44] http://servat.unibe.ch/icl/si00000_.html

ments and scholarships for the German-speaking minority in Slovenia. Since this group was mentioned explicitly in the agreement, the Austrian foreign minister claimed that the "Old Austrian" minority had been recognised by Slovenia.[45]

The real issue are Bosniaks, Croats and Serbs, who have migrated to this country. Each outnumbers the official national minorities of Hungarians and Italians. Their societies get some funding by the Ministry of Culture, but they do not enjoy minority rights. There is also the issue of the so-called "izbrisani" ("erased" ones). In 1992 about 18 000 residents, people from other former Yugoslav republics were deleted from the civil registries by the Slovene government. The authorities have to date not acted to fully redress this violation of human rights.

These examples show the fluidity of the term minority – its legal application depends upon respective political interest. With respect to those groups not considered by law, we have to reflect their Janus-like character of both being hidden and hiding themselves. For those small ethnic groups which we call hidden minorities, the following general statements vis-à-vis their legal treatment and self-organisation can be made:

- The nation state is by nature not interested in having too many ethnic minorities; it hesitates to give minority rights to all possible groups. This is valid in particular for weak communities, which are exposed to wilful assimilation and to objective factors of homogenisation (education, emigration to urban centres). The restricted number of ethnic groups legally recognised as minorities in Austria and Slovenia speaks for this strategy.
- But it should also be considered that the nation state itself is *involuntarily producing* its own minorities. By imposing the concept of the single nation it induces various groups to become aware of their different "cultural" traits. Some of them will be recognised as national minorities.[46] But what is more, we can even observe the *wilful production* of new minorities during the last fifteen years. Some years ago the Italian centre-left government widened the scope of minority protection. This was also the case in Hungary and to a greater extent – however surprising and possibly deceptive the impression may be – in Croatia during the last years. Even neighbouring Bosnia and Herzegovina and Serbia and Montenegro – which are otherwise not considered in this book – passed in 2002 new laws for the protection of national minorities.[47] Their approach is less idealistic than pragmatic: In Bosnia

---

[45] Cf. http://www.parlament.gv.at/PG/DE/XXI/I/I_00563/pmh.shtml.

[46] Cf. Brunnbauer, Einleitung. In: U. Brunnbauer, Umstrittene Identitäten pp. 11-29, here 22.

[47] In Bosnia and Herzegovina the legal protection of the seventeen minorities listed in the law still has still not been implemented; in Serbia only half of twenty ethnic groups have formed Minority councils – cf. the respective reports at http://www.coe.int/t/e/human_rights/minorities/

and Herzegovina, Croatia and Serbia and Montenegro, the respective laws were passed to overtly show their compliance with the regulations of the Framework Convention for the Protection of National Minorities. And, what is more, if a state decides that its small and ever diminishing minorities should be present in public, this can also be explained by the state's will to place them under public control.

- Hidden minorities – those autochthonous ethnic groups either not willing to be recognised as a national minority or too small to develop their own representation – can serve as an instrument and as a *quid pro quo* of foreign policy. "Changes in groupness – short term fluctuations as well as long term developments – are cognitively mediated, depending on changes in the distribution of propagation of groupist representation, or on changes in their accessibility, activation, salience or resonance." (Brubaker)[48] Through ethnic and political entrepreneurs from outside, even a rather weak ethnic group can become a legally recognised minority or – to put it more clearly – at least its representatives can improve their symbolic status. This can be the case when political reasons and foreign policy require such procedures. Such promotions took place recently with the representatives of the Slovenes in the Austrian province of Styria ("Styrian Slovenes") and those of the "Old Austrians" in Slovenia.
- A continuity of *three generations* maintaining cultural and linguistic traits is the precondition for the legal recognition of an ethnic and/or national minority in most countries of concern here (the only exception is Croatia). From the viewpoint of the state, this argument has some logic: The third generation of not so recent migrant groups are often highly assimilated, since no institutional means (instruction in mother language etc.) existed in order to integrate them into their native culture. Empirical studies on the descendants of migrants therefore prove the consistency of this *normative concept*.[49] In the case of autochthonous hidden minorities, by contrast, the three generation model is not characterised by a sharp caesura such as migration from one country to another. The scholar has to locate the *first* generation, which is the *last* generation in full possession of the traditional cultural and linguistic traits of a local community. But having fixed this "first" generation, the process of assimilation (roughly, exclusive competence of the minority language in the first generation, bilingualism of the second, and almost

2._framework_convention_%28monitoring%29/2._monitoring_mechanism/3._state_reports_and_unmik_kosovo_report/2._second_cycle/List_2nd_Cycle_StateReports_en.asp.

[48] Brubaker, Ethnicity without Groups, p. 80.

[49] Cf. Marijana Jakimova, Mojca Ravnik and Biljana Sikimić in this volume.

> exclusive use of the majority language in the third generation) is working along the same lines as in the case of migrant communities.[50]

Whatever strategy will be applied by the state, it is virtually impossible to include all possible minorities. There will always be hidden minorities, groups which are not legally recognised and still have a collective memory of their cultural/linguistic uniqueness.

> In its cognitive dimensions, groupness can only be understood as depending not simply on the content of representations [...] but on the distribution of such representations within a population [...] and – not least – on the relative ease with which they 'slot' into the 'interlock' with other key cultural representations.[51] (Rogers Brubaker)

4. About this book

The common interest of the authors in this volume is to contribute to the concept of hidden minorities with theoretical insights and new research results. They come from a variety of disciplines – jurisprudence, historiography, ethnology, social anthropology, cultural studies, linguistics and educational theory.

A sample of case studies on small ethnic groups in the intermediate area between Central Europe and the Balkans forms the backbone of the volume. These case studies are not exhaustive, but they provide a better understanding of the concept of hidden minorities. As the subtitle of the volume – language and identity – suggests, case studies require a broader understanding of language and identity within the given geographical setting. The practical implementation of minority laws, furthermore, has to be reflected both among recognised and hidden minorities. This is why we have put the adjective of the term hidden minorities in brackets in the title of this book. Additional case studies deal with the role of changing borders and their effect on the population concerned. State borders in the region have changed at least three times in the course of the 20th century and have affected the identity strategies of the local population. We therefore have to investigate situations, both where hidden minorities are clearly present and where a situation seems to be free of such issues. Only then we can acquire insights into how far hidden minorities develop a particular pattern of general linguistic and identity strategies in the region. Finally, we have to ask, if issues of language and identity in this intermediate area of Europe are only a concomitant of modernity, or if it would also pay off to look into the more distant past.

---

[50] Cf. Tanja Petrović in this volume.

[51] Brubaker, Ethnicity without Groups, p. 80.

The volume is divided into four sections. It was the unanimous view of the editors that within each chapter the papers be presented in alphabetical order so as to avoid the involuntary imposition of symbolic geographies.

The first section deals with ***Theory and Law*** and begins with **Marija Jurić Pahor's** contribution on the theoretical discussion on minority and identity concepts. By concentrating on the Slovenes in Carinthia and the Province of Trieste, she provides general insights into processes of adaptation and assimilation during the last one and a half centuries. Jurić Pahor notes that the scale of possible identities among the minority population includes a variety of diverse and ambiguous strategies. They cannot be reduced to the rigid distinction between majority and minority. Essential myths or 'grand narratives' of these distinctions have therefore to be interpreted in a new way. Her keywords for describing these strategies are those of *passing* and *mimicry* vis-à-vis the dominant nation.

Mirjam Polzer-Srienz concentrates on the significance of legal protection for hidden minorities. She deals with it on an international level as well as at the local level of local representation for ethnic groups. The principle of equality is often not sufficient to protect minorities. They require a special status, which not only guarantees equality on an individual but also on a collective level. For the latter she considers different models of representation and participation. Her case study puts a special focus on the normative minority protection in Austria in comparison with that in Slovenia, referring both to the German-speaking minority in Slovenia and to the Slovene minority in the Austrian Federal Province of Styria.

The paper by **Christian Promitzer** discusses such issues by explicitly applying the research concept of hidden minorities. In his geographical scope, Promitzer reaches beyond the intermediate area between Central Europe and the Balkans. He elaborates the historically changing view of ethnic groups which could have been considered hidden minorities in a respective period. He furthermore gives an outline of possible fields of research with respect to hidden minorities and serves as an introduction to the following section.

The second section, ***Hidden Minorities – Case Studies,*** is dedicated to empirical research on autochthonous and migrant hidden minorities in the intermediary area between Central Europe and the Balkans:

Klaus-Jürgen Hermanik writes about the hidden Slovene minority in the Austrian Federal Province of Styria. He concentrates on the area of Soboth close to the Austrian-Slovenian border. He shows how the Slovene-speaking group living there was *hidden* by the government and at the same time developed survival strategies of *hiding* itself. Hermanik furthermore dwells on identity constructions of people 'living at and with the border' and facing the pressure of assimilation at the same time.

Marijana Jakimova discusses the shifting of identities among Bulgarian gardeners and their descendants in the Austrian city of Graz. Bulgarian gardeners migrated to this city in the first decade of the 20th century to consequently become a serious rival for Austrian gardeners in the vegetable market. Since the Bulgarian migrants were restricted to a special professional segment, linguistic and cultural assimilation was delayed until after the Second World War. Jakimova traces the gradual assimilation of the descendants of the Bulgarian gardeners into the third generation and compares them with new migrants from Bulgaria after 1989.

Oto Luthar discusses aspects of Roma cultural practices and survival strategies in the region of Prekmurje in north-eastern Slovenia. The local cultural melting pot in Prekmurje together with very complex extended family structures among the Roma led to dispersal and the imposition of varieties of the majority culture. In this situation, according to Luthar, Roma had to invent new forms of self-representation and of the presentation of their neighbours. In the process of name changing they even assumed the names of famous Slovenes or of well known pop icons.

Tanja Petrović applies sociolinguistic methods in order to describe the situation of four Serbian villages in the southern Slovenian region of Bela Krajina. In dealing with local language behaviour she also applies statistical and cultural anthropological methods. Petrović interprets census results in various institutional contexts in detail. Today only few inhabitants of the four villages confront actively the slow death of their native vernacular, the consequence of the increase of mixed marriages with Slovenes. Petrović finally tackles issues of 'language vitality' and 'language ideology' with respect to the concept of hidden minorities.

Ivica Šarac focuses on the rather anonymous Catholic Serbs in and around the Dalmatian city of Dubrovnik. This example is noteworthy, since it contradicts the general assumption that Serbs are Orthodox and Croats are Catholic. Šarac provides an historical overview on the evolution of this group from the early 19th century until the present. This group had already vanished from public life with the first Yugoslav state. After 1991, being faced with new political circumstances, they went totally "undercover"; only scattered remnants of this group still preserve their ethnic identity.

Biljana Sikimić applies an ethno-linguistic approach in her case study of the Serb community living on the island of Csepel, Hungary. By giving some examples out of a vast number of interviews she has collected in the field, Sikimić illustrates the status of bilingualism (Hungarian-Serbian) as well as the tenacity of Serbian rituals (Christmas, wedding and funeral customs, calendar feasts etc). She puts a special focus on descendants of Bulgarian gardeners who have migrated to Csepel at a later period and in the course of time have merged into the Serbian community, forming a specific variant of a hidden minority.

Eduard G. Staudinger, finally, deals with the German-speaking population in the Abstall Basin in northern Slovenia. His approach is a historical one. Four crucial periods can be recognised in the historical development of the Basin and its population: the first one until 1918, when it was under Habsburg rule and had a predominantly German-speaking population; the second in the years 1918-1941, when its was part of the Kingdom of Yugoslavia during which demography shifted in favour of the Slovenian population; the third period under Nazi rule saw the region submitted to the general policy of Germanising and deportation of the Slovene population; and the last period after 1945 led to the internment and expulsion of most of the local German population. Only a few of them returned to their homes and stayed there as a hidden minority.

The third section of the book deals with ***Crossing borders – Living with Borders***. It treats the situation in border areas or short-distance migrations across state borders, where national / ethnical self-ascriptions of individuals and ascriptions by the states they are living in, are not always congruent.

Duška Knežević-Hočevar discusses the role of changing identities among the inhabitants of the upper Kolpa Valley on the state border between Slovenia and Croatia, which came into being after the demise of Yugoslavia in 1991. She investigates the identity constructions of the people living on the two river banks as well as their persisting trans-national relationships. Knežević-Hočevar describes furthermore linguistic and ethnic boundaries among the members of a kinship living on both sides of the river. By discussing the construction of national and linguistic identities she reveals strategies which can be also observed in the case of hidden minorities

The article by **Mojca Ravnik** discusses both migration and the impact of state borders. She deals with the role of family and kinship among migrants from Slovene Istrian villages in the Italian city of Trieste by investigating their life stories. Migration from the hinterland to the city had several aspects; it was a movement from one linguistic and cultural setting to another and a movement from a rural environment to an urban one. What is more, after the Second World War the city and its hinterland became separated by state borders. Ravnik focuses on the linguistic and national affiliation of the migrants and their links to the kinship that has remained in the original villages. By doing so, she poses issues of cultural continuity and discontinuity with respect to the local vernacular and ethnic/national identity.

The last chapter puts its focus more on the subtitle of this book by dealing with ***Languages and Language Contacts in Medieval Times***. It shows that the issue of language and identity in the Alpine-Adriatic region is not only a modern one. We can trace it back into the medieval period, as **Giorgio Ziffer** demonstrates. His paper deals with the *Gospel of Nicodemus*, a literary source of the High Middle Ages, and its meaning for German-Slavic language interactions in that period. Ziffer concentrates on linguistic features and lexemes and compares them with Church Slavonic texts. By doing so, he demonstrates that language contacts can be also found in historical epochs where adequate sources are rare.

Bibliography:

BARTH, Frederic: Introduction. In: F. Barth (ed.), Ethnic groups and Boundaries: The Social Organization of Cultural Difference. Bergen – London 1969, pp. 9-38.

BIRÓ, Anna-Mária/KOVÁCS, Petra (eds.): Diversity in action. Local public management of multi-ethnic communities in Central and Eastern Europe. Budapest 2001.

BREZOVSKY, Ernst-Peter/SUPPAN, Arnold/VYSLONZIL, Elisabeth (eds.): Multikulturalität und Multiethnizität in Mittel-, Ost- und Südosteuropa. Frankfurt/M. et al. 1999.

BRUBAKER, Rogers: Ethnicity without Groups. Cambridge (MA) – London 2006, p. 17.

BRUNNBAUER, Ulf (ed.): Umstrittene Identitäten. Ethnizität und Nationalität in Südosteuropa. Frankfurt/M. et al. 2002.

BUFON, Milan: Minorities, Regional Transformation and Integration in Borderlands: A Case Study. *Annales* 13 (2003), pp. 1-8.

ČEDE, Peter/FLECK, Dieter: Die Steirischen Slowenen im Spiegel der amtlichen Volkszählungen. *Razprave in Gradivo – Treatises and Documents* 46 (2005), pp. 167-194.

ELWERT, Georg: Boundaries, Cohesion and Switching. In: B. Brumen/Z. Šmitek (eds.), MESS: Mediterranean Ethnological Summer School, Piran, Slovenia, 1994-1995. Ljubljana 1995 (= Knjižnica Glasnika Slovenskega etnološkega društva 24), pp. 105-121.

FASSEL, Horst/WAACK, Christoph (eds.): Regionen im östlichen Europa – Kontinuitäten, Zäsuren und Perspektiven. Tübingen 2000.

FIELITZ, Wilhelm: Das Stereotyp des Wolhyniendeutschen Umsiedlers. Popularisierungen zwischen Sprachinselforschung und nationalsozialistischer Propaganda. Marburg/Lahn 2000 (= Schriftenreihe der Kommission für deutsche und osteuropäische Volkskunde in der Deutschen Gesellschaft für Volkskunde e.V. 82).

GELLNER, Ernest: Nationalismus. Kultur und Macht. Berlin 1999.

GEYER, Ingeborg: Sprachinseln. Anmerkungen zu Definition und Forschungstradition.. In: P. Wiesinger/W. Bauer/P. Ernst (eds.), Probleme der oberdeutschen Dialektologie und Namenkunde. Vorträge zum 100. Geburtstag von E. Kranzmayer. Vienna 1999, pp. 150-170.

GIORDANO, Christian et al. (eds.): Interkulturelle Kommunikation im Nationalstaat. Freiburg 1998 (= Studia Ethnographica Friburgensia. 20).

GIORDANO, Christian: Ethnizität und Territorialität. Zur sozialen Konstruktion von Differenz in Mittel- und Osteuropa. *Ethnologica Balcanica* 3 (1999), pp. 9-43.

GUY, Will (ed.): Between past and future. The Roma of Central and Eastern Europe. Hertfordshire 2001.

HABERL-ZEMLJIČ, Andrea: Die Sprache im Dorf lassen. Festhalten und Aufgeben der slowenischen Sprache in Radkersburg und Umgebung. Graz 2004 (= Wissenschaftliche Schriftenreihe des Pavelhauses 6).

HASSINGER, Hugo: Lebensraumfragen der Völker des europäischen Südostens. In: K.H. Diezel/O. Schmieder/H.Schmitthenner (eds.), Lebensraumfragen europäischer Völker, vol. 1. Leipzig 1941, pp. 594-612.

HASSINGER, Hugo: Mitteleuropa, Donaueuropa, Südosteuropa. *Volkstum im Südosten* 3 (1941), pp. 173-176.

HERMANIK, Klaus-Jürgen: Eine versteckte Minderheit. Mikrostudie über die Zweisprachigkeit in der steirischen Kleinregion Soboth. Weitra 2007.

HEUBERGER, Valeria/SUPPAN, Arnold/VYSLONZIL, Elisabeth (eds.): Brennpunkt Osteuropa. Minderheiten im Kreuzfeuer des Nationalismus. Vienna – Munich 1996 (= Schriftenreihe des Österreichischen Ost- und Südosteuropa-Instituts XXIV).

HILPOLD, Peter: Modernes Minderheitenrecht. Eine rechtsvergleichende Untersuchung des Minderheitenrechts in Österreich und in Italien unter besonderer Berücksichtigung völkerrechtlicher Aspekte. Vienna et al. 2001.

HINDERLING, Robert/EICHINGER, Ludwig M. (eds.): Handbuch der mitteleuropäischen Sprachminderheiten. Tübingen 1996.

HIRSCHHAUSEN, Ulrike v./LEONHARD, Jörn (eds.): Nationalismen in Europa. West- und Osteuropa im Vergleich. Göttingen 2001.

HÖSCH, Edgar: Kulturgrenzen in Südosteuropa. *Südosteuropa* 47/12 (1998), pp. 601-623.

JOHN, Michael/LUTHAR, Oto (eds.): Un-Verständnis der Kulturen. Multikulturalismus in Mitteleuropa in historischer Perspektive. Klagenfurt – Ljubljana – Vienna 1997.

KAPPELER, Andreas (ed.): The formation of national elites. Aldershot et al. 1992 (= Comparative studies on governments and non-dominant ethnic groups in Europe [1850 – 1940] 6).

KASER, Karl/GRAMSHAMMER-HOHL, Dagmar/PICHLER, Robert (eds.): Europa und die Grenzen im Kopf. Klagenfurt – Vienna – Ljubljana 2003 (Wieser Enzyklopädie des Europäischen Ostens 11).

KASER, Karl: Freundschaft und Feindschaft auf dem Balkan. Euro-balkanische Herausforderungen. Klagenfurt – Vienna – Ljubljana 2001.

KEUPP, Heiner et al.: Identitätskonstruktionen. Das Patchwork der Identitäten in der Spätmoderne. Reinbeck 1999 (= rowohlts enzyklopädie 55634).

KLEMENČIČ, Vladimir: Narodne manjšine kot element politične, prostorske, socialne in ekonomske stvarnosti v Alpsko-Jadransko-Panonskem prostoru. In: Arbeitsgruppe Minderheiten der ARGE Alpen Adria et al. (eds.), Minderheiten im Alpen-Adria-Raum. Konferenzbericht. Ljubljana 1994, pp. 1-8.

KOMLOSY, Andrea et al.: Kulturen an der Grenze. Vienna 1995.

KRIŽMAN, Mirko: Jezikovna razmerja. Jezik pragmatike in estetike v obmejnih predelih ob Muri. Maribor 1997.

KÜPPER, Herbert: Das neue Minderheitenrecht in Ungarn. Munich 1998 (= Untersuchungen zur Gegenwartskunde Südosteuropas 36).

LIENAU, Cay/STEINDORFF, Ludwig (eds.): Ethnizität, Identität und Nationalität in Südosteuropa. Munich 2000 (= Südosteuropa-Studien 64).

LORD, Christopher (ed.): Central Europe: Core or periphery? Copenhagen 2000.

LÖWE, Heinz-Dietrich/TONTSCH, Günther H./TROEBST, Stefan (eds.): Minderheiten, Regionalbewußtsein und Zentralismus in Ostmitteleuropa. Cologne-Weimar-Vienna 2000 (= Siebenbürgisches Archiv 3/35).

MARKO, Joseph: Der Minderheitenschutz in den jugoslawischen Nachfolgestaaten. Slowenien, Kroatien und Mazedonien sowie die Bundesrepublik Jugoslawien mit Serbien und Montenegro. Bonn 1996 (= Minderheitenschutz im östlichen Europa 5).

MEINHOF, Ulrike H. (ed.): Living (with) borders. Identity discourses on East-West borders in Europe. Aldershot 2002.

MINNICH, Robert G.: Homesteaders and Citizens: An Ecology of Person and Self-realization among Slovene Speaking Villagers on the Austro-Italian Frontier. Bergen 1992.

MINNICH, Robert G.: Speaking Slovene – Being Slovene. Verbal Codes and Collective Self-images: Some Correlations between Kanalska Dolina and Ziljska Dolina. *Slovene Studies* 10/2 (1988), pp. 125-147.

MORITSCH, Andreas (ed.): Alpen-Adria. Zur Geschichte einer Region. Klagenfurt – Ljubljana – Vienna 2001.

MÜLLER, Dietmar: Southeastern Europe as a Historical Meso-region: Constructing Space in Twentieth-Century German Historiography. *European Review of History* 10/2 (2003), pp. 393-408.

OKUKA, Miloš (ed.): Lexikon der Sprachen des europäischen Ostens. Klagenfurt – Vienna – Ljubljana 2002 (Wieser Enzyklopädie des Europäischen Ostens 10).

ÖSTERREICHISCHES VOLKSGRUPPENZENTRUM (ed.): Internationales und Europäisches Volksgruppenrecht. Klagenfurt 1995 (= Österreichische Volksgruppenhandbücher 8).

PAULIK, Antal/SOLYMOSI, Judit: Language policy in Hungary. *Noves SL. Revista de Sociolingística*, Spring-summer 2004, http://www6.gencat.net/llengcat/noves/hm04primavera-estiu/ paulik 1_2. htm

PROMITZER, Christian: Verlorene Brüder. Die Geschichte der zweisprachigen Region Leutschach in der südlichen Steiermark (19. – 20. Jahrhundert). Graz 1996 (unpublished doctoral dissertation).

RAUTZ, Günther: Die Sprachenrechte der Minderheiten. Ein Rechtsvergleich zwischen Österreich und Italien. Bozen 1998 (unpublished doctoral dissertation).

SEEWANN, Gerhard: Bibliographisches Handbuch der ethnischen Gruppen Südosteuropas, 2 vol. Munich 1997.

SFIKAS, Thanasis D./WILLIAMS, Christopher (eds.): Ethnicity and nationalism in East Central Europe and the Balkans. Aldershot et al. 1999.

SIKIMIĆ, Biljana (ed.): Skrivene manjine na Balkana/Hidden Minorities in the Balkans. Belgrade 2004 (= Srpska akademija nauka i umetnosti, Balkanološki institut, posebna izdanja 82).

SUNDHAUSSEN, Holm: Der Balkan: Ein Plädoyer für Differenz. *Geschichte und Gesellschaft* 29 (2003), 608-624.

SUNDHAUSSEN, Holm: Europa balcanica. Der Balkan als historischer Raum Europas. *Geschichte und Gesellschaft* 25 (1999), pp. 626-653.

SUNDHAUSSEN, Holm: Südosteuropa und Balkan: Begriffe, Grenzen, Merkmale. In: U. Hinrichs (ed.), Handbuch der Südosteuropa-Linguistik. Wiesbaden 1999, pp. 27-49.

TANNER, Arno (ed.): The forgotten minorities of Eastern Europe. The history and today of selected ethnic groups in five countries. Helsinki 2004.

THER, Philipp/SUNDHAUSSEN, Holm (eds.): Regionale Bewegungen und Regionalismen in europäischen Zwischenräumen seit der Mitte des 19. Jahrhunderts. Marburg 2003 (= Tagungen zur Ostmitteleuropa-Forschung 18).

TODOROVA, Maria: Der Balkan als Analysekategorie: Grenzen, Raum Zeit. *Geschichte und Gesellschaft* 28 (2002), pp. 470-492.

TODOROVA, Maria: Historische Vermächtnisse als Analysekategorie. In: K. Kaser/D. Gramshammer-Hohl/R. Pichler (eds.), Europa und die Grenzen im Kopf, pp. 227-252.

TODOROVA, Maria: Imagining the Balkans. New York – Oxford 1997.

TROEBST, Stefan: Ethnien und Nationalismen in Osteuropa. *Österreichische Zeitschrift für Geschichtswissenschaft* 5:1 (1993), pp. 7-22

TRUBETA, Sevasti/VOSS, Christian (eds.): Minorities in Greece – Historical issues and new perspectives. Munich 2003 (= Jahrbücher für Geschichte und Kultur Südosteuropas 5).

VERMEULEN, Hans/GOVERS, Cora (eds.): The Anthropology of ethnicity. Beyond 'Ethnic groups and boundaries'. Amsterdam 1996, second edition.

VERMEULEN, Hans/GOVERS, Cora (eds.): The Politics of Ethnic Consciousness. New York 1997.

VILFAN, Sergij (ed.): Ethnic Groups and Language Rights. Comparative Studies on Governments and Non-dominant Ethnic Groups in Europe, 1850-1940. Aldershot 1993.

WILSON, Thomas/DONNAN, Hastings (eds.): Border Identities. Cambridge 1998.

WINGFIELD, Nancy (ed.): Creating the other. Ethnic conflict and nationalism in Habsburg Central Europe. New York – Oxford 2003.

WOLFF, Stefan (ed.): German minorities in Europe. Ethnic identity and cultural belonging. New York – Oxford 2000.

ZEITLER, Klaus: Raumbezogene Identität – ein Entwicklungsfaktor für den ländlichen Raum? Eine soziologische Analyse der Determinanten und Inhalte ländlicher Raumentwicklung. Augsburg 2001 (= Angewandte Sozialgeographie 42).

Part I.

Theory and Law

Hidden Identities within National Minority Groups: The Case of Slovenes in Carinthia and in the Province of Trieste

Marija Jurić Pahor

Introduction

The Slovenes in Austrian Carinthia (Carinthian Slovenes) and the Slovenes living in the Province of Trieste (Friuli Venezia Giulia Region) have a status of national minorities. This is confirmed in the reports submitted by Austria and Italy pursuant to Article 25, paragraph 1 of the Framework Convention for the protection of National Minorities of the Council of Europe (FCNM), which was ratified at the beginning of 1995 and entered into force on 1 February 1998.[1] In the reports the terms *Volksgruppen* and *minoranze linguistiche,* as the common legal expression in Austria and Italy, are used in accordance with the wording of the FCNM and are thus recognised as *national minorities.* Although the Framework Convention does not provide a clear concept of national minorities, because it was impossible to arrive at a definition acceptable to all Council of Europe member States (Explanatory report, paragraph 12), in Article 5, paragraph 1, the "essential elements of their identity, namely their religion, language, traditions and cultural heritage" are considered key elements. National minorities are therefore minorities that differ from the majority population in one of the above-mentioned criteria. It must be stressed that we are referring to minorities considered "official minority groups" on a state by state basis. Within Austria and Italy a distinction is made between these groups (six in Austria and twelve in Italy), which are legally defined and recognised as minorities, and other ethno-cultural groups, such as Roma and Sinti (especially in Italy)[2], Jews, asylum seekers and other immigrants. These other groups do not have a special legal status as "official minority groups" although they are *de facto* minorities. This consideration also suggests that categories like "national minority", "Volksgruppe" or "minoranza linguistica" initiate a community-building discourse, reminiscent of the establishment of the modern territorial nation state.

The decisive impulse for this development was given by the French Revolution. It should be noted that from 1789 on, the nation started to consider itself

---

[1] The text of the FCNM including the Exploratory report are available at: http://www.coe.int/t/e/human_rights/minorities/2._FRAMEWORK_CONVENTION_%28MONITORING%29/.

[2] The Roma (and Sinti) in Austria were officially recognised as a national minority (Volksgruppe) in 1993. Five larger groups of Roma can be distinguished in Austria today: Burgenland Roma, Sinti, Lovara, Kalderaš and Arlije.

as a collective singular, which means that it is defined by other nations (rejecting those who represent a "nation in the nation"[3], especially those who are territorially difficult to localise clearly) and in the relationship with its citizens (rejecting those who do not meet the criteria of the postulated national ideal). The nation, in accordance with the equation "one state – one nation", or better, "one nation – one state", unifies the social field in an internally inclusive and externally exclusive "unity". Hence the minorisation[4] of nations in its primary meaning of the word, i.e. the state of being both the (numerical) minority and an "alien body" to be both assimilated and rejected. The nation and all its citizens should be inspired by the same spirit. Differences were considered divisive and therefore treacherous. It is only in this fact that the main cause of "hidden identities" phenomenon should be considered. As will be demonstrated, this phenomenon will necessarily be present inside "minority" communities. The process of national unification implied in fact the "principle of choice", more or less in terms of choosing between the status quo and a future, unified nation state. Nevertheless this principle contained its negation since the decision for the new and future state was compulsory. The nation therefore became not only a prospective, but also an amalgamating, expansionist idea, that forced the "old" nation/community underground or – closely related with this – into the desire and finally the claim for autonomy, as very clearly expressed by the myth of the "millenarian dream of the nation about its own state". Miroslav Hroch, who on the basis of comparative studies developed a three-phase periodisation of small national movements in Central and Eastern Europe, concludes that this claim appears massively in the third phase, the very late phase of national movements.[5] This is true also for the modern national consciousness in Carinthia and in the Trieste region, which reached the masses of the Slovene-speaking population only in the last third of the 19th century. Among the German and Italian-speaking and in general among the population of the Alpine and Adriatic region it was not very different.[6] Nevertheless we must consider that in that period, and especially after the collapse of the Habsburg monarchy, the idea started to spread among intellectuals and the political

[3] Clermont-Tonnerre spoke in the National Assembly on 23.12.1789 on the emancipation of the Jews: "We must refuse everything to the Jews as a nation and accord everything to Jews as individuals (…) They must be citizens individually". What France cannot tolerate, Clermont-Tonnerre insisted, is a "nation in the nation". Detlev Claussen: Grenzen der Aufklärung. Zur gesellschaftlichen Geschichte des modernen Antisemitismus. Frankfurt/M. 1987, pp. 73-74.

[4] Lat. *minor*, that which is less, or inferior in comparison with another, the term being employed as well of things as of persons. Cf. The Catholic Encyclopedia, vol. X. New York 2003, Online Edition.

[5] Miroslav Hroch: Social Preconditions of National Revival in Europe: A Comparative Analysis of the Social Composition of Patriotic Groups among the Smaller European Nations. New York 2000.

[6] Andreas Moritsch (ed.): Vom Ethnos zur Nationalität. Der nationale Differenzierungsprozeß am Beispiel ausgewählter Orte in Kärnten und im Burgenland. Vienna – Munich 1991 (= Wiener Beiträge zur Geschichte der Neuzeit. Volume 18); Marina Cattaruzza (ed.): Nazionalismi di frontiera. Identità contrapposte sull' Adriatico nord-orientale. Catanzaro 2003.

elite that the world by definition belongs to strong (nation) states and that "smaller and marginal" or "late" nations lacked the right of self-determination or even to exist.

Hence the policy of assimilation by which individuals were persuaded (and sometimes coerced) into abandoning their original identity, accepting membership in the dominant community and adopting its official language and culture. The consequences of such policies were and (partly) still are especially visible in Carinthia. The characteristic of the Slovene minority in Carinthia was its gradually increasing semi-visibility, non-visibility or even its disappearance. This is suggested in studies[7] often based on census data. Already in 1826, Urban Jarnik in his essay "Andeutungen über Kärntens Germanisierung" ("Hints on the Germanisation of Carinthia") wrote that this people (i.e. the Slavs, the Slovenes) still live in German Carinthia, only their language has been changed as the old dress for the new.[8]

Although an assimilation policy was implemented in Friuli Venezia Giulia, the Slovenes in this region (especially in the Trieste area, less in Gorizia) resisted vehemently at the end of the 19th century, but mainly at the beginning of the 20th century, which had the effect of undermining its intended goals. This effect was even stronger because this community had close relations with the "(South) Slavic block", which was stimulated by the restrictive assimilation policy. A relatively strong liberal middle-class and working class, the presence of national banks, a series of political, cultural and economic associations of the liberal, catholic and proletarian type, the "political" acceptance of the Slovene community in the city centres (Trieste and Gorizia) by the central authorities, conditions that did not exist for Slovenes in Carinthia, contributed to these developments. The contemporary existence of these elements and their expansion are also present in the assumption that in that period less "nationally eager" Slovenes of the Trieste region also chose the appearance of the eager – in everyday talk also "pure" or *d.o.c.,* i.e. self-described "genuine Slovenes". In the years before 1914 in Trieste the process that would inevitably bring to the redistribution of power between the Italian and the Slovene group began to crystallise to suddenly be interrupted by the outbreak of the First World War, followed by the collapse of the Habsburg monarchy and later by fascism.[9]

---

[7] Vida Obid et al.: Haiders Exerzierfeld. Kärntens SlowenInnen in der deutschen Volksgemeinschaft. Vienna 2002.

[8] Theodor Domej: O skupinski identiteti na Koroškem v prednacionalnem obdobju, p. 56.

[9] Cattaruzza: Sloveni e Italiani a Trieste, pp. 57-58.

From "nation" to nation

Before moving on to the phenomenon of the hidden identities among the Slovenes of Carinthian and Trieste, I wish to point out that by the middle of the 18th century, the expression *natio* existed only in the Romance languages; in German the word *Volk* was used, the Latin the word *natio* or *natie* was perhaps used by the aristocratic or educated classes[10]; in Slovenian the words *rod* and later *narod* were employed. The above-mentioned notions had very similar semantic contents. Dictionaries often connect *rod* with the words *roditi* (from Latin *nascior*, to be born, *natus*, born) or "birth", in French *naissance*, in Italian *nascita, origine*. Nation is therefore a collective term that defines a community of people as inhabitants of a certain country or native land, i.e. of people who were born in a particular place and are organised on the basis of common characteristics as language, culture, religious rites or traditions. Nations are certainly not all identical and none of them include all the above-mentioned characteristics, in the academic but also in the everyday discourse, they are subject to very different interpretations.[11] However, we can state that nations appeared as an attempt to develop a meaningful order for a complex social reality – with the classification of people into distinctive nations the "chaos" of different groups of people was to be avoided. Nations had already been used in the ancient Rome as a definition of non-Romans, that is, "foreigners" not born in Rome (they were usually concentrated in certain parts of the city called "quarters"). The Romans themselves never called themselves *natio*, but always "populus romanus" and their sign was SPQR (Senatus Populusque romanus, the Roman Senate and the Roman people).[12] Especially since the late Middle Ages, nation can be found as an antonym to *patria, civitas* and/or *civitas Dei*. It was sometimes scornfully connected with societies personified by mother-goddesses or societies, in which descent was traced through the women (i.e. matrilineal societies)[13] It was also associated with the members of pagan or syncretic religions, as suggested by the word *pays natal*, in Italian *paese natio*, later eas-

---

[10] Eric J. Hobsbawm: Nationen und Nationalismus. Mythos und Realität seit 1780. Frankfurt/M. 1991, pp. 26-27.

[11] Hobsbawm, Nationen und Nationalismus, pp. 25-29; Suzanne Citron: Nacionalni mit. Pretres zgodovine Francije. In: R. Rizman (ed.), Študije o etnonacionalizmu. Ljubljana 1991, pp. 207-208.

[12] In an analogous position to Roman nations, in ancient Greek towns the various *metics* (*metoiki*) were inhabitants who were not citizens.

[13] The existence of such societies is clear in the equation *natio* = *natio* or in Slovene *matica* = *matica*. In old Greek the equivalent is *meter* = *metris*. Even Cicero, a proud Roman citizen and member of the "civitas", said that the goddess of birth was called *natio*. "Natio quoque dea putanda est, quia partus matronarum tucatur, a nascentibus Natio nominata est". (De Natura Deorum, III) In the Slovene language the Slovene nation and also the Slovene nation state have been stubbornly identified with the terms *matica* or *motherland* and never with the terms *očetnjava* or *fatherland*. The attempts to "patriarchise" were unsuccessful on a terminological level. See Marija Jurić Pahor: Narod, identiteta, spol. Trieste/Trst 2000, pp. 155-195.

ily identified by the lexicographers with the "province".[14] The words "pays" and "paese" derive from *pagus*, from which derive "paysan", "paesano" (peasant) and "paien", i.e. "pagano" (pagan, non-Christian). It is interesting to note that also the word "ethnicity", a derivation from the Greek term *ethnicos*, initially defined people that did not belong to the main or "true" religion. In the Christianised context the word, "ethnic" (sometimes spelled "hethnic") recurred in the sense of "heathen" or, in German, "Heide". The English language has retained the pagan memory of "ethnic", secularised in the often negative sense of ethnic as "other".[15] This linguistic technique carries with it all the connotations that have and had the function of separating between "us" as a Godly-chosen or secularised chosen people and "them/others".

The Alpine-Adriatic space had its own "nations". The term defined the immigrants in the strict and in the broad sense of the word; i.e. groups of people that came from the neighbouring countryside especially into big cities. This is evidenced, for example in a letter of the Levantine bishop Vinzenz Joseph Schrattenbach to the emperor Joseph II dated 9 June 1783, in which he argues against the creation of a "common seminary" in Graz where students from the regions of Carinthia, Styria, Carniola and Friulia could study. He calls them *Nationen* and thought that they differ both in "habits, characteristics, virtues" and also in the approach to the "spiritual guidance" of the priests. This difference was for the bishop the reason for – under the clear influence of the process of modern nationalisation – fighting for the Klagenfurt seminary. He thought that in the planned *common* seminary, "divided into four nations, the patriotism of each nation would influence the other, and the directorship would hardly be able to control the prejudices, hating attitudes, conjures among the young men."[16]

In Trieste after 1719, that is, after the declaration of the city as a free port that included more religious freedom, newcomers such as Jews, Greek and Serbian Orthodox, Protestants (especially Lutherans from Germany and Swiss Calvinists from Graubünden), and Armenians, whose members would soon reach the apex of the mercantile elite, were called *nazione*, or, in plural, *nazioni*[17]; a part of these nations had existed in their nuclear form already since the late Middle Ages. The petition of the "Carniolan community" of 1783 shows that it also formed its own "nation" – the "nazione cragnolina". The petition, written in Italian, is interesting not only because it shows evidence of the cohesion of the

---

[14] Hobsbawm, Nationen und Nationalismus, p. 28.

[15] Werner Sollors: Beyond Ethnicity: Consent and Descent in American Culture. New York – Oxford 1986, p. 25.

[16] Domej, O skupinski identiteti na Koroškem, pp. 47-48. I am very grateful to the author for checking again the term *Nationen* in the archive.

[17] Louis C. Dubin: The Jews of Trieste: Between *Mitteleuropa und Mittelmeer*, 1719-1939. In: E. Lappin (ed.), Jüdische Gemeinden, Kontinuitäten und Brüche. Berlin – Vienna 2002, p. 26; Roberto Finzi/Giovanni Panjek (eds.): Storia economica e sociale di Trieste. La città dei gruppi 1719-1918. Trieste 2001.

Carniolan or "central-Slovene" immigrant people in Trieste, but also because it turns to the local Church authority in order to preserve the sermon in the church of the former Jesuit order attended by "many Carniolans" and held in the "Carniolan" language[18], i.e. in the language that would become the Slovene language and gradually replace the ethnonyms "windisch/Winde/Wende", "krainerisch/Krainer" and "cragnolino/Cragnolini" as German and Italian synonyms for the "Slovene language" and the "Slovenes".[19] On the basis of registry records of the city parishes of Trieste, it is possible to state that in the 18th century, about two thirds of the newcomers came from the traditional Slovene-speaking hinterland and from Gorizia-Gradisca, Carniola and Istria; a large part of the newcomers had their origin in Friuli (and nearby Carinthia).[20]

At first glance it seems that the "nazioni" were organised religiously, which can be seen even today in religious buildings, gathered in the heart of Trieste (but also in other Alpine-Adriatic cities, especially in Istria) which were homes to the little-known and publicly invisible or semi-visible communities or *nazioni*. Their different architectural styles (oriental, neo-Byzantine, neo-classic, neo-gothic, eclectic), expressing a symbolic axis between the Orient and Occident, show that the idea of territory or (imagined) *locus* of origin was stressed more than the idea of religion, a fact which also becomes clear in the contemporary use of the terms *nazione ebraica (israelitica), nazione greca, nazione illyrica, nazione alemanna, nazione elvetica, nazione armenica.* The members of the latter, mostly Ottoman subjects from the East Mediterranean were, because of their dress and their religious celebrations with oriental rites, often the target of negative comments. Nevertheless, it must be added that the population of such minorities were very small; in 1776 39 Armenian immigrants lived in Trieste, the next year only 26.[21] The *nazione cragnolina* also found itself under the watchful eye of ascetic-nationalistic views. This group, together with the indigenous Slovene native speakers was not only considered "peasant", "heretic" and "hethnic" (very clearly by the "reformed" bishop

---

[18] Aleksej Kalc: Poti in usode. Selitvene izkušnje Slovencev z zahodne meje. Koper – Trst 2002, pp. 21-22.

[19] Domej, O skupinski identiteti na Koroškem, pp. 62-63. Jernej Kopitar was the first to use the ethnonym *Slovene/slowenisch* at the beginning of the 19th century. It must be added that the Slovene language had not been subject to "purification" up to then, which means that it still contained many loan-words from other, especially neighbouring languages. This was true both in the literary language and in the dialects. The terms "krainerisch/Krainer", "cragnolino/Cragnolini" and "kranjski/Kranjec" referred to Carniola, from 15th century on the only region with an almost complete Slovene population. Therefore the Slovene language was identified with the "Carniolans" and the "Carniolan" language (especially its Upper Krain variety – gorenjščina), which became the basic norm in the unification of Slovene into a language that was to be "one and the same" for everybody; Slovene dialects became inferior, secondary.

[20] Kalc, Poti in usode, pp. 15-16. The census from 1900 shows for Triest 1755 Carinthians and 2268 Styrians, and between them also migrants "di lingua slovena". Pierpaolo Dorsi: La collettività di lingua tedesca. In: Finzi/Panjek (eds.), Storia economica, p. 558.

[21] See Tullia Catalan. Cenni sulla presenza armena a Trieste tra fine Settecento e primo Ottocento. In: Finzi/Panjek (eds.), Storia economica, pp. 606-608.

Bonomo and even more clearly by his then student and vicar Primož Trubar, who will become the main personality of Slovene Protestantism), and therefore not yet "civilised", but also someone who could not be a member of the urban elite, which *mostly* communicated in Italian, or better in its local version, known as *tergestino*.[22] However, it is true that the Slovene language in the city was the "domestic language or the language used mostly by some trade groups. The Slovene language was in fact one of the (at least) three languages fluently used by the Triestine aristocracy"[23].

Nevertheless the idea that Trieste was an "Italian" city spread obstinately, as all the other towns and cities on the Adriatic coast were considered "Italian", and all the towns and cities in Styria, Carinthia and even Carniola were "German". This idea coincides with the idea of an "ethnic and linguistic boundary" in which the Slovenes of the hinterland, in this case the hinterland of Trieste, had lived – at least up to the 19th century – *ante muros*, i.e. before the doors of the city and that they had been up to then a "peasant nation without its own ruling class" and therefore an "ahistorical nation".[24] Several studies have drawn our attention to the fact that the Slovenes (and members of some other communities) had been *constantly* present in Trieste. Some of them were even aristocrats or "*cives* by full right"[25], which cannot be said for St. Veit/Šentvid and Klagenfurt/Celovec, the former and the present capital of Carinthia. (Nevertheless, the rite of investiture of the Carinthian dukes points to the fact that people of Slav or Slovene origin also lived in Carinthia, who could be defined using terms like *cives* or *civitas* [as the whole body of *cives*]; and who held, in the period of the ancient *Carantania* leading functions.[26])

---

[22] On the phenomenon of the Triestine dialect (*tergestino*), which changed after 1719 its physiognomy in the direction of modern *triestino* see Mario Doria: Storia del dialetto triestino, Trieste 1978. The "pure Italian" or "Toscano" in its consciously conservative and purist form began to be used only at the end of the 19th century.

[23] Paolo Merkù: La presenza slovena nella città preemporiale. In: Finzi/Panjek (eds.), Storia economica, p. 288.

[24] See for example Angelo Ara/Claudio Magris: Triest. Eine literarische Hauptstadt in Mitteleuropa. Munich – Vienna 1987, p. 39.

[25] Merkù, La presenza slovena, pp. 288-289.

[26] The rite of investiture was carried out in Slovene and the last one took place in 1444. It was closely related with *Civitas carantana* that had its headquarters in the Castle of Kamburg on Zollfeld, on the road between Klagenfurt and St. Veit. Between the 7th and the 8th centuries, this castle was also the centre of the poly-ethnic Duchy of Carantania, mainly composed and led by people of Slav origin. In the 9th century a Carolingian Palatinate was established and Slav people were Christianised during this period, but not without rebellions. The rite of the investiture of Carantanian leaders played an important role, especially because it included an oath to the Christian religion. Nevertheless the rite conserved clear pagan or "matriarchal" oriented concessions, which among other things are also evident in the fact that Carantania was not only governed by dukes (Valuk, Borut, Gorazd, Hotimir, Valhun, Pribislav(ka), Semika, Stojmir and Edgar). The name "Pribislavka", in written documents quoted as "Priwizlauga", is not a male, but a "female form, and it certainly denotes a duchess", as Jožko Šavli recently discovered. And there were probably also women among the so-called *cives* (free peasants called *kosezi,* in German *edlinger,* sometimes *ritter, gepawer).* It is interesting that the famous Duke's Throne, on which especially

A document for the city of Trieste from the year 1202 quotes among 360 *cives,* 30 names of Slav origin; the percentage of Slovene-speaking people in the city at the beginning of the 18th century, when the total population numbered a little more than 3,000 people, was significantly bigger.[27] In the writings of Boris Pahor it becomes clear that at that time in Trieste, native speakers not only arrived from the hinterland, but also from Carniola and Istria: "Documents from 1382, 1395, 1401, 1463 are full of names like Nedeljko, Tomaž, Babič and Stojan. [...] In Cavana Street in 1454 Miha Babič has his own house; close to it lived Ivan and Martin Babič. [...] The artisans are: shoemakers Zobec, Zorko and 'Pietro from Lubiana'; the barber Just Mirec, the hatter 'Martin from Castua', the dressmaker 'Tomaso from Postojna' [...]." The Slovenes were also part of the mercantilists' elite, among them, especially, members of the *nazione cragnolina.* Their names appear among factory and warehouse owners who, in spite of limited possibilities, participated as shareholders in the Imperiale Privilegiata Compagnia Orientale (Oriental Imperial Privileged Company) established in 1719 for overseas trading in the Levant and the West Indies, and among the high imperial officials.[28]

The fact is that the "nations" were, especially after 1719, in spite of suggested or apparent "concentration", dynamic, heterogeneous and mostly united entities, more open "to the world" than withdrawn from it. Religion, that is, "religious" organisation, represented, however, the only link within the individual communities, even if it was often an unclear and weak link. Many people were included in the process of crossing geographical borders – "from the Adriatic and the Levant", or more modestly "from the hinterland and the city" (in which Trieste as the main port of the Habsburg monarchy undoubtedly had an outstanding role in the Alpine-Adriatic region). Their loyalties did not belong "only to their own communities", but also to two (or more) places, religions, cultures and people. It was this fluctuating way of life and belonging that made them know that their "national" identity and what it is believed to imply can

---

this class of people invested the Carantanian dukes, was also defined by the term *civitas* or *civitate*, and it was also connected with the Latin name "Maria in Solio" (Gospa Sveta, Maria Saal) or the word *solium* as a definition of Duke's throne (*stuol*). The Carantanian *kosezi* disappeared from the political scene as soon as the rite did. Both are still known only as a "European characteristic" or as a peculiar, even funny relict. In the 12th and 13th centuries the *kosezi* were identified with the ministerial aristocracy; later they were only peasants with special rights. In the 16th century they lost also their special rights and were included among simple subjects. See Marko Vidic et al. (eds.): Ilustrirana zgodovina Slovencev. Ljubljana 2001, pp. 34-87; Marija Wakounig: Das Alpen-Adria Gebiet im hohen und späten Mittelalter. In: A. Moritsch (ed.), Alpen-Adria. Zur Geschichte einer Region. Klagenfurt – Ljubljana – Vienna 2001, pp. 133-136; Jožko Šavli: St. Domitian amd St. Modestus of Carantania, http://www.carantha.net/st__domitian_and_st__modestus_of_carantania.htm.

[27] Milan Bufon: Trst, Trieste. In: Enciklopedija Slovenije, vol. 13. Ljubljana 1999, p. 352; Boris Pahor, O slovenski pričujočnosti v Trstu. In: M. Pirjevec (ed.), Tržaška knjiga. Ljubljana 2001, p. 8.

[28] Marta Verginella: Sloveni a Trieste tra Sette e Ottocento. In Finzi/Panjek (ed.), Storia economica, pp. 449-445.

shift or change in time. In this case marriage played a major role, because it seldom happened that complete families immigrated. This inevitably led to the "formation of couples of often very diverse origin and culture"[29] and therefore also to interpersonal cultural confrontation, that could have different forms. However this confrontation did not coincide with a conscious desire of breaking with the original "nation", that is, with the community a person belonged to "by birth". Such a desire became acute only with the modernist-oriented intellectual and political elite's assumption that nations and ethno-cultural communities, which insist on their *native's point of view* – we could also say in their primary matrix – are "societies against the state"[30], or that they had not yet entered the arena of European or Western civilisation, which means that they did not want a nation or state strongly enough. Whatever the modern nation was, it never lacked a desire for stateness. And, especially, it did not lack a clear falogocentrism[31] that demanded a radical entrance in the "world of history", that is, in a specifically human world of "programmed consensus" and removal from the libidinal dimension, connected with the primary dyad mother-child; it is a process that included a detachment from traditions and cultural practices of the original community. The revolutionary abbot Sieyès, who repudiated his own order, was the herald and greatest executor of this alchemy. In February 1789 he wrote in his work "Qu'est-ce que le Tiers État?": "The nation is before everything, it is the origin of everything. Its will is always legal, it is the law itself".[32] With this *credo*, which reads like a revolution that carries its holiness in itself and eventually in the nation, nationalism starts to exist as an all-embracing phenomenon.

Nation – Passing – Mimicry

The process of creation of the modern nation coincides with the "desire of unity", of "a single whole", and can be identified with the phenomenon summed up by Robert W. Connel in the idea of "hegemonic masculinity" (the "revolutionary" nation was considered a "fraternity" that did not accept women[33]). However it also coincides with the assumption that "nationalism is primarily a principle which holds that the political and national unit should be

---

[29] Marco Breschi et al.: La nascita di una città. Storia minima della popolazione di Trieste, secc. XVIII-XIX. In: Finzi/Panjek (eds.), Storia economica, pp. 166-181.
[30] Pierre Clastres: Society against the State. Essays in Political Anthropology. New York 1987.
[31] Falogocentrism (Jacques Derrida) is the fusion of falocentrism and logocentrism. Falocentrism defines the system that privileges the phallus as the symbol of origin and power. Logocentrism defines the main current of occidental thought that privileges Logos as a metaphysical presence.
[32] Citron, Nacionalni mit, p. 213.
[33] Erna Appelt: Geschlecht, Staatsbürgerschaft, Nation. Politische Konstruktionen des Geschlechterverhältnisses in Europa. Frankfurt/M. – New York 1999.

congruent."[34] We may add that this principle also implies that the political duty of propagators of nation building to the society, which encompasses and represents the nation, overrides all other political obligations and in extreme cases, such as wars, all other obligations as such. This implication distinguishes modern nationalism from other and less demanding forms of "national" or group identification. But modern nationalism coincides more than everything with the claim that the "desire of unity" should be realised in the form of the sovereign state. What creates the "unity" of a nation? According to Ernest Gellner, nationalism is not what it seems: "Admittedly, nationalism uses the pre-existing, historically inherited proliferation of cultures and of cultural wealth, though it uses them very selectively and most often transforms them radically".[35] Side by side with this process of national unification, feelings of local or regional identity persisted to a powerful degree, supported by images about independent cultural traditions and separate linguistic habits. National identity is now defined according to the ideal of "purity", the loyalty to one's own origin, language and national culture, formulated and partly reproduced in the national discourse. Where the equation "one nation – one state – one culture" had become a political, the opinion arose that the co-habitation of different human groups would lead to a weakening of character; the mixture of peoples and cultures were now considered as a sin against the unitary force usually referred to as the soul, mind or spirit of a people, described in Hegel's terms as the *Volksgeist* or the character of a nation (state). And precisely this force finally led to the absolutist recognition of the uniqueness of the nation and with it to the idea of the "contamination" through the other, for example the potpourri of "ethnic groups, 'nations', religions and languages".

It was not until the nineteenth century that we find Europe divided into clearly defined nation states – even as late as 1861 or 1871 in the case of Italy and Germany. It is precisely from this period onwards that the nation state is recognised as the unit of political power par excellence, its form being taken as a model "not only in Western Europe but also in the rest of the world".[36] Therefore, it was also the model for (Central-) Eastern Europe and even more precisely for the national movement in Carinthia and in the province of Trieste, where it will find its suitable expression in the proclamation of national liberation and inclusion of Slovenia into the first Yugoslav state (29 October 1918). Soon, on 1 December 1918, Slovenia united with the victorious Serbia into the Kingdom of Serbs, Croats and Slovenes. Today consensus is spreading on the fact that this movement should primarily be seen as an answer to the existing national movements of other, dominant nations, which were imitated by Slovene national representatives. Their purpose was not only to develop a strong national "we" consciousness amongst the Slovene-speaking population,

---

[34] Ernest Gellner: Nations and Nationalism. Oxford 1983, p. 1.

[35] Gellner, Nations, p. 55.

[36] Montserrat Guibernau: The Nation-State and Nationalism in the Twentieth Century. Cambridge 1996, p. 57.

but also to defy national marginalisation more efficiently. The driving force behind this was a mostly German and Italian *mission civilisatrice,* which defined Slovenes as well as all (southern) Slavs as not sufficiently civilised peoples.[37] Such stereotypes can be found even today in scientific publications. The most drastic example – at least among the more influential theorists – is Ernest Gellner. In two of his last works[38] he put South-East Europe into the third "time zone" and reiterated a myth, which is rooted in the Trieste province in particular and which expresses disdain towards the Slovenes and Central European "Ruritanians", whom he considers potentially dangerous and violent, but also as non-compatible with the heritage of modern *nation building*. Gellner refers to the nationalism west of Trieste as mostly benign, while nationalism east of Trieste as "mostly appalling".[39] His diction coincides also with the thesis of the "supremacy of the city", which both in the Triestine and in the Carinthian context most often proves to be *porte-parole* and classifies hierarchically "Italianity" or "Germanity" vis-à-vis "Slovenity". John Himka writes: "Here we have an instance of the larger problem of the relation between what has been variously called a 'non-historical', 'plebeian', 'submerged', 'small' nation with one that is 'historical', 'state', 'dominant' and 'great' [...] It is the Ruritanian-Megalomanian nexus."[40] Slovene "peasant society" proves to be an antithesis to "modern society" – as if it developed "independently" from it. I want to underline the fact that this "nexus" contributed fundamentally to the reinforcement of the hegemonic position to which Carinthian and Triestine Slovenes were exposed – although in different ways – in the last third of the 19th century, and especially after the First World War, when in the Republic of Austria and imperialistically enlarged Italy, minorities were considered undesirable, almost unacceptable. It also contributed strongly to the "violence of justification" (*violence de fondation*, in Étienne Balibar's words), which is also a fundamental condition of a so-called hidden identity. It is closely related with the relation domination-subordination and with the process of stigmatisation. The classical Greeks used the word "stigma" to refer to brands or body markings exposing people that were to be avoided; they were proclaimed to be ritually unclean and therefore outlawed. In most cultures physical marking or stigmatisation disappeared, though the stigma kept many of the original connotations. The term refers to being different in some undesirable way. People use this difference in order to drive others away or to avoid them. In this sense, the institution of stigma is also very effective at the establishing of "norm/alisation" or "normality". Most people do not want to be seen as differ-

---

[37] A highly important factor here was the fear that a united Slovene national territory could threaten access to the Adriatic. There was only one possible solution to this problem – the Slovene national movement and Slovene nationality must never really exist.

[38] Ernest Gellner: Language and Solitude: Wittgenstein, Malinowski and the Habsburg Dilemma. Cambridge 1998; Ernest Gellner: Nationalismus. Kultur und Macht. Berlin 1999.

[39] Ernest Gellner: Nationalismus, pp. 98-99.

[40] John-Paul Himka: Slovaks and Hungarians, Ruritanians and Megalomanians. In: http://www.h-net.msu.edu/~habsweb/archives/threads/szarka.html.

ent or "abnormal".[41] This means that some strategies are developed to permit them to repress or hide those characteristics of their identity that are considered undesirable or even illegal. In the following I will introduce two strategies for avoiding "stigma" that I consider most characteristic in relations between members of dominant and non-dominant communities.

Passing: This strategy is often called "going to the other side" or "crossing over"; the term is often used in literature and refers to the relationships between whites and blacks (i.e. *passing for white*), but it can also be transferred to other majority-minority contexts. At its centre is the concealment of stigma or of the characteristics that are connected with it, and it usually presents itself as the change of identity or, more acutely, as assimilation (< lat. *assimilatio*, becoming more similar, identical; from lat. *ad*, to, towards + *similes*, similar). The main reason for passing must be sought in the conditions of massive political, economic and social inequality between the dominant and non-dominant communities, in the power hierarchy that forces the individuals to "wish" or "want" to hide their origin or completely abandon it (often to the point of radically refusing it) in favour of certain advantages. These advantages are often associated with a better life and – in extreme cases – even with survival. One of these can be the access to certain resources (for example to education or work) or the mitigation of stressful situations connected with the weaker and stigmatised community (for example social control, inferiorisation, and expulsion). Both passing and assimilation are not a predictable and linear process that "necessarily" leads to a unified culture with homogeneous cultural practices. The assumption that these strategies end in the disappearance of specific cultural characteristics of minority communities must therefore be verified critically. How could we otherwise explain the different phenomena associated with so-called "ethnic revival" or "re-assimilation" or the phenomenon of partial identification or non-identification with the national community in the modern sense?

Mimicry: As opposed to passing or assimilation, this strategy is not (so much) an identification with the dominant community in the sense of a tendency to integrate into it. Neither is it the well-known exercise of dependent relations through "narcissistic identification". In the foreground of this strategy are procedures with which people adapt to the predominant conditions through deception. It is actually a kind of "hide and seek", in which the subversive protest and cultural or ethnic *difference* (even if it looks so small) plays an important role. The observations of Ruža Petrović, on the difference between ethnic origin and ethnic orientation (*etničko poreklo* and *etnička opredeljenost*) in former Yugoslavia, are interesting. Even if people often considered themselves "Yugoslavs" in censuses and/or changed their ethnic or national identities in the course of their lives, it is clear from official statistics that they most often

[41] Erving Goffman: Stigma. Über Techniken der Bewältigung beschädigter Identität. Frankfurt/M. 1967.

died with the identity given "at birth", for example as Roma, Albanians, Serbs; this classification was given them by their relatives.[42] As in passing, an essential role is also played by the unequal power relations between "we" and "the others" in the processes of mimicry. However, these relations may change. For example, a non-dominant, stigmatised community may obtain power or even predominance, which may lead to open resistance or to new hierarchical relations and therefore to sharpened reciprocal borders. This process will also be visible in mimicry, which is, similar to passing, always also a form of identity discourse at the crossroads of what is known and permissible and what, though known, must be kept concealed. The wearing of the mask of heroism or the stressing of the "love for one's own people" are well known and permitted, while well known but concealed would remain "non-heroism" or the tendency to identity with the other; hence, for example, the fear of expressing the "primary", "soft" attributes of identity and fear of "contamination" (connoted in the unconscious with the mother-woman). It is not possible to draw clear lines between the two strategies; the *passing* strategy is more characteristic for the Carinthian Slovenes, while the *mimicry* strategy (especially the mimicry of heroism) is more characteristic for the Triestine Slovenes. Under the classification "Slovene" I include here both the national, i.e. self-defined or openly "Slovene" Slovenes, and those people, who are native speakers of Slovene and at least in private or on the local level use in one or another form Slovene linguistic and cultural "codes". This definition is based on the premise that precisely these people were, at least partly, important co-creators of what we today call the "Slovene nation", even if they were often the "target" of (German, Italian, Slovene) national elites, which necessarily influenced the transformation of their identities.

The Slovenes in Carinthia

I consider it suitable to approach the *passing* identity strategy with the example of Carinthian Slovenes. It is closely related to the "liberal call to assimilate" that Zygmunt Bauman rightly defined as "the most specifically, authentically modern of the nation-state policies" that "obliquely reaffirms what has to be proved – the superiority [...] of the native rulers".[43] This authority was in Carinthia centred in the hands of liberally-oriented German elites and groups that from the second third of the 19th century onwards followed an expansionistic policy, partly with the imperialistic or "Great German" undertones. This development can be clearly seen in the censuses about the colloquial language,

[42] Ger Duijwings: Die Erschaffung von Ägypten in Kosovo und Makedonien. In: U. Brunnbauer (ed.), Umstrittene Identitäten. Ethnizität und Nationalität in Südosteuropa. Frankfurt/M. et al. 2002, pp. 123-148.

[43] Zygmunt Bauman: Modernity and Ambivalence. Cambridge 1991, pp. 69-70.

about which Emil Brix thinks that they were not only the expression of objective statistical analysis but primarily the expression of political and economic power, which on the bilingual territory of Carinthia clearly privileged "Germanity". This is also evidenced in the various types of pressure during censuses, which strongly hastened the national differentiation between the German-speaking and the Slovene-speaking population in Carinthia.[44] However this pressure was not as successful among "common people" as one would imagine. In the 1880 census, when, within the framework of the Habsburg Monarchy, the population had to decide about their "colloquial language" for the first time, 85,051 persons in Carinthia identified themselves as Slovene-speaking persons; in 1891 Slovene was used by 84,667 persons. But in the following two decades everything changed. The Slovene-speaking people in Carinthia followed what they considered the norm and avoided any mention about their colloquial language. The 1910 census indicates only 66,463 Slovene-speaking persons. A rapid decrease follows, from 34,436 persons in 1923 to 24,857 persons in 1934. This number increases again in 1951, when 42,095 persons declare they speak Slovene, but it decreases again, like soon after the plebiscite – the 1961 census reveals only 24,911 persons speaking Slovene in one form or another and this number continues to fall: 1971: 20,972; 1981: 16,552; 1991:14,580; 2001: 12,568.[45]

According to Albert F. Reiterer this unsteadiness of persons identifying themselves as Slovene-speaking is a clear indicator of the fact that statistical information depends on socio-political circumstances and the execution of the census; that they do not reveal any factual information about the Slovene language in Carinthia.[46] This was precisely the situation that Reiterer examined in 1999 with the help of a micro-census and detailed interviews. He came to unexpected results: today there are still only between 12,000 and 13,000 persons in Carinthia that consider themselves as belonging to the Slovene national community, but the group of those who "are not ethnically Slovene (any more)", but who have a certain, limited Slovene linguistic competence, is rising constantly, reaching 60,000 persons. They are mostly people "with Slovene roots", which they still remember, even if with an emotional touch that goes from a neutral to very negative feeling -- as if these roots pointed towards a "shadow", to an alter ego, the existence of which they despise.[47] This is an internalised stigma (for example "slowenisch is *schiach*", "*awful*"; "windisch is *jugo*",

---

[44] Emil Brix: Die Umgangssprachen in Altösterreich zwischen Agitation und Assimilation. Die Sprachenstatistik in den zisleithanischen Volkszählungen 1880 bis 1910. Vienna et al. 1982.

[45] See table in: Vida Obid et al.: Haiders Exerzierfeld. Kärntens SlowenInnen in der deutschen Volksgemeinschaft. Vienna 2002, p. 13.

[46] Albert F. Reiterer: The Slovene Language in Carinthia – Symbolic Bilingualism. *Razprave in gradivo* 43 (2003), pp. 186-201.

[47] Reiterer, The Slovene Language; Albert F. Reiterer: Lebenswelt Muttersprache. Das Slowenische und seine heutige Wahrnehmung ein Bericht. *Kärntner Jahrbuch für Politik* 2000, pp. 340-362. I am grateful to Albert F. Reiterer, who sent me both articles by e-mail, from where I quote.

"*yugo*"[48]), hastened and forced as a result of German nationalism. Nietzsche clearly described this process: "The reputation, name, and appearance, the usual measure and weight of a thing, what it counts for – originally almost always wrong and arbitrary, [...] – all this goes from generation unto generation, merely because people believe in it, until it gradually grows to be part of the thing and turns into its very body. What at first was appearance becomes in the end, almost invariably, the essence and is effective as such".[49] However, Reiterer states that Slovene also evokes "softer" memories, for example, when he refers to an "old Windisch woman" (according to Reiterer, a woman of Slovene origin, not willing to declare herself as such) saying that she sometimes talks "Windisch" with her (half-)brothers, because it was something her mother "most certainly liked to *see* (italics by M.J.P.)".[50] The relationship with her mother is often mentioned in this context. The author then assesses a "discrete *outing* of Slovene-speaking Carinthians".[51] The language choice thus becomes a rational-choice matter, as any other linguistic skill.

We should ask ourselves whether this *outing* also *and perhaps particularly* implies a latent identification with Slovene-speaking ancestors as a form of a protest, as we see today in the phenomenon of "ethnic revival." This latter phenomenon is especially prevalent among groups, which have previously been subjected to a severe assimilation policy adopted by the dominant society, their native languages being generally believed to be facing rapid extinction. Those Slovenes that for some reason decided to mask their Slovene origin were consistently labelled *nemškutarji*, renegades by the for the most part conservative-clerical-oriented Slovene national representatives. Later the term was also identified with the concept *Windisch*.[52] The expression *nemškutarji* (also *nemčur*) first appeared in 1848 as a definition for people "born by a simple Slovene mother, who learnt some German at school and in the army, who live among Slovenes, but hate and persecute Slovenes and their language [...] and consider themselves Germans".[53] It must be read as an expression of the ruling national-

---

48 Reiterer, Lebenswelt Muttersprache.
49 Cited after Maria Todorova: Imagining the Balkans. New York – Oxford 1997, p. 19.
50 Reiterer, Lebenswelt Muttersprache.
51 Ibidem.
52 The term *Windisch* or *Windische* contains two aspects. The first is the linguistic aspect, where people say: "this is a Slovene dialect". This definition of Windisch corresponds with the fact that Windisch was a synonym for the Slovene-speaking people. However it implies a second aspect, the assumption that Windisch differs politically from Slovene, which can be clearly stereotyped differentiation: "The Slovenes are for the Slovenia of (former) Yugoslavia" or "The Slovenes are for Slovenia under Tito, they are Tito communists". This stereotype has its historical appearance in the so-called *Windischentheorie*, founded by the Carinthian historian Martin Wutte (1927) with the aim of promoting the pan-Germanic idea and to discredit the so-called self-described or *zavedni* Slovenes (the people, pushed into this category, will latter find themselves in concentration camps). This theory assumes the Windische as a separate nation, which is more in line with the Germans than with the Slovenes (*deutschfreundlich*) or as Germans with their own linguistic and cultural tradition (*eigensprachige Kulturdeutsche*).
53 Vidic et al. (eds.): Ilustrirana zgodovina Slovencev, p. 245.

ist logic that did not allow people to live "together" any more, assumed a clear separation of *either* Germans *or* Slovenes. This necessarily created quite stressful situations, especially among Slovene-speaking people that were often compelled to "define themselves as Germans", because this was the only way for them to get a higher social status, better living conditions; sometimes it was a simple matter of social and – especially after the 1920 plebiscite – even physical survival. This was despite the fact that in 1920, 60% of the South-Carinthian population voted for "German" Austria – and the "Slovene votes" were decisive.

The continuous reproof of being renegades, which was apparent already at the beginning of the 20th century, was very painful for many Slovene-speaking people; it was a *factum brutum*, which they experienced as an unjust expression of the falsification of their identity. This falsification is also shown in the fact that the group, which was the target of this reproof, was so diverse in its social structure and its reasons that it could possibly be reduced only to the characteristic of *wilful* de-ethnisation or de-nationalisations, this being the main contents of the term *nemškutarj*. People gravitating towards passing or assimilation maintained or cultivated in part, strong relationships with their origin and tradition, even when they identified themselves as Germans. This is what, for example, was stressed by the most famous Slovene *Burger* and renegade Dragotin Dežman (also Deschmann), who in 1867 wrote in the Laibacher Tagblatt that "also *nemškutars* love their mother tongue and hope it will develop".[54] This diction can be found everywhere in the press of German nationalists written in Slovene language and intended for the Slovene Carinthian countryside. This press is even more interesting because it had to consider first the feelings of the readers intended to be won over to the "German side". That this was not easy is clear in the fact that even in 1909, sentences like the following can be found: "'Nemčurji'! Incomprehensible and stupid is this word. We have never re-baptised or changed anybody. Who is Slovene, is and remains Slovene, also in our party".[55]

Avguštin Malle writes that in around 1870, teachers, who according to Austrian and Carinthian elites, were to become one of the primary driving forces of assimilation, still showed some understanding for Slovene as a language of instruction and were not indifferent towards Slovene demands for equality of the Slovene language at school. Some teachers and students of education even organised Slovene celebrations at school and actively took part in Slovene national demonstrations. Malle goes on: "No doubt many teachers were germanised, but the process took much longer than we usually believe; it became pronounced when school authorities no longer permitted any more doubt about its German nationalist orientation".[56]

---

[54] Vidic et al. (eds.): Ilustrirana zgodovina Slovencev, p. 245.

[55] Janko Pleterski: Narodna in politična zavest na Koroškem. Ljubljana 1965, p. 235.

[56] Avguštin Malle: "Tabori na Koroškem." *Zgodovinski časopis*, 41/2 (1987), pp. 603-604.

Equally interesting is Oswin More's observation regarding the character of Carinthian workers, who sought work outside their domestic, rural and catholic environment, although they kept in touch with it all the time and retained "many inherited habits in their lifestyle."[57] Nevertheless, the Slovene national elites defined Slovene teachers, and especially workers, as *nemčurji*, that is, people presenting a certain danger of *passing*. And from their point of view this danger was present in all those who were not strongly rooted in a "protected" Catholic rural milieu.

It is certainly symptomatic that Carinthia in the period of Nazism did not only prove to be "the most loyal of all the Fuhrer's Alpine fiefs" (as is often accurately suggested, although this is a very general position), but also one of the less loyal and from the viewpoint of prominent Nazis, distinctly inconsistent and unreliable countries. Joško Tischler, the then leading Carinthian Slovene politician, observed in autumn 1938 that repression, i.e. "the fact that people are not allowed to speak Slovene" generated a new phenomenon, i.e. that "unconscious elements are consciously starting to speak Slovene".[58] "Until recently unknown documents" referring to the expulsion of Carinthian Slovenes to the German Reich or Nazi concentration camps, prove that Nazism failed to (completely) undermine ethnic ties and "basic foundations of human and neighbourly solidarity". This expulsion stirred up a lot of fear and some protests even amongst the population oriented towards a German national identity; the doubt about the rightfulness of forceful "ethnic cleansing" was very strong.[59]

Alois Maier Kaibitsch, the chief organiser of the expulsion, on July 10th 1942 on the occasion of the Gauamt meeting in Klagenfurt, spoke before the state and provincial representatives as well as leaders of the NSDAP stating "that the people of Carinthia had little understanding of their duties along the border, having altogether forgotten what it was all about…" He reluctantly admitted that, immediately after the expulsion, the Slovene language was hardly heard anywhere, but was now again beginning to be spoken: "There are even mayors, peasant leaders, members of the BDM and the HJ that speak Windisch; this is especially true of Jauntal and Rosental".[60]

Here we are dealing with a tendency that has survived until today. Of course it is true, that a considerable part of the population inhabiting the bilingual terri-

[57] Pleterski, Narodna in politična zavest, p. 319.

[58] Teodor Domej: Prvo leto koroških Slovencev pod kljukastim križem. In: A. Malle/V. Sima (eds.), Der "Anschluß" und die Minderheiten in Österreich. "Anšlus" in manjšine v Avstriji. Klagenfurt/Celovec 1989, p. 83.

[59] Teodor Domej: O ponemčevanju južne Koroške za časa nacizma in odmevi nanj (1938-1942). In: A. Malle/V. Sima (eds.), Narodu in državi sovražni. Pregon koroških Slovencev 1942. – Volks- und staatsfeindlich. Die Vertreibung von Kärntner Slowenen 1942. Klagenfurt/Celovec 1992, pp. 210-231.

[60] See the reprint in Tone Ferenc: Quellen zur nationalsozialistischen Entnationalisierungspolitik in Slowenien 1941-1945. Maribor 1980, pp. 452-461.

tory of Carinthia was more or less strongly permeated with German nationalism, partly even (post)Nazism, but it is likewise true that ties with Slovene ethnic "roots" – i.e. traditions or latently ongoing patterns of life that have been shaped in close neighbourly relations and coincide neither with the majority nor with minority nationalism – are still alive or are going through a process of revival.

The Slovenes in the Province of Trieste

I will now discuss the situation in the Province of Trieste. It can be said that the national polarisation there took a different course than in Carinthia and that it had different results. While the status of German nationalism in Carinthia has always been monopolistic, this is not true of Italian nationalism. Already at the beginning of the 20th century, and especially before the First World War, the Slovene national movement in the Trieste region was of such economic, cultural and political strength that the national balance tipped in its favour. This prevented forced assimilation, so that "Italians" and "Slovenes" stood one against another like two incompatible monoliths in seeming homogeneity and supposed uninterchangeable specificity. Slovenes have – also due to the ample and continually growing share of the population from the Slovene hinterland – established themselves even in the city centre, as shown by the slogan "Trieste belongs to us", as well as by exclamations ("Long live Slovenes, long live Trieste!") on different occasions, attended also by other (southern) Slavs. Angelo Ara and Claudio Magris notice: "The Adriatic city acquires for the Slovenes the meaning of the moral and natural capital of Slovenia, the symbol of its national resurrection, the aim to which it is worth tending to."[61]

The occupation of the then Austrian Littoral (November 1918), which coincided with the re-establishment of the expansionist Italian nationalism and later fascism, which in Italy was extremely repressive especially against Slovenes and Croats, hindered the realisation of Slovene national goals, but did not stop them completely. This is especially true of fascism, which triggered or strengthened the tendency of Slovenes (especially young men with strong feelings of ethnic affiliation) to unite and act in the direction of militant "irreversible polarisation".

The Italian invasion of Yugoslavia and the occupation of the province of Ljubljana aggravated the relations between the two nations. A vast number of Slovenes of Trieste and the Littoral joined the national liberation struggle, which, after the fall of Mussolini, was mostly directed against Nazism, or, to be more precise, against Nazi-fascism; it ended with the "victory" or "liberation of

---

[61] Ara/Magris, Triest, p. 69.

the Littoral". This "victory", which right after the war was manifested in revenge upon the executors of fascist violence and the collaborators, as well as in the persistent stereotype of "the brave and rebellious people of the (Slovene) Littoral", has been presented in Italian (and not only nationally oriented) public discourse to this day as a kind of inferno. A similar argument can be found in the report of the Slovene-Italian Historical and Cultural Commission (established at the initiative of the Foreign Ministries of Slovenia and Italy). According to the report, the atmosphere on the Italian-Yugoslav border after 1945 was that of "a clash between civilisations".[62] Fascist totalitarian violence and "struggle for borders" strengthened the calls for national unity ("all forces have to be lined up in a united fight") and binary opposition (up to 1954: "pro-Slovenian/pro-[Yugo] Slav bloc" – "pro-Italian bloc").

Interviews with Slovenes from Trieste born after 1945 clearly show that this constellation has a strong impact upon the identity of the Slovene people from the Trieste region.[63] On an abstract level this resulted in an "identity-in-difference" that implied a relationship between two "fraternal" communities. This relationship is based on the homo-social desire (what Luce Irigaray with a pun calls hommo-sexuality[64]), i.e. on repressed and therefore despised "soft" feelings that are closely related to the primary, "oceanic" unity with the mother. These feelings continue to live in the human being in a latent form and can go back to regression to this unity, which societies with a phallocentric ideology – often linked with the desire or need for "a fight, or rebellion" – want to impede with all their might. It is a mechanism that – in reference to mental processes and national identification especially in the Trieste region – psychoanalyst Pavel Fonda suggests, suit the "group-defensive posture in every war".[65]

The fact is that fascism and later Nazism greatly influenced the people of the Trieste region; between the years 1920 and 1954 they lived in a permanent state of war. And precisely this state of war created an attitude among many Triestine Slovenes that exists even today, even if in a mitigated way, understood as "heroism" or "rebellious heroism" – which is among other things visually well "documented" by the series of national-defensive or partisan monuments and memorial plaques, present in almost every Slovene or bilingual village (in Trieste there are none, because this would, according to the ruling diction, "infect" the "Italianity" of the city). Even if this attitude looks

[62] Slovene-Italian historical and cultural commission: Slovene-Italian Relations 1880-1956. Ljubljana 2001: pp. 55, 103, 150. The report was published in Slovene, Italian and English.
[63] Jurić Pahor, Narod, pp. 291-331.
[64] hommo-sexuality: from the French *hom(m)osexualité*; homme: man, human. The use of a double "m" expresses the privileged status of the "male" in any conception of gender and sexuality. See Luce Irigaray: Speculum. Spiegel des anderen Geschlechts. Frankfurt/M. 1980, pp. 124-132.
[65] Pavel Fonda: Psihični proseci in narodnostna identifikacija. In: F. Clavora et al., Ednina, dvojina, večina. Petnajst prispevkov k vprašanju identitete, sožitja in življenja v narodnostno mešanem okolju. Trst 1987, p. 89.

"normal" – as a habit or an inherent "part" of the mental or somatic "nature" – in a more detailed analysis it reveals itself as superficial, as mimicry or masquerade. It is nevertheless an attitude that does not act only as a negative or exclusive code, it is also a sanction and – very pertinently – as the law of a discourse that separates the speakable from the unspeakable (creates boundaries and builds the field of the unspeakable) and the legitimate from the illegitimate. In other words, those who do not speak or act in accordance with the image implied in the figure of the "heroic rebel" may be explicitly or implicitly "excommunicated"; they will not be "seen or heard" on the public scene of the community.

Only recently have some voices come to the foreground that reveal how the described attitude works. Some younger historians[66] have noticed both the absence of written records and a preliminary selection of the documentation produced on the war. This absence is visible especially in the fact that the connection with the figures of the "hero" or the "heroic community" cancelled the traces of fear, worry, powerlessness, disappointment characteristic for the state of war. A more detailed analysis of this documentation, and especially the analysis of oral material, further reveals that it is impossible to draw "clear boundaries between perpetrators and victims, between heroes and cowards, between "'our people' and 'the others'".[67] It can furthermore be said that the image of heroic people greatly contributed to contemptuous talk about identities that are regarded "assimilatable" (typically "Carinthian", according to popular belief), "split", "soft" or disharmonious with the radical national or national-revolutionary political action. This is manifested in the fact that victims of concentration camps (be they alive or dead) are still an "unwelcome guest" (Boris Pahor) in the collective consciousness of the Trieste Slovenes. "Victims were ignored and even despised, while partisans were enwrapped into the 'glory of heroism'."[68] Victims also represent something that – as suggested by the Triestine-Slovene national discourse – should not exist: in a way even the living were already dead, destroyed as "personalities"; they kept on living despite their all but "militant posture". Slavoj Žižek arrived at a similar conclusion: "No matter how horrible it sounds, it is in a way easier to understand executioners in concentration camps than their victims; an executioner identifies himself with the phantasmagorical image of a Nazi evildoer who enjoys torturing people, [...] he is just an extreme point of the scale, where, on the one end, there is a courageous hero willing to sacrifice his life for his homeland, and on the other end a cruel executioner – but as for the victim, there is simply no place for him".[69] The "heroic posture" is to be found in the logics of history:

---

[66] Marta Verginella et al.: Ljudje v vojni. Druga svetovna vojna v Trstu in na Primorskem. (Knjižnica Annales 9). Koper 1995.

[67] Verginella, Ljudje v vojni, p. 12.

[68] Ivanka Hergold: Zapiski o Pahorjevi Nekropoli. In: M. Pirjevec/V. Tuta Ban (eds.), Pahorjev zbornik. Spomini, pogledi, gradivo. Trst 1993, p. 169.

[69] Slavoj Žižek: Jezik, ideologija Slovenci. Ljubljana 1987, p. 215.

it was triggered by fascism and its consequence, anti-fascism. It is furthermore handed down to the younger generations and therefore makes the spontaneous human relationships and co-habitation more difficult. Let me illustrate this with one single quotation from an interview: “My Italian friend often asks me: ‘Why are you talking to me with your prejudice and defensive posture?’ And then it happens that I often interpret his answers as assaults upon myself. My first reaction is always: ‘Is this anything against me?’ I am very careful, always very careful.”[70]

Conclusion

This short fragmentary outline, referring to the phenomenon of “passing” (in Carinthia) as well as to the phenomenon of “mimicry”, created by the acute national polarisation (in the Trieste region) suffice to point out that in majority and minority discourse strongly defined by nationalism, there are many blind spots that have yet to be made visible and elaborated conceptually. These blind spots point out the fact that, if we look under the surface, national – but also ethnic – identities always turn out to be multilayered, controversial and heterogeneous phenomena, which know neither monolith unity nor linear expressions of belonging. They also point to the vision that national identities are not static or fixed, but are changing and varying and may acquire different forms. National identities may be imposed or refused, manipulated in order to become gradually lost, revived or (newly) imagined. They may also lead to a nobody’s country (“I belong neither here nor there”) or “somewhere between” (“I am neither this nor that”). I consider it important that a “reflective change” is taking place in this field. It is strongly supported by people that were or are exposed to different forms of stigmatisation, theoreticians or authors striving in promising research studies for the affirmation of an alternative symbolic system, i.e. a system, that does not propagate an abstract unity under some transcendent leadership, but imagines concrete reality as a condition, in which a person can be different without fear. Some of these scholars work within the framework of European Unity, which is no longer a project or a fantasy, but a material reality that cannot “be opposed” and presents a great chance in its challenges.

Translated by Vesna Bajc

[70] Jurić Pahor, Narod, p. 320.

Bibliography:

APPELT, Erna: Geschlecht, Staatsbürgerschaft, Nation. Politische Konstruktionen des Geschlechterverhältnisses in Europa. Frankfurt/M. – New York 1999.

ARA, Angelo/MAGRIS, Claudio: Triest. Eine literarische Hauptstadt in Mitteleuropa. Munich – Vienna 1987.

BAUMAN, Zygmunt: Modernity and Ambivalence. Cambridge 1991.

BILLIG, Michael: Spomin na vsakdanji nacionalizem. In: M. Nastran Ule (ed.), Predsodki in diskriminacije. Ljubljana 1999, pp. 157-183.

BRESCHI, Marco et al.: La nascita di una città. Storia minima della popolazione di Trieste, secc. XVIII-XIX. In: R. Finzi/G. Panjek (eds.), Storia economica e sociale di Trieste, vol. 1: La città dei gruppi, Trieste 2001, pp. 166-181.

BRIX, Emil: Die Umgangssprachen in Altösterreich zwischen Agitation und Assimilation. Die Sprachenstatistik in den zisleithanischen Volkszählungen 1880 bis 1910. Vienna et al. 1982.

BUFON, Milan: Trst, Trieste. In: *Enciklopedija Slovenije,* vol. 13, Ljubljana 1999, pp. 352-356.

CATALAN, Tullia: Cenni sulla presenza armena a Trieste tra fine Settecento e primo Ottocento. In: R. Finzi/G. Panjek (eds.), Storia economica e sociale di Trieste, vol. 1: La città dei gruppi, Trieste 2001, pp. 483-558.

CATTARUZZA, Marina (ed.): Nazionalismi di frontiera. Identità contrapposte sull' Adriatico nord-orientale. Catanzaro 2003.

CATTARUZZA, Marina: 'Sloveni e Italiani a Trieste, la formazione dell' identità nazionale'. In: *Clio. Rivista trimestrale di studi storici* 25/1 (1989), pp. 28-58.

CITRON, Suzanne: Nacionalni mit. Pretres zgodovine Francije. In: R. Rizman (ed.), Študije o etnonacionalizmu. Ljubljana 1991, pp. 191-220.

CLASTRES, Pierre: Society against the State. Essays in Political Anthropology. New York 1987.

CLAUSSEN, Detlev: Grenzen der Aufklärung. Zur gesellschaftlichen Geschichte des modernen Antisemitismus. Frankfurt/M. 1987.

DOMEJ, Teodor: Prvo leto koroških Slovencev pod kljukastim križem. In: A. Malle/V. Sima (ed.), Der "Anschluß" und die Minderheiten in Österreich. "Anšlus" in manjšine v Avstriji. Klagenfurt/Celovec 1989, pp. 66-88.

DOMEJ, Teodor: O ponemčevanju južne Koroške za časa nacizma in odmevi nanj (1938-1942). In: A. Malle/V. Sima (eds.), Narodu in državi sovražni. Pregon koroških Slovencev 1942. – Volks- und staatsfeindlich. Die Vertreibung von Kärntner Slowenen 1942. Celovec/Klagenfurt 1992, pp. 210-231.

DOMEJ, Theodor: O skupinski identiteti na Koroškem v prednacionalnem obdobju. In: A. Moritsch (ed.), Matija Majar Ziljski. Klagenfurt/Celovec 1995, pp. 43-65.

DORSI, Pierpaolo: La collettività di lingua tedesca. In: R. Finzi/G. Panjek (eds.), Storia economica e sociale di Trieste, vol. 1: La città dei gruppi, Trieste 2001, pp. 547-582.

DUBIN, Louis C.: The Jews of Trieste: Between *Mitteleuropa und Mittelmeer*, 1719-1939. In: E. Lappin (ed.), Jüdische Gemeinden, Kontinuitäten und Brüche. Berlin – Vienna 2002, pp. 23-42.

DUIJZINGS, Ger: Die Erschaffung von Ägyptern in Kosovo und Makedonien. In: U. Brunnbauer (ed.), Umstrittene Identitäten. Ethnizität und Nationalität in Südosteuropa. Frankfurt/M. et al. 2002, pp. 123-148.

FERENC, Tone: Quellen zur nationalsozialistischen Entnationalisierungspolitik in Slowenien 1941-1945. Maribor 1980.

FINZI, Roberto/PANJEK, Giovanni (eds.): Storia economica e sociale di Trieste. La città dei gruppi 1719-1918. Trieste 2001.

FONDA, Pavel: Psihični proseci in narodnostna identifikacija. In: F. Clavora et al., Ednina, dvojina, večina. Petnajst prispevkov k vprašanju identitete, sožitja in življenja v narodnostno mešanem okolju. Trieste 1987, pp. 68-111.

GELLNER, Ernest: Nations and Nationalism. Oxford 1983.

GELLNER, Ernest: Language and Solitude: Wittgenstein, Malinowski and the Habsburg Dilemma. Cambridge 1998.

GELLNER, Ernest: Nationalismus. Kultur und Macht. Berlin 1999.

GOFFMAN, Erving: Stigma. Über Techniken der Bewältigung beschädigter Identität. Frankfurt/M. 1967.

GUIBERNEAU, Montserrat: The Nation-State and Nationlism in the Twentieth Century. Cambridge 1996.

HERGOLD, Ivanka: Zapiski o Pahorjevi Nekropoli. In: Pirjevec/Tuta Ban (eds.), Pahorjev zbornik. Spomini, pogledi, gradivo. Trieste/Trst 1993, pp. 159-174.

HIMKA, John-Paul: Slovaks and Hungarians, Ruritanians and Megalomanians. In: http://www.h-net.msu.edu/~habsweb/archives/threads/szarka.html

HOBSBAWM, Eric J.: Nationen und Nationalismus. Mythos und Realität seit 1780. Frankfurt/M. 1991.

HROCH, Miroslav: Social Preconditions of National Revival in Europe: A Comparative Analysis of the Social Composition of Patriotic Groups among the Smaller European Nations. New York 2000.

IRIGARAY, Luce: Speculum. Spiegel des anderen Geschlechts. Frankfurt/M.1980.

JURIĆ-PAHOR, Marija: Narod, identiteta, spol. Trieste 2000.

KALC, Aleksej: Poti in usode. Selitvene izkušnje Slovencev z zahodne meje. Koper – Trieste 2002.

MALLE, Avguštin: "Tabori na Koroškem." *Zgodovinski časopis*, 41/2 (1987), pp. 599-622.

MERKÙ, Paolo: La presenza slovena nella città preemporiale. In: R. Finzi/G. Panjek (eds.), Storia economica e sociale di Trieste, vol. 1: La città dei gruppi, Trieste 2001, pp. 273-291.

MORITSCH, Andreas (ed.): Vom Ethnos zur Nationalität. Der nationale Differenzierungsprozeß am Beispiel ausgewählter Orte in Kärnten und im Burgenland. Vienna – Munich 1991 (= Wiener Beiträge zur Geschichte der Neuzeit. Volume 18).

OBID, Vida et al.: Haiders Exerzierfeld. Kärntens SlowenInnen in der deutschen Volksgemeinschaft. Vienna 2002.

PAHOR, Boris: O slovenski pričujočnosti v Trstu. In: M. Pirjevec (ed.), Tržaška knjiga. Ljubljana 2001, pp. 17-19.

PLETERSKI, Janko: Narodna in politična zavest na Koroškem. Ljubljana 1965.

REITERER, Albert F.: 'Lebenswelt Muttersprache. Das Slowenische und seine heutige Wahrnehmung ein Bericht.' In: *Kärntner Jahrbuch für Politik* 2000, pp. 340-362.

REITERER, Albert F.: The Slovene Language in Carinthia – Symbolic Bilingualism. *Razprave in gradivo* 43 (2003), pp. 186-201.

SLOVENE-ITALIAN HISTORICAL AND CULTURAL COMMISSON: Slovene-Italian Relations 1880-1956. Ljubljana 2001.

SOLLORS, Werner: Beyond Ethnicity: Consent and Descent in American Culture. New York – Oxford 1986.

TODOROVA, Maria: Imagining the Balkans. New York – Oxford 1997.

VERGINELLA, Marta et al: Ljudje v vojni. Druga svetovna vojna v Trstu in na Primorskem. Koper 1995 (= Knjižnica Annales 9).

VERGINELLA, Marta: Sloveni a Trieste tra Sette e Ottocento. In: R. Finzi/G. Panjek (eds.), Storia economica e sociale di Trieste, vol. 1: La città dei gruppi. Trieste 2001, pp. 441-481.

VIDIC et al. (eds.), Ilustrirana zgodovina Slovencev. Ljubljana 2001.

WAKOUNIG, Marija: Das Alpen-Adria-Gebiet im hohen und späten Mittelalter. In: A. Moritsch (ed.), Alpen-Adria. Zur Geschichte einer Region. Klagenfurt/Celovec – Laibach/Ljubljana – Vienna/Dunaj 2001, pp. 123-172.

ŽIŽEK, Slavoj: Jezik, ideologija Slovenci. Ljubljana 1987.

The Representation of Small Ethnic Groups by State Bodies: The Case of Austria and Slovenia

Mirjam Polzer-Srienz

Introduction

Over the last decade, minority protection has gained increased importance in Europe. The collapse of the Union of Soviet Socialist Republics (USSR), the Socialist Federal Republic of Yugoslavia (SFRJ) and the flaring up of ethnic conflicts have all drawn increasing attention to this area. This violent escalation of ethnic tensions was the impulse for a more vehement development of international minority protection. The UN Declaration on the Rights of Persons Belonging to National or Ethnic, Religious and Linguistic Minorities was adopted in 1992; the Council of Europe developed the Framework Convention for the Protection of National Minorities and the European Charter for Regional or Minority Languages. In addition the OSCE – faced with the fact that legal arrangements alone are insufficient to regulate conflicts – introduced, as an early warning system, the position of the High Commissioner on National Minorities. However, despite multiple efforts on national and international levels, great deficits still exist.

1. Minority protection on the international level

No definition of national and ethnic minorities is generally accepted in international law.[1] Nevertheless, some general criteria can be distilled from the documentation. A minority can thus be defined as:

(1) an autochthonous community that settles as a special ethnic or national group

(2) either in a closed area or dispersed throughout a state,

(3) whose members are citizens of that state

(4) and who distinguish themselves through ethnic, linguistic or cultural characteristics from the remaining citizens of that state and who are

(5) willing to preserve these characteristics.[2]

---

[1] Rainer Hofman: Minderheitenschutz in Europa – Überblick über die völker- und staatsrechtliche Lage. *Zeitschrift für ausländisches öffentliches Recht und Völkerrecht* 52 (1992), p. 3.

[2] See also the definition in article 2, Draft Supplementary Protocol to the European Convention on Human Rights. In: Österreichisches Volksgruppenzentrum (ed.), Internationales und

International law guarantees different minority rights. But it is questionable to what extent valid international law guarantees internal political representation for minorities.[3] The UN International Covenant on Civil and Political Rights of 16th September 1966, guarantees in article 25 every citizen and therefore also persons belonging to ethnic groups the right to participate directly or through freely chosen representatives in the organisation of public matters. However, this right is an individual right and does not apply to a minority claiming political representation as a group. Similarly, the UN Declaration for the Rights of Persons Belonging to National or Ethnic, Religious and Linguistic Minorities of 18th December 1992 speaks only of individual rights. In accordance with article 2 (3) of the declaration, persons belonging to minorities have the right to an effective representation on decisions in those matters, which concern the minority to which they belong. But the concrete rendering of these minority rights is left to the national legislator. Furthermore, the declaration is not legally binding; it only makes recommendations for the political representation of minorities.

Article 3 of the 1st Supplementary Protocol of 4th November 1950 to the European Convention on Human Rights describes the right of citizens to participate in the execution of state power. Again, here the right is defined only as an individual right the concrete rendering of which is left to the individual state.

International minority protection has been improved through the adoption of the Council of Europe's Framework Convention for the Protection of National Minorities and the European Charter for Regional or Minority Languages.[4] Yet the Framework Convention contains no collective rights with regard to the participation and representation of ethnic groups; the Charter protects not ethnic or national groups, but regional and minority languages.

Within the framework of the OSCE, a considerable catalogue of minority protective measures has been compiled. Since, however, the different declarations are not legally binding, these political declarations of will are dependent on the individual states for their enforcement. Yet with the "Lund Recommendations on the Effective Participation of National Minorities in Public Life" of 1999 explicit and detailed recommendations to states to issue special measures in this field were made for the first time. Although the Lund recommendations are again, not legally binding, they are of great political importance since representation and participation of ethnic groups has to date been prevented in some states while the explicit reference to the need for self-determination has been lacking.

Europäisches Volksgruppenrecht. Vienna 1995 (= Österreichische Volksgruppenhandbücher 8), p. 104.

[3] The term minority is used neutrally in this article and includes both small and/or hidden ethnic groups.

[4] http://conventions.coe.int/treaty/en/Treaties/Html/148.htm; http://conventions.coe.int/treaty/en/Treaties/Html/157.htm.

Within the framework of the EU, no obligations concerning the right to representation and participation of minorities exist. Minorities seem to be twofold dependent on the goodwill of the nation state in which they live: on the one hand, the states must involve themselves as subjects of international law for minority protection; on the other hand, these states must adopt these norms from international law into their national legal system. This is a reason why even in the 21st century still no generally accepted minority right protection on international level exists.

2. The need for representation of ethnic groups

The state does not only consist of a single people as it formulated the idea of the nation state "Volk = Staat = Nation" but of different ethnic groups. Therefore, it is necessary that all ethnic groups support the state. If the state, is understood as Renan's daily plebiscite[5], then the integration of the different ethnic groups is taken as given, otherwise the state suffers from a legitimisation deficit. However, the incorporation of ethnic groups should not mean assimilation but integration. Integration means that several parts establish a unit while maintaining their unique characteristics. Thus integration requires recognition of the differences in ethnic groups.[6]

Depending on how the recognised difference of the ethnic groups is handled, two models are possible: the "constitution of identity through the exclusion of difference" and "the maintenance of autonomy through inclusion of difference".[7] While the fiction of identity of individuals and nations excludes the political and legal recognition of difference and has the consequence of assimilation and/or segregation, the legal recognition of difference allows the maintenance of autonomy and integration.[8]

The integration of ethnic minorities is of special importance since there is a crucial difference between political and ethnic minorities. Political minorities need not always remain a minority; if they succeed in developing a strong opposition policy, then the circumstances can change with the next election. Ethnic minorities, on the other hand, are in a permanent situation of being a minority. Such minorities often cannot protect their interests.

---

[5] Ernest Renan: "Was ist eine Nation?", lecture in Sorbonne 11.3.1882. In: L. Gall/R. Koch (eds.), Der europäische Liberalismus im 19. Jahrhundert, vol. 3, Frankfurt/M. et al. 1981, p. 132.

[6] Cf. Michael Brems: Die politische Integration ethnischer Minderheiten aus staats- und völkerrechtlicher Sicht. Frankfurt/M. 1995, p. 5; Rudolf Smend: Staatsrechtliche Abhandlungen. Berlin 1968; Rudolf Smend: Verfassung und Verfassungsrecht. Munich/Leipzig, 1928. See also Hans Kelsen: Der Staat als Integration. Vienna 1930.

[7] Joseph Marko: Autonomie und Integration: Rechtsinstitute des Nationalitätenrechts im funktionellen Vergleich. Vienna et al. 1995, p. 163.

[8] Marko, Autonomie und Integration, p. 108.

Representation and participation offer a form of institutionalisation of conflict resolution mechanisms. Diverging interests of the minority and majority populations can be discussed harmonised and controlled democratically and serve for the peaceful settlement of ethnic tensions and the protection of interests of ethnic groups. Political integration into state bodies is of great importance because representation and participation guarantees self-determination; the ethnic group is no longer dependent on the majority and freedom and equality of all people can be realised.

The largest ethnic group often dominates a state. This group is then able to successfully assert its own interests, even against the will of ethnic minorities. Therefore, its understanding of the basic principles of democracy considerably influences the organisation of minority protection systems. Equality is for this reason of special importance as a central basic right of democratic states. The question arises as to how the special characteristics of people or groups should be protected if one requires formal equal treatment? Can an exception[9] be justified or is it even required in specific cases? Especially if one uses the equality of groups as a standard of comparison, it is clear that ethnic groups experience disparities despite or due to formally equal treatment. An unequal treatment of individuals can often only be noticed when groups are used as a standard of comparison and persons belonging to one ethnic group are compared with persons belonging to another group. Only then can unequal treatment, which is traced back to the affiliation to the group, be spotted.

Collective rights are thus as important as individual rights for an effective protection of ethnic groups. Individual rights are important for the protection of individuals from discrimination; however, they cannot guarantee the existence of groups. Moreover, many minority rights are only conceivable as collective rights. If collective rights are refused, the protection of minorities is also considerably limited. Especially in the field of political representation, the political civil rights of every single individual are as necessary as the collective right of the minority group to political representation. Rights to self-government, representation and participation, "privileges" in electoral law as well as participation in government are only conceivable as group rights. Individual rights can indeed protect individuals from discrimination but they cannot guarantee appropriate participation of the minority as a group.

National minority protection systems are influenced by specific historical and political evolution. As an example, group related or individual legal protection

[9] "Dignity and equality for all individuals and groups are essential components of democracy. The realization of these rules, by way of non-discrimination and special rights and measures, furthers the fruits of participatory development and improves the quality of life for both, minorities and the society as a whole. This approach reduces internal tensions, prevents dismemberment of states and helps keep the peace." Gudmundur Alfredsson: Minority Rights: Non-Discrimination, Special Rights and Special Measures. In: F. Ermacora/H. Tretter/A. Pelzl (eds.), Volksgruppen im Spannungsfeld von Recht und Souveränität in Mittel- und Osteuropa. Vienna 1993, p. 149.

can be mentioned. Collective rights are recognised mostly in the so-called states of the "new democracies" like in Slovenia and Hungary.

In the "older" liberal nation states of the West, however, ethnic groups often do not receive legal protection as minorities because of a group phobia which is linked to the concept of the nation state postulating the indivisibility and the unity of the body politic. This group phobia is due to the fact that the interest of a national minority, as Peter Pernthaler emphasises, is the same as that of the state nation – namely "free existence". Due to Pernthaler a national minority is a "nation on a small scale"; it therefore does not compete with other partial groups of society, but with the interest of the whole nation in its "free existence", i.e. with the nation's claim for sovereignty. The liberal nation state therefore is not opposed against individual members of a national minority, but against the national minority as a whole.[10] With other words, individual rights and equal treatments of individual members of ethnic groups are granted in the pluralistic social order of the "older" liberal nation states, but they have no desire to recognise ethnic groups as national minorities by collective rights.

3. Normative minority protection in Austria

After the dissolution of the Austria-Hungarian monarchy in 1918, conflicts concerning the drawing of the border between Austria and the Kingdom of the Serbs, Croats and Slovenes developed. These conflicts also affected the minorities in the two states. The boundary conflict had negative results for the Carinthian Slovenes in particular[11]; and had important consequences for the Croats in Burgenland[12] and the Slovenes in Styria.[13]

---

[10] Cf. Peter Pernthaler: Der Schutz der Gemeinschaften durch individuelle Rechte. *Europa Ethnica* (1962), p. 59.

[11] Mirjam Polzer-Srienz: The Croat and the Slovene Minority in Austria. In: K. Cordell/S. Wolff (eds.), Ethnopolitical Encyclopaedia of Europe. Basingstoke, New York 2004, pp. 28-45.

[12] Gerhard Baumgartner: 6 x Österreich. Geschichte und aktuelle Situation der Volksgruppen. Klagenfurt 1995 (= Edition Minderheiten 1); Österreichisches Volksgruppenzentrum (ed.): Burgenländische Kroaten. Vienna 1993 (= Österreichische Volksgruppenhandbücher 5); Herbert Gassner: Unterlassungssünden gegenüber den Kroaten. In: R. Henke (ed.), Leben lassen ist nicht genug. Vienna 1988, p. 117; Herbert Gassner: Die Rechtslage der Kroaten im Burgenland. In: S. Geosits (ed.), Die burgenländischen Kroaten im Wandel der Zeit. Vienna 1986, p. 350.

[13] Österreichisches Volksgruppenzentrum (ed.): Steirische Slowenen. Vienna 1996 (= Österreichische Volksgruppenhandbücher 9); Janko Pleterski: Slovenci na avstrijskem štajerskem in člen 7 pogodbe o Avstriji. In: B. Jesih et al. (eds.), Slovenci v avstrijski zvezni deželi Štajerski. Zbornik referatov na znanstvenem srečanju v Mariboru, 25.-27. maja 1993. Lubljana 1994 (= narodne manjšine 3), p. 235; Tom Priestly: Zur Rechtfertigung des Unentschuldbaren: Politische Manipulation ethnischer Beziehungen in Gebieten mit slowenischen Minderheiten in Österreich und Ungarn. In: C. Stenner (ed.), Slowenische Steiermark: Verdrängte Minderheit in Österreichs Südosten. Vienna – Cologne – Weimar 1997 (= Zur Kunde Südosteuropas II/23), p. 297.

In Austria, the protection of ethnic groups is incomplete and fragmented. Norms for the protection of minorities are included in legal regulations dating from the monarchy, in international treaties and internal regulations. Article 19 Staatsgrundgesetz (StGG), articles 66-69 of the Treaty of St. Germain, article 7 Treaty of Vienna, article 8[14] of the Austrian federal constitution (B-VG), the law of ethnic groups (Volksgruppengesetz (VGG)) and the laws for minority education (Minderheitenschulgesetze) in Carinthia and Burgenland are the most important of these.

The Republic of Austria made an explicit commitment to respect, protect and promote the language, culture, existence and maintenance of autochthonous ethnic groups in the new section 2 of article 8 B-VG (Bundes-Verfassungsgesetz), revised in 2000.

Article 19 StGG guarantees equal rights and the inviolable right to protection and promotion of national traditions and language. But the validity of article 19 StGG has been controversial both in theory and its jurisdiction since the adoption of the treaty of St. Germain.

It is of vital importance for minority protection in Austria because it has a normative content that is more far-reaching than the regulations of the treaty of St. Germain (article 19 StGG) and the treaty of Vienna; article 19 StGG guarantees an inviolable right to protection and promotion of identity to all ethnic groups as well as the equal rights of all languages of the country[15] in schooling, administration and public life. According to a judgement of the imperial constitutional court, languages were country-specific when they were spoken by more than 3.5% of the population.[16] Article 19 StGG recognises ethnic groups as subjects and in part recognises a collective protection of groups.[17] All other constitutional regulations concerning minorities guarantee only individual rights.

The differentiation of collective and individual rights is especially important in questions of legal protection. If ethnic groups are not recognised as subjects, they have no legal basis for claiming their collective rights as for example the bilingual topographic names. Hidden minorities thus have to claim their minority rights as individuals. Especially in areas where ethnic groups have often been matter of conflict, this means that individuals have to declare their belonging to a specific – often with negative prejudice burdened – group and expose themselves.

The articles 66-69 of the Treaty of St. Germain are without doubt valid; they guarantee rights for persons belonging to ethnic groups. Article 66 guarantees

---

[14] *Austrian Federal Gazette*, BGBl.I 68/2000.

[15] Article 7 Treaty of Vienna guarantees only the additional use and not the equality of language.

[16] Cf. Theo Öhlinger: Die Rechtslage ethnischer Gruppen in Österreich. In: Österreichisches Volksgruppen-zentrum (ed.), Volksgruppenreport 1996. Vienna 1996, p. 159.

[17] Stefan Hammer: Der gruppenrechtliche Gehalt des Artikel 19 StGG als Ansatzpunkt für die Neugestaltung des österreichischen Volkgruppenschutzes. In: Österreichisches Volksgruppenzentrum (ed.), Volksgruppenreport 1997. Vienna 1997, p. 226.

the equal treatment of all citizens of Austria, also in respect to political rights. However, article 67 does not only guarantee equal legal treatment, it also says that special rights for ethnic groups will have to be realised. In 1981 the constitutional court decided in the so-called KEL-ruling that a schematic equalisation of persons belonging to minorities could not always satisfy.[18] This shows that the protection of a person belonging to a minority sometimes justifies or even requires a special treatment of the minority.

The Treaty of St. Germain is intended for all minorities existing in Austria. Article 7 Treaty of Vienna is only valid for the Slovene and Croat minorities in Styria, Carinthia and Burgenland.[19] Article 7 Treaty of Vienna is the only legal provision that mentions explicitly the rights of Slovenes in Styria.

As executing law to article 7 Treaty of Vienna, the law on ethnic groups (Volksgruppengesetz – VGG)[20] was passed on 7th July 1976. Slovenes, Croats, Hungarians, Czechs and Slovaks were recognised as minorities in the Volksgruppengesetz (VGG); the Roma[21] were recognised as a minority in 1993.

Minority advisory boards (Volksgruppenbeiräte) were established at the level of the Chancellor's office. Their task is to advise the Federal Government and the Federal Ministers, protecting and representing the cultural, social and economical interest of their respective constituent minorities. The advisory boards can also introduce proposals for the improvement of the situation of minorities. If it is requested, the advisory boards can also counsel regional governments.

The federal government appoints the members of the advisory boards for four years. Only individuals from whom the representation of minority interests can be expected can be appointed. The composition of the advisory boards indicates the function of the advisory board as a body of representation of interests, not the function of an expert body.

Which ethnic groups are recognised in Austria as minorities is determined by the Federal Government by decree. The appropriate parliamentary committee and the regional government concerned are also permitted to take a position.

The veto of the Styrian government has prevented the establishment of a separate advisory board for the Styrian Slovenes, but the enlargement of the advisory board of the Carinthian Slovenes for persons belonging to the Styrian Slovene minority has been fulfilled in early 2004. Before, the latter had been

[18] Decision of the Austrian constitutional court *VfSlg.* 9224/1981, p. 19. The Koroška Enotna Lista/Kärntner Einheitsliste, a political party of the Slovenes in Carinthia, then had in vain protested against the organisation of constituencies in that Austrian federal province, since it would discriminate Slovene voters.

[19] See the interpretation of article 7: Ernest Petrič: Mednarodno pravno varstvo narodnjih manjšin. Ljubljana 1977, p. 228; Ralf Unkart: Ein Beitrag zur Auslegung des Artikel 7 des Staatsvertrages 1955. *Österreichische Juristen-Zeitung* 29/4 (1974), pp. 91-98; Felix Ermacora: Österreichs Staatsvertrag und Neutralität. Frankfurt/M. 1957.

[20] *BGBl 396*/1976.

[21] *BGBl 323*/1993.

only accepted as observing members of the Carinthian Slovene advisory board and had no right to vote.

Let us have a look backward: Since the establishment of advisory boards, a discussion about whether the ethnic Slovene communities living in different regions of Austria should be treated as one single ethnic group or as different ones has developed. The formulation found in article 7 Treaty of Vienna, which defines “the rights of the Slovene and Croat minority in Styria, Carinthia and Burgenland” is unclear. Even if the dispersed populations are understood as a single group,[22] the different regional views and needs of Carinthian and Styrian Slovenes could justify either the establishment of separate Styrian Slovene advisory boards or at least the granting of voting rights in the Carinthian Slovene advisory board. In the most recent legal decision[23] the administrative court failed to see significant political and ideological differences between Carinthian and Styrian Slovenes that would prevent the appointment of specific regional representatives to the Carinthian Slovene advisory board. The appointment of the advisory board members has to consider the representation of essential political views and ideological orientations of the relevant ethnic group. Since there are due to the mentioned decision of the administrative court no relevant differences regarding political and ideological opinions between Carinthian and Styrian Slovenes, the composition of the advisory board of the Carinthian Slovenes has so far not been unlawful.

We also have to consider in general that the advisory board arranged at the federal chancellor’s office is no representation body in order to authorise the minority to participate effectively in the state will formation process. Rather, the advisory board is a consultative body of the federal chancellor office[24], and that is why it is arranged on an administrative level. Therefore, the advisory boards alone cannot guarantee effective representation and participation.

4. Normative minority protection in Slovenia

With the end of the Second World War Germans[25] in Slovenia hat to face measures of retaliation. They became the aim of revenge not simply because they were Germans, but because the conviction prevailed, that they were re-

---

[22] Cf. Ralf Unkart: Die Minderheitenrechte der Slowenen in der Steiermark und ihre Realisierung. In: Jesih, Slovenci, pp. 257-262.

[23] Beschluss des Verwaltungsgerichtshofes v. 26.5.2003, ZL 98/12/0528-12.

[24] Cf. Bundespressedienst (ed.): Grundlagenbericht der Bundesregierung über die Lage der Volksgruppen in Österreich. Vienna s.d. [1991], p. 35.

[25] The term is used as synonym for German-speaking ethnic group/minority in Slovenia.

sponsible for Nazi crimes committed. This was also comparable to post-war Allied politics in Germany itself.[26]

After the end of the Second World War, the majority of Germans left Slovenia. The small number who did not or could not leave their homes was exposed to massive reprisals. This led to the nearly total disappearance of Germans in Slovenia; their numbers decreased steadily until 1981. Since 1981 the number of Germans increased again, although this growth has mainly been due to immigration from abroad.

An essential question requisite for recognition and special legal status is the question whether the Germans living in Slovenia are an autochthonous ethnic group as per the definition of the Slovenian constitution. If yes, they should be granted collective rights in addition to their already existing individual rights.

While developing the new Slovenian constitution, several proposals were made as to what form of minority protection should be adopted. Slovenia finally decided to adopt a "positive concept"[27] of minority protection since the Yugoslav constitution of 1974 also had adopted this "positive concept".[28] It considers both individual persons belonging to a minority and the minority as such as legal subjects. The special rights of minorities are individual and collective rights at the same time. This dual protection is only granted to autochthonous ethnic groups recognised as such.

In the following existential rights are named which are particularly important for allochthonous ethnic groups, i.e. for the Germans, too. These regulations guarantee basic rights on individual level:

In the chapter II "human rights and basic freedoms" of the Slovenian constitution from 1991, the prohibition of discrimination is regulated in article 14. All are equal before the law. Article 61 guarantees every individual the right to confess freely his affiliation to his nation[29] or his ethnic group[30], the right to preserve his culture and the use of language and writing. Article 62 is procedural; everyone has the right to use his own language and writing before state authorities.

The Slovenian constitution explicitly treats in article 63 any incitement to national, racial, religious or other discrimination as unconstitutional. Unconstitutional actions to article 63 are especially fatal, if political parties commit them,

---

[26] Dušan Nečak: Nemci na Slovenskem 1945-1955 v luči nemških in avstrijskih dokumentov. In: D. Nečak (ed.), "Nemci" na Slovenskem 1941-1955. Ljubljana 1998, p. 207.

[27] Institute for Ethnic Studies (ed.): Ethnic Minorities in Slovenia. Ljubljana 1994, p. 18.

[28] Mirjam Polzer-Srienz: 'Die rechtliche Stellung der autochthonen italienischen und ungarischen Volksgruppe in Slowenien'. *Europa Ethnica* 3-4/97, pp. 115-137; Mirjam Polzer-Srienz: Minderheitenschutz. In: N. Brandt/M. Polzer-Srienz/M. Polzer (eds.), Handbuch des politischen Systems Sloweniens, Vienna – Munich 2005, pp. 512-536.

[29] "Nation" is interpreted here as ethnic category.

[30] Italians and Hungarians outside the autochthonous settlements.

because in this case, the constitutional court is the competent authority (article 160).[31]

The status of Germans is mentioned explicitly in the bilateral agreement between Austria and Slovenia. The bilateral agreement about co-operation in the field of culture, education and science between Austria and Slovenia[32] refers to the legal status of the German-speaking ethnic group. Slovenia stresses within this agreement the legal status of Germans guaranteed in article 61 of the Slovenian constitution.

The Slovenian constitution guarantees in article 64 detailed rights to the autochthonous Italian and Hungarian minorities. These minorities also have the right to representation and participation (including a veto right), both in local self-government and in parliament. These rights are guaranteed irrespective of the number of persons belonging to the minorities.

In order to be able to observe representation and participation, a special organisational structure for ethnic groups is needed. Therefore the Italian and Hungarian minority as well as the ethnic group of Roma are organised in national self-government communities. These communities have essential tasks in the field of political participation. Minorities can also participate in state bodies through co-operation with political parties.

As in many countries, Slovenia differentiates between ethnic groups in allochthonous and autochthonous groups. Special legal status is guaranteed only for autochthonous groups while some individual rights are also guaranteed for allochthonous minorities. These regulations create a basis for protection. It remains to be seen how Slovenia will manage the concrete execution of these constitutional provisions.

5. "The Framework Convention for the Protection of National Minorities" and the "Charter for Regional or Minority Languages"

The Republic of Slovenia determines the following minorities subjected to the Framework Convention:

Considering that the Framework Convention for the Protection of National Minorities does not contain a definition of the notion of national minorities and it is therefore up to the individual Contracting Party to determine the groups which it shall consider as national minorities, the Government of the Republic of Slovenia, in accordance with the Constitution and internal legislation of the Republic of Slovenia, declares that these are the autochthonous Italian and Hungarian National Minorities. In accordance with the Constitution and internal legislation of the

[31] Cf. Miro Cerar: Ustava Republike Slovenije, Človekove pravice in temeljne svoboščine (III). *Pravna praksa* 11/2 (1992), p. 3.

[32] See the text of the agreement on the homepage of the Austrian parliament, http://www.parlament.gv.at/PG/DE/XXI/I/I_00563/pmh.shtml.

Republic of Slovenia, the provisions of the Framework Convention shall apply also to the members of the Roma community, who lives in the Republic of Slovenia.[33]

While the German-speaking minority is not mentioned here, its status is mentioned in its state report.[34]

The Republic of Austria declares:

[…] for itself, the term 'national minorities' within the meaning of the Framework Convention for the Protection of National Minorities is understood to designate those groups which come within the scope of application of the Law on Ethnic Groups (*Volksgruppengesetz*, Federal Law Gazette No. 396/1976) and which live and traditionally have had their home in parts of the territory of the Republic of Austria and which are composed of Austrian citizens with non-German mother tongues and with their own ethnic cultures.[35]

Austria submitted its state report in 2000 and refers in it to the status of Slovenes living in Styria.[36]

By ratifying the Charter for Regional or Minority Languages, the Republic of Slovenia informed the Secretary General of the Council of Europe that "the Italian and Hungarian languages were regional or minority languages on the territory of the Republic of Slovenia. In addition, Slovenia informed the Secretary General that the provisions from Article 7, Paragraph 1-4 would be applied *mutatis mutandis* to the Romany language." In the Report by the Republic of Slovenia on the implementation of the European Charter for Regional or Minority Languages from March 2002 in point 1 the status of the German-speaking ethnic group in Slovenia is stressed. In the report the agreement between the government of the Republic of Austria and the government of the Republic of Slovenia on Co-operation in Culture, Education and Science signed in Ljubljana on the 30th April 2001 is mentioned.

The provision of Article 15 stipulating that the ministries of both countries will include in their working programmes 'the projects for the benefit of wishes and needs of the members of the German-speaking ethnic group in Slovenia, important in terms of culture, education and science (e.g. projects in the fields of language learning and preservation of monuments, scholarships, etc.)' is of significant, perhaps even of vital importance for the development of this group. By mentioning the existence of this group in an international agreement, an additional legal framework has been created for the protection and development of specific ethnic features of this group.

---

[33] http://conventions.coe.int/Treaty/Commun/ListeDeclarations.asp?NT=157&CM=3&DF=2/22/05&CL=ENG&VL=1.

[34] Cf. the report submitted by the Republic of Slovenia pursuant to art. 25, paragraph 1 of the Framework Convention: http://www.coe.int/t/e/human_rights/minorities/2._framework_convention_%28monitoring%29/2._monitoring_mechanism/3._state_reports_and_unmik_kosovo_report/1._first_cycle/PDF_1st_SR_Slovenia_en.pdf. The "German ethnic group" is also mentioned in the Second Report submitted by Slovenia in July 2004: http://www.coe.int/t/e/human_rights/minorities/2._framework_convention_%28monitoring%29/2._monitoring_mechanism/3._state_reports_and_unmik_kosovo_report/2._second_cycle/PDF_2nd_SR_Slovenia_en.pdf.

[35] http://conventions.coe.int/Treaty/Commun/ListeDeclarations.asp?NT=157&CM=3&DF=2/22/05&CL=ENG&VL=1.

[36] Cf. http://www.coe.int/t/e/human_rights/minorities/2._framework_convention_%28monitoring%29/2._monitoring_mechanism/3._state_reports_and_unmik_kosovo_report/1._first_cycle/PDF_1st_SR_Austria_en.pdf.

Footnote 5 of the report concretises further:

It would not be correct to state that the German-speaking ethnic group was officially recognised by signing the cultural agreement. If we follow the interpretation by F. Capotorti, Special Rapporteur of the Sub-Commission on Prevention of Discrimination and Protection of Minorities, a certain minority may be recognised in various ways: by recognising for it the status of legal person, by adopting special measures for the protection of its identity or by guaranteeing certain rights only. Since the state financially supports cultural activities of German cultural associations (although modestly), the state formally and legally meets at least one of the criteria for the recognition of [a] German-speaking ethnic group.[37]

Austria declares in the instrument of ratification that minority languages within the meaning of the Charter in the Republic of Austria include Burgenland-Croatian, Slovenian, Hungarian, Czech, Slovakian languages and Romany. While with regard to the Slovenes in Styria, in the first report individual requirements had been listed, in the second one from 2006 the recognition of the Slovene minority was treated as having been implemented.[38] This prompted the Advisory Committee on the Framework Convention on 11th June 2009 to express the following opinions:

The Advisory Committee welcomes the increasing recognition and support that have been given to the culture and identity of the Slovene minority in Styria, which reportedly contributed to increasing numbers of persons declaring Slovenian as the language spoken in everyday life in the 2001 census. […] The Advisory Committee notes that, despite the encouraging developments mentioned above, more measures need to be taken to raise awareness of the culture and language of the Slovenes of Styria and ensure their development, notably in the field of education.[39]

Both the Framework Convention for National Minorities and the European Charter for Regional or Minority Languages of the Council of Europe are the first international legally binding instruments in the sphere of minority or language protection. The monitoring procedure guarantees a specific form of publicity that could increase the sensibility of state authorities in minority issues. Both documents clearly express the intention to maintain the linguistic, cultural and ethnic diversity of Europe. If these minority protection instruments are taken seriously, they can give impetus for a new stage of minority policy in several states of Europe.

Conclusion

When we compare the situation of the Styrian Slovenes in Austria and the Germans in Slovenia we can see a similar paradoxical situation. The Styrian

---

[37] www.coe.int/t/dg4/education/minlang/Report/PeriodicalReports/SloveniaPR1_en.pdf.

[38] http://www.coe.int/t/e/human_rights/minorities/2._framework_convention_%28monitoring%29/2._monitoring_mechanism/3._state_reports_and_unmik_kosovo_report/2._second_cycle/PDF_2nd_SR_Austria_en.pdf.

[39] http://www.coe.int/t/e/human_rights/minorities/2._framework_convention_%28monitoring%29/2._monitoring_mechanism/4._opinions_of_the_advisory_committee/1._country_specific_opinions/2._second_cycle/PDF_2nd_OP_Austria_en.pdf.

Slovenes enjoy the same constitutional rights on an individual level as every autochthonous minority in Austria. They enjoy an even more comprehensive protection through article 7 Treaty of Vienna. But until recently, Styrian Slovenes were confronted with the fact that their rights are to a large extent had not been fulfilled, and even after their formal recognition the state has to take more measures to ensure the development of this group.

The German-speaking people in Slovenia are not recognised as an autochthonous group but nevertheless they enjoy individual rights that are guaranteed in the constitution. Although the protection of Styrian Slovenes is regulated in more detail in the Austrian constitution, both ethnic groups must fight for the realisation of their existential rights.

The right to effective participation exists in Austria neither for autochthonous nor for allochthonous ethnic groups. Slovenia guarantees the representation and participation in state bodies to autochthonous minorities; allochthonous minorities do not have a special right to political representation.

Some basic rights are especially important for minority ethnic groups. In addition to freedom of expression and freedom of assembly, the freedom of association is of special importance. Freedom of association offers the possibility to support the formation of opinion and focusing of interests. The formation of political opinion in associations confirms the self-confidence of the persons belonging to these ethnic groups. However, minority associations are not usually set up as representative minority organisations; instead they are used for different association purposes and calm the need for social formation of groups. However, political interests are of course pursued from time to time in minority associations.

Without the possibility to associate, minorities would be separated and fragmented. As a special form of the freedom of association, party freedom is also of elementary importance. While freedom of association protects private groups against the state, part freedom and the party rights guarantee participation in state structures. Minority parties could constitute the only possibility for political participation of minorities, although they are often already limited from the beginning since they should be formed as closely as possible and integrate all classes, interests and groups.

Specific regulations for minority parties are hardly guaranteed in the constitutions of European states. Without special regulations in the electoral law (division of electoral districts, blocking clause and other mandate forms) the chances for a mandate for minority parties are very small. Agreements and/or alliances with other parties could offer a possible solution.

The Styrian Slovenes now, by the back entrance, got a representation in a state body, while legal adoptions for the Germans in Slovenia are still underway. Both must attempt to realise their interests also in alternative ways. If parliamentary representation and participation is not realisable, there are nevertheless alternatives for ensuring a certain minimum of representation for ethnic groups.

Models such as a minority commissioner exist in Europe. Ombudsmen for minorities and parliamentary committees for minorities can further influence and increase consciousness for minority problems. The constructive and tolerant co-habitation of different ethnic groups can be realised.

Finally, the principle must be realised that the state, especially in the case of small and dispersed minorities which in the past were confronted with assimilation, does not need to be protected from them, but vice versa that these minorities need the protection of the state. Minorities are a component of European cultural diversity.

Bibliography:

ALFREDSSON, Gudmundur: Minority Rights: Non-Discrimination, Special Rights and Special Measures. In: F. ERMACORA/H. TRETTER/A. PELZL (eds.): Volksgruppen im Spannungsfeld von Recht und Souveränität in Mittel- und Osteuropa. Vienna 1993, pp. 149-158.

BAUMGARTNER, Gerhard: 6 x Österreich. Geschichte und aktuelle Situation der Volksgruppen. Klagenfurt 1995 (= Edition Minderheiten 1).

BREMS, Michael: Die politische Integration ethnischer Minderheiten aus staats- und völkerrechtlicher Sicht. Frankfurt/M. 1995.

BUNDESPRESSEDIENST (ed.): Grundlagenbericht der Bundesregierung über die Lage der Volksgruppen in Österreich. Vienna s.d. [1991].

CERAR, Miro: Ustava Republike Slovenije, Človekove pravice in temeljne svoboščine (III). *Pravna praksa* 11/5 (1992), Ljubljana, pp. 2-3.

ERMACORA, Felix: Österreichs Staatsvertrag und Neutralität. Frankfurt/M. 1957.

GASSNER, Herbert: Unterlassungssünden gegenüber den Kroaten. In: R. Henke (ed.), Leben lassen ist nicht genug. Vienna 1988, pp. 117-120.

GASSNER, Herbert: Die Rechtslage der Kroaten im Burgenland. In: S. Geosits (ed.), Die burgenländischen Kroaten im Wandel der Zeit. Vienna 1986, pp. 330-344.

HAMMER, Stefan: Der gruppenrechtliche Gehalt des Artikel 19 StGG als Ansatzpunkt für die Neugestaltung des österreichischen Volkgruppenschutzes. In: Österreichisches Volksgruppenzentrum (ed.), Volksgruppenreport 1997. Vienna 1997, pp. 226-234.

HOFMAN, Rainer: Minderheitenschutz in Europa – Überblick über die völker- und staatsrechtliche Lage. *Zeitschrift für ausländisches öffentliches Recht* 52 (1992), pp. 1-65.

INSTITUTE FOR ETHNIC STUDIES (ed.): Ethnic Minorities in Slovenia. Ljubljana 1994.

KELSEN, Hans: Der Staat als Integration. Vienna 1930.

MARKO, Joseph: Autonomie und Integration: Rechtsinstitute des Nationalitätenrechts im funktionellen Vergleich. Vienna et al. 1995.

NEČAK, Dušan: "Nemci" na Slovenskem 1945-1955 v luči nemških in avstrijskih dokumentov. In: D. Nečak (ed.), "Nemci" na Slovenskem 1941-1955. Ljubljana 1998, pp. 173-244.

ÖHLINGER, Theo: Die Rechtslage ethnischer Gruppen in Österreich. In: Österreichisches Volksgruppenzentrum (ed.), Volksgruppenreport 1996, Vienna 1996, pp. 157-172.

ÖSTERREICHISCHES VOLKSGRUPPENZENTRUM (ed.): Burgenländische Kroaten. Vienna 1993 (= Österreichische Volksgruppenhandbücher 5).

ÖSTERRREICHISCHES VOLKSGRUPPENZENTRUM (ed.): Internationales und Europäisches Volksgruppenrecht. Klagenfurt 1995 (= Österreichische Volksgruppenhandbücher 8).

ÖSTERREICHISCHES VOLKSGRUPPENZENTRUM (ed.): Steirische Slowenen. Vienna 1996 (= Österreichische Volksgruppenhandbücher 9).

PERNTHALER, Peter: Der Schutz der Gemeinschaften durch individuelle Rechte. In: *Europa Ethnica* 19 (1962), pp. 50-89.

PETRIČ, Ernest: Mednarodno pravno varstvo narodnjih manjšin. Ljubljana 1977.

PLETERSKI, Janko: Slovenci na avstrijskem štajerskem in člen 7 pogodbe o Avstriji. In: B. Jesih (ed.), Slovenci v avstrijski zvezni deželi Štajerski. Zbornik referatov na znanstvenem srečanju v Mariboru, 25.-27. maja 1993. Ljubljana 1994 (= narodne manjšine 3), pp. 235-242.

POLZER-SRIENZ, Mirjam: Die rechtliche Stellung der autochthonen italienischen und ungarischen Volksgruppe in Slowenien. *Europa Ethnica* 3-4 (1997), pp. 115-137.

POLZER-SRIENZ, Mirjam: The Croat and the Slovene Minority in Austria. In: K. Cordell /S. Wolff (eds.), Ethnopolitical Encyclopaedia of Europe. Basingstoke, New York 2004, pp. 28-45.

POLZER-SRIENZ, Mirjam: Minderheitenschutz. In: N. Brandt/M. Polzer-Srienz/M. Polzer (eds.), Handbuch des politischen Systems Sloweniens. Vienna – Munich 2005, pp. 512-536.

PRIESTLY, Tom: Zur Rechtfertigung des Unentschuldbaren: Politische Manipulation ethnischer Beziehungen in Gebieten mit slowenischen Minderheiten in Österreich und Ungarn. In: C. Stenner (ed.), Slowenische Steiermark: Verdrängte Minderheit in Österreichs Südosten. Vienna – Cologne – Weimar 1997 (= Zur Kunde Südosteuropas II/23), pp. 297-344.

RENAN, Ernest: "Was ist eine Nation?", In: Gall/Koch (eds.), Der europäische Liberalismus im 19.Jahrhundert, vol 3. Frankfurt/M. et al. 1981, pp. 132-152.

SMEND, Rudolf: Staatsrechtliche Abhandlungen. Berlin 1968.

SMEND, Rudolf: Verfassung und Verfassungsrecht. Munich – Leipzig, 1928.

UNKART, Ralf: Ein Beitrag zur Auslegung des Artikel 7 des Staatsvertrages 1955. *Österreichische Juristen-Zeitung* 29/4 (1974), pp. 91-98.

UNKART, Ralf: Die Minderheitenrechte der Slowenen in der Steiermark und ihre Realisierung. In: B. Jesih (ed.), Slovenci v avstrijski zvezni deželi Štajerski. Zbornik referatov na znanstvenem srečanju v Mariboru, 25.-27. maja 1993. (= narodne manjšine 3) Lubljana 1994, pp. 257-262.

Small is Beautiful: The Issue of Hidden Minorities in Central Europe and the Balkans[1]

Christian Promitzer

> …the heroes of the play are not only Czechs, Slovaks, Hungarians etc., but Masurians and Cassubians, Slovinians and Slovenes, Uskoks and Hanaks, Cumans and Iasygians, Valachians and Armenians, Gypsies and Jews, Szeklers, Ruthenes, Cossacks, Lemkos, Boykos and by whatever names the innumerable ethnic, social or ethnosocial groups of the region were called in various epochs.
>
> The history of Europe, let alone of the world, is too vast to do these groups justice; history understood in terms of the modem nation states is too teleological to care about those which did not eventually develop into full-fledged modem nations. The 'medium scale' of regional history seems to be the only chance to render them their due, to avoid ahistorical determinism and to treat ethnic or social groups according to their real significance in the given epoch, not according to their future fate. (Maciej Janowski)[2]

This chapter deals with the issue of small ethnic groups in Central Europe and the Balkans theoretically. It will try to formulate a common platform for the application of the research results on "hidden minorities" and possible consequences for further empirical research. Thereby I want to show that hidden minorities seem to be a transitory phenomenon of modernity. They should be understood as satellites of nation building, and researching them can open new perspectives on the development of nations and ethnic groups.

I. The general framework: how to deal with something too small to be relevant

Within the enlarged European Union, *ethnic* identities like class struggles seem to be something outmoded. This wishful thinking has to do with the fact that the established "old" nations in the Western part of the continent tend to consider such issues a product of backwardness and folklore. Only in East Central Europe they do seemingly still play a certain role. Such a view is often connected with the fact that this part of the continent has been historically disadvantaged to different extents. The way in which the enlargement of the European Union is being pushed through in East Central Europe is paved with the optimistic language of neo-liberal expansionism. On this journey, nobody is

---

[1] I want to thank Klaus-Jürgen Hermanik, Marijana Jakimova, Tanja Petrović, Eduard Staudinger, and Ivica Šarac for their collaboration in the project P-15080 on "Hidden Minorities between Central Europe and the Balkans", financed by the Austrian Science Fund FWF; without their foregoing research this article would have never been written.

[2] Maciej Janowski: Pitfalls and opportunities: the Concept of East-Central Europe as a Tool of Historical Analysis. *European Review of History* 6/1 (1999), pp. 91-100, here 95.

eager to look into the rear-view mirror and confront the fact that the Western part of Europe only overcame the age of nationalist passions with the end of the Second World War. Western European nation states only recently lost their aggressiveness; and even this statement is relativised if we take into account the harsh measures and xenophobic movements against migrants and asylum seekers and the still unsolved Bask and northern Irish issues.[3]

In general, though, the nation states in the elder part of the EU seem to have overcome their nationalist struggles, for they had once used violent means of domination and assimilation of those deviating from the majority population; the state used its institutions of socialisation (schools, police, military service and other mechanisms of power) in order to create a single nation. Only in peripheral regions could different ethnic identities and local traditions survive for a certain period, but even there the majority of the population was attracted by the affluence of the urban nation and by the perspective of careers in the ranks of the dominating nation, so that the successful formation of a plausible model of the nation was underway. Only those who were not swallowed by the dominant nation and still insisted on their different ethnic identities were granted a framework of minority rights.

According to the Viennese Declaration on Multiculturalism and Multiethnicity in East Central and South-East Europe of 1998 the place where issues of national minorities and of ethnic identities have not lost their impact has to be sought in East Central Europe, i.e. just in those countries which are gradually being integrated into the European Union. According to the declaration, forty million people in East Central Europe can be considered members of national and ethnic minorities.[4] In the last one and a half decades – since the fall of the Eastern European Communist regimes, if not even slightly before – we can observe processes of "ethnic revival" and of "(re)discovery and (re)creation of identity".[5] What is more, these developments are not restricted to East Central Europe anymore; they have spilled over even into the marginal zones of countries, which were Western during the Cold War, as in the case of the Slovene minorities in Italy and Austria.[6]

---

[3] These thoughts may be interpreted as a critical reflection of Ernest Gellners zones of nationalism in Europe – cf. Ernest Gellner: Nationalismus. Kultur und Macht. Berlin 1999, pp. 88-97.

[4] Cf. Arnold Suppan: Multikulturalität und Multiethnizität in Mittel-, Ost- und Südosteuropa und die Wiener Deklaration vom 30. September 1998. *Österreichische Osthefte* 41/2 (1999), p. 10.

[5] László Kürti/Juliet Langman: Introduction. Searching for identities in the new East Central Europe. In: L. Kürti/J. Langman (eds.), Beyond borders. Remaking cultural identities in the new East and Central Europe. Boulder, Colorado – Oxford 1997, p. 8; Hanns Haas: Ethnikum und Nation in der dörflichen Lebenswelt eines deutsch-tschechischen Dorfes. In: V. Rajšp/E. Bruckmüller (eds.), Vilfanov zbornik: Pravo-zgodovina-narod/Recht-Geschichte-Nation. Ljubljana 1999, p. 557.

[6] In Italy the range of minority rights for the Slovene minority has been expanded recently, while in Austria the issue of a possible Slovene minority in the federal province of Styria has been under intense discussion.

The evocation of a common treaty for the EU indicates the topicality of a second issue: Will the unification of a multitude of nations and ethnic groups give rise to a future pan-European identity?[7] For the anthropologist Ernest Gellner there is only one obvious answer, "In the industrial age only high cultures in the end effectively survive. Folk cultures and little traditions survive only artificially, kept going by language and folklore preservation groups".[8] The term "artificially", can also include a legal framework of minority protection. But even if linguistic and cultural diversity will be preserved in this way, it will have to be based upon the hardly achievable ideal of "unity in diversity". The realisation of such an ideal, which is typical for the nineties of the last century, has no successful historical forerunners in the modern age: multiethnic empires facing the challenges of modernity, as case of the Habsburg Monarchy vividly demonstrates, came to an end, since no viable solution could be found that would formulate a passable recipe for common (then dynastic) rule and ethnic (national) diversity. The issue of imposing a common democratic rule is today one of the serious difficulties of the Russian Federation, a multiethnic entity and true heir of the still more multifaceted Soviet Union.

II. The issue of hidden minorities

The issue of ethnic identities is therefore an important question for the future of the European Union. This being the case, we have to explain why our focus is not on the ardent issue of national minorities, but on small ethnic groups which we call hidden minorities? Why should we deal with such marginal and only partly visible phenomena that apparently have never influenced the course of history?

The first argument we could throw into the discussion, is that quantity cannot be the sole guideline of academic interest. In our case, even the investigation of small communities may reveal something fundamental about mechanisms of inclusion and exclusion, about the relationship between private and public. Our interest is directed towards ethnic groups which *hide themselves* from the public or are, by various means, *hidden by the authorities* of the states they are living in. The issues of *hiding* or *being hidden* are closely connected with the emergence of the public sphere in modern societies. The latter determines which issues are of public and which of private interest. But it can happen that matters of possible public interest are isolated within a *taboo zone*. In order to prevent possible conflicts with the majority population and to avoid coming too

[7] Cf. Krzysztof Glass/Janez Kranjc/Oto Luthar: Vorwort. In: K. Glass/J. Kranjc/O. Luthar (eds.), Grenzlandidentitäten im Zeitalter der Eurointegration. Vienna – Poznań 1998, p. 9; Suppan, Multikulturalität.

[8] Ernest Gellner: Nations and nationalism. Reprint: Oxford 1988, p. 117.

closely into contact with the wheels of modern society, some societal groups will formulate strategies, which try to play down some of their peculiarities. One of these strategies is the practice of *hiding*.

These considerations can be seen among migrants in foreign countries. They are inevitably compelled to show an overt conformity with the majority population, hiding their original cultural traits. The latter are restricted to the private sphere.[9] As long as they form a constitutive element of their everyday life, it would be appropriate to name these groups hidden minorities. It is of interest that after the First World War some of these groups were even recognised as national minorities. This was the case with the Czech and Slovak migrants in Vienna. Other groups, like the Bulgarian gardeners, who also started to come to Central Europe around the turn of the 20th century, would remain a hidden minority that finally became assimilated.[10] This was also the case with Slovene and Croat migrants from Istria who settled in the city of Trieste.[11]

But there are also autochthonous small ethnic groups, often living on new or old state borders, which form a possible subject for the concept of hidden minorities. They have in common that they have never been recognised as national minorities. For a long time they have been neglected by academic research. It is mainly these groups that we want to address as hidden minorities.[12]

Such clarifications, however, still do not answer the questions, which have been posed: What is the purpose of dealing with ethnic groups which are simply too small to be treated within the traditional canon of research on national minorities?[13] Is it antiquarianism, the search for "dying Europeans"[14] and the possible fight for the cultural survival of those groups in question? If this would be the reason, one should better watch out that he will not wind up as a constructor of a human *Jurassic Park*.

The reasonability of the study of small ethnic groups has to be sought elsewhere and can be answered with a remark of Carlo Ginzburg, the doyen of micro history, who said that the improbable and exceptional source is often the

---

9 "Hiding" only works, when cultural differences with the majority population are not too great. It works to a lesser extent for migrants of Muslim belief or for migrants of different physical appearance (e.g. Africans).
10 Cf. the article by Marijana Jakimova in this volume.
11 Cf. the article by Mojca Ravnik in this volume.
12 Cf. a similar approach in two readers on "hidden or 'forgotten' minorities in the Balkans and in Eastern Europe": Biljana Sikimić (ed.): Skrivene manjine na Balkanu/Hidden Minorities in the Balkans. Belgrade 2004; Arno Tanner (ed.): The forgotten minorities of Eastern Europe. The history and today of selected ethnic groups in five countries. Helsinki 2004.
13 Cf. Boris Jesih: So "male" manjšine drugačne od "velikih"? – Sind "kleine" Volksgruppen anders als große? In: K. Anderwald/P. Karpf/V. Smrtnik, (eds.), Die europäische Dimension des Volksgruppenrechtes. Sprachminderheiten: Herausforderung und Chance. Klagenfurt 1997, pp. 112-120.
14 Cf. Karl-Markus Gauß: Die sterbenden Europäer. Unterwegs zu den Sepharden von Sarajevo, Gottscheer-Deutschen, Arbereshe, Sorben und Aromunen. Vienna 2001.

potentially more abundant one.[15] In European (and even global) history, the process of nation building is of central interest for the explanation of group formation in the last two centuries. The majority of studies, which deal with this phenomenon concentrate on nations and on the role of intellectuals and of new technologies that made them possible.[16] But prototypical case studies, at least with respect to East Central Europe, dealing with the implementation of nation building at a given location and with the plausibility of the nation concept in rural areas have also been published. These concentrate on ethnically heterogeneous environments, where after the First World War national minorities – in a legal sense – came into being.[17] *European intermediate areas* are forming the focus of a new branch of research interested in why and when the nation model asserted itself vis-à-vis competing models of societal affiliation.[18] Intermediate areas are environments in which we can also observe the phenomenon of hidden minorities. Here, however, we rarely encounter the labour of local intellectuals who try to persuade the local population to become a national minority.[19] *Ethnic engineers* of the majority population (teachers, priests, civil servants) rather, try to convince them to become part of the dominant nation. The interplay between these intellectual missionaries and the local population – be the subsequent reaction assimilation or resistance – can reveal the range and plausibility of nation building. Consequently, the research of hidden minorities explores those circumstances responsible for the formation of national minorities. Not only the population and the pressure of referential nations (so-called "mother nations"), but also the will of the respective population were decisive for the establishment of national minorities after the First World War.

Let us formulate an interim result: the historical study of hidden minorities can contribute to a direct and overarching understanding of how competing models of nation building were implemented in rural areas. Because of their initial

---

[15] Carlo Ginzburg: Mikro-Historie. Zwei oder drei Dinge, die ich von ihr weiß. *Historische Anthropologie. Kultur-Gesellschaft-Alltag* 1/2 (1992), p. 191.

[16] Cf. Benedict Anderson: Imagined communities. Reflections on the origin and spread of nationalism. Revised ed: London – New York 1995; Gellner, Nations; Gellner, Nationalismus; Miroslav Hroch: Social preconditions of national revival in Europe. A comparative analysis of the social composition of patriotic groups among the smaller European nations. New York 2000.

[17] Cf. Haas, Ethnikum; Peter M. Judson: Nationalizing rural landscapes in Cisleithania, 1880-1914. In: N. Wingfield (ed.), Creating the other. Ethnic conflict and nationalism in Habsburg Central Europe. New York – Oxford 2003, pp. 127-148; Heinz-Dietrich Löwe/Günther H. Tontsch/Stefan Troebst (eds.): Minderheiten, Regionalbewusstsein und Zentralismus in Ostmitteleuropa. Cologne – Weimar – Vienna 2000, pp. 121-184; Robert Gary Minnich: Homesteaders and citizens. Collective identity formation on the Austro-Italian-Slovene border. Bergen 1998; Andreas Moritsch (ed.): Vom Ethnos zur Nationalität. Der nationale Differenzierungsprozeß am Beispiel ausgewählter Orte in Kärnten und im Burgenland. Vienna – Munich 1991.

[18] Philipp Ther/Holm Sundhaussen (eds.): Regionale Bewegungen und Regionalismen in europäischen Zwischenräumen seit der Mitte des 19. Jahrhunderts. Marburg 2003.

[19] Exceptions from this rule are the Catholic Serbs of Dubrovnik, who indeed were a product of intellectuals. They are treated in this volume by Ivica Šarac.

cultural difference vis-à-vis the majority population that would form the core of the future dominant nation, we get a photographic negative, by which we can acquire a better understanding of the ways and methods of nation building in East Central Europe.

III. How to grasp hidden minorities in history

By introducing hidden minorities, we are inevitably compelled to clarify their relationship with national minorities.[20] This is not an easy task, since hidden minorities seem to form ever existing, but seldom addressed, *quantités négligeables*, firstly, within the process of nation building and, secondly, within the formation of national minorities. Both latter phenomena are of a fluid nature, since they are a result of complex historical processes dependent on internal developments and external political decisions. In some cases, for example, large ethnic groups, which previously were treated neither as national minorities nor as "hidden" ones, were given the status of nations, as was the case with the Montenegrins and Bosniaks (Bosnian Muslims) in Socialist Yugoslavia. And once hidden minorities, like the Macedonians in the Kingdom of Yugoslavia, could even become a nation. Slovenes in Fascist Italy, then a hidden minority, gained the status of a national minority after the Second World War. Other groups have emerged as "visible" ethnic groups for a short time, but then – because of political decisions of the government of the state they were living in – disappeared again from the scene. Examples for such phenomena are the "Slavic minority" in Northern Greece which disappeared after 1925 and the Macedonians in south-western Bulgaria which were "existent" only in a short period after the Second World War.[21] Other ethnic groups again, like the Roma and German-speaking communities in Slovenia and the Slovenes in the Austrian federal province of Styria, are still stuck in the process of formal recognition as national minorities.[22] There are also uncertainties with respect to designation, since possible national minorities in the Bulgarian constitution of 1990 for example, are only quoted as "ethnic groups" or as "Bulgarians of dif-

---

[20] With respect to national minorities, various conventions of the international community, like the CSCE (OSCE), the Council of Europe or the United Nations use different terms for this phenomenon such as "national minorities", "ethnic, religious and language minorities" or "national, ethnic, religious and language minorities"; cf. Vladimir Ortakovski: Minorities in the Balkans. Skopje – Štip 1998, pp. 34. To be short and unambiguous in the comparison with hidden minorities, the term national minority will be used throughout to denote legally recognised ethnic groups.

[21] Cf. Hugh Poulton: The Balkans. Minorities and state in conflict. New edition: London 1993, pp. 107-108, 175-182; Ortakovski, Minorities, pp. 165-167; Gerhard Seewann/Péter Dippold (eds.): Bibliographisches Handbuch der ethnischen Gruppen Südosteuropas, vol. 2. Munich 1997, pp. 1291-1295.

[22] Cf. the articles by Oto Luthar and of Klaus-Jürgen Hermanik in this volume.

ferent ethnic origin."[23] We also have to deal with small ethnic groups, which tend to hide within larger national minorities, as is the case with small Muslim communities like the Pomaks, Torbeshes and Poturs and Islamised Roma populations in the southern Balkans, whose position can be described as "intermediary groups".[24] These small groups are attached to larger ethnic groups of Muslim origins, such as the Turks in Bulgaria and Greece and the Albanians in the Republic of Macedonia and in Kosovo.[25] Occasional examples can be also found among Orthodox groups as for instance among descendants of Bulgarian gardeners in Hungary, which merged with the local Serbian community.[26] Finally, not all possible members of hidden minorities want to be addressed as such; rather they adopt strategies of mimicry and of passing, of "crossing over" to the majority population or as "passing" for members of it.[27]

It is thus impossible to give a satisfying definition of hidden minorities vis-à-vis national minorities at this point in the discussion. For the time being it should be sufficient to say that the decisive criterion is the legal recognition of a given ethnic group. From a historical point of view this would mean that national minorities could, until their legal recognition as such, be likewise treated as hidden minorities. But since the term hidden minorities is a construction *a posteriori*, it should mainly refer to small ethnic groups in Central Europe and the Balkans which until the present time do not have explicit minority rights. The following historical survey will nonetheless treat all mentioned aspects of the notion of hidden minorities.

In the late 19th century, national and ethnic issues began to dominate political discussions in the Habsburg Empire, and they were also topics of intense debate in Russia and in the ever retreating Ottoman Empire. In retrospect we can even say that the "innumerable ethnic, social and ethno-social groups", made up the fabric and one of the key factors of this area in the 19th and early 20th century.[28] Within multiethnic empires and in the Habsburg Empire in particular, contemporary legal treatment of ethnic groups referred to those nations or "nationalities", as they were called at that time, which were able to impose their agenda on the foundation of alleged "historical rights", or – in the case of the "ahistorical" nations of the Slovenes or Slovaks – simply due to the existence of a national movement. Others, like the Ruthenians, were a bone of contention between rivalling empires so that their national self-assertion was stimulated by external factors.[29]

---

[23] Cf. Ortakovski, Minorities, p. 264.
[24] Yulian Konstantinov: An account of Pomak conversions in Bulgaria (1912-1990). In: G. Seewann (ed.), Minderheitenfragen in Südosteuropa. Munich 1992, pp. 343-357, here 344.
[25] Cf. Poulton, Balkans, pp. 55, 117, 209.
[26] Cf. the article by Biljana Sikimić in this volume.
[27] Cf. the article by Marija Jurić Pahor in this volume.
[28] Maciej Janowski: Pitfalls, p. 95; cf. Miller: Russia, p. 39.
[29] For the discussions among Austrian Social democrats like Karl Renner and Otto Bauer for possible political solutions of these ardent issues cf. Günther Sandner: Austromarxismus und

Such discussions seldom considered those small ethnic groups treated in this book; they were simply too small to warrant such awareness. At first glance this seems to be true for the Balkans as well. Beginning in the 19th century, nation states were founded on the European territory of the Ottoman Empire, but they only asserted themselves based on the will of the Great Powers, as the Greek uprising, the Congress of Berlin and the peace negotiations after the first Balkan War of 1912-1913 show. The Great Powers provided, at least nominally, for the legal protection of the vast religious, mainly Muslim, minorities in international treaties.[30] But what is of greater interest here is that scholarly research in the Balkan states already in that period touched on the forerunners of later hidden minorities. This focus upon small ethnic groups was a possible side-effect of the relatively small size of these states (namely Serbia, Greece, Romania and Bulgaria) vis-à-vis the vast multiethnic empires, so that even low-ranking ethnic phenomena crossed the threshold of perception. Such awareness was also a consequence of the ethnic fragmentation of the Balkans, resisting the Western European and German programmatic ideal of nationally homogeneous states. This situation required a more sophisticated approach in order to assess the varieties of small groups that differed from the predominant nation by confession, language or, simply, by local tradition.

Examples of contemporary scholars, who were engaged in the study of small ethnic groups, can demonstrate the plausibility of this argument. In the last two decades of the 19th century, the Czech historian Konstantin Jireček, who was minister of education in Bulgaria for a short time in the early 1880s, treated a multitude of small ethnic groups in his own country[31] as well as examples of former or contemporary Romance-speaking groups in the Western Balkans (Muslim *Aromanians*, Orthodox *Morlacs* and *Vlachs*). Jireček called some of these communities "nations" ("*Völker*"), while he addressed the smaller ones as "ethnographic groups".[32] This term was also adopted by the Serbian ethnologist and geographer Manojlo Smiljanić, who in 1905 wrote an interesting article on "ethnographic grouping of the nations of the Balkan peninsula". Smiljanić stated that the various small ethnic groups once had had strong national back-

---

Multikulturalismus. Karl Renner und Otto Bauer zur nationalen Frage im Habsburgerstaat. In: Kakanien revisited, www.kakanien.ac.at/beitr/fallstudie/GSandner1.pdf. For the legal treatment of minorities in the Habsburg and Ottoman Empires in general cf. Ortakovski: Minorities, pp. 44-53.

[30] For a detailed overview cf. Ortakovski, Minorities, pp. 53-99. Treating the mentorship of the Habsburg Empire upon Christian groups in the Ottoman Empire would go beyond the frame of this discussion.

[31] Among these are the remnants of Turkish-speaking *Cumans* and *Pechenegs*, the nomadic and Turkish-speaking Muslim *Yuruks*, the *Gagauz* and *Surguch* peoples, who were Orthodox, but spoke Turk vernaculars, the Bulgarian-speaking Muslim *Pomaks*, further Catholic Bulgarians called *Paulicians*, and *Shopi,* who formed a transient group with their own tradition in the *intermediate area* between Bulgaria and Serbia.

[32] Cf. Helena Bočkova: Ethnische Gemeinschaften und ethnische Prozesse auf dem Balkan im Werke Konstantin Jirečeks. *Ethnologia Slovaca et Slavica* XXIV-XXV (1992-93), pp. 227-229, 237-240.

grounds, which they had irretrievably lost in the course of history. Due to convenient geographical circumstances, however, they had managed to preserve some of their ethnographic traits.[33]

Because of the ethnic heterogeneity of their own countries, intellectuals from the Balkans considered their own nation states deficient with respect to ethnically allegedly much more homogenous nation states like France, Italy, and, most of all, the German Reich. Multiethnic empires like Russia and the Habsburg Empire were no ideals in this respect, their actual power in the fields of military and foreign policy notwithstanding. Such thinking can be seen in the case of the Bulgarian physicist Stefan Vatev, who at the turn to the 20th century adopted a German physical anthropological model for assessing the "racial composition" of ethnic Bulgarians vis-à-vis "other nations resident in the Bulgarian principality." Vatev also assessed the "racial composition" of the Bulgarian Diaspora outside the principality.[34] Similarly, the Slovene historian and ethnologist Niko Županič, a proponent of the Yugoslav ideal, concentrated upon the investigation of isolated small ethnic groups of apparent or imagined South Slavic origin.[35]

Vatev and Županič are only two noteworthy figures with respect to the scholarly treatment of small ethnic groups in this period. An overall treatment of this phenomenon in the Balkans, however, was formulated by the Serbian geographer Jovan Cvijić. Within a general reflection about ethnic identities in the Balkans he explained their existence through migrations that took place during Ottoman rule and had formed "exotic population oases."[36]

---

[33] Cf. Manojlo B. Smiljanić: Etnografsko grupisanje naroda Balkanskoga poluostrva. *Godišnjica Nikole Čupića* XXIV (1905), p. 102.

[34] Cf. S[tefan] Wateff: Anthropologische Beobachtungen an den Schülern und Soldaten in Bulgarien. *Correspondenz-Blatt der deutschen Gesellschaft für Anthropologie, Ethnologie und Urgeschichte* XXXII/4 (1901), pp. 29-30; S[tefan] Wateff: Anthropologische Beobachtungen der Augen, der Haare und der Haut bei den bulgarischen Schulkindern in der europäischen Türkei. *Correspondenz-Blatt der deutschen Gesellschaft für Anthropologie, Ethnologie und Urgeschichte* XXXIII/3 (1903), pp. 23-24; S[tefan] Wateff: Anthropologische Beobachtungen der Augen, der Haare und der Haut bei den Schulkindern von den Türken, Pomaken, Tataren, Armenier[n], Griechen und Juden in Bulgarien. *Correspondenz-Blatt der deutschen Gesellschaft für Anthropologie, Ethnologie und Urgeschichte* XXXIV/7-8 (1903), pp. 58-60.

[35] These groups were the hitherto almost unknown and isolated villages of Serbs on the border of Croatia with Carniola and the inhabitants of a Greek village close to Athens called "Hrvati" (Harvati, present-day Pallini), who according to Županič, were of Croat descent, although the inhabitants of the villages spoke an Albanian vernacular and designated themselves as Greeks. On these investigations by Županič cf. Christian Promitzer: "Gute Serben". Ethnologen und Politiker über die Identität der Serben in der slowenischen Bela krajina. In: U. Brunnbauer (ed.), Umstrittene Identitäten. Ethnizität und Nationalität in Südosteuropa. Frankfurt/M. et al. 2002, pp. 176-183; Niko Županič: Hrvati kod Atine. Prilozi antropologiji i istorijskoj etnologiji. *Starinar – Organ Srpskog Arheološkog Društva* new series VI (1911), pp. 95-152; on the Serbs in Bela Krajina cf. the article by Tanja Petrović in this volume.

[36] Jovan Cvijić: Balkansko poluostrvo. Reprint: Belgrade 1987, pp. 127, 133, 143-144, 167.

After the demise of the traditional multiethnic empires of East Central Europe, new borders between new, often only nominally nation states were drawn. Consequently, a legal framework for national minorities who happened to live outside their referential states was developed in the Paris peace treaties, concomitant minority treaties, and finally, in the system of the League of Nations.[37] This system created obligations only for the small and politically weak states in Central and Eastern Europe. It would not have been possible to create any kind of minority protection system that would apply to all members of the League of Nations, where the majority, inclined towards assimilation of minorities, would not allow any limitation of their sovereignty in favour of the minorities.[38]

The legal issue of "national minorities" was a complete reformulation of how national issues had been treated in the multiethnic empires. Where they had once been a case of domestic policy, they now became a matter of international law. Such an approach, of course, had to be selective; it comprised only those groups, which were quantitatively strong enough and at the same time had appropriate support from the states of their referential nations. But as the case of the suppression of the Slovenes in Fascist Italy and various other examples in the Balkans show, even these qualities often were not sufficient to grant treatment as a national minority.

One has to remember, of course, that not all of these groups were interested in subjecting their status to norms of international law and of emerging minority laws. But even in such cases, they could become topic of scholarly scrutiny. Central European academics took over the discourse of visualisation of small ethnic groups, as it had manifested itself in the Balkans (Jireček, Smiljanić, Vatev, Županič, Cvijić) before the First World War: In the case of German minorities who had settled in East Central Europe in the medieval period, the adoption of the discourse of visualisation developed into the ideological concept of German *Volksboden* and German *Kulturboden*. This concept posited a historical role of German settlers in the European east as missionary propa-

[37] On the legal provisions for national minorities in the interwar period cf. Ortakovski, Minorities, pp. 109-118; Ognjana Chrisimova: "Mirnite" Balkani sled N'oj. Obštestvoto na narodite kato faktor na statukvoto i malcinstvenija mir (1919-1939). In: S. Eldărov (ed.), Balkanite meždu mira i vojnata XIV-XX vek. Sbornik naučni izsledvanija. Sofija 2002, pp. 267-283; cf. also Dietmar Müller: Staatsbürger auf Widerruf. Juden und Muslime als Alteritätspartner im rumänischen und serbischen Nationscode. Ethnonationale Staatsbürgerschaftskonzepte 1878-1941. Wiesbaden 2005 (= Balkanologische Veröffentlichungen 41), pp. 211-248. There is a huge amount of literature dealing with historical aspects of emerging minority issues in Central Europe and the Balkans. Since most of it deals with national minorities and not so much hidden minorities, it will suffice to cite a few outstanding examples: Valeria Heuberger/Arnold Suppan/Elisabeth Vyslonzil (eds.): Brennpunkt Osteuropa. Minderheiten im Kreuzfeuer des Nationalismus. Vienna – Munich 1996; Löwe/Tontsch/Troebst, Minderheiten; Gerhard Seewann (ed.): Minderheitenfragen in Südosteuropa. Munich 1992. For an exhaustive bibliography cf. Seewann/Dippold, Bibliographisches Handbuch.

[38] Ortakovski, Minorities, p. 117.

gators and radiators of "German culture" among the native populations, which had not reached a similar "stage of civilisation".[39] Academic representatives of this approach did not restrict themselves to the investigation of closed German minority groups, they would also assess small "linguistic islands" (*Sprachinseln*) – hidden minorities, therefore – which were treated as cells of German *Kulturboden*, if they were not able to meet the higher norms of German *Volksboden*.[40] This concept was an ideological forerunner of the ideal of *Lebensraum* propagated by the Third Reich.

In Central Europe itself one could observe government actions against hidden minorities that went beyond conventional linguistic and cultural assimilation. Such was the case with the surveillance of the Slovene population at the southern border of Austrian Styria by the provincial government. Here, the local Slovenes – unlike those in the neighbouring province of Carinthia – had not constituted themselves as a visible minority, but they were nonetheless considered a possible source of South Slavic irredentism and an obstacle for the prospective re-conquest of the southern parts of the province that had become part of the Yugoslav Kingdom after the First World War.[41]

Such measures, of course, have to be considered within the broader geographical context of measures against ethnic diversity in East Central Europe in general. In addition to the expulsion of Muslim groups in the course of the establishment and augmentation of Balkan nation states throughout the 19th century up to the Balkan Wars of 1912/13, major population exchanges took place in the Balkans mediated by the Great Powers. This was the case with the Greco-Bulgarian and Greco-Turkish conventions on voluntary and obligatory exchange of populations after the First World War.[42] After the example of these "ethnic cleansings" which were conducted with international approval, further population exchanges, such as of the Bulgarian and Romanian populations of the region of Dobrudja in 1940, and the resettling of German minorities in satellite states of the Third Reich in East Central Europe in the first years of the Second World War, took place. These measures initially aimed at the realisation of the ideal of ethnic homogeneity; later they have to be interpreted as a corollary of the "new order" imposed by the Third Reich.[43] With respect to our question, it is important to stress that population exchanges often also extermi-

---

[39] Cf. Albrecht Penck: Deutscher Volks- und Kulturboden. In: C.C. von Loesch (ed.), Volk unter Völkern. Für den deutschen Schutzbund. Breslau 1925, pp. 62-73.

[40] Various examples of this discussion can be found in Michael Fahlbusch: Wissenschaft im Dienst der nationalsozialistischen Politik? Die „Volksdeutschen Forschungsgemeinschaften" von 1931-1945. Baden-Baden 1999.

[41] Cf. Christian Promitzer: Body, race and the border. Notes on a paradigm of German national thinking on the Slovenes. In: O. Luthar/J. Perovšek (eds.), Zbornik Janka Pleterskega. Ljubljana 2003, pp. 597-608; for more on this small ethnic group cf. the arcticle by Klaus-Jürgen Hermanik in this volume.

[42] Cf. Ortakovski, Minorities, pp. 196-206.

[43] As highlighted in the case of the "ethnic cleansing" of Serbs in the fascist "Independent State of Croatia". For an overview cf. Ortakovski, Minorities, pp. 209-224.

nated small ethnic groups who were treated as part of the "Turkish", "Bulgarian", "Romanian" etc. populations, which were to be resettled.[44]

The Second World War is remembered for the Holocaust and the genocide of the Roma population. The Nazi control of East Central Europe led furthermore to population transfers and expulsions which effected the further existence of small ethnic groups. This fate meet the great majority of the German population of East Central Europe during and after the retreat of the German *Wehrmacht*. Ironically, these ethnic homogenisation policies would altogether "ease" minority issue politics in this part of Europe in the years after the Second World War. With respect to hidden minorities, Communist modernisation led to a further assimilation of small ethnic groups, which were compelled to abandon their traditional way of live[45], not to mention the national programmes that were being realised in the context of Socialism in that period.[46] The Soviet model of the positive treatment of "nationalities" was most authentically pursued in Socialist Yugoslavia, which offered some ethnic groups a possibility to abandon the status of former hidden minorities. Compared to the established Western model of inclusion of minorities, this approach was more complex, since it offered a differentiated hierarchy of ethnic affiliation (i.e. "nations" and "nationalities"). Although the range of possible beneficiaries of minority rights was widened, their members had nevertheless to adapt to the predominant discourse of the ruling elite.[47]

Communist rule in East Central Europe led to the recognition of ethnic groups not recognised in the interwar period, even if their existence exhausted itself in folklorist performances. Other groups, which had been recognised in the interwar period (primarily Jews and Germans), had been exterminated, expelled or suppressed.

In Yugoslavia the end of Communism led to the establishment of ethno-nationalist regimes, which each rallied its citizens based on claimed mass crimes of "ethnic cleansing" and expulsion in times of war and peace. The Communist regime in Bulgaria tried, in its last days, to play this card with respect to the Turkish and other Muslim populations.[48] In former Yugoslavia, the recent wars have led to the flight and expulsion of larger ethnic groups, and in their wake,

---

[44] This was the case with the Islamised Megleni Vlachs, which were torn apart by the Balkan Wars and the Greek-Turkish population transfer of 1923 – cf. Thede Kahl: Zur Islamisierung der meglenitischen Vlachen (Meglenorumänen). Das Dorf Nânti (Nótia) und die "Nântinets" in der heutigen Türkei. *Zeitschrift für Balkanologie* 38/1-2 (2002), pp. 31-55.

[45] Thus the nomadic *Sarakatsani* or *Karakatsani*, a transhumant Greek-speaking group of shepherds were finally compelled to settle down in the process of the establishment of agricultural co-operatives. The Sarakatsani lost their visibility as a different ethnic group and became a hidden minority – cf. Ženja Pimpireva: Karakačanite v Bălgarija (ot nomadstvo kăm usednalost). Sofia 1995, pp. 93-98.

[46] Cf. Ortakovski, Minorities, pp. 263-282, 299-325.

[47] Cf. ibidem, pp. 328-331.

[48] This was a continuation of similar measures set in the late 1940s and early 1950s – cf. Poulton, Balkans, pp. 119-120, 129-161; Ortakovski, Minorities, pp. 275-282.

of various hidden minorities in the region – as in the case of Croatia (Slavonia), Bosnia and Herzegovina and Kosovo in particular after the intervention of NATO in 1999.[49] The demise of federal Yugoslavia meant furthermore that ethnic groups that had been recognised as "nationalities" in the common Socialist state, had to queue up in order to be recognised as national minorities in the successor states, as was the case with the Roma in Slovenia or with the Muslims (Bosniaks) both there and in Croatia. Other ethnic groups, like the Germans in Croatia, used the new opportunities to gain minority protection.

As a dark legacy of the misshapen and distorted Communist welfare project in former Yugoslavia, and to a lesser extent also in other Balkan states, we can observe a general political disorientation of the populace; it opened a path for populist strategies in politics and in the public sphere. Consequently, social issues were re-interpreted as national ones in the successor states. Instead of finding solutions for critical social problems in the transformation of Communism to capitalism, populist politicians sought scapegoats among ethnic minorities. The end of Communism, however, must not only be interpreted negatively, it also made room for the discussion of disputed ethnic identities. In some cases, small ethnic groups either could manifest themselves within a new political framework or at least find attention among the scholarly community.[50]

It is no coincidence that just in these years the international community passed a number of conventions for the protection of national minorities, among which the 1994 Framework Convention for the Protection of National Minorities of the Council of Europe is maybe the best known. It was due to the independence of Slovenia that a new awareness for the Slovene population in Austrian Styria emerged[51] and that Italy passed in 2001 an extended minority law for the Slovenes. Similar observations can be made in the case of Greece. After the Greek Civil War in 1949, the state and its institutions became engaged in the suppression of minorities so as to realise an ethnically homogeneous nation state, but since the early 1990s, under the eyes of the NGO-led human rights associations, the Greek public has been compelled to tackle with the issues of hidden ethnic minorities and to get used to the idea that more than just one minority, defined locally as "Muslim", is living in the country.[52]

---

[49] For more on the present situation of hidden minorities in the Balkans cf. Sikimić, Skrivene manjine.

[50] Cf. Poulton, Balkans; Brunnbauer, Umstrittene Identitäten; Pimpireva, Karakačanite; Cay Lienau/Ludwig Steindorff (eds.): Ethnizität, Identität und Nationalität in Südosteuropa. Munich 2000; Sikimić, Skrivene manjine.

[51] Boris Jesih (ed.): Narodne manjšine 3: Slovenci v avstrijski zvezni deželi Štajerski. Zbornik referatov na znanstvenem srečanju v Mariboru, 25.-27. maja 1992. Ljubljana 1994; Christian Stenner (ed.): Slowenische Steiermark. Verdrängte Minderheit in Österreichs Südosten. Vienna – Cologne – Weimar 1997; cf. also the article by Klaus-Jürgen Hermanik in this volume.

[52] Cf. the focus on "Minorities in Greece – historical issues and new perspectives" in*: Jahrbücher für Geschichte und Kultur Südosteuropas* 5 (2003). Cf. also Poulton, Balkans, pp. 175-192; Sevasti Trubeta: Die Konstitution von Minderheiten und die Ethnisierung sozialer und

The end of Communism in general and the break up of former Yugoslavia in particular are only single elements of the revival of ethnic issues. An enhanced awareness for ethnic groups and ethnic issues can be observed in Western Europe since the end of the 1970s.[53]

In summary, some hidden minorities have certainly become subject of legal treatment in the past two centuries. Others – due to "ethnic cleansing" in the Balkans – disappeared for good. Others – be they in the Balkans or in Central Europe – remained hidden, either because they were already assimilated to such a degree that they did not have the power to do so or because they simply had no desire to reveal themselves in such a way.

IV. At the end of the road: Are hidden minorities unsuccessful national minorities?

This short and limited historical survey of the treatment of groups considered fit to be national minorities and of those who were not, provides a first impression of an *external* view of the phenomena of issue. It has demonstrated that contemporary hidden minorities are those small ethnic groups, which never or only for a short period had the opportunity to proliferate themselves as national minorities. Any discussion of hidden minorities remains one-sided, as long as the *internal* point of view of the respective groups, which was often one of not wanting to be treated as national minorities despite being subject to assimilation strategies, is not considered.

The road is short, if hidden minorities were solely to be considered from a juridical point of view.[54] This would mean treating hidden minorities only as yet undiscovered or still unrecognised national minorities. This may be correct in certain cases, where representatives of hidden minorities are interested in official recognition, but it does not cover a great variety of cases.

Still, we cannot avoid touching on the juridical definitions for national minorities, for without mentioning them it would be much more difficult to grasp some major traits of hidden minorities. By doing so, we have first to be aware of the lack of conceptual clarity with respect to juridical definitions of national

politischer Konflikte. Eine Untersuchung am Beispiel der im griechischen Thrakien ansässigen Moslemischen Minderheit. Frankfurt/M. et al. 1999.

[53] We have also to take into account the discovery of regionalism since the 1970s, which led to an increasing awareness of ethnicity; cf. Gerhard Sonnert: Nationalismus und Krise der Moderne. Theoretische Argumentation und empirische Analyse am Beispiel des neueren schottischen Nationalismus. Frankfurt/M. 1987, pp. 200-211.

[54] Cf. the article by Mirjam Polzer-Srienz in this volume.

minorities.[55] One of the shortest of various definitions characterises national minorities in their "identifiability, differential power, differential and pejorative treatment, and group awareness".[56] With respect to small ethnic groups, "group awareness" is a complicated term. Who is observing group awareness – a scholar, a state, or a jurist? With respect to possible legal recognition of a given ethnic community, "group awareness" is supposed to be public, it should not be a phenomenon restricted only to claims of solidarity among a local population, even if the latter could otherwise also be characterised in terms of "identifiability, differential power, differential and pejorative treatment". Hidden minorities, however, are often interested just in avoiding public recognition and this especially with respect to their "identifiability". In extreme cases, these groups even try to hide any apparent feeling of solidarity among their own group from the public, since this could be misunderstood as the wish to preserve deviating cultural (i.e. ethnic) traits.[57]

A subjective perception of social exclusion and a feeling of cultural otherness, on the other hand, are nonetheless present among the groups in question. In some cases, there may have even been individual attempts by members of these communities to attain recognition of their traditions from the majority population, without immediately claiming rights as minorities, but most often these small communities have tried to leave no suspicious traces of their existence in the public sphere. Their otherness is restricted to the private sphere. In extreme cases, hidden minorities have even rejected the potential support of their alleged referential ("mother"-) nation, since this would only threaten their hitherto non-existing political role in their country of residence.[58]

This common sense of contemporary hidden minorities – their interest in endogamy and the preservation of specific cultural traits in the private sphere, but not to manifest them in public[59] – clearly shows, where the road ends, when we compare them with recognised national minorities. This also means that methods of jurisprudence and of political history, which have dominated to date, cannot be of help any longer if we want to understand the internal point of view of ethnic groups living below the level of officially recognised minorities.

---

[55] Jennifer Jackson Preece: National Minorities and the European Nation-States System. Oxford 1998, pp. 14-15, 27-29.

[56] Anthony Gary Dworkin/Rosalind J. Dworkin: The Minority Report. An Introduction to Racial, Ethnic and Gender Relations. 3rd ed.: Fort Worth et al. 1993, p. 17.

[57] For similar thoughts cf. Dieter Blumenwitz: Das Recht auf Gebrauch der Minderheitensprache. Gegenwärtiger Stand und Entwicklungstendenzen im europäischen Völkerrecht. In: K. Bott-Bodenhausen (ed.), Unterdrückte Sprachen. Sprachverbote und das Recht auf Gebrauch der Minderheitensprachen. Frankfurt/M. et al. 1996, p. 160.

[58] Paul Smith: Introduction. In: P. Smith (ed.), Ethnic groups in international relations. Aldershot 1991, p. 8.

[59] In the Balkans the Bulgarian Pomaks seem to form a prototype for such behaviour – cf. Konstantinov, Pomak conversions, p. 354.

Other approaches are necessary for studying the purpose and use of the term ethnicity in the everyday life of those small communities denoted hidden minorities.

V. Multiple identities versus assimilation: complementary or competing features?

Ethnicity is no magic word; nevertheless, like the term minority it has no generally accepted definition.[60] Scholarly approaches towards the term ethnicity have changed in the last decades: The primordialist approach, which focused upon "'objective features' such as shared language, religion, territory or history"[61] was replaced by a situationalist one, which shifted attention from the "cultural stuff" towards the organisation and mobilisation of ethnic affiliation through self-ascription and ascription by the others.[62] Such criticism finally led to constructivist interpretations of nation and ethnicity, which put the supratemporal character of identity and ethnicity into question.[63]

Considering these general arguments, four issues are most interesting with respect to hidden minorities:

1. Ethnicity is not a constant factor; "Ethnicity can [...] increase or weaken in its importance, or even disappear."[64]

2. The constructivist approach opens a path to the perception of "switching identities"[65] and

3. of local social identities which do not fit into an obviously "preset canon" of nations and ethnic groups; the relation of these local identities towards the encompassing majority population can and is interpreted as ethnic difference.[66]

---

[60] Christian Giordano: Ethnizität: Prozesse und Diskurse im interkulturellen Vergleich. In: Hettlage/Deger/Wagner (eds.), Kollektive Identität in Krisen. Ethnizität in Region, Nation, Europa. Opladen 1997, pp. 58-59.

[61] Cf. the critical treatment of these notions by Hans Vermeulen/Cora Govers: From political mobilization to the politics of consciousness, in: H. Vermeulen/C. Govers (eds.), The politics of ethnic consciousness. New York 1997, p. 5.

[62] Frederic Barth: Introduction, in: F. Barth (ed.), Ethnic groups and boundaries: the social organization of cultural difference. Bergen – London 1969, pp. 9-38.

[63] Anderson, Imagined communities.

[64] Reinhart Kößler/Tilman Schiel: Nationalstaaten und Grundlagen ethnischer Identität, in: R. Kößler/T. Schiel (eds.), Nationalstaat und Ethnizität. Frankfurt/M. 1994, p. 11.

[65] Georg Elwert: Boundaries, Cohesion and Switching. In: B. Brumen/Z. Šmitek (eds.), MESS: Mediterranean Ethnological Summer School, Piran, Slovenia, 1994-1995. Ljubljana 1995, pp. 105-121.

[66] As has been demonstrated on the macro level by Iver B. Neumann: Uses of the other. Manchester 1999.

4. It is possible to recognise multiple or plural identities even within one individual, so that in extreme cases, issues of mutual exclusiveness and of ethnic boundaries cut through one and the same person.[67]

These issues have to be interpreted within the context of three different assumptions which seem to contradict each other but with care can be combined to develop further insights for the explanation of hidden minorities:

a) Multiple and plural identities cannot be selected arbitrarily since they are not a result of wishful multicultural thinking but of adaptation.

b) In contradiction to presuppositions of radical constructivism, ethnic affiliations even among small groups demonstrate a surprising tenacity.

c) The conscience of being ethnic distinct alone can hardly be accountable for the preservation of hidden minorities, since ethnic affiliations are always reproduced in contact with the outside world.

Ad a) In the case of hidden minorities one has to be careful not to idealise plural ethnic identities as an echo of post-modern multiculturalism; rather, they seem to be a product of historical survival strategies of a particular population, long before the idea of multiculturalism established itself in history. One has to ask whether the adoption of more than one ethnic identity is an *additive* or a *subtractive* process, a process evolving along the same lines as bilingualism.[68] In the first (ideal and often only pre-modern) case, an individual from a minority population will show his loyalty to the majority population of the state in which he lives by accepting offers to take over its concept of identity but will nonetheless retain his own original ethnic identity in a complementary way, so that in the end his cultural and ethnic tradition reaches beyond that of the majority population. In the second (contemporary and therefore more realistic) case, the concept of identity of the majority population, which is pushed through by the power of various state institutions and which enjoys a higher social status, will in the long term replace the other identities and their cultural values, although for a certain period of transition the identity concepts of the minority play a certain role.[69] Even without quoting particular cases, it becomes clear that most modern hidden minorities are of the second variety; the transition from one ethnic and national identity to another together with the concomitant linguistic and cultural assimilation.

---

[67] Janek Musek: The psychological basis of multiple identity. In: S. N. Lukanovič (ed.), Overlapping cultures and plural identities/Cultures partielles et identités multiples. Ljubljana 1995, pp. 9-28.

[68] Josiane Hamers/Michel Blanc: Bilinguality and Bilingualism. Cambridge et.al. 1989, p. 56.

[69] This has been demonstrated in the case of the remnants of the Romance-speaking Aromanian (Vlach) community in Bulgaria – cf. Thede Kahl: Wandlung von ethnischen Identitätsmustern bei den Aromunen (Vlachen) Bulgariens und ihre Folgen. In: Lienau/Steindorff, Ethnizität, pp. 19-47, here 37, 40-41. For the theoretical implications of double identities, although not exemplified as hidden minorities – cf. Stephen Shulman: Competing versus complementary identities: Ukrainian-Russian relations and the loyalties of Russians in Ukraine. *Nationalities Papers* 26/4 (1998), pp. 615-632.

Ad b) Even if we want to avoid being criticised for using essentialist "objective features" for the description of ethnicity, we still cannot deny that *historically oriented ethnological research* in the field will discover common socio-cultural patterns, common historical and contemporary experiences, images of a common origin and, consequently, collective identities and concomitant boundaries between different populations, which gradually acquired the quality of being perceived as "ethnic".[70] The origin of these phenomena has to be sought in specific "historical memories" and specific "cultural codes"[71] that can help to unmask arbitrary interpretations of ethnicity. Even if we accept the constructivist character of ethnic and national affiliations, it is not true that "anything goes": ethnic identities are not independent of reality.[72] And – apart from the notion of "switching identities" – we have to take into account a certain tenacity of ethnic phenomena, which at the same time must not be mistaken with alleged „invariability", as was the belief of the pre-constructivist era. In this tenacity we have also to seek the resistance of small ethnic groups that hide among the majority population from cultural and linguistic assimilation. Hidden minorities therefore, say something about the completeness of nation building, since they form fragments not fully integrated into this process or were overwhelmed by it in a rather late phase.

Ad c) Even if we accept that specific cultural patterns were and are responsible for the intrinsic continuity of a given population, this population still exists in interplay with the outside world:

1. We should not misunderstand the character of this interplay. In focussing on the difference of hidden minorities vis-à-vis their surroundings, we risk falling into the trap of overusing the term "ethnic identity"; we may tend to qualify specific cultural traits as ethnic because they often bear only the character of locality, or better said, of local culture – like a specific local dialect deviant from the standard language.[73]

---

[70] Friedrich Heckmann: Ethnische Minderheiten, Volk und Nation. Soziologie inter-ethnischer Beziehungen. Stuttgart 1992, p. 46; Friedrich Heckmann: Ethnos, Demos und Nation, oder: Woher stammt die Intoleranz des Nationalstaates gegenüber ethnischen Minderheiten. In: G. Seewann (ed.), Minderheitenfragen in Südosteuropa. Munich 1992, p. 17.

[71] Jan Assman: Kollektives Gedächtnis und kulturelle Identität. In: J. Assman/T. Hölscher (eds.), Kultur und Gedächtnis, Frankfurt/M. 1988, pp. 9-19.

[72] Vermeulen/Govers, The politics, pp. 20-21.

[73] This was demonstrated by the Bulgarian anthropologist Yulian Konstantinov, who came to the conclusion that the younger generation of Bulgarian Pomaks tries to explain their intermediate position through regional and not ethnic peculiarities – cf. Konstantinov, Pomak conversions, p. 344. For a different point of view considering such views of the younger generation (i.e. school children) as a way to evade stigmatisation – cf. Jordanka Telbizova-Sack: Die Pomaken Bulgariens zwischen Identitätsverlust und Selbstbehauptung. In: Lienau/Steindorff, Ethnizität, pp. 71-88, here 78. For comprehensive views from scholars of non-Bulgarian origin cf. Ulf Brunnbauer: Diverging (hi-) stories: the contested identity of the Bulgarian Pomaks. *Ethnologia Balkanica* 3 (1999), pp. 35-50; Evangelos Karagiannis, Fremdzuschreibung und Minderheit: Bemerkungen zu den Pomaken Bulgariens. *Zeitschrift für Balkanologie* 39/1 (2003), pp. 37-51.

2. Exchange with the modern outside world will finally lead to the assimilation of small ethnic groups despite the above-mentioned tenacity, which for a certain period could help to preserve their specific cultural traits and a feeling of group awareness on a local level. Although measures of assimilation in general have the consequence that affected groups will finally give in, the threatening of the identity of an ethnic group by the authorities of the majority population may in some cases, as among the Bulgarian Pomaks, have the effect that "the differentiation between them and the majority population has become very pronounced and sharply cut".[74] This should not blind us to the fact, however, that in most other cases, it is only a matter of time until assimilation (and not differentiation!) will be successful. In the course of this trajectory, members of hidden minorities show similar attitudes. In the private and local sphere they remain attached to their group by various (hidden) means; vis-à-vis the outside world, however, they organise their lives and careers in accordance with the norms and practices of the majority population due to their fears of being recognised and treated as different. And there are even examples which show that, in spite of strategies of adaptation engaged in by members of hidden minorities, their overt conformity is not sufficient to evade stigmatisation by the majority population.[75] Exactly these circumstances make fieldwork difficult and demand an empathic competence from the researcher in order to allow for the "representation of the other"[76] which is realised by various modes of hiding, assimilation and of preservation of cultural traditions. The issue of preservation again shows that for most hidden minorities, group awareness is closely connected with the respective regional setting and local *identity*[77], rather than with a diffuse notion of ethnicity.

VI. Possible methods of research and the geographical focus of the research of hidden minorities

Using this theoretical framework, we can try to assess methods of research and its possible topics: Ideally, research methods should be multidisciplinary or at least interdisciplinary, comprising the disciplines of history, ethnology and linguistics.

Historical research opens the way to archival sources and contextualises the emergence and political treatment of hidden minorities within the respective

[74] Konstantinov, Pomak conversions, p. 356.
[75] Cf. Telbizova-Sack, Pomaken, pp. 81-82.
[76] Eberhard Berg/Martin Fuchs (eds.): Kultur, soziale Praxis, Text. Die Krise der ethnographischen Repräsentation, Frankfurt/M. 1995.
[77] Christian Giordano: Ethnizität und Territorialität. Zur sozialen Konstruktion von Differenz in Mittel- und Osteuropa. *Ethnologia Balkanica* 3 (1999), pp. 9-34.

political developments of a given period.[78] But if it is not done with the help of multidisciplinary approaches like historical anthropology or oral history, this method will run the risk of relying exclusively on biased sources written by regional and local elites (such as priests, teachers and civil servants) and reduce itself to a view from outside. On the basis of detailed case studies, applying ethnographic and linguistic research methods, a cross-cultural and historical comparison can help, however, to assess, refine and correct common features of hidden minorities.

It is one of the main tasks of ethnographic fieldwork among hidden minorities to assess those factors, which have guaranteed the cultural survival and the intrinsic consistency of these small ethnic groups. Since culture imparts meaning and orientation, it is necessary to define those codes and symbols by which the uniqueness of these groups is expressed in the context of their respective 'life worlds' and determine their room for manoeuvre.[79] This includes the already mentioned assessment of the role of ascribed and self-ascribed boundaries that distinguished the respective group from the majority population. Narratives and modes of *self-ascription* in particular lead to insights of personal and collective identity constructions.[80] This leads to the assessment of the role of symbols and myths, especially of the myth of common descent, within the discussion of ethnicity and national affiliation. Like an iceberg, hidden minorities are in most cases only partly visible through their different *cultural signs*. But symbols and myths about "the others", which are handed down by members of the majority population, indicate that something went "wrong" in the process of national homogenisation. They reveal fears of the "other" on the one hand; and motives for assimilation on the other. Such an approach brings to light latent, subconscious features among both members of the hidden minorities and their neighbours among the majority population. These features are even manifest among "traitors" of recognised national minorities who, despite their descent, do not want to identify themselves as members of the minority but prefer to stay anonymous and therefore form a special case of a hidden minority beside the official minority. In their case and in the case of small ethnic groups – i.e. hidden minorities in the narrower sense of the meaning – these

---

[78] For a paradigmatic reader cf. Heinz-Gerhard Haupt/Michael G. Müller/Stuart Woolf (eds.): Regional and national identities in Europe in the XIX and XXth centuries/Les Identités régionales et nationales en Europe aux XIXe et XXe siècles. The Hague-London-Boston 1998.

[79] For prototypical case studies cf. Zdeněk Uherek: The Czech minority in Sarajevo and its symbols. In: B. Jezernik (ed.), Urban symbolism and rituals. Proceedings of the international symposium organised by the IUAES Commission on Urban Anthropology. Ljubljana, June 23-25, 1997, Ljubljana 1999, pp. 69-79; Zdeněk Uherek: Bosnian Czechs: A lesson from the theory of ethnicity. *Ethnologia Balkanica* 3 (1999), pp. 141-154.

[80] Cf. Aleida Assmann/Heidrun Friese (eds.): Identitäten. Erinnerung, Geschichte. Frankfurt/M. 1998; Ulrike Meinhof/Heidi Armbruster/Craig Rollo: Identity discourses on East-West borders in Europe: an introduction. In: U. Meinhof (ed.), Living (with) borders. Identity discourses on East-West borders in Europe. Aldershot 2002, pp. 10-13.

subconscious features can survive the process of assimilation and can still play a role when ethnically defined group awareness has long gone lost.[81]

Linguistics, but foremost its sub-discipline socio-linguistics, provides even more detailed answers to the scale of strategies used by members of hidden minorities, although restricted to a lower bandwidth than ethnographic fieldwork. If language is one of the key factors in the process of identification, then an integrated and methodologically homogenous approach with respect to the roles of language and language strategies among small ethnic groups and hidden minorities in particular is still at its beginnings.[82]

With respect to the geographical focus of research on hidden minorities, we cannot ignore that most such minorities live in border areas, are fragmented by new borders which ideally have respected linguistic frontiers in general, but have also taken into account geopolitical or geographic demands for "smooth" and strategic borderlines by the states concerned: "Because of their liminal and frequently contested nature, borders tend to be characterised by identities which are shifting and multiple."[83] The study of hidden minorities can therefore be considered investigations of the historical impact of nation building on state borders. It forms part of an increasing academic interest in borders and *intermediate areas* (Ther/Sundhaussen). In this respect we are confronted with the double meaning of border: Border areas are sensitive regions, where state power is interested in the loyalty of the population and initiates nationalising measures. At the same time, border areas are often regions of economic underdevelopment and marginalisation; bilingualism, however, can make cross-border traffic easier. This can be an economic argument for the preservation of plural identities or, respectively, of denationalising borders.[84]

VII. How to grasp assimilation

The goal of research on hidden minorities is not the discovery of yet another "forgotten" group. Every scholar who is successful in this respect – and the Balkans will offer further possibilities in the future – can (in private) truly be

[81] For similar observations in the case of the (not totally hidden) minority of Slovenes in Carinthia cf. Dietmar Larcher: Soziogenese der Urangst. In: K. B. Boeckmann et al. (eds.), Zweisprachigkeit und Identität. Klagenfurt 1988, pp. 15-64; cf. also the article of Marija Jurić Pahor in this volume.

[82] Cf. the articles by Tanja Petrović and Biljana Sikimić in this volume.

[83] Thomas M. Wilson/Hastings Donnan: Nation, state and identity at international Borders. In: T. M. Wilson/H. Donnan (eds.), Border identities: nation and state at international frontiers. Cambridge 1998, p. 13. pp. 1-30. For changing identities in the course of recently established state borders cf. the article by Duška Knežević-Hočevar in this volume.

[84] Cf. Hans Knippenberg/Jan Markusse (eds.): Nationalising and denationalising European border regions, 1800-2000: views from geography and history. Dordrecht – Boston – London 1999.

proud of himself, but he should be always aware not to stumble into the traps of nostalgic discourse that would end in the above-mentioned *human Jurassic Park*. The issue, rather, which we want to address deals with the assessment of the crucial historical point, when the pre-modern features of collective identities, which in some cases were reinforced by exponents of their referential nations, crumble and are no longer plausible as means for guaranteeing the independent existence of these small ethnic groups vis-à-vis the victorious nation state.

A survey of Central Europe and the Balkans plainly shows that this crucial point was reached in the north at an earlier stage in history; in the south the process is still ongoing. This difference is due to the delayed establishment of nation states, or rather of national affiliation, as, for example, in the Balkans.[85] Defining the period in time, when the assimilation of small ethnic groups was enforced in different national and geographic settings, however, will only be of superficial use, if we do not make use of a decisive working principle of hidden minorities. Ethnic solidarity, in their case, is reduced to a local level and functions in the absence of extensive cultural and educational institutions; it is therefore always based on the passing on of tradition within the family. This means that only a focus on the role of *family* and *kinship* can give further information on how long specific cultural patterns of hidden minorities have been preserved, on the one hand, and when they started to fail vis-à-vis the modern state, which offered viable subsistence alternatives and even career possibilities within or without the traditional local frame.

The penetration of society by the modern state in the Balkans took place in a later period than in Central Europe, often only in the form of state socialism. In Central and Western Europe, the nuclear family formed an ideal basis for making "peasants into Frenchmen".[86] However, the different systems of kinship and inheritance in the Balkans, or at least their residues, which had been in the research focus of Karl Kaser[87], made it much more difficult for the state to conquer and colonise the rural masses and to lay the groundwork for the modern principle of national homogeneity. This seems to be the main

[85] In the case of Central Europe the above-mentioned spill-over of the discourse on small ethnic groups from the Balkans after the First World War is irrelevant; in Austria it only re-enforced the assimilation of native hidden minorities by the state, since the population of Austria, although small in size, had the advantage of being nationally overwhelmingly homogeneous, while Yugoslavia, as an authentic heir to the multiethnic empires, had many more problems in dealing with large and compact national minorities than with small ethnic groups which did not impose any threat to the existence of this state.

[86] Cf. Eugen Weber: Peasants into Frenchmen: the modernization of rural France, 1870-1914. London 1977.

[87] For concise overviews on kinship and inheritance, collective identities and family cf. Karl Kaser: Verwandschaft und Abstammung. Familie und Geschlechterbeziehungen. In: K. Kaser/S. Gruber/R. Pichler (eds.), Historische Anthropologie im südöstlichen Europa. Eine Einführung. Vienna – Cologne – Weimar 2003, pp. 131-174; Ulf Brunnbauer: Vom Selbst zum Eigenen. Kollektive Identitäten. In: ibidem, pp. 377-402.

reason, why we can observe different degrees of assimilation of small ethnic groups in Central Europe and in the Balkans.

Be it in the Balkans or in Central Europe, the comparison shows that one feature of cultural and linguistic assimilation seems to be common. In each case we are able to grasp it in the course of *three generations within one family*. It is only the question of assessing the point in time, when the last generation that comprises all cultural traits, which ideally form the essence of the given hidden minority, retires from the stage. The following generation is already open towards new incentives of modern society, offered by the nation state. Some members of this second generation will show this openness towards modernity by practising exogamy, which was taboo for the parental generation. While the second generation may still cling to local tradition (including the partial use of the imparted vernacular), it will be the third generation, which will finally abandon the spell of local tradition in the face of complete integration into the majority population. In their case, the issue of hidden minorities seems to have come to an end. It can only be traced on the subconscious or symbolic levels where family tradition may still form a secondary feature for constructing individual identities.[88]

This pattern of assimilation within three generations is a well-known pattern to describe the integration of migrants into a new society.[89] It makes sense, therefore, to compare the assimilation of hidden minorities, which remain in their local setting, with various sample groups of migrants.[90]

Assimilation seems to be the final fate of hidden minorities. There is nothing nostalgic about this fact, as long as it represents the will of the members of these populations, be it accentuated or vague. And we have to accept their will, even if historical research shows that this consciousness is the result of a colonising violence by the state in its desire to create ethnically homogeneous territories. In such cases, scholars can only assess the transition from hidden *minorities* towards hidden *identities* represented by individual members of such small ethnic groups, who try to cope with the submergence of their local community. It is an issue of respect, of how to interpret the local "wisdom" of such outstanding, for the most part elderly and male persons on which every fieldworker will stumble, when he deals with hidden minorities.[91] Bearers of hidden

[88] This is the case among the descendants of Czechs in Sarajevo and of Bulgarian gardeners in Austria – cf. Uherek, Czech minority; Uherek, A lesson, and the article by Marijana Jakimova in this volume.

[89] Mojca Ravnik: Bratje, sestre, strniči, zermani. Družina in sorodstvo v vaseh v Slovenski Istri, Ljubljana – Koper 1996; Meinhof/Armbruster/Rollo, Identity discourses, pp. 6-7.

[90] It has to be investigated, however, if the process of assimilation took the same form in the case of the Czechs and Slovaks in Vienna which at an early stage got the protection by minority laws.

[91] The author himself came into repeated contact with two elderly male individuals from among the Serbs of Bela Krajina (Southern Slovenia) and the Slovene-speaking remnants in Southern Styria (region of Leutschach). Discussion showed striking similarities between these two representatives of two totally different hidden minorities, concerning history and language.

identities therefore have to be considered within their environment, which is at a late stage in the process of assimilation and where group awareness is less and less determined by divergent cultural traits. They may impose themselves on the fieldworker as authentic representatives of once hidden minorities, as those, who did not keep pace with the ongoing process of assimilation. Such individuals are still affected by the colonial aspect of assimilation; they do not want to be addressed in public – sometimes not even at the local level. Only if the story of the hidden minorities is finished and the younger generations have switched to the majority culture/language will some of them open up and talk about their local community's past, since they are too old to be attacked as possible advocates of "ethnic revival".

VIII. What about the ethnic revival of hidden minorities?

If hidden minorities are doomed to disappear, how are we to deal with certain observations dealing with aspects of their "ethnic revival"? Attempts at such secondary *identity constructions* are a genuine issue today. In northern Greece, for example, the so-called "Rainbow" party, has been working towards the official recognition of the Slavic population in the region as a national minority. This party and the intellectuals rallied around it have only partly succeeded in interesting the concerned population in their aims, since most of the latter want to stay anonymous, even if this would mean the prolongation of the ongoing process of colonisation by the Greek nation state.[92]

In Kosovo, the rule of Slobodan Miloševič had the side-effect of creating an Egyptian minority of Roma descent, which – although not putting into question the minority rights of this hitherto hidden minority, which can look back on a long local history – had the instrumental purpose of reducing the role of the suppressed Albanian majority.[93]

In southern Slovenia the hitherto hidden Serbian minority of some four villages was discovered in 1988 by nationalist Serbian journalists, who tried to impose themselves as their advocates and wanted to show that this population had been the subject of ethnic assimilation by the institutions of the then still Socialist Republic of Slovenia, although the villagers in concern indignantly rejected these accounts and preferred the perspective of peaceful assimilation.[94]

---

[92] Cf. Christian Voss: Sprachdiskurse in minoritären Ethnisierungs und Nationalisierungsprozessen – Die slawischsprachige Minderheit in Griechenland. *Südosteuropa. Zeitschrift für Gegenwartsforschung* 52/1-3 (2003), pp. 116-135.

[93] Ger Duijzings: Die Erschaffung von Ägyptern in Kosovo und Makedonien. In: Brunnbauer, Umstrittene Identitäten, pp. 123-148.

[94] Cf. Promitzer, "Gute Serben", pp. 192-194.

Similarly, the Austrian government and the Graz-based "Alpenländischer Kulturverein Südmark" have recently tried to make use of the remnants of German minorities (so-called "Altösterreicher") in Slovenia to impose themselves into the discourse of Slovenia joining the European Union.[95] It will be a matter of bilateral politics, if the "artificial" survival (in the sense of Ernest Gellner) of these groups will be achieved.

In Austria, finally, we can also observe a case similar to the situation in northern Greece, although it is still more extraordinary in its implications. Here we are dealing with an association intent on recognising the Slovene-speaking population in southern areas of the province of Styria. The so-called "Article-VII-Cultural Society" (Artikel-VII-Kulturverein für Steiermark), founded in the late 1980s, can in fact lean upon the Article 7 of the Austrian State Treaty of 1955, where, among other things, minority rights of the Slovene-speaking population of the province of Styria, are foreseen. The society is demanding these minority rights although the affected population seems uninterested. As a matter of fact, apart from some respected, but isolated individuals from the autochthonous Slovene population, the society consists mainly of members of migrant families from Slovenia and of sympathetic German-speaking Austrians.

These examples pose the issue of the role of real and would-be advocates of hidden minorities. These small ethnic groups have undergone decades of assimilation, which in some cases could be described as human rights violations. By now many of them have lost that group awareness, which would legitimise such ethnic revival endeavours. Therefore we have to speak of phenomena of *ethnical entrepreneurship* and *identity-management* coming from without but seldom from within. If the latter is the case, the discussion of *ethnic revival* and of *identity-management* has also to consider emerging trans-national networks which, like in the case of descents of Slavic Macedonians from Greece or of the Germans of the Slovene region of Kočevje (Gottschee), had an echoing effect upon the remaining members of such communities in their home countries.[96]

The common starting point of advocates of these small ethnic groups is nonetheless the "misguided claim" of nationalist ideology[97]; they consider hidden minorities "sleeping beauties" which – if we adopt an allegory by Ernest Gellner for the role of intellectuals in the creation of nations – have only to be kissed awake in order to function like recognised national minorities. But such approaches do not consider the fact that hidden minorities often do not want to

[95] Cf. Stefan Karner: Die deutschsprachige Volksgruppe in Slowenien. Aspekte ihrer Entwicklung 1939-1997. Klagenfurt – Ljubljana – Vienna 1998; cf. the article of Eduard Staudinger in this volume.

[96] Cf. Loring M. Danforth: The Macedonian conflict. Ethnic nationalism in a transnational world. New Jersey 1995.

[97] Gellner, Nations, pp. 47-48.

be kissed awake and be deprived of their until now, successful and protective concealment.

Of course, recent *ethnic-engineering* and *identity-management* initiatives, which are often directly dependent upon the role of the respective *referential nations,* also have their positive side; they were responsible for the insight that the issue of hidden minorities is a topic of interest for academic research. But research is not advocacy. The decisive difference is that while academic research into hidden minorities and their difficult existence includes a basic sympathy for all aspects in their life worlds and respect for all possible individual variants and strategies, it does not work as a missionary. Descriptions of the often unfavourable context of hidden minorities, which naturally have to include the concrete naming of human rights violations, are only descriptions of strategies. These strategies comprise those of the authorities of the majority population, including either peaceful and violent assimilation, or even something in-between, often the playing off of one ethnic group against another.[98] But also hidden minorities have their strategies in giving in, hiding out or showing resistance.

IX. Conclusion

It is worthwhile to deal with hidden minorities: it should be evident that the study of small ethnic groups may shed additional light upon the relativity of issues of ethnicity ands help in explaining nation building in Europe – or at least in Central Europe and the Balkans.

One further argument has to be made: One could say that it is only a matter of labels, when we name certain small ethnic groups "hidden minorities". The term "hidden minorities", however, can sharpen the focus on those small ethnic groups, which do not fit into the traditional filter of nation building in Central Europe and in the Balkans. Since the denomination has the most serious drawback of being an academic construction *a posteriori*, it can only have an operational character, not an essentialist one. Its study, however, can contribute to the general knowledge of how once "laterally separated petty communities of the lay members of the society" were subjected to "the general imposition of a high culture".[99]

This essay started with a quotation about heroes of a traditional play which is no longer performed; it ends mentioning a second play, a modern play on nationalism. Small ethnic groups, which were seldom invited to observe the spectacle, were nonetheless compelled to make their own interpretations of the

[98] Cf. Poulton, Balkans, p. 210.
[99] Gellner, Nations, pp. 9-10, 57.

snippets of the plot they manage to hear outside the theatre. The "plural identities" of these small ethnic groups were a way of coping with this, mostly bad news, nothing else.

Bibliography:

ANDERSON, Benedict: Imagined communities. Reflections on the origin and spread of nationalism. Revised ed.: London – New York 1995.

ASSMAN, Jan: Kollektives Gedächtnis und kulturelle Identität. In: J. Assman/T. Hölscher (eds.), Kultur und Gedächtnis, Frankfurt/M. 1988, pp. 9-19.

ASSMANN, Aleida/FRIESE, Heidrun (eds.): Identitäten. Erinnerung, Geschichte. Frankfurt/M. 1998.

BARTH, Frederic: Introduction, in: F. Barth (ed.), Ethnic groups and boundaries: the social organization of cultural difference. Bergen – London 1969, pp. 9-38.

BERG, Eberhard/FUCHS, Martin (eds.): Kultur, soziale Praxis, Text. Die Krise der ethnographischen Repräsentation, Frankfurt/M. 1995.

BLUMENWITZ, Dieter: Das Recht auf Gebrauch der Minderheitensprache. Gegenwärtiger Stand und Entwicklungstendenzen im europäischen Völkerrecht. In: K. Bott-Bodenhausen (ed.), Unterdrückte Sprachen. Sprachverbote und das Recht auf Gebrauch der Minderheitensprachen. Frankfurt/M. et.al. 1996, pp. 159-202.

BOČKOVA, Helena: Ethnische Gemeinschaften und ethnische Prozesse auf dem Balkan im Werke Konstantin Jirečeks. *Ethnologia Slovaca et Slavica* XXIV-XXV (1992-93), pp. 225-244.

BRUNNBAUER, Ulf: Diverging (hi-) stories: the contested identity of the Bulgarian Pomaks. *Ethnologia Balkanica* 3 (1999), pp. 35-50.

BRUNNBAUER, Ulf (ed.): Umstrittene Identitäten. Ethnizität und Nationalität in Südosteuropa. Frankfurt/M. et al. 2002.

BRUNNBAUER, Ulf: Vom Selbst zum Eigenen. Kollektive Identitäten. In: K. Kaser/S. Gruber/R. Pichler (eds.), Historische Anthropologie im südöstlichen Europa. Eine Einführung. Vienna – Cologne – Weimar 2003, pp. 377-402.

CHRISIMOVA, Ognjana: "Mirnite" Balkani sled N'oj. Obštestvoto na narodite kato faktor na statukvoto i malcinstvenija mir (1919-1939). In: S. Eldărov (ed.), Balkanite meždu mira i vojnata XIV-XX vek. Sbornik naučni izsledvanija. Sofija 2002, pp. 267-283.

CVIJIĆ, Jovan: Balkansko poluostrvo. Reprint: Belgrade 1987.

DANFORTH, Loring M.: The Macedonian conflict. Ethnic nationalism in a transnational world. New Jersey 1995.

DUIJZINGS, Ger: Die Erschaffung von Ägyptern in Kosovo und Makedonien. In: U. Brunnbauer (ed.), Umstrittene Identitäten. Ethnizität und Nationalität in Südosteuropa. Frankfurt/M. et. al. 2002, pp. 123-148.

DWORKIN, Anthony Gary/DWORKIN, Rosalind J.: The minority report. An introduction to racial, ethnic and gender relations. 3rd ed.: Fort Worth et al. 1993.

ELWERT, Georg: Boundaries, Cohesion and Switching. In: B. Brumen/Z. Šmitek (eds.), MESS: Mediterranean Ethnological Summer School, Piran, Slovenia, 1994-1995. Ljubljana 1995, pp. 105-121.

FAHLBUSCH, Michael: Wissenschaft im Dienst der nationalsozialistischen Politik? Die „Volksdeutschen Forschungsgemeinschaften" von 1931-1945. Baden-Baden 1999.

GAUSS, Karl-Markus: Die sterbenden Europäer. Unterwegs zu den Sepharden von Sarajevo, Gottscheer-Deutschen, Arbereshe, Sorben und Aromunen. Vienna 2001.

GELLNER, Ernest: Nations and nationalism. Reprint: Oxford 1988.

GELLNER, Ernest: Nationalismus. Kultur und Macht. Berlin 1999.

GINZBURG, Carlo: Mikro-Historie. Zwei oder drei Dinge, die ich von ihr weiß. *Historische Anthropologie. Kultur-Gesellschaft-Alltag* 1/2 (1992), pp. 169-192.

GIORDANO, Christian: Ethnizität: Prozesse und Diskurse im interkulturellen Vergleich. In: R. Hettlage/P. Deger/S. Wagner (eds.), Kollektive Identität in Krisen. Ethnizität in Region, Nation, Europa. Opladen 1997, pp. 56-72.

GIORDANO, Christian: Ethnizität und Territorialität. Zur sozialen Konstruktion von Differenz in Mittel- und Osteuropa. In: *Ethnologia Balkanica* 3 (1999), pp. 9-34.

GLASS, Krzysztof/KRANJC, Janez/LUTHAR, Oto: Vorwort. In: K. Glass/J. Kranjc/O. Luthar (eds.), Grenzlandidentitäten im Zeitalter der Eurointegration, Vienna – Poznań 1998, pp. 7-11.

HAAS, Hanns: Ethnikum und Nation in der dörflichen Lebenswelt eines deutsch-tschechischen Dorfes. In: V. Rajšp/E. Bruckmüller (eds.), Vilfanov zbornik: Pravo-zgodovina-narod/Recht-Geschichte-Nation. Ljubljana 1999, pp. 555-588.

HAMERS, Josiane/BLANC, Michel: Bilinguality and Bilingualism. Cambridge et al. 1989.

HAUPT, Heinz-Gerhard/MÜLLER, Michael G./WOOLF, Stuart (eds.): Regional and national identities in Europe in the XIX and XXth centuries/Les Identités régionales et nationales en Europe aux XIX et XXe siècles. The Hague-London-Boston 1998.

HECKMANN, Friedrich: Ethnische Minderheiten, Volk und Nation. Soziologie inter-ethnischer Beziehungen. Stuttgart 1992, p. 46.

HECKMANN, Friedrich: Ethnos, Demos und Nation, oder: Woher stammt die Intoleranz des Nationalstaates gegenüber ethnischen Minderheiten? In:

G. Seewann (ed.), Minderheitenfragen in Südosteuropa. Munich 1992, pp. 9-36.

HEUBERGER, Valeria/SUPPAN, Arnold/VYSLONZIL, Elisabeth (eds.): Brennpunkt Osteuropa. Minderheiten im Kreuzfeuer des Nationalismus. Vienna – Munich 1996.

HROCH, Miroslav: Social preconditions of national revival in Europe. A comparative analysis of the social composition of patriotic groups among the smaller European nations. New York 2000.

JAHRBÜCHER *für Geschichte und Kultur Südosteuropas* 5 (2003), Focus: Minorities in Greece – historical issues and new perspectives.

JANOWSKI, Maciej: Pitfalls and Opportunities. The Concept of East-Central Europe as a Tool of Historical Analysis. *European Review of History* 6/1 (1999), pp. 91-100.

JESIH, Boris (ed.): Narodne manjšine 3: Slovenci v avstrijski zvezni deželi Štajerski. Zbornik referatov na znanstvenem srečanju v Mariboru, 25.-27. maja 1992. Ljubljana 1994.

JESIH, Boris: So "male" manjšine drugačne od "velikih"? – Sind "kleine" Volksgruppen anders als große? In: K. Anderwaldl/P. Karpf/V. Smrtnik (eds.), Die europäische Dimension des Volksgruppenrechtes. Sprachminderheiten: Herausforderung und Chance, Klagenfurt 1997, pp. 112-120.

JUDSON, Peter M.: Nationalizing rural landscapes in Cisleithania, 1880-1914. In: N. Wingfield (ed.), Creating the other. Ethnic conflict and nationalism in Habsburg Central Europe. New York – Oxford 2003, pp. 127-148.

KAHL, Thede: Wandlung von ethnischen Identitätsmustern bei den Aromunen (Vlachen) Bulgariens und ihre Folgen. In: C. Lienau/L. Steindorff (eds.), Ethnizität, Identität und Nationalität in Südosteuropa. Munich 2000, pp. 19-47.

KAHL, Thede: Zur Islamisierung der meglenitischen Vlachen (Meglenorumänen). Das Dorf Nânti (Nótia) und die „Nântinets" in der heutigen Türkei. *Zeitschrift für Balkanologie* 38/1-2 (2002), pp. 31-55.

KARAGIANNIS, Evangelos: Fremdzuschreibung und Minderheit: Bemerkungen zu den Pomaken Bulgariens. *Zeitschrift für Balkanologie* 39/1 (2003), pp. 37-51.

KARNER, Stefan: Die deutschsprachige Volksgruppe in Slowenien. Aspekte ihrer Entwicklung 1939-1997. Klagenfurt – Ljubljana – Vienna 1998.

KASER, Karl: Verwandschaft und Abstammung. Familie und Geschlechterbeziehungen. In: K. Kaser/S. Gruber/R. Pichler (eds.), Historische Anthropologie im südöstlichen Europa. Eine Einführung. Vienna – Cologne – Weimar 2003, pp. 131-174.

KNIPPENBERG, Hans/MARKUSSE, Jan (eds.): Nationalising and denationalising European border regions, 1800-2000: views from geography and history. Dordrecht – Boston – London 1999.

KÖSSLER, Reinhart/SCHIEL, Tilman: Nationalstaaten und Grundlagen ethnischer Identität, in: R. Kößler/T. Schiel (eds.), Nationalstaat und Ethnizität. Frankfurt/M. 1994, pp. 1-21.

KONSTANTINOV, Yulian: An account of Pomak conversions in Bulgaria (1912-1990). In: G. Seewann (ed.), Minderheitenfragen in Südosteuropa. Munich 1992, pp. 343-357.

KÜRTI, László/LANGMAN, Juliet: Introduction. Searching for identities in the new East Central Europe. In: L. Kürti/J. Langman (eds.), Beyond borders. Remaking cultural identities in the new East and Central Europe. Boulder, Colorado – Oxford 1997, pp. 1-16.

LARCHER, Dietmar: Soziogenese der Urangst. In: K. B. Boeckmann et. al. (eds.), Zweisprachigkeit und Identität. Klagenfurt 1988, pp. 15-64.

LIENAU, Cay/STEINDORFF, Ludwig (eds.): Ethnizität, Identität und Nationalität in Südosteuropa. Munich 2000.

LÖWE, Heinz-Dietrich/TONTHSCH, Günther H./TROEBST, Stefan (eds.): Minderheiten, Regionalbewußtsein und Zentralismus in Ostmitteleuropa. Cologne-Weimar-Vienna 2000.

MEINHOF, Ulrike/ARMBRUSTER, Heidi/ROLLO, Craig: Identity discourses on East-West borders in Europe: an introduction. In: U. Meinhof (ed.), Living (with) borders. Identity discourses on East-West borders in Europe. Aldershot 2002, pp. 1-13.

MINNICH, Robert Gary: Homesteaders and citizens. Collective identity formation on the Austro-Italian-Slovene border. Bergen 1998.

MORITSCH, Andreas (ed.): Vom Ethnos zur Nationalität. Der nationale Differenzierungsprozeß am Beispiel ausgewählter Orte in Kärnten und im Burgenland. Vienna – Munich 1991.

MÜLLER, Dietmar: Staatsbürger auf Widerruf. Juden und Muslime als Alteritätspartner im rumänischen und serbischen Nationscode. Ethnonationale Staatsbürgerschaftskonzepte 1878-1941. Wiesbaden 2005 (= Balkanologische Veröffentlichungen 41).

MUSEK, Janek: The psychological basis of multiple identity. In: S. N. Lukanovič (ed.), Overlapping cultures and plural identities/Cultures partielles et identités multiples. Ljubljana 1995, pp. 9-28.

NEUMANN, Iver B.: Uses of the other. Manchester 1999.

ORTAKOVSKI, Vladimir: Minorities in the Balkans. Skopje – Štip 1998.

PENCK, Albrecht: Deutscher Volks- und Kulturboden. In: C. C. von Loesch (ed.), Volk unter Völkern. Für den deutschen Schutzbund. Breslau 1925, pp. 62-73.

PIMPIREVA, Ženja: Karakačanite v Bălgarija (ot nomadstvo kăm usednalost). Sofia 1995.

POULTON, Hugh: The Balkans. Minorities and states in conflict. New edition: London 1993.

PREECE, Jennifer Jackson: National Minorities and the European Nation-States System. Oxford 1998.

PROMITZER, Christian: "Gute Serben". Ethnologen und Politiker über die Identität der Serben in der slowenischen Bela krajina. In: U. Brunnbauer (ed.), Umstrittene Identitäten. Ethnizität und Nationalität in Südosteuropa. Frankfurt/M. et. al. 2002, pp. 173-199.

PROMITZER, Christian: Body, race and the border. Notes on a paradigm of German national thinking on the Slovenes. In: O. Luthar/J. Perovšek (eds.), Zbornik Janka Pleterskega. Ljubljana 2003, pp. 597-608.

RAVNIK, Mojca: Bratje, sestre, strniči, zermani. Družina in sorodstvo v vaseh v Slovenski Istri, Ljubljana – Koper 1996

SANDNER, Günther: Austromarxismus und Multikulturalismus. Karl Renner und Otto Bauer zur nationalen Frage im Habsburgerstaat. In: Kakanien revisited, www.kakanien.ac.at/beitr/fallstudie/GSandner1.pdf.

SEEWANN, Gerhard (ed.): Minderheitenfragen in Südosteuropa. Munich 1992.

SEEWANN, Gerhard/DIPPOLD, Péter (eds.): Bibliographisches Handbuch der ethnischen Gruppen Südosteuropas, vol. 2. Munich 1997.

SHULMAN, Stephen: Competing versus complementary identities: Ukrainian-Russian relations and the loyalties of Russians in Ukraine. *Nationalities Papers* 26/4 (1998), pp. 615-632.

SIKIMIĆ, Biljana (ed.): Skrivene manjine na Balkanu/Hidden Minorities in the Balkans. Belgrade 2004.

SMILJANIĆ, Manojlo B.: Etnografsko grupisanje naroda Balkanskoga poluostrva. *Godišnjica Nikole Čupića* XXIV (1905), pp. 102-123.

SMITH, Paul: Introduction. In: P. Smith (ed.), Ethnic groups in international relations. Aldershot 1991, pp. 1-11.

SONNERT, Gerhard: Nationalismus und Krise der Moderne. Theoretische Argumentation und empirische Analyse am Beispiel des neueren schottischen Nationalismus. Frankfurt/M. 1987.

STENNER, Christian (ed.): Slowenische Steiermark. Verdrängte Minderheit in Österreichs Südosten. Vienna – Cologne – Weimar 1997.

SUPPAN, Arnold: Multikulturalität und Multiethnizität in Mittel-, Ost- und Südosteuropa und die Wiener Deklaration vom 30. September 1998. *Österreichische Osthefte* 41/2 (1999), pp. 187-194.

TANNER, Arno (ed.): The forgotten minorities of Eastern Europe. The history and today of selected ethnic groups in five countries. Helsinki 2004.

TELBIZOVA-SACK, Jordanka: Die Pomaken Bulgariens zwischen Identitätsverlust und Selbstbehauptung. In: Lienau C./Steindorff L. (eds.), Ethnizität, Identität und Nationalität in Südosteuropa. Munich 2000, pp. 71-88.

THER, Philipp/SUNDHAUSSEN, Holm (eds.): Regionale Bewegungen und Regionalismen in europäischen Zwischenräumen seit der Mitte des 19. Jahrhunderts. Marburg 2003.

TRUBETA, Sevasti: Die Konstitution von Minderheiten und die Ethnisierung sozialer und politischer Konflikte. Eine Untersuchung am Beispiel der im griechischen Thrakien ansässigen Moslemischen Minderheit. Frankfurt/M. et. al. 1999.

UHEREK, Zdeněk: The Czech minority in Sarajevo and its symbols. In: B. Jezernik (ed.), Urban symbolism and rituals. Proceedings of the international symposium organised by the IUAES Commission on Urban Anthropology. Ljubljana, June 23-25, 1997, Ljubljana 1999, pp. 69-79.

UHEREK, Zdeněk: Bosnian Czechs: A lesson from the theory of ethnicity. *Ethnologia Balkanica* 3 (1999), pp. 141-154.

VERMEULEN, Hans/GOVERS, Cora: From political mobilization to the politics of consciousness, in: H. Vermeulen/C. Govers (eds.), The politics of ethnic Consciousness. New York 1997, pp. 1-30.

VOSS, Christian: Sprachdiskurse in minoritären Ethnisierungs und Nationalisierungsprozessen – Die slawischsprachige Minderheit in Griechenland. In: *Südosteuropa. Zeitschrift für Gegenwartsforschung* 52/1-3 (2003), pp. 116-135.

WATEFF, S[tefan]: Anthropologische Beobachtungen an den Schülern und Soldaten in Bulgarien. *Correspondenz-Blatt der deutschen Gesellschaft für Anthropologie, Ethnologie und Urgeschichte* XXXII/4 (1901), pp. 29-30.

WATEFF, S[tefan]: Anthropologische Beobachtungen der Augen, der Haare und der Haut bei den bulgarischen Schulkindern in der europäischen Türkei. *Correspondenz-Blatt der deutschen Gesellschaft für Anthropologie, Ethnologie und Urgeschichte* XXXIII/3 (1903), pp. 23-24.

WATEFF, S[tefan]: Anthropologische Beobachtungen der Augen, der Haare und der Haut bei den Schulkindern von den Türken, Pomaken, Tataren, Armenier[n], Griechen und Juden in Bulgarien. *Correspondenz-Blatt der deutschen Gesellschaft für Anthropologie, Ethnologie und Urgeschichte* XXXIV/7-8 (1903), pp. 58-60.

WEBER, Eugen: Peasants into Frenchmen: the modernization of rural France, 1870-1914. London 1977.

WILSON, Thomas M./DONNAN, Hastings: Nation, state and identity at international Borders. In: T. M. Wilson/H. Donnan (eds.), Border identities: nation and state at international frontiers. Cambridge 1998, p. 13. pp. 1-30.

ŽUPANIĆ, Niko: Hrvati kod Atine. Prilozi antropologiji i istorijskoj etnologiji. *Starinar – Organ Srpskog Arheološkog Društva* new series VI (1911), pp. 95-152.

Part II.

Hidden Minorities – Case Studies

The Hidden Slovene Minority in Styria

Klaus-Jürgen Hermanik

Introduction

This study focuses on the small Slovene communities in the Austrian Federal Province of Styria in three separate areas at the Austrian-Slovenian border[1]; it gives some insights into the complex identity constructions of people "living at and with the border".[2] Examples will be drawn from Soboth/Sobota area. This ethnic group did not and still does not possess essential material, social and psychological resources[3], which would enable them to develop and realise the idea of being a minority – of being a *we group* in contrast to the *others* – and thus acquiring official minority status.[4] Their case will be discussed within the new research concept of *hidden* minorities, also because of the increasing assimilation pressure in the Austrian-Slovenian borderlands since the second half of the 19th century. We can observe, since that time, a shift from Slovene monolingualism via German-Slovene bilingualism to German monolingualism, which is today dominated by a German and Austrian identity; remnants of the Slovene identity are in most cases deeply hidden.

1. Slovenes in Styria

It is still little known that a German *and* Slovene-speaking bilingual minority is living in the south of Styria that has been more or less assimilated into the German-speaking majority.[5] Among the initiatives for the advancement of mi-

[1] This case study is part of FWF-Project P 15080 "Hidden Minorities between Central Europe and the Balkans", financed by the Austrian Science Fund FWF; it is based on my book: Eine versteckte Minderheit. Mikrostudie über die Zweisprachigkeit in der steirischen Kleinregion Soboth. Weitra 2007. The term "Styrian Slovenes" was introduced some twenty years ago to designate all Slovenes living in that Austrian province. It does not refer to the Slovene population of Lower or Slovene Styria (Štajerska, in Slovene), which became a part of Yugoslavia and later Slovenia.

[2] Cf. Thonmas M. Wilson/Hastings Donnan: Nation, state and identity at international borders. In: T. Wilson/H. Donnan (eds.), Border Identities. Cambridge 1998, pp. 1-30.

[3] Heiner Keupp et al.: Identitätskonstruktionen. Das Patchwork der Identitäten in der Spätmoderne. Reinbeck 1999 (= rowohlts enzyklopädie 55,634), p. 53.

[4] Friedrich Heckmann: Ethnische Minderheiten, Volk und Nation. Soziologie interethnischer Beziehungen. Stuttgart 1992; Albert F. Reiterer: Soziale Identität. Frankfurt/M. et al. 1998 (= Europäische Hochschulschriften XII/321).

[5] Cf. Mirko Križman: Die slowenische Minderheit in der Österreichischen Steiermark (Radkersburger Winkel). In: R. Hinderling/L. Eichinger (eds.), Handbuch der mitteleuropäischen

norities within the Federal Republic of Austria[6], also representatives of the *Article-VII-Cultural Society* (Kulturno društvo člen 7) demand that this group be recognised as a minority according to the Article 7 of the Austrian State Treaty of 1955[7], which guarantees minority rights for various ethnic groups in Austria and in which the federal province of Styria is listed explicitly. The *Article-VII-Cultural Society* represents only a small part of the substantial interests of the Styrian Slovenes[8], who for the most part neither want to be recognised as a minority nor are they "willing to preserve their characteristics".[9] This is certainly one main characteristic of hidden minorities in general.

Three main compact and autochthonous Styrian Slovene settlements can be distinguished at the Austrian-Slovenian border[10]: the Radkersburg triangle/Radgonski trikotnik in the south-east corner of the province, the area south of Leutschach/Lučane and the area of Soboth/Sobota to the southwest. The first two named areas in the 1990s have been treated in two monographs[11], while for the Soboth area at the time only an ethnological reader on the settlement Laaken/Mlake, a momentary glimpse of the dying village during the late eighties of the 20th century, was existing.[12] In 2007 however, I published an extensive

Sprachminderheiten. Tübingen 1996, p. 173; Boris Jesih (ed.): Slovenci v avstrijski zvezni deželi Štajerski. Zbornik referatov na znanstvenem srečanju v Mariboru, 25.-27. maja 1993. Lubljana 1994 (= narodne manjšine 3).

[6] Ursula Hemetek (ed.): Wege zu Minderheiten. Ein Handbuch. Klagenfurt 1998.

[7] Cf. Gerhard Baumgartner: 6 x Österreich. Geschichte und aktuelle Situation der Volksgruppen. (= Edition Minderheiten 1) Klagenfurt 1995, p. 52. In early 2004 the advisory board of the Carinthian Slovenes was enlarged for a person belonging to the "Styrian Slovene minority".

[8] The officials of the *Article-VII-Cultural Society* are not members of the autochthonous ethnic group and their activities can be seen as *ethnic engineering* from outside; nearly all Styrian Slovenes call these officials 'self-appointed representatives' and not 'their representatives'. They reject the programme of the society and avoid contact with the *Article-VII-Cultural Society* as best they can.

[9] Mirjam Polzer-Srienz: Die Repräsentation ethnischer Gruppen im staatlichen Willensbildungsprozeß. Ein Rechtsvergleich Österreich-Slowenien. Graz 1999 (unpublished doctoral dissertation). Mirjam Polzer-Srienz refers to I Art.2 1e) of the basic rights of European ethnic groups – cf. Österreichisches Volksgruppenzentrum (ed.): Internationales und Europäisches Volksgruppenrecht. Klagenfurt 1995 (= Österreichische Volksgruppenhandbücher 8), p. 104.

[10] Cf. Matjaž Klemenčič: Jezikovna struktura prebivalstva na z avtohtonim slovenskim prebivalstvom poseljenem območju Avstrijske Štajerske od srede 19. Stoletja do leta 1971. *Časopis za zgodovino in narodopisje*, 49 (1978), pp. 120-144.

[11] Andrea Haberl-Zemljič: Die Sprache im Dorf lassen. Festhalten und Aufgeben der slowenischen Sprache in Radkersburg und Umgebung. Graz 2004 (= Wissenschaftliche Schriftenreihe des Pavelhauses 6); Mirko Križman: Jezikovna razmerja. Jezik pragmatike in estetike v obmejnih predelih ob Muri. Maribor 1997, pp. 117-222; Christian Promitzer: Verlorene Brüder. Geschichte der zweisprachigen Region Leutschach in der südlichen Steiermark (19.-20. Jahrhundert). Graz 1996 (unpublished doctoral dissertation).

[12] In 1992 the *Institute of Ethnology and Cultural Anthropology* at the *Karl-Franzens-University* Graz published a research study about the village Laaken/Mlake: Johannes Moser/Elisabeth Katschnig-Fasch (eds.): Blatten. Ein Dorf an der Grenze. Graz 1992 (= Kuckuck. Notizen zu Alltagskultur und Volkskunde Sonderband 2); cf. Elisabeth Katschnig-Fasch/Johannes Moser/: Sprache und Identität. In: B. Jesih (ed.), Slovenci v avstrijski zvezni deželi Štajerski. Zbornik referatov na znanstvenem srečanju v Mariboru, 25.-27. maja 1993. Lubljana 1994 (= narodne

historical and ethnological study on this area which is placed within the general context of the hidden minorities in South-East Central Europe and forms the basis for this chapter.[13]

Why did I just select the Soboth area as topic of research? The hidden minority of Soboth/Sobota and the two settlements Laaken/Mlake and Rothwein/Radvanje[14], which are geographically part of the Soboth area, are not even mentioned in the 1996 *Handbook of Central European language minorities*.[15] And finally, it has to be stressed that this hidden minority is to disappear within the next generation(s).

The term Soboth implies two different things. It is firstly is a village (1065 m) with 492 inhabitants in south-western Styria; it is also a mountainous area reaching from the Slovenian border up to the Koralpe mountain.

The whole area had to be "newly defined" after the establishment of the border in 1919/20 due to total marginalisation. Until that time, all traffic routes from Soboth had gravitated to the Drau/Drava Valley, which was granted to Slovenia, i.e. the Kingdom of Serbs, Croats and Slovenes (Yugoslavia). Especially for the Styrian Slovenes a period followed which would irritate their *feeling of local identity*.[16] Tradition and (rare) social contacts in such mountainous rural areas form the individual local identities more vigorously than in (sub-) urban areas; the radius of social contacts played and still plays a main role for the individual *feeling of local identity*. This social contact was cut off by the new international border.[17]

Before I move on to describing this "most unknown" area of a (former) Slovene area of settlement in Styria, I will draw a short outline of the Slovene population of Styria and what made and still makes their Slavic identity a hidden one. Thereafter I will mark the specifics of their ethnic identity to finally

---

manjšine 3), pp. 26-31. Johannes Moser: Zwischenwelt. Auf der Suche nach Anerkennung und Identität in einem Dorf an der Grenze. In: C. Stenner (ed.), Slowenische Steiermark. Verdrängte Minderheit in Österreichs Südosten. Vienna – Cologne – Weimar 1997 (= Zur Kunde Südosteuropas II/23), pp. 235-250.

[13] Klaus Jürgen Hermanik: Eine versteckte Minderheit. Mikrostudie über die Zweisprachigkeit in der steirischen Kleinregion Soboth. Weitra 2007.

[14] In the years 1919/20, the villages of Laaken/Mlake and Rothwein/Radvanje were divided by the border. In the case of Laaken, the border separated the Austrian settlement from the core of the village, which was on Yugoslav territory. On 1 January 1954, the formerly independent community of Laaken/Mlake became part of the community of Soboth; Rothwein/Radvanje became part of the community of Aibl on 1 January 1969.

[15] Cf. Križman: Die slowenische Minderheit.

[16] Cf. Klaus Zeitler: Raumbezogene Identität – ein Entwicklungsfaktor für den ländlichen Raum? Eine soziologische Analyse der Determinanten und Inhalte ländlicher Raumentwicklung. Augsburg 2001 (= Angewandte Sozialgeographie 42), p. III.

[17] In comparison, see, for the Leutschach-region: Christian Promitzer: Ecotype – Mentality – Nationality: Dominant Agricultural System and the Process of National Diffentiation at the German-Slovene Linguistic Border. In: M. Jovanović/K. Kaser/S. Naumović (eds.), Between the Archives and the Field: A Dialogue on Historical Anthropology of the Balkans. Münster 2004 (= Studies on South East Europe 1), pp. 141-157.

deal with the effects of the establishment of the border in 1919/20 and the restoration of the border in 1945.

1.1 Ethnic identity in the borderlands of Austria and Slovenia

1.1.1. Border identity

Border areas, located at the fringes of nation states, usually lack precise boundaries[18] and have always been attractive to scholars interested in both the separating effect of the border and its economical and cultural bridging function. "As barriers they repel, as transitions they attract and disclose dynamic interstitial zones of 'nor more' and 'not yet', yet also of 'as well', crystallization points of multiculturalism, intercultural contact and crossover."[19]

Initially, we are attracted by the separating aspects of borders and their semantic references – national border, language border, periphery of a closed economic area, and many others – but secondly we need also pay attention to trans-border connections, which create a border identity[20] – neighbourhood and relatives, bilingualism, trans-border economic and cultural activities. Identities of people living at and with the border are categorised by scholars of ethnicity like Wilson/Donnan by establishing three main groups:

> i) those who share ethnic ties across the border *as well as* with those residing at their own state's geographical core; ii) those who are *differentiated* by cross-border ethnic bonds from other residents of their state; and iii) those who are members of the national majority in their state, and have no ethnic ties across the state's borders.[21]

Historically, most of the *small ethnic groups* in Central Europe were very much affected by the effects of the establishment of new borders; they were cut off from their relatives, friends and neighbours. During the historical rise of nations and nation states[22] borders represented not only national but also ethnic and cultural boundaries, and for separated small ethnic groups there seemed to be no place within the several 'new' nations. Within this context it is evident that political boundaries create cultural dissimilarities in the very border areas and that borderlines hardly ever can be treated as "natural facts", because

---

[18] Cf. Anthony Cohen: Boundaries of Consciousness, Consciousness of Boundaries. Critical questions for Anthropology. In: H. Vermeulen/C. Govers (eds.), The Anthropology of Ethnicity. Beyond "Ethnic groups and boundaries". Amsterdam 1994, pp. 59-79.

[19] Cf. Tobias Wendl/Michael Rösler: Frontiers and borderlands. The rise of an anthropological research genre. In: T. Wendl/M. Rösler (eds.), Frontiers and borderlands. Anthropological Perspektives. Frankfurt/M. et al. 1999, p. 1.

[20] Cf. Ulrike H. Meinhof (ed.): Living (with) Borders. Identity discourses on East-West borders in Europe. Aldershot 2002, pp. 1-13.

[21] Wilson/Donnan, Nation, state and identity at international borders, p. 14.

[22] Cf. Anthony D. Smith: Nationalism and Modernism. A critical survey of recent theories of nations and nationalism. London – New York 1998, pp. 182-183.

historically most of the modern border areas tended to overlap; therefore the definition of national identities in borderlands was and is a very complex task.[23]

1.1.2 The ethnic identity of Slovenes in Styria

Determining or evaluating *ethnic identity* of Slovenes in Styria is very complex;[24] like an iceberg, hidden *minorities* and hidden *identities* are in most cases only partly visible through their different cultural signs. Some hidden elements include:

a) the differentiation between WE (the bilingual minority) AND THE OTHER (the German-speaking majority) at present has no value for the bilingual people – in most cases they had and still have fears of belonging "only" to a minority instead of being treated as "real" Austrians[25];

b) distinctive signs of a specific ethnic culture[26] are not present in public, being limited to the private sphere of life; and the bilingual inhabitants are careful to say whether they speak Slovene or German[27], because a public identification with Slovene codes is socially stigmatised.[28] In the case of such complex ethnic structures[29] anthropologists use the term of *switching identity* or *code-switching* to describe the oscillation between the Slovene origin and the German assimilation;

---

[23] Cf. Duška Knežević-Hočevar: Studying International Borders in Geography and Anthropology: Paradigmatic and Conceptual Relations. In: M. Orožen-Adamič (ed.), *Geografski Zbornik XXXX*, Ljubljana 2000, p. 91.

[24] Michael G. Müller/Rolf Petri (eds.): Die Nationalisierung von Grenzen. Zur Konstruktion nationaler Identität in sprachlich gemischten Grenzregionen. Marburg/L. 2002, pp VII-XVI; Robert G. Minnich: Wie man an den Rändern moderner Staaten zu Bürgern wird. Einige Überlegungen zur politischen Implikation der Ethnizität, wie sie von mehrsprachigen Dorfbewohnern im "Dreiländereck" erlebt wird. In: Stenner, Slowenische Steiermark, pp. 261-295; F. Heckmann, Ethnische Minderheiten, pp. 30-33.

[25] Especially before Slovenia became independent in 1991 the members of the Slovene-speaking minority expressed their belonging to Austria very strongly, because they did not want to be identified *as Yugoslavs*. cf. Johannes Moser/Ernst Töscher: "Bezeichnet werden wir schon als Jugoslawen". Einige Überlegungen zu Identität in einem grenznahen Ort. In: J. Moser/E. Katschnig-Fasch (eds.), Blatten, p. 31.

[26] Cf. Stuart Hall: Ethnizität: Identität und Differenz. In: J. Engelmann (ed.), Die kleinen Unterschiede. Der Cultural Studies-Reader. Frankfurt M. – New York 1999, pp. 83-122.

[27] Cf. Andrea Haberl-Zemljič: Želja po nevidnosti v Radgonskem kotu. In: V. Klopčič (ed.), Živeti z mejo. Materinščina, dejavnik osebne in skupnoste narodnoste identitete. Ljubljana 2000 (= narodne manjšine 4), pp. 269-282.

[28] Cf. Robert Gary Minnich: Homesteaders and Citizens. Collective identity formation on the Austro-Italian-Slovene frontier. Bergen 1998, p. 259 f.

[29] Cf. Ralf Unkart: Sind die Slowenen in der Steiermark eine eigene Volksgruppe? In: In: C. Stenner (ed.), Slowenische Steiermark. Verdrängte Minderheit in Österreichs Südosten. Vienna – Cologne – Weimar 1997 (= Zur Kunde Südosteuropas II/23), pp. 345-365.

c) a common minority structure of 'Styrian Slovenes' has never played a major role. The dislocated areas – Soboth, Leutschach and Radkersburg are isolated from each other by a distance of up to about 100 km – and political oppression have made it impossible until now. As opposed to Carinthian Slovenes, they never had a public feeling of mutual solidarity.[30] Nevertheless there still exist forms of a collective subconscious[31] of being a small ethnic group, although they never developed into ethnically defined group awareness;

d) links to the Slovene hinterland (relatives, weddings, Austrian landowners with possessions in Slovenia, economics and traffic) became difficult after the establishment of the border in 1919/20. Even before the First World War, the German national influence was stronger than the Slovene one.[32]

e) the influence of the nation state or of supra-regional political institutions and the assimilation-pressure are very strong in border areas[33]: After the First World War the *Deutscher Schulverein Südmark* for example (in collaboration with the *Landesschulrat* of the Government of Styria) declared the *Germanisation* of the Austrian-Slovene border areas in Styria its main target[34];

f) bilinguality (German-Slovene) is the most significant cultural sign for distinguishing the hidden minority from the majority. But at present the Slovene language is consciously held distant from the public, a fact, which demands a high amount of sensibility during field work.

g) there is a generational rift between the bilingual elderly, born at the beginning of the 20th century or at least before the Second World War,[35] and their German-speaking grandchildren, who at present are often interested in their cultural past and who sometimes try to learn the Slovene language, too.

---

[30] "Na žalost med štajerskimi Slovenci na avstrijskem ozemlju zgodovina ni mogla izoblikovati tako močnega subjektiva dejavnika […]" ("In the past unfortunately could never grow up a strong subjective determinant within the group of Styrian Slovenes in Austria […]") – Janko Malle: Položaj Slovencev na Avstrijskem Štajerskem. *Znamenje* 1 (1987), p. 58.

[31] Mario Erdheim: Die gesellschaftliche Produktion von Unbewusstheit. Eine Einführung in den ethnopsychoanalytischen Prozeß. Frankfurt/M. 1988 (= suhrkamp taschenbuch wissenschaft 465).

[32] Thus the Slovene intellectual Jožef Muršec in 1847 warned "[…] that in about 10-20 years the Slovene Soboth will be totally German," quoted after Tone Zorn: Slovenci na Avstrijskem Štajerskem. *Časopis za Zgodovino in Narodopisje* 15/1-2 (1979), p. 434; more about that in Christian Promitzer: Body, race and the border: Notes on a paradigm of German national thinking on the Slovenes. In: Luthar/Perovšek (eds.), Zbornik Janka Pleterska. Ljubljana 2003, pp. 597-608.

[33] Cf. Wilson/Donnan, Nation, state and identity at international borders, p. 7 f.

[34] see also section 2.3 of this article.

[35] Cf. Malle, Položaj Slovencev, p. 61.

1.2. Effects of the establishment of the border – the years 1919/20 and 1945

At the end of the First World War, the German-Austrian "Abwehrkampf" or as it was known in Slovenia, "the Fight for the Northern Border" in 1919/20 was particularly significant for the new borderlands.[36] Radkersburg/Radgona and Soboth were occupied by Yugoslav troops until 1920, which proved to be a deep cut into social and economic life.[37] Families, relatives and friends were separated from each other and they became conscious that they did not belong to a multiethnic, polyglot state any longer[38] but to an Austria defined as German – "Deutschösterreich".

A second border struggle would take place at the end of the Second World War. Since autumn 1944 in the south-western part of Styria – above all in Soboth area – heavy fighting between Slovene partisans of the "Lackov odred" (unit "Lacko"), to whom a small group of Austrian partisans was attached, with military formations of the Third Reich took place.[39] The interwar border was restored after the Second World War, but in the peace negotiations Yugoslavia made claims to Soboth area, which were dismissed by the Allies. In the same time there were rallies in Soboth underlining the wish of the people to remain in Austria. The Yugoslav claims, however, were converted into a minority paragraph (mentioning Styria explicitly) in the Austrian State Treaty of 1955.

The border to Yugoslavia was closed entirely until 1955; the Slovene-speaking population of Styria were robbed of their contacts in their former hinterland and to relatives, friends and neighbours for many years.

But even after the Austrian State Treaty of 1955, the bilingual minority did not receive political recognition as defined in Article 7. In general, the period until the 1960s was characterised by the pressure to assimilate and by emigration from the borderlands. The overt use of the Slovene language would have been taken as proof that the speakers wanted to be Yugoslavs rather than Austrians,

---

[36] On 6 October 1918 the "Narodno vijeće Slovenaca, Hrvata I Srba" (National council of Slovenia, Croatia and Serbia) was constituted in Zagreb demanding that the whole "ethnographic territory" be included in the new SHS-state. On 1 November 1918 Major Rudolf Maister from Maribor took over military command of Slovene troops in northern Slovenia; on 27 November he – in the meantime a General – and the French Colonel Passy signed a contract allowing Maister the occupation of bilingual areas at the Slovenian-Austrian border.

[37] Cf. Jurij Fikfak: Geschichten über die Grenze. In: Moser/Katschnig-Fasch, Blatten, pp. 72-73.

[38] Cf. Hans Vermeulen/Cora Govers: From Political Mobilization to the Politics of Consciousness. In: Vermeulen/Govers, Ethnic Consciousness, pp. 1-30.

[39] Wehrmacht, Waffen-SS, Gestapo and Gendarmerie-corps (HIGA etc.) were active in the Soboth region fighting Partisans. cf. Christian Fleck: Koralmpartisanen: Über abweichende Karrieren politisch motivierter Widerstandskämpfer. Vienna – Cologne 1986 (= Studien zur historischen Sozialwissenschaft 4); Milan Ževart: Lackov odred. Maribor 1988. Clashes continued for some time after the official end of the war on 8 May 1945, as witnessed by graves and monuments in this region.

which in common thinking included being a communist, a Titoist or a Partisan. The fighting at the end of the Second World War for a long time was present in the memory of the people and the terms "Yugoslav", "Partisan" or "Communist" denoted enemies; any form of antifascist liberation or political resistance against the Nazis was denied completely, the exact opposite of the positions being taken on the other side of the border (in Yugoslavia). The members of the bilingual minority were always compelled to demonstrate that they were "normal" Austrians, and they accepted the conditions of assimilation, hiding their second ethnic identity, their Slavic origin, as best they could.[40]

2. Examples from the Soboth area from the last two centuries
2.1. Economy

Traditionally, the Soboth area was cultivated by forest-farmers and lumber workers and was very poor until the 19th century, when the glass industry changed the economical structure. Many workers were needed in the local forests, for charcoal-production and for transport. By the 1890s, many farmers had sold their forest property to the *Hüttenberger Eisenwerksgesellschaft* and after the closing of the glassworks at the beginning of the 20th century, emigration started, which is continuing to date.

The establishment of the border in 1919/20 dealt another blow to the regional economy, which became totally marginalised: On the one hand, the present-day road from the south-western part of Austrian Styria up to Soboth was only built in the 1930s, on the other hand, the economically important traffic route to the Drau Valley in the south became nearly impassable due to the new border between Austria and the SHS state, which imposed strong customs regulations. Lumber workers had a wood surplus but were not able to sell it at a fair price on the market due to the unfavourable transportation situation. Therefore, smuggling became an important economic factor[41] – for Slovene-speaking persons it was also an important link to their former neighbours beyond the border.

The survival of the Slovene language depended on the stock of people living in the area; the subsistence from agriculture together with employment possibilities in the lumbering industries at least delayed the emigration of the

[40] Cf. in general Heckmann, Ethnische Minderheiten, pp. 162-164.

[41] Cf. Georg Oswald/Josef Lipp: Strategien zur Behauptung dörflichen Bewußtseins. In: Moser/Katschnig-Fasch, Blatten, pp. 53-54; Irene Gassenbauer: Steirische Grenzlandbezirke: Das Schicksal einer Region als "Stiefkind" der Wirtschaft; eine Analyse der Sozial- und Wirtschaftsstruktur der steirischen Grenzlandbezirke Deutschlandsberg, Leibnitz und Radkersburg. Graz 1992 (unpublished Master's thesis).

autochthonous Slovene population.[42] Assimilation put further pressure on the Slovene language. The association *Deutscher Schulverein Südmark* – a so-called "Schutzverein", defending the German population against Slavic cultural infiltration – built a model farm in Rothwein/Radvanje in 1929, which became an effective instrument of Germanisation.[43] The main goal of such *development aid* was the ideological affiliation of the population to the association *Südmark* and its German national interests, that is to say, to change Slovene and/or bilingual farmers into German "Grenzbauern" (frontier farmers).[44]

After the Second World War, when economic growth in Styria was rapid, the borderlands remained marginalised; conditions which again and again forced people to emigrate. Absolute numbers among the bilingual minority decreased rapidly in the 1950s and 1960s; the community of Rothwein/Radvanje lost about 30 percent of its inhabitants in this decade.[45] Emigration has not stopped to date and many of the houses in the Soboth area are owned by emigrants, who visit their property on holidays if they have not been sold to weekend-tourists.

2.2. Church

The parish of Soboth, part of the Seckau diocese since 1788, was transferred to the predominantly Slovene diocese Maribor in 1859; whole passages of the church-chronicle of Soboth from 1859 until 1920 are therefore written in the Slovene language. But even then, the Slovene influence on the Roman Catholic Church was not very strong in the Soboth community; masses were still held in Latin, sermons and hymns were in the German language.[46]

Bilingual priests and chaplains held their services (weddings, funerals, baptisms etc.) in German or in Slovene, depending on the dominant language of the respective groups of *parishioners*. After the middle of the 19th century, when German nationalism increased significantly, the Catholic Church remained an important supporter of bilingualism.[47] Even in such isolated areas

---

[42] Anton Klug: Weststeirisches Bauerntum im Wandel der sozialen und wirtschaftlichen Verhältnisse. Graz 1995 (unpublished Master's thesis).

[43] Cf. Südweststeirisches Grenzland. Das Wirken des Deutschen Schulvereins Südmark im Raume von Soboth bis Kleinradl. Graz 1937, p. 61; Eduard G. Staudinger: Die Südmark. Aspekte der Programmatik und Struktur eines deutschen Schutzvereines in der Steiermark bis 1914. In: H. Rumpler/A. Suppan (eds.), Geschichte der Deutschen im Bereich des heutigen Slowenien. 1848-1941. Munich – Vienna 1988, pp.130-154; Sigrid Kiyem: Der deutsche Schulverein "Südmark" 1818-1938. Vienna 1995 (unpublished Master's thesis).

[44] Cf. Promitzer, Verlorene Brüder, p. 263.

[45] In 1969 the elementary-school of Laaken/Mlake had to be closed because of lack of pupils.

[46] cf. Ante Beg: Slovensko-nemška meja na Štajerskem. Kulturno zgodovinski in narodopisni doneski. Ljubljana 1905, pp.19-29.

[47] Cf. Promitzer, Verlorene Brüder, pp.127-128.

like in that one of the Soboth, however, the use of German language, especially in the village of Soboth and the immediate environs increased. The bilingual priest Jozef Kostanjevec asked people from Untersoboth in the year 1905, for example, why they did not use their Slovene mother tongue any more. They answered him in a corrupted Slovene: "Ker dajtsch je bolj nobel šprah" ("because German is the more noble language").[48]

After the First World War the parish of Soboth came again under the jurisdiction of the Seckau diocese, although it still formally belonged to the Maribor diocese.[49] As a consequence, no Slovene priests were installed any longer; the possibility of bilingual services disappeared.

Before the establishment of the border in 1919/20, the community of Laaken/Mlake belonged to the parish of Pernice/Pernitzen and the community of Rothwein/Radvanje to the parish of Sv. Jernej/St. Bartlmä, which were both incorporated into the Kingdom of the Serbs, Croats and Slovenes.

For many decades, bilingual inhabitants from the Austrian part of Laaken/Mlake went to their "lost" parish Sv. Simon at Pernice/Pernitzen across the border and people from Rothwein/Radvanje crossed the border to the church of Sv. Jernej/St. Bartlmä.[50] In these two parishes sermons and hymns were in the Slovene language; thus we can say that the *traditional* church habits preliminarily contributed to the survival of the local Slovene language. During the closing of the border from 1945 to 1955 this attendance at the Slovene churches of Sv. Jernej and Sv. Simon by Styrian Slovenes became impossible and were not resumed afterwards.[51]

2.3. School

Elementary schools were the most important places of language and cultural assimilation. From the 19th century until the interwar period the children of farmers or lumber workers, who spoke Slovene at home, had their first contact with the German language at school.

The system of classes was "utraquistic", bilingual classes could be held in both languages, but in practice, bilingual classes were only held until the pupils un-

---

See further Klaus-J. Hermanik: Die Arnfelser Pfarrchronik des Matthias Ljubša. Auf den Spuren der Zweisprachigkeit in der pfarrlichen Seelsorge des 19. Jahrhunderts. *Blätter für Heimatkunde* 74/1-2 (2000), Graz, pp. 12-26.

[48] Parish chronicle Soboth, p. 45.

[49] Cf. Amon /Liebmann (eds.): Kirchengeschichte der Steiermark. Graz 1993, p. 422.

[50] Cf. Archive of the Diocese Graz-Seckau (Graz), "Dekanatliche Visitationen, Dekanat Schwanberg", Kirchenvisitationen 1926-1939.

[51] Since that time – until the present – a decline in rates of strong belief and of attendance at mass can be observed, even in rural areas.

derstood as much German as needed to follow instruction. This method of instruction was usual in many of the bilingual areas – where German was one of the two languages – of the Cisleithanian part of the Habsburg monarchy and it guaranteed the unchallenged status of the German language.[52]

After the First World War the *Deutscher Schulverein Südmark* made the whole Soboth area one of their main targets. In Laaken/Mlake and Rothwein/Radvanje it founded new schools in farm houses since most of the old schools now lay beyond the border. Later the society erected new school buildings in Laaken/Mlake and Rothwein/Radvanje and gave them names in the German-national tradition. In 1926 the *Deutscher Schulverein Südmark* finished the extension of the "Grenzlandschule" in the village of Soboth and named it after Gustav Gross, who was the chairman of the society at that time. In 1930 they opened the new school at Rothwein/Radvanje named after Hans Klöpfer, who was a local author of poems, some of which were in the spirit of Germanisation. In 1931 they finally opened the school in Laaken/Mlake named after Franz Xaver Mitterer, who was one of the founders of the society.[53]

But not only the school buildings belonged to the *Südmark Society*, they also had great influence on the hiring of teachers, who therefore were consequent followers of the ideas of the society and tried to contribute to overcoming bilingualism.[54] In the 1930s the Styrian ethnologist Victor Geramb observed that half of the pupils in Rothwein/Radvanjewere of Slovene origin, and saw the borderland-schools as a "noble weapon" [55] in the fight against the influence of the Slovene language.

Most of the children were very poor and each school in the border area was "adopted" by German-national societies, which paid the expenses for a daily school lunch. Before Christmas, during the so-called *Weihnachtsaktion,* each pupil received a present such as worn clothes or old shoes donated by students of the German-nationalist fraternity *Thalia* from Graz. Local interviewees, including those that were bilingual, saw these gifts positively. On the one hand, they did not want to ask, if it was questionable or not, to receive presents from a German-national society and on the other hand, the *Weihnachtsaktion* was welcomed by the poor children and was sometimes more important than Christmas itself.[56]

---

[52] Promitzer, Verlorene Brüder, p. 142; Klaus-Jürgen Hermanik/Christian Promitzer (eds.): Grenzenlos zweisprachig. Die Erinnerungen des Keuschlersohnes Anton Šantel (1845-1920) an seine Kindheit in Leutschach und Jugend in Marburg. Graz 2002, pp. 50-71.

[53] Cf. Julij Felaher: Slovenci v Avstriji. *Gospodarski Koledar za leto 1958* (1958), p. 34.

[54] Cf. Herbert Nikitsch: "Lebendiges Ganzkorn". Anni Gamerith und die Suche nach dem "Urwissen bäuerlicher Überlieferung". *Österreischische Zeitschrift für Volkskunde* LIV/103 (2000), p. 296. (Anni Gamerith was a teacher in Laaken from 1928-1935.)

[55] Cf. Viktor Geramb: An der Grenze. *Alpenländische Monatshefte* 4/1 (1927-28), p. 45.

[56] On *Weihnachtsaktionen* in the school of Rothwein/Radvnaje – cf. Schulchronik St. Lorenzen, p. 289.

The strong German-national influence in the schools was continued during the National Socialist period (1938-1945).

Official attitudes with respect to the Slovene origin of the pupils in the Soboth area did not change after the Second World War. It lasted up to the 1990s until a small group of pupils signed up for Slovene language courses in the nearby small market town of Eibiswald/Ivnik in their leisure time; offering the possibility of learning Slovene language in regular elementary school lessons is still not a priority for the supervisory school authority in Styria.

2.4. The present situation

The issue of bilingual minorities in Styria is a subject of repression still today. Nearly everybody who living in the borderland speaks of a warm and friendly atmosphere with respect to their neighbours, and some of them regret that they could not speak Slovene as well as the Slovenes speak German. This is meant in respect to speaking Slovene in Slovenia or with Slovenes visiting Austria, but speaking Slovene with each other is to be strictly avoided by Austrian citizens.

In 1997 a commission from the Government of Styria, which investigated the case of a "Slovene minority" in Styria visited the communities Radkersburg-Umgebung, Glanz/Schloßberg and Soboth to collect information with respect to a possible recognition of such a minority.[57]

Before this planned visit the local mayor's office of Soboth published a resolution on 4 April 1997, which was supported by 200 signatures of the local community. This resolution begins with the sentence that *never ever (sic!) did live Slovene* speaking persons on the territory of the village and that therefore, such a minority could not exist.[58] The bilingual persons living in Laaken and Untersoboth, which are today parts of the municipality of Soboth, did not want to be officially mentioned as a minority either and did not protests against the resolution. Strong reactions in the Austrian press regarding this "minority-problem" in a small village, which was nearly unknown before, compelled the mayor of Soboth to defend the resolution against journalists, and he spoke of the fear that Soboth could be incorporated into Slovenia after EU-expansion, and declared that this was the reason why the people living there had to react against the

[57] Cf. P.K.: Steirische Slowenen: Weitere Hearings in den Grenzgemeinden. *Neue Zeit* 18.04.1997, p.14.

[58] Resolution of the *Gemeinderat* of the community of Soboth. (1997) (Pavelhaus – Laafelder Archiv für Steiermark/Štajerska – LASŠ) (Archive of Laafeld für Styria/ Štajerska).

argument that in the Soboth-area there would live a Slovene-speaking minority.[59]

The commission from the Styrian government itself, then, came to no significant answer. The head of this commission was a member of the conservative Austrian People's Party (ÖVP). The conservatives had always denied the existence of a bilingual minority in Styria – and did so again on 24 June 1997 in the community of Soboth[60], the populist Austrian Freedom Party (FPÖ) joined in this opinion. The Austrian Social-democratic Party (SPÖ) was neutral, while the Greens (Grüne) and the Liberal Party (LIF) made an effort in favour of minority rights, which had been guaranteed in the Austrian State Treaty of 1955.

Conclusion

The preceding has illustrated why we have to speak of a hidden minority in this situation. The triad of 1) assimilation and Germanisation, 2) political oppression and renunciation and 3) economic marginalisation lead to "hiding". On the one hand, it forced the bilingual community in Styria in general, and in the Soboth area in particular, to hide from public view; on the other hand, they were "hidden".

The hidden part of the identity construction of each bilingual individual remains essential and justifies the use of the term hidden identity to describe the present ethnic situation in the Soboth area.

This also means that this hidden minority is about to disappear within the next generation(s). Neither political agreement between the Government of Styria and the Slovene Government nor the identity managers from of the *Article-VII-Cultural Society* (Kulturno društvo član 7) will likely change the situation significantly. There does not exist any solidarity of collective belonging among the bilingual community, which is otherwise still one of the main characters of *the consciousness of being an ethnic or national minority.*

---

[59] *Der Standard* 18.4. 1997, p. 15. These *fears* of a Slovene and/or a Yugoslav take-over had a long tradition since the establishment of the border in 1919/20 and were sometimes articulated in political argumentation.

[60] The political event itself passed quietly. The inhabitants of Soboth delivered presents of wine to the politicians from the Styrian Government and the debates never engaged the essential point of the local minority discussion of the Soboth area.

Appendix: Linguistic relations in Soboth area reflected in censuses

The census from 1880 was the first to give information on linguistic relations on a local level. The censuses from 1880, 1890, 1900 and 1910 illustrate two things: 1) The use of Slovene as colloquial language in the Soboth area at the end of the 19th and at the beginning of the 20th century, contradicting recent statements of the absence of Slovene speaking people throughout history. 2) Processes of assimilation and in particular, a shift back and forth in the villages of Laaken and Rothwein.

Table 1: Censuses from 1880 to 1910 of the municipality of Soboth[61]:

Year	*Inhabitants*	*German as colloquial language*	*Slovene as colloquial language*	*relation % rounded*
1880	886	701	184	79 : 21
1890	780	722	57	93 : 07
1900	786	774	12	98 : 02
1910	708	670	38	95 : 05

Table 2: Census of the village of Laaken/Mlake[62]:

Year	*Inhabitants*	*German as colloquial language*	*Slovene as colloquial language*	*relation % rounded*
1880	280	43	234	16 : 84
1890	300	48	250	16 : 84
1900	284	86	194	31 : 69
1910	218	89	129	41 : 59

61 Cf. Klemenčič, Jezikovna struktura prebivalstva, p. 147.
62 Cf. ibidem.

Table 3: Census of the village of Rothwein[63]:

Year	*Inhabitants*	*German as colloquial language*	*Slovene as colloquial language*	*Relation % rounded*
1880	179	98	81	55 : 45
1890	185	0	185	0 : 100
1900	180	86	94	48 : 52
1910	179	56	123	31 : 69

In the interwar period the first census was held in the year 1923 for which most of the Styrian data for colloquial language use has been lost. In the census of 1934, 74 persons using Slovene as colloquial language were registered in the Soboth area (1910: 290).[64]

Even after the Second World War and the founding of the "Second Austrian Republic", the census practice of *splitting & splaying* was maintained. In 1951, those people of the autochthonous population using Slovene as colloquial language – who were not willing to put their cross in the category colloquial language "German" from the start – put it into the category "Sonstige, unbekannt" (Others, not known):

Table 4: Census of the communities Soboth, Laaken and Rothwein from the year 1951 – category "Sonstige, unbekannt" ("other, unknown") with regard to colloquial language for the:[65]

Community	*Inhabitants*	*"Sonstige, unbekannt"*
Soboth	776	6
Laaken	156	2
Rothwein	183	15

[63] Cf. ibidem.

[64] Cf. Matjaž Klemenčič: Im Lichte der sprachlichen Statistik: Slowenisch- und Deutschsprachige in der Süd- und Untersteiermark 1830-1991. In: Stenner, Slowenische Steiermark, p. 96.

[65] Österreichisches statistisches Zentralamt (ed.): Ergebnisse der Volkszählung vom 1. Juni 1951 nach Gemeinden. Vienna 1952, Steiermark, pp. 6-7.

Table 5: Census regarding "Slovene colloquial language" for the communities Aibl and Soboth from the years 1981 and 1991[66]*:*

Community	*Year*	*Inhabitants*	*Austrian citizens*
Aibl	1981	2	2
Soboth	1981	0	0
Aibl	1991	4	3
Soboth	1991	0	0
Aibl	2001	2	1
Soboth	2001	2	1

These examples from Soboth area illustrate the state of *being hidden* by the Styrian Government. They show the vanishing of Slovene colloquial language use and of course the *hiding* of the Slovene speaking people, who did not declare themselves during a census.

Bibliography:

AMON, K./LIEBMANN, M. (eds.): Kirchengeschichte der Steiermark. Graz 1993.

BAUMGARTNER, Gerhard: 6 x Österreich. Geschichte und aktuelle Situation der Volksgruppen. Klagenfurt 1995 (= Edition Minderheiten 1).

BEG, Ante: Slovensko-nemška meja na Štajerskem. Kulturno zgodovinski in narodopisni doneski. Ljubljana 1905.

COHEN, Anthony: Boundaries of Consciousness, Consciousness of Boundaries. Critical questions for Anthropology. In: H. Vermeulen/C. Govers (eds.), The Anthropology of Ethnicity. Beyond 'Ethnic groups and boundaries'. Amsterdam 1994, pp. 59-79.

ERDHEIM, Mario: Die gesellschaftliche Produktion von Unbewusstheit. Eine Einführung in den ethnopsychoanalytischen Prozeß. Frankfurt/M. 1988 (= suhrkamp taschenbuch wissenschaft 465).

FELAHER, Jurij: Slovenci v Avstriji. *Gospodarski Koledar za leto 1958* (1958), pp. 29-40.

FLECK, Christian: Koralmpartisanen: Über abweichende Karrieren politisch motivierter Widerstandskämpfer. Vienna – Cologne 1986 (= Studien zur historischen Sozialwissenschaft 4).

FIKFAK, Jurij: Geschichten über die Grenze. In: J. Moser/E. Katschnig-Fasch (eds.), Blatten. Ein Dorf an der Grenze. Graz 1992 (= Kuckuck. Notizen zu Alltagskultur und Volkskunde. Sonderband 2), pp. 62-79.

[66] Rothwein nowadays is part of the community of Aibl, and Laaken is part of the community of Soboth – cf. footnote 13. Census data are taken from Statistik Austria, database ISIS.

GASSENBAUER, Irene: Steirische Grenzlandbezirke. Das Schicksal einer Region als "Stiefkind" der Wirtschaft; eine Analyse der Sozial- und Wirtschaftsstruktur der steirischen Grenzlandbezirke Deutschlandsberg, Leibnitz und Radkersburg. Graz 1992 (unpublished Master's thesis).

GERAMB, Viktor: An der Grenze. *Alpenländische Monatshefte* 4/1 (1927-28), pp. 45-46.

HABERL-ZEMLJIČ, Andrea: Die Sprache im Dorf lassen. Festhalten und Aufgeben der slowenischen Sprache in Radkersburg und Umgebung. Graz 2004 (= Wissenschaftliche Schriftenreihe des Pavelhauses 6).

HABERL-ZEMLJIČ, Andrea: Želja po nevidnosti v Radgonskem kotu. In: V. Klopčič (ed.), Živeti z mejo. Materinščina, dejavnik osebne in skupnoste narodnoste identitete. Ljubljana 2000 (= narodne manjšine 4), pp. 269-282.

HALL, Stuart: Ethnizität: Identität und Differenz. In: J. Engelmann (ed.), Die kleinen Unterschiede. Der Cultural Studies-Reader. Frankfurt/M. – New York 1999, pp. 83-122.

HECKMANN, Friedrich: Ethnische Minderheiten, Volk und Nation. Soziologie interethnischer Beziehungen. Stuttgart 1992.

HEMETEK, Ursula (ed.): Wege zu Minderheiten. Ein Handbuch. Klagenfurt 1998.

HERMANIK, Klaus-Jürgen: Die Arnfelser Pfarrchronik des Matthias Ljubša. Auf den Spuren der Zweisprachigkeit in der pfarrlichen Seelsorge des 19. Jahrhunderts. *Blätter für Heimatkunde* 74/1-2. Graz 2000, pp. 12-26.

HERMANIK, Klaus Jürgen: Eine versteckte Minderheit. Mikrostudie über die Zweisprachigkeit in der steirischen Kleinregion Soboth. Weitra 2007.

HERMANIK, Klaus-Jürgen/PROMITZER, Christian (eds.): Grenzenlos zweisprachig. Die Erinnerungen des Keuschlersohnes Anton Šantel (1845-1920) an seine Kindheit in Leutschach und Jugend in Marburg. Graz 2002.

JESIH, Boris (eds.): Slovenci v avstrijski zvezni deželi Štajerski. Zbornik referatov na znanstvenem srečanju v Mariboru, 25.-27. maja 1993. Lubljana 1994 (= narodne manjšine 3).

KEUPP, Heiner et al.: Identitätskonstruktionen. Das Patchwork der Identitäten in der Spätmoderne. Reinbeck 1999 (= rowohlts enzyklopädie 55 634).

KIYEM, Sigrid: Der deutsche Schulverein "Südmark" 1818-1938. Vienna 1995 (unpublished Master's thesis).

KLEMENČIČ, Matjaž: Jezikovna struktura prebivalstva na z avtohtonim slovenskim prebivalstvom poseljenem območju avstrijske Štajerske od srede 19. Stoletja do leta 1971. *Časopis za zgodovino in narodopisje* 49 (1978), pp. 120-144.

KLEMENČIČ, Matjaž: Im Lichte der sprachlichen Statistik: Slowenisch- und Deutschsprachige in der Süd- und Untersteiermark 1830-1991. In: C. Stenner (ed.), Slowenische Steiermark. Verdrängte Minderheit in Österreichs Südosten. Vienna – Cologne – Weimar 1997 (= Zur Kunde Südosteuropas II/23), pp. 69-106.

KLUG, Anton: Weststeirisches Bauerntum im Wandel der sozialen und wirtschaftlichen Verhältnisse. Graz 1995 (unpublished Master's thesis).

KNEŽEVIĆ-HOČEVAR, Duška: Studying International Borders in Geography and Anthropology: Paradigmatic and Conceptual Relations. In: M. Orožen-Adamič (ed.), Geografski Zbornik XXXX, Ljubljana 2000, pp. 81-93.

KRIŽMAN, Mirko: Die slowenische Minderheit in der Österreichischen Steiermark (Radkersburger Winkel). In: R. Hinderling/L. Eichinger (eds.), Handbuch der mitteleuropäischen Sprachminderheiten Handbuch der mitteleuropäischen Sprachminderheiten. Tübingen 1996, pp. 169-198.

KRIŽMAN, Mirko: Jezikovna razmerja. Jezik pragmatike in estetike v obmejnih predelih ob Muri. Maribor 1997, pp. 117-222.

MALLE, Janko: Položaj Slovencev na Avstrijskem Štajerskem. *Znamenje* 1 (1987), pp. 53-64.

MEINHOF, Ulrike H. (ed.): Living (with) Borders. Identity discourses on East-West borders in Europe. Aldershot 2002.

MINNICH, Robert G.: Homesteaders and Citizens. Collective identity formation on the Austro-Italian-Slovene frontier. Bergen 1998.

MINNICH, Robert G.: Wie man an den Rändern moderner Staaten zu Bürgern wird. Einige Überlegungen zur politischen Implikation der Ethnizität, wie sie von mehrsprachigen Dorfbewohnern im "Dreiländereck" erlebt wird. In: C. Stenner (ed.), Slowenische Steiermark. Verdrängte Minderheit in Österreichs Südosten. Vienna – Cologne – Weimar 1997 (= Zur Kunde Südosteuropas II/23), pp. 261-295.

MOSER, Johannes: Zwischenwelt. Auf der Suche nach Anerkennung und Identität in einem Dorf an der Grenze. In: C. Stenner (ed.), Slowenische Steiermark. Verdrängte Minderheit in Österreichs Südosten. Vienna – Cologne – Weimar 1997 (= Zur Kunde Südosteuropas II/23), pp. 235-250.

MOSER, Johannes/KATSCHNIG-FASCH, Elisabeth (eds.): Blatten. Ein Dorf an der Grenze. Graz 1992 (= Kuckuck. Notizen zu Alltagskultur und Volkskunde. Sonderband 2).

MOSER, Johannes/KATSCHNIG-FASCH, Elisabeth: Sprache und Identität. In: B. Jesih (ed.), Slovenci v avstrijski zvezni deželi Štajerski. Zbornik referatov na znanstvenem srečanju v Mariboru, 25.-27. maja 1993. Lubljana 1994 (= narodne manjšine 3), pp. 26-31.

MOSER, Johannes/TÖSCHER, Ernst: "Bezeichnet werden wir schon als Jugoslawen". Einige Überlegungen zu Identität in einem grenznahen Ort. In: J. Moser/E. Katschnig-Fasch (eds.), Blatten. Ein Dorf an der Grenze. Graz 1992 (= Kuckuck. Notizen zu Alltagskultur und Volkskunde. Sonderband 2), pp. 24-45.

MÜLLER, Michael G./PETRI Rolf (eds.): Die Nationalisierung von Grenzen. Zur Konstruktion nationaler Identität in sprachlich gemischten Grenzregionen. Marburg/L. 2002.

NIKITSCH, Herbert: "Lebendiges Ganzkorn". Anni Gamerith und die Suche nach dem "Urwissen bäuerlicher Überlieferung". *Österreischische Zeitschrift für Volkskunde* LIV/103 (2000), pp. 283-307.

ÖSTERREICHISCHES VOLKSGRUPPENZENTRUM, (ed.): Internationales und Europäisches Volksgruppenrecht. Klagenfurt 1995 (= Österreichische Volksgruppenhandbücher 8).

OSWALD, Georg/LIPP, Josef: Strategien zur Behauptung dörflichen Bewußtseins. In: J. Moser/E. Katschnig-Fasch (eds.), Blatten. Ein Dorf an der Grenze. Graz 1992 (= Kuckuck. Notizen zu Alltagskultur und Volkskunde. Sonderband 2), pp. 46-61.

POLZER-SRIENZ, Mirjam: Die Repräsentation ethnischer Gruppen im staatlichen Willensbildungsprozeß. Ein Rechtsvergleich Österreich-Slowenien. Graz 1999 (unpublished doctoral dissertation).

PROMITZER, Christian: Body, race and the border: Notes on a paradigm of German national thinking about the Slovenes. In: O. Luthar/J. Perovšek (eds.), Zbornik Janka Pleterska. Ljubljana 2003, pp. 597-608.

PROMITZER, Christian: Ecotype – Mentality Nationality: Dominant Agricultural System and the Process of National Differentiation at the German-Slovene Linguistic Border. In: M. Jovanović/K. Kaser/S. Naumović (eds.), Between the Archives and the Field: A Dialogue on Historical Anthropology of the Balkans. Münster 2004 (= Studies on South East Europe 1), pp. 141-157.

PROMITZER, Christian: Verlorene Brüder. Geschichte der zweisprachigen Region Leutschach in der südlichen Steiermark (19.-20.Jahrhundert). Graz 1996 (unpublished doctoral dissertation).

REITERER, Albert F.: Soziale Identität. Frankfurt/M et al. 1998 (= Europäische Hochschulschriften 321).

SMITH, Anthony D.: Nationalism and Modernism. A critical survey of recent theories of nations and nationalism. London – New York 1998.

STAUDINGER, Eduard G.: Die Südmark. Aspekte der Programmatik und Struktur eines deutschen Schutzvereines in der Steiermark bis 1914. In: H. Rumpler/A. Suppan (eds.), Geschichte der Deutschen im Bereich des heutigen Slowenien. 1848-1941. Munich/Vienna 1988, pp.130-154.

SÜDWESTSTEIRISCHES GRENZLAND. Das Wirken des Deutschen Schulvereins Südmark im Raume von Soboth bis Kleinradl. Graz 1937.

UNKART, Ralf: Sind die Slowenen in der Steiermark eine eigene Volksgruppe? In: C. Stenner (ed.), Slowenische Steiermark. Verdrängte Minderheit in Österreichs Südosten. Vienna – Cologne – Weimar 1997 (= Zur Kunde Südosteuropas II/23), pp. 345-365.

VERMEULEN, Hans/GOVERS, Cora: From Political Mobilization to the Politics of Consciousness. In: H. Vermeulen/ C. Govers (eds.), The Politics of Ethnic Consciousness. New York 1997, pp. 1-30.

WENDL, Tobias/RÖSLER, Michael: Frontiers and borderlands. The rise of an anthropological research genre. In: T. Wendl/M. Rösler (eds): Frontiers and borderlands. Anthropological Perspektives. Frankfurt/M. et al. 1999.

WILSON, Thomas M./DONNAN, Hastings: Nation, state and identity at international borders. In: T. M. Wilson/H. Donnan (eds.), Border Identities. Cambridge 1998, pp. 1-30.

ZEITLER, Klaus: Raumbezogene Identität – ein Entwicklungsfaktor für den ländlichen Raum? Eine soziologische Analyse der Determinanten und Inhalte ländlicher Raumentwicklung. Augsburg 2001 (= Angewandte Sozialgeographie 42).

ZORN, Tone: Slovenci na Avstrijskem Štajerskem. *Časopis za Zgodovino in Narodopisje* 15/1-2 (1979), pp. 430-447.

ŽEVART, Milan: Lackov odred. Maribor 1988.

Migration and Assimilation. The Case of the Bulgarian Gardeners in Austria[1]

Marijana Jakimova

1. Going abroad to make a living

Going abroad to make a living is a traditional part of the Bulgarian population's enterprising spirit and drive for improving its standard of living. As defined by the Bulgarian Encyclopaedia, "going abroad to make a living" – this is the general idea behind the Bulgarian terms *gurbet*, *gurbetčijstvo* – meaning practising a trade abroad (home tailoring, masonry, coal mining, coppersmithing, gardening). The phenomenon of going abroad to make a living first appeared during Ottoman rule and grew to become very popular during the Bulgarian Renaissance in the 19th century. It usually lasts from nine to ten months a year, and sometimes continues as long as two to three years. The extensive period of time spent abroad is a prerequisite to the formation of novel relationships between masters, apprentices and journeymen.[2] In the agricultural sector, going abroad to make a living is expressed mainly by the migration of labour from the mountains to the rich plains and river valleys during harvest season.[3]

For the migrant the first step on "terra incognita" has to do with initial familiarisation and communication; the economic aspect of migration follows naturally at a later stage, which is then logically evolved into the pursuit of profits and information exchange and finally – trading. In such a manner the original meaning of the term "going abroad to make a living" has been extended and popularised in almost all Balkan countries (Serbia, Montenegro, Croatia, Bosnia and Herzegovina, Macedonia, Bulgaria, Albania, Greece and Turkey). Going abroad to make a living also includes the offering of specific professional capabilities characteristic of certain geographical regions where financial and intellectual prosperity is being pursued and nostalgia is being suppressed. Men working abroad became strangers and wanderers. They spend their nights in tents like gypsies and look for new strategies for survival – a traditional part of the entrepreneurial spirit and drive for a higher standard of living.[4]

---

[1] This case study is part of FWF-Project P 15080 "Hidden Minorities between Central Europe and the Balkans", financed by the Austrian Science Fundation FWF.

[2] Cf. Gurbetčijstvo. In: Enciklopedija Bălgarija, vol. 2. Sofia 1981, p. 197.

[3] Cf. Petko Christov: Gurbetčijstvoto/pečalbarstvoto v centralnata čast na Balkanite kato transgraničen obmen. In: M. Karamichova (ed.), Da živeeš tam, da sanuvaš tuk. Emigracionni procesi v načaloto na XXI vek. Sofia 2003, pp. 223-235.

[4] Cf. Christov, Gurbetčijstvoto/pečalbarstvoto.

2. Phases of Bulgarian gardeners' emigration until the Second World War

Going abroad to make a living by gardening began at the end of 17th and the beginning of 18th century as an indirect result of the numerous wars led by the Ottoman Empire against the Austro-Hungarian monarchy and Russia. The maintenance of the Turkish army of many thousands was ensured through the employment of workers at the garrisons to grow vegetables. Later these workers, together with homespun, woollen braid manufacturers and horse dealers attending to the army's needs, were granted special privileges beyond those of the rest of the non-Muslim population.[5]

Already in the 1830s we can observe Bulgarian gardeners living in the Serbian capital Belgrade.[6] After the liberation of Bulgaria and until the beginning of the First World War, we can find Bulgarian gardeners in Romania and Serbia, and even in Russia; the total number of gardeners in the first years of the 20th century going abroad annually during the gardening season was roughly between 12,000 and 17,000.[7]

The possibility for quick realisation of profit abroad and accumulation of property and capital attracted many Bulgarians. It was no secret that every gardener's goal was to earn enough money to build his own house, which should prove his well-being and the fact that he was head of his own household. With respect to the husband's household patrilocality was consequently transformed into neolocality. Until the present day there exist dozens of houses of Bulgarian gardeners who had worked abroad, built in the period between the two world wars. They are located in the village of Draganovo and the outskirts of the district of Veliko Tărnovo, which became the centre of gardener emigration.

In the period between the two world wars, the process of seasonal and permanent migration was motivated additionally by the difficult economic situation in Bulgaria after the First World War. The outcome of the war was catastrophic: within a period of six years Bulgaria had taken part in three wars – the First Balkan War (1912-1913), the Second Balkan War (1913) and the First World War (1915-1918). The country lost Southern Dobrudja and Western Thrace with its outlet to the Aegean Sea to its neighbours. Thousands of people were killed, wounded or disappeared without trace; the national economy col-

[5] Cf. Stefan Băčvarov: Bălgarsko gradinarstvo. Sofia 1986, p. 12.

[6] Cf. Kliment Džambazovski: Privredne veze Bugara s Kneževinom Srbijom u doba kneza Miloša Obrenovića i Ustavobranitelja. Belgrade 1986 (= Srpska akademija nauka i umetnosti, Balkanološki institut, posebna izdanja 28), pp. 75-88.

[7] Cf. Micheline Billaut: Les migrations externs en Bulgarie. In: D. Eeskaute-Bardery (ed.), Migrations balkaniques et danubiennes. Paris 1991, pp. 20-21.

lapsed. And what is more, the country owed huge sums for reparations as envisaged by the Treaty of Neuilly (1919).

Therefore the number of Bulgarian emigrants remained high. From 1932 until the beginning of the Second World War the number of Bulgarian gardeners leaving the country reached an annual average of about 4,800 persons; their main destinations were Hungary, Austria, Czechoslovakia, Poland and the Yugoslav Kingdom. During these years their migration became less and less seasonal and many decided not to return to their home country during the winter season.[8]

Traian Stoianovich, a Canadian expert on the Balkans says of this period and its longer term effects: "Garden cultivation was stimulated by the growth of cities and availability – but also scarcity – of water. [...] In parts of Hungary, including the rural area around Budapest, many of the ablest vegetable gardeners were Bulgarians whose ancestors had brought their skills northward from the garden cultures of the south."[9]

3. The migration of Bulgarian gardeners to Austria

Bulgarian gardeners have been living in Austria since the beginning of the 20th century. As a small, isolated professional group they have been able to preserve their ethnic identity for several decades. Bulgarian gardeners were responsible for the dissemination of new kinds of vegetables and for an advance in the variety of vegetable species in horticulture.

It was the growth of the cities and consequently of their food markets, which made it possible for Bulgarian gardeners to lay the foundations for a passable existence in the Habsburg Empire. In Vienna for instance, the number of inhabitants more than doubled between 1869 and 1910 from almost one million to two million and represented a rich market for gardeners. The second largest city of today's Austria, Graz, experienced a rapid growth of 150,000 inhabitants between 1900 and 1910. A similar increase can be observed for other cities of the Habsburg Empire.[10]

---

[8] Cf. Billaut, Les migrations externs en Bulgarie, p. 31-33; Băčvarov: Bălgarsko gradinarstvo, pp. 58-59; Istorija na bălgarskoto gradinarstvo. Jubileen sbornik po slučaj 10 godini ot osnovavane na Bălgarski Gradinarski săjuz 1928-1938. Sofia 1938, pp. 257-281.

[9] Traian Stoianovich: Balkan Worlds. The First and Last Europe. New York – London 1994, p. 334.

[10] Cf. Michael John/Albert Lichtblau: Schmelztiegel Wien einst und jetzt. Zur Geschichte und Gegenwart von Zuwanderung und Minderheiten. Vienna – Cologne – Weimar 1993, p. 12; Gemeindelexikon der im Reichsrate vertretenen Königreiche und Länder. Steiermark. Vienna 1904, p. 2; Spezialortsrepertorium für Steiermark. Vienna 1917, p. 1; William H. Hubbard: Auf dem

When the Austro-Hungarian monarchy collapsed, unemployment became a widespread phenomenon. Inflation reached unprecedented levels. In order to help the gardeners to overcome the economic crisis, the Austrian government provided them with certain privileges regarding visa application procedures and labour rights. The rapid development of Bulgarian gardening in Austria was due to the necessity for a regular supply of vegetables to the markets in the post-war period and later in the global economic depression in 1929. Vegetables turned out to be the cheapest food; they could be grown quickly, were rich in vitamins and could be preserved fresh or canned for the winter. Bulgarian gardeners grew sufficient quantities of vegetables for the satisfaction of every family's needs. They developed agricultural technology for mass production and applied unique manufacturing methods adapted to the local climatic and soil conditions and introduced many new vegetable species and varieties unknown to the Austrian population before. They contributed a great deal to the supply of tomatoes, pepper, eggplant, cabbage and beans, as well as for the popularisation of new varieties among the local population. In foreign seeds catalogues various sorts of Bulgarian pepper or onion were listed by their original names.[11]

Bulgarian gardeners were consequently treated as dangerous rivals by their Austrian competitors, because of their monopoly on completely new vegetables. As a consequence, in order to protect Austrian gardeners, the Bulgarian gardeners were not allowed to the Viennese markets in 1935 and 1936.[12] And in early 1938 the Austrian government in its last days passed a law, which forbade foreign gardeners to rent property beyond a certain size.[13]

In March, 1938, Austria was annexed to the Third Reich. Due to the friendly relations between Bulgaria and the Third Reich at this time, Bulgaria entered into a contract which obliged her to submit resources and labour forces to Germany in order to satisfy the agricultural needs of the latter. These agreements were known as labour force exchange contracts despite them being a one-way labour transfer. Due to similar conventions, by the middle of 1939 37,000 Italians, 15,000 Yugoslavians, 12,000 Hungarians and 5,000 Bulgarians were occupied in the agricultural sector of the Third Reich.[14]

From 1939 to 1944 4,064 persons (544 organisers and 3,520 workers) were members of the Vienna branch of the Society of Bulgarian Gardeners; they tilled 523 gardens with an overall surface of 2,088 hectares; i.e. each worker

---

Weg zur Großstadt. Eine Sozialgeschichte der Stadt Graz 1850-1914. Vienna 1984 (= Sozial- und wirtschaftshistorische Studien 17), pp. 10-13.

[11] For example the *Kalinkov* and *Marinovski* pepper or the *Ljaskovski* and *Kaba Samovodska* onion – cf. Băčvarov, Bălgarsko gradinarstvo, pp. 101-103.

[12] Cf. John/Lichtblau, Schmelztiegel Wien, p. 64;

[13] Cf. Bundesgesetz zum Schutze der gärtnerischen Erzeugung. *Bundesgesetzblatt für den Bundesstaat Österreich*. 22.1.1938, pp. 187-189.

[14] Cf. Ulrich Herbert: Fremdarbeiterpolitik und Praxis des "Ausländer-Einsatzes" in der Kriegswirtschaft des Dritten Reiches. Berlin – Bonn 1985, p. 56.

cultivated an area of about half a hectare.[15] During the course of the Second World War Bulgarian gardeners increasingly replaced German ones, who had to go to the army. This was the reason why after 1945, the Bulgarian government accused them of having collaborated with the Nazis.

After the Second World War the establishment of communist regimes in Eastern Europe and in Bulgaria prevented legal emigration to the West and to Austria. The remaining Bulgarian gardeners in Austria lost contact with their relatives and friends in Bulgaria. This situation lasted until the fall of the Iron Curtain in 1989. The end of the Second World War became a caesura for the Bulgarian gardeners in Austria. After that period they lost their importance. No successors came from Bulgaria and in Austria it came to a silent assimilation of the second and third generations of the migrants.

The best time for the Bulgarian gardeners in Austria was therefore the interwar period; they filled a gap in the supply of the citizenry with vegetables. They used other horticultural techniques than their Austrian competitors and as a result, they could produce more effectively.

4. Technologies and work organisation

Usually, the Bulgarian gardeners rented estates of 5 to 10 hectares immediately outside the cities, since they had to apply a complex system of canals for irrigation. They were pioneers in the use of the water wheel for irrigation, and later of the water pump. They used the same patch for different vegetable varieties, which ripened in different seasons.[16]

These horticultural techniques were new for the Austrian society. Social distance between the locals and the migrants was predominant. This was a reason for professional segregation and can be assessed as a cultural division of the labour market. In the case of Bulgarian gardeners their traditional repertoire of skills emphasised their peculiarity, but they also proved be a possible cultural enrichment for the local society. Since many of the vegetables introduced by the Bulgarian gardeners in Austria are now common in this country, cultural enrichment did definitely take place in this case.

In the interwar period the gardeners working abroad were organised in small cooperatives (the so-called *zadruga*) of seven or eight members whereby membership was fixed or variable. They borrowed the organisation structures, legal relations and profit allocation methods from *zadruga*s, which had developed during the Bulgarian Renaissance in the country. The organiser of the *zadruga*

[15] Cf. Kiril Filipov: Jubileen doklad po slučaj 50 godini ot sazdavaneto na bălgarskoto gradinarsko družestvo văv Viena. Vienna 1986, p. 4.
[16] Cf. John/Lichtblau, Schmelztiegel Wien, p. 64.

(the *gazda*) and the workers lived together in a household. In some cases two brothers organised a group together with seasonal workers. Initially only family members could participate in the group, later, unrelated Bulgarians were accepted into the group as well. Their membership was organised by the *gazda*. While the majority of the members returned to Bulgaria during the winter season, at least one of them remained behind to guard the garden sites and sell the produce during this period. The *zadruga* was a combination of older patterns with newer forms; it combined Bulgarian traditions with capitalist principles. Each member acted at a strictly defined hierarchical level and contributed with a specific amount of capital, but also participated in the sharing of the profit. Without being able to draw regular loans, the gardeners had to increase investments through borrowing money from other cooperatives. All relations between the members of the zadruga were regulated by customary law.[17] The *zadruga* was a very effective variant of a kinship network. This network rested on a consistent number of families, which were the pioneers of this mode of professional migration to Central Europe.

In 1936 the Bulgarian gardeners founded a professional association, the Society of Bulgarian Gardeners. The new association would subsequently legitimate the mutual financial support system of the *zadruga*s in Austria. But it also dealt with other legal issues and aimed at defending the gardeners' interests' vis-à-vis the Bulgarian state, on the one hand, and with governments of the gardener's respective host countries.[18]

5. A gardener family between assimilation and integration

In the following I will concentrate upon the settlement of Bulgarian gardeners in the city of Graz, the capital of the Austrian Federal Province of Styria: Here the Bulgarian colony came into being in the early 20th century. Parts of the Bulgarian cultural and ethnic identity among the gardeners' families have survived until today. How did these Bulgarian migrants, who had a social and cultural microstructure of their own, adapt to the local society?

Three issues will be treated in this context. I will take a look at the causes and motives of this migration movement connected with certain villages in central Bulgaria and organised by a kinship network. Secondly, I will say something about the shifting of identities between tradition and integration in the new surroundings. And finally, I will ask if a relationship exists between Bulgarian gardeners who came to Austria before 1945 and the Bulgarian migrants who came after 1989.

---

[17] Cf. Marijana Jakimova: Kulturna identičnost na bălgarskata gradinarska emigracija v Avstrija. Sofia 2000 (unpublished Master's thesis), p. 25.
[18] Cf. Filipov, Jubileen doklad, p. 4.

a) Causes and motives for migration

Push and pull factors were responsible for the migration of Bulgarian migrants into foreign countries. Among the pull factors was the growth of the cities in Central Europe and the increasing need to supply them with vegetables, as mentioned above. Among the push factors in Bulgaria, one has to cite the gradual decomposition of complex families. They were replaced by nuclear families. The reasons for the demise of complex families are manifold and the best analyses of this phenomenon focus on the Western Balkans. The decline of complex families had the effect that the sons left the parental household earlier and the often emigrated. A second reason was the growth in population, which reached its climax around 1930, during the world economic crisis, which hit the farmers in the Balkans in particular.[19]

But how did emigration from Bulgaria to Austria work under these circumstances? This can be illustrated using the example of a family of Bulgarian gardeners that came to Graz in the early 20th century. The pioneer of this family was Grigori Boneff (Bonev). He was born in 1894 in the village of Draganovo near Veliko Tărnovo in Central Bulgaria. The family property was too small to nourish the whole family. So Grigori left for Austria in 1908 at the age of fourteen. In Graz he worked as a seasonal gardener. Each winter he returned to his family in Bulgaria. His elder brother, who had remained in Bulgaria lived with his wife and the children in the parental household; emigration of the younger son proved to be a survival strategy for the whole family.[20]

After Grigori's marriage in 1918, things changed: In 1921 his first child, a son, was born. Grigori and his wife took up permanent residence in Graz. Here he rented a flat and became chief of a group of seasonal workers from Bulgaria. But their son remained in Bulgaria under the custody of his grandparents. Grigori and his wife lived in Graz, but they built a house in their home village of Draganovo. The son came to his parents only after he turned eleven, in 1932. The second child, a daughter, Magdalena, was born in Austria in 1936.[21]

This example shows how the gradual decline of the complex family is intertwined with the phenomenon of modern migration. The economic situation made it necessary for the youngest son to go abroad in order to earn money for the family. For some ten years his earnings were crucial for them. But after his marriage and after he had become a leading figure among the emigrants responsibility gradually shifted. Grigori's first child was still raised by his grandparents, who were being supported by Grigori. He also regularly sent money back home to his brother. But Grigori's second child, his daughter Magdalena,

[19] Karl Kaser: Familie und Verwandschaft auf dem Balkan. Geschichte und Verbreitung eines kulturellen Musters. Vienna – Cologne – Weimar 1995, p. 150.
[20] Interview with Magdalena Penkova. Graz, 17.6.1998.
[21] Interview with Magdalena Penkova. Graz, 17.6.1998.

was raised in Austria. And she would stay there. Her brother had enjoyed the protection of a complex family in decline; for her the modem nuclear family was and is the dominant horizon.

Grigori was initially a seasonal worker adopted into a *zadruga*. Later he became the *gazda* of a *zadruga* himself and stayed in Austria permanently. Since the *zadruga* was a patriarchal organisation, participating women were exposed to multiple stresses, as Magdalena testifies: "The whole day my mother used to cook and to wash for twenty persons. And she went to the market to sell the vegetables. In the evening she used to sew, to weave and to knit for the children. I wonder how she ran the household. She was incredibly strong".[22]

b) Shifting identities

What impact did the process of migration have on the identities of the Bulgarian gardeners who both had to deal with their traditional Bulgarian heritage and their integration into Austrian society?

The ethnic and cultural identities of the Bulgarian migrants were to a certain extent dependent upon their repertoire of images and values or, briefly, upon the cultural memory of their country of origin. We have to consider that the act of migration with all its consequences was a challenge to the cultural horizon of the migrants. The migrants had to develop images of themselves and the other. They were furthermore exposed to a cultural change which forced them to adapt to the conditions of their host countries. This is valid for existential caesurae such as birth, childhood, puberty, marriage, illness and death. Other factors, however, had a conservative effect and strengthened their indigenous ethnic and cultural identities, including language, traditional rituals, their existence within a professional group, the seasonal return to the complex of family and kinship.[23]

But after the Second World War Two links to Bulgaria were cut off. It has already been mentioned that the Bulgarian government accused the gardeners of collaboration with the Nazi regime. Many of the Bulgarian gardeners in Austria decided to give up their seasonal return and to stay in Austria for good. Those who had worked in Germany and Austria and came back to Bulgaria were shot in the name of the Republic. Grigori Boneff, for instance, had built a modern house in his home village of Draganovo. The house was finished towards the end of war. It was built in Austrian style, had central heating, which was a novelty in a Bulgarian village like Draganovo at that time. But Grigori and his wife

[22] Interview with Magdalena Penkova. Graz, 17.6.1998.

[23] Cf. Marijana Jakimova: Die bulgarischen Wandergärtner in der Steiermark. Historische und anthropologische Aspekte. Graz 2003 (unpublished Master's thesis), pp. 67-100.

decided not to go back; the house remained empty. Grigori and his wife died in the 1970s without having ever lived there. Such empty houses are not only common in Draganovo, but in the whole region of Veliko Tărnovo.[24]

The broken contact to Bulgaria already became apparent in the second generation and only became stronger in the third generation, as can be seen for Magdalena and her children. Magdalena was nine years old in 1945. She did not go to Bulgaria until 1981, when she was invited to visit the country on the occasion of the 1300th anniversary of its foundation. After 1989 she has regularly been on holiday in Bulgaria.

Magdalena calls Bulgarian her mother language, hut her command of Bulgarian is only oral. In the Austrian school there was no possibility to learn Bulgarian. Her Bulgarian has a German accent and is mixed with German words. But the solidarity among the Bulgarian migrants was so strong that voluntary endogamy was common for the second generation. Magdalena married the son of another Bulgarian gardener. They have three sons which were born in the 1960s. All of them have a Bulgarian name, which shows some cultural continuity (Boris, Sasha, Simeon), but they do not speak Bulgarian. Today Magdalena regrets that she did not teach her mother language to her sons, but the circumstances were not favourable at that time.[25]

Whether immigrant families conserve their mother tongue or not, is dependent upon internal and external social factors. The latter are above all stereotypes about "superior" and "inferior" languages, i.e. a consequence of ethnocentrism engaged by the majority population against minority languages. Living in Austria, Magdalena was worried that the Eastern European origin of her sons could be made out, a fear which was amplified by Cold War enmity against Communist countries.

There were also other reasons why the sons did not develop a Bulgarian identity. For one, they only had Austrian friends and they had little interest in becoming gardeners like their grandparents. Already their father had chosen to become an insurance clerk. Magdalena's elder brother had also abandoned the family trade. He studied in Germany and became a chemist.

The assimilation of the offspring of Bulgarian gardeners happened peacefully, and it worked according to the following general model.[26]

The first generation adapts itself to the country of arrival only in economic and social terms while it tries to preserve its culture by ethnic grouping. A key element in this ethnic grouping is the *zadruga* with its kinship network. The first generation is very devout. They have a comprehensive orthodox outlook on life. According to the traditional male-female roles in patriarchal society, where

---

[24] Interview with Magdalena Penkova. Graz, 17.6.1998.
[25] Interview with Magdalena Penkova. Graz, 17.6.1998.
[26] Charles Price: The Study of Assimilation. In: J. A. Jackson (ed.), Migration, Cambridge University Press 1969, p. 181-237, here p. 183.

the women are tied to the household, the men have a better command of German than the women.

The second generation still tries to preserve the culture of their parents within the family, and endogamy is still is of importance. But this generation, having Austrian citizenship, is already adapting itself to the culture of the host country. It lives in two cultures with different standards of values. This is best seen in Magdalena's use of German words when she speaks Bulgarian. But it is also apparent that the children of the migrants tend to prefer the use of German rather than of Bulgarian. They communicate in German in order to hide their origin. Their living in two cultures leads them to attempt to overcome the gap between them. Thus a retired gardener from a town near Graz, for example, regrets that Bulgaria had not abandoned the Cyrillic alphabet and adopted the Latin one.[27] The second generation is not as religious as the previous generation. They are not aware of the theological background of the Bulgarian Orthodox Church, but they respect religion, since it has to do with tradition

The third generation gives up the culture of their parents and grandparents and adapts completely to the "core culture" of the host country. Members of the third generation hardly ever speak the mother language of their parents or grandparents. But there is another aspect which is a common quality of modern societies which do not function any longer according to traditional models: parents are no longer examples and mentors for their children. Instead, educational institutions, circles of friends and the media assume this role.[28] In the case of the third generation of Bulgarian migrants this can be applied with respect to the use of the mother language of their parents and to their religion. Consequently, the third generation is either atheist or indifferent to the church.

The gradual overtaking of one culture by another can be observed primarily among the second and third generations. The acculturation is completed with the third generation. Acculturation can be described as a learning process of adaptation during which a person adopts cultural characteristics, guidelines and behavioural patterns from the host society.[29] But the process can also be bluntly considered as assimilation piloted by social pressure and by voluntary submission. Integration would have meant the inclusion of migrants with respect for their specific identity. This did not happen. The third generation is in most cases completely assimilated. Is their even a connection between them and the new migrants from Bulgaria since 1989?

---

[27] Interview with Dimităr Penkov, Gratkorn, 1.3.1999.

[28] Cf. Margaret Mead: Der Konflikt der Generationen. Jugend ohne Vorbild. Olten 1971, pp. 110-111.

[29] Cf. Hartmut Esser: Aspekte der Wanderungssoziologie. Assimilation und Integration von Wanderern, ethnischen Gruppen und Minderheiten. Eine handlungstheoretische Analyse. Darmstadt 1980, p. 20.

c) New developments since 1989

After the fall of the Iron Curtain a new generation of migrants came from Bulgaria to Austria. Modernisation and changing political circumstances have finally replaced the gardeners, persons of a narrow professional segment, by manifold forms of professional migration. The general crisis of a country in transition from one societal system to another and the concomitant high rate of unemployment represent the main factors for emigration.[30]

These new immigrants are often highly qualified individuals, many of them with university degrees, but they seldom find jobs in Austria, which would correspond to their qualifications. Compared to the female gardeners with their traditionally submissive role, the new female immigrants are much more independent. In Bulgaria they had enjoyed a higher social status and education. And what is more, they overwhelmingly have an urban background. Contrary to stereotypes still prominent in Austria, traditional patriarchal family relations are no longer relevant among Bulgarian migrants today. These women look differently on sexual relationships and often live together with men without marrying them. Among immigrant women the institution of marriage is being discussed vehemently. In some exceptional cases even divorce has become an option, although one could think that the bands of marriage would be strengthened by living in a foreign country.

There are already two generations of new immigrants from Bulgaria in Austria. The children of the immigrants are confronted with the same issues as the second generation of Bulgarian gardeners. Not all of them have a positive attitude toward their origin. Many of them adopt basic attitudes typically Austrian and feel ashamed of their mother tongue, their parents and their origin. They want to adopt an Austrian identity, although they often look like somebody from the "south". Contrary to their parents, and having close contact with Austrian friends, they successfully suppress their foreign accent, if even present, when they speak German. Some already have their Austrian citizenship. Those who came later together with their parents have to fight against ever more restrictive immigration laws.[31] Even if they wanted to, there is almost no possibility to gain insight into the culture of their origin; they have almost no knowledge of Bulgarian history and culture and there is almost no possibility to learn Bulgarian in a systematic way. In the city of Graz a Bulgarian teacher attempted to organise instruction in Bulgarian in a few schools, but the idea had

---

[30] Cf. Daniela Bobeva: Migration aus und nach Bulgarien in Vergangenheit, Gegenwart und Zukunft, in: H. Fassmann/R. Münz (eds.), Migration in Europa. Frankfurt/M. et al. 1996, pp. 305, 312-315.

[31] This situation was only partly eased by the EU membership of Bulgaria because of the Austrian government applies a restrictive transitional regulation of incoming labour force from new EU members.

to be abandoned for economic reasons and the fact that there were not enough pupils.[32]

Are there any contacts between the descendants of the Bulgarian gardeners and the new migrants? They are organised sporadically on an intergenerational level. The second generation of Bulgarian gardeners, which is now in its sixties, has some contact with the first generation of new immigrants, which is mainly in its thirties and forties. There are informal annual meetings in restaurants which have the purpose of conjuring up a common origin. These events are characterised by superficiality, gossip and embarrassment, like meetings between distant relatives whose only linkage is their long distant common origin, if there is not the accidental possibility of establishing business contacts. They do not have the character of informal networks like the ethnic grouping of the first generation of Bulgarian gardeners in Austria. The third generation of the old immigrants does not participate in the meetings, since it has already adopted an Austrian identity. The second generation of the new immigrants, children and teenagers do participate, but for the most part as a result of the fact that a young person has to obey the will of their parents without protest.

These sporadic meetings are nevertheless of importance. Gossip, for instance, has a widely underestimated social function. For the descendants of the Bulgarian gardeners, these meetings represent a symbolic revival of their ethnic identity as Bulgarians. They enjoy meeting countrymen after the long separation of the Cold War. For the new immigrants these meetings at least are an assurance that they are not the first to come from Bulgaria to Austria, and even if they have different values, they can listen to the experience of their older predecessors.

Conclusion

In conclusion, one can observe a slow and peaceful process of cultural assimilation of Bulgarian immigrants in Austria. That the Bulgarian identity is not any longer determined by traditional and patriarchal values restricted to agriculture and horticulture is demonstrated by the arrival of new immigrants after the fall of the Iron Curtain. Even if there may be a huge gap between the descendants of the Bulgarian gardeners and the new immigrants, there is a desire for communication, in meetings visited by both people arriving in Austria during the last decade and people who have lived half a century in Austria or are even born in Austria. Thus a breaching of the gap between pioneers and new emigrants is at least partly being realised. Although they represent a colourful mosaic, they continue to speak of themselves as "we Bulgarians."

[32] Interview with Linda Tascheva (Taševa), Graz, 15.4.1998.

Bibliography

BĂČVAROV, Stefan: Bălgarsko gradinarstvo. Sofia 1986.

BILLAUT, Micheline: Les migrations externs en Bulgarie. In: D. Eeskaute-Bardery (ed.), Migrations balkaniques et danubiennes. Paris. 1991 pp. 11-50.

BOBEVA, Daniela: Migration aus und nach Bulgarien in Vergangenheit, Gegenwart und Zukunft, in: H. Fassmann/R. Münz (eds.), Migration in Europa. Frankfurt/M. et al. 1996, pp. 303-322.

BUNDESGESETZ ZUM SCHUTZE DER GÄRTNERISCHEN ERZEUGUNG. *Bundesgesetzblatt für den Bundesstaat Österreich.* 22.1.1938, pp. 187-189.

CHRISTOV, Petko: Gurbetčijstvoto/pečalbarstvoto v centralnata čast na Balkanite kato transgraničen obmen. In: M. Karamichova (ed.), Da živeeš tam, da sanuvaš tuk. Emigracionni procesi v načaloto na XXI vek. Sofia 2003, pp. 223-235.

DŽAMBAZOVSKI, Kliment: Privredne veze Bugara s Kneževinom Srbijom u doba kneza Miloša Obrenovića i Ustavobranitelja. Belgrade 1986 (= Srpska akademija nauka i umetnosti, Balkanološki institut, posebna izdanja 28).

ESSER, Harmut: Aspekte der Wanderungssoziologie. Assimilation und Integration von Wanderern, ethnischen Gruppen und Minderheiten. Eine handlungstheoretische Analyse. Darmstadt 1980, p. 20.

FILIPOV, Kiril: Jubileen doklad po slučaj 50 godini ot sazdavaneto na bălgarskoto gradinarsko družestvo văv Viena. Vienna 1986.

GEMEINDELEXIKON der im Reichsrate vertretenen Königreiche und Länder. Steiermark. Vienna 1904.

GURBETČIJSTVO. In: Enciklopedija Bălgarija, vol. 2. Sofia 1981, p. 197.

HERBERT, Ulrich: Fremdarbeiterpolitik und Praxis des "Ausländer-Einsatzes" in der Kriegswirtschaft des Dritten Reiches. Berlin – Bonn 1985.

HUBBARD, William H.: Auf dem Weg zur Großstadt. Eine Sozialgeschichte der Stadt Graz 1850-1914. Vienna 1984 (= Sozial- und wirtschaftshistorische Studien 17).

ISTORIJA NA BĂLGARSKOTO GRADINARSTVO. Jubileen sbornik po slučaj 10 godini ot osnovavane na Bălgarski Gradinarski săjuz 1928-1938. Sofia 1938.

JAKIMOVA, Marijana: Die bulgarischen Wandergärtner in der Steiermark. Historische und anthropologische Aspekte. Graz 2003 (unpublished Master's thesis).

JAKIMOVA, Marijana: Kulturna identičnost na bălgarskata gradinarska emigracija v Avstrija. Sofia 2000 (unpublished Master's thesis).

JOHN, Michael/LICHTBLAU, Albert: Schmelztiegel Wien einst und jetzt. Zur Geschichte und Gegenwart von Zuwanderung und Minderheiten. Vienna – Cologne – Weimar 1993.

KASER, Karl: Familie und Verwandschaft auf dem Balkan. Geschichte und Verbreitung eines kulturellen Musters. Vienna – Cologne – Weimar 1995.

MEAD, Margaret: Der Konflikt der Generationen. Jugend ohne Vorbild. Olten 1971, pp. 110-111.

PRICE, Charles: The Study of Assimilation. In: J. A. Jackson (ed.), Migration, Cambridge University Press 1969, pp. 181-237.

SPEZIALORTSREPERTORIUM FÜR STEIERMARK. Vienna 1917.

STOIANOVICH, Traian: Balkan Worlds. The First and Last Europe. New York – London 1994.

An Invisible Community between Dispersal and a New Sense of Belonging: Roma Survival Strategies in Prekmurje – Slovenia

Oto Luthar

Introduction

This article is on aspects of Roma cultural practices and their survival strategies in Prekmurje, the most inter- and multicultural region in the north-eastern part of Slovenia. It is about the set of phenomena that I came across together with a group of students from the pedagogical faculty in Maribor when comparing patterns of self-representation and presentation of the Other in this region, the only point in Europe where conglomerates of Romany, Germanic, Slav and Hungarian culture(s) meet. I will only discuss some aspects of this dynamic process, in particular the self-representation of the Romany people in this area and the invention and re-invention of their identity. The article deals further with their survival strategies and their opposition to dispersal and the imposition of varieties of majority culture. It is about their way of establishing a new sense of belonging and their ability to recognise their chances to survive outside the traditional narrative.

The question of visibility

The concept of "hidden minorities" is particularly appropriate for this purpose, first because it unambiguously suggests that the process or phenomenon we are dealing with must first be uncovered. I also understand the term as an invitation to analyse the phenomenon in the past. Moreover, the use of the word *hidden* anticipates a process of decoding or deconstructing inscribed meaning(s). It also anticipates an active role of the interpreter. According to the English historian Keith Jenkins, historians not only have to locate what is happening in "non-narrative present actuality [...] in a longer, contextualising narrative form", they also have to be aware of "hidden mechanisms of ideological power in our current social formations that simultaneously permit us to operate within all [...] usual gate-keeping paraphernalia" such as academic standards, publication controls and all sorts of "latent, ostracizing power".[1] Jenkins further points out that most academic historians do not think in this way. They still

[1] Keith Jenkins: Refiguring History. New thoughts on an old discipline. London – New York 2003, pp. 17-18.

continue to strive for "real historical knowledge, for objectivity, for the evidentially-based synoptic account and for truth-at-the-end-of-enquiry" that leads to so called "interpretative closures". Therefore, he suggests – and this is the point where I am willing to join him – the exact opposite, he is convinced "that in the name of interminable openness and unthought possibilities we *ought* to have an implacable opposition to every type of closure", firstly, because of the logically unavoidable openness of the historical text, and secondly, because such unavoidable openness demands new "disrespectful, contentious, radical readings and re-readings, writings and rewritings of the past".[2]

Along this and similar lines, the concept of hidden minorities can be helpful in stressing the primary problems related to the discussion of Romany life and culture. In the first place, the problem concerns numbers. Like in all parts of Europe and the world, there exists also in Slovenia a significant difference between official data and the real figure of the Romany population. According to the official statistics, approximately 7,000 Romany people live in two Slovene regions (Prekmurje and Dolenjska); according to non-official data they number about 10,000. Therefore they are at least partly hidden or even invisible in the official statistics.

They remain a more or less non-existent entity from the perspective of Slovene legislation; they are mentioned in the Slovene constitution, they have been promised separate laws/legislation, but have to date never received more than an eleven-point document saying that they, as an "autochthonous and specific ethnic community should get separate legislation/laws".[3]

Meanwhile, the quality of life of some Roma families, particularly in the Dolenjska region, has deteriorated. The following case is exemplary for the contemporary situation. It is the story of a Roma family who bought a house in the village of Maline some 40 km from the Slovene capital Ljubljana but were never allowed to move in.

Invisible

The Maline case is interesting also because of the media coverage of the event:

> Even though the events involved a concrete Romany family, they were given the opportunity to make their standpoints known in only two accounts [...] On the contrary, the other side expressed their standpoints very often – both those directly involved in the conflict (the villagers of Maline and surrounding places, the mayors of the municipalities, municipal officials) and those

---

[2] Jenkins, Refiguring History, p. 3.

[3] Mladen Tancer: Vzgoja in izobraževanje Romov na Slovenskem. Maribor 1994. p. 65. – The Roma in Slovenia have at least one satisfaction. In Article 65 of the new Slovene constitution they are mentioned as a separate ethnic group for the first time. Before that they were hidden under the umbrella term "ethnic groups".

who were not directly affected by the event (presidential candidates, representatives of the church, of political parties, etc.).[4]

In analysing such accounts the authors of the book *We About the Roma* realised that journalists did not relate their own observations, but instead relayed the voice of the majority population. Another problem contributing to "[...] the extremely deficient citing of Romany sources is the distribution of the information sources across [...]"[5] the whole coverage. "Even when journalists chose to quote Romany sources, their standpoints were not given independently but were invariably presented together with those of the majority population."[6].

Finally the case became an enormous media event that showed that Slovene "media are not interested in their (Romany people's) difficulties unless they turn into a conflict that also threatens to affect the majority population."[7]

Visible, but somehow out of focus...

The Roma interviewed in Prekmurje did not face this kind of problem, although they were well aware that they were far from the status of the two other ethnic groups (Hungarians and Italians) in Slovenia which already had official minority status.

But before going on I should explain more about the fieldwork for the *Eni in drugi* ("One and the Other") project: The main goal was to reconstruct the fine nuances of the wide spectrum of relationships between different cultural practices. Prekmurje is – in otherwise ethnically and religiously quite uniform Slovenia – a vast mixture of languages and cultures. Among the approximately 90,000 people who live in this region, some 4,000 are Roma, 8,500 are Hungarian and a very small community are German-speaking. In addition, Prek-

---

4 Karmen Erjavec/ Sandra B. Hrvatin/ Barbara Kelbl: We About the Roma. Discriminatory Discourse in the Media in Slovenia. Ljubljana 2000, p.14.

5 Ibidem.

6 Ibidem, p. 15.

7 Ibidem, p. 7.

In their analysis of media writing about the Maline case on the one hand, and media writing about "Romany problems" in general, the authors argue that the "prevalent mood of coverage could be summed up with a single word – 'PROBLEMS'. In their view "the media write about ethnic minorities only when they are involved in some conflict". According to the authors, "Journalistic writing rests on the assumption that the Roma are 'different from us'". Their analysis shows that media are full of stereotypes and generalisations. In this "concocted media image" the Romany people are presented as a threat to the social order. They are described as aggressive and dangerous, lazy and idle, un-adaptable and problematic. — This bilingual (Slovene/English) booklet also shows that "Roma are clearly underprivileged in terms of communication and excluded from the shaping of media agenda. [...] Even though the events involved a concrete Romany family they were given the opportunity to make their standpoints known in only two accounts" out of 99 – cf. ibidem, pp.14-15.

murje is the only Slovene province where Catholic and Protestant (Lutheran and Calvinist) communities coexist. The region is the only remaining Slovenian region with a continuous tradition of co-habitation of all kinds of central European cultural and religious entities. Before the Nazi deportation of the Lendava Jews in 1944, it also included two strong Jewish communities.[8]

Prekmurje, as a typical region between East and West, has its own expressly multicultural structure. But although it can in many ways be seen as Central Europe in miniature, the region lacks some of the elements that define Central Europe as a whole. It seems that usual, conflicting/controversial national narratives coloured by moral indignation, historical speculation and nostalgic transfiguration are alien to the people living in this region. The different ethnic groups of Prekmurje do not appear to posses different historical maps and milestones and the people living there do not seem to feel the need to draw attention to the national and cultural peculiarities of their respective nationalities. It seems that they do not wish to be seen as something special, unique or inimitably original. They do not share the typical Central European relationship to "Others". They live detached from the mainstream of Slovene trends; so they did not join the endeavour of a part of the members of the Slovene intelligentsia, who were imbued with the mission to uncover and cultivate the linguistic individuality of a new or reborn nation, to produce what István Bibo would call "linguistic nationalism".[9] Therefore, the situation seems less complicated than in most Central European regions with a similarly high degree of multiculturalism.

The reason for this, at least in part, can be found in Yugoslav minority legislation which is still in effect. It is the legislation which enabled the occasional development of inter-cultural practices, not only in Prekmurje but also in other parts of the former Yugoslavia, in Istria, the northern Adriatic coastal region, Vojvodina, Macedonia and, until the beginning of the 1980s, in Kosovo as well. The research in Prekmurje therefore supports the view that we can criti-

---

[8] At the end of the 15th and the beginning of the 16th century, after the decree of emperor Maximilian (1496), the Jews were expelled from all central Slovene regions (Carinthia, Styria and Carniola). Later we find Jews as a constituent part of economic and cultural life only at the border between Italy and Slovenia, in Trieste/Trst and less so in Gorizia/Gorica, and of course in Prekmurje. These two regions are today border regions in Slovenia, the former to the west and the latter to the east. Both are the most multicultural regions in the country.

[9] In Bibo´s view, linguistic nationalism was born out of the existential fear for the community and limited the Western European construction of nationality in that it produced a distinctly anti-democratic nationalism in which the liberation of the community was not connected to the liberation of the individual. — Furthermore, the from the West imported difficulty of living with difference was even worse due to the perception of being trapped between Western cultural imperialism and local attempts to revive pure and indigenous regional cultures which had their source in the "oriental treat" from the South or the Southeast. Here is a typical example of what Emmanuel Levinas would call "self-centred 'egology'", which on the one hand takes advantage of the narcissism of newborn or re-born nations and yet stems from the existential fear that sees henchmen, enemies and traitors on all sides – cf. István Bibo/Tibor Huszár/Jenő Szűcs: Regije evropske povijesti. Zagreb 1995.

cise the former communist regime in Yugoslavia for many things, but certainly not for improper treatment of minorities and nationalities. On the contrary, the ideology of post war Yugoslavia strongly emphasised the development of "brotherhood and unity" between all citizens of the People's Republic.

Discrete multiculturalism

This clearly democratic legal environment, and the improved school curricula, freed Prekmurjans (and our interviewees) from second thoughts about relationship between, Romany people and "civilians"[10]; the latter term being used by the Roma of Prekmurje for all non-members of the three *nests*. The term *nest* was used by a highly respected member of the Pušča community also called Gypsy prince. In an open interview he explained that the Prekmurje Roma each belong to one of three *nests* rooted in various groups coming to Prekmurje from Hungary.

Along with legal, constitutional and educational regulations[11], another essential contributor to an atmosphere of coexistence is the construction of local loyalties. As shown by the empirical results of the project, through the formation of a local identity in the post-war period, an inter-ethnic and inter-cultural alliance successfully took shape.[12] This demonstrates that in a distinctly multicultural

[10] To the question whether they think that some minority (religious, national, cultural, etc.) threatens the Slovene homogeneity, only 9.97 percent gave affirmative answers, which is about 80 percent less than the national average.

[11] Cf. the most recent Slovene primary school curricula that deals with the instruction of „ethics and society". This subject could round off public education and help lay the groundwork of an educational programme that could help pupils understand, apart from various issues of economy, also ideas such as democracy, pluralism, cooperation, cultural unity and diversity, conflicts and changes and migrations. This subject, also called "education for the culture of peace" is combined with intercultural and multicultural education and teaching against racism and xenophobia. In the development of curricula of such content, a significant alternation in the equality of education occurred. For example: the chapter title "Differences between people" was replaced in the final draft of a programme by "Communication" and "Generations and cultures – inter-personal communication." The chapter "Man and major religions of the world" was replaced by "Religion and belief", a title which does not discriminate against minor non-Christian religions – cf. Milan Divjak: Šola in človekove pravice: vzgoja in pouk za človekove pravice v osnovni šoli. Ljubljana 1998 (= Slovenija in Svet Evrope 4).

[12] I use the term inter-cultural/inter-culturalism rather than multiculturalism to stress the difference between the two. In my opinion, multiculturalism relates the idea that there is always a possibility for interaction between different cultures, whenever they are close to each other. The term inter-culturalism, on the other hand, also describes the possibility of the creation of new cultures which under certain conditions take shape when representatives of two or more cultures meet. I stand for such a redefinition of the concept "multiculturalism" which is not just a simple description of a given situation. Being opposed to its descriptive use, I am interested in the detection and analysis of those practices and procedures which discredit intercultural practices, most often from the perspective of great nationalist ideas.

environment the majority of differences, which is evident between the representatives of different cultures, can be surmounted by their instinct for self-preservation; the latter is subconsciously supported by a feeling of being equally treated, which in turn generates similarity. Their "other" is thus kept outside of themselves. To give a concrete example: people in Prekmurje say that under the former regime, everyone was equally privileged or unprivileged, while now there is a new state, which, "due to exaggerated centralisation, neglects this region". In this perception of self, more than 70 percent of those living in this north-eastern part of the country, feel that they are more hospitable, more open and more direct than their fellow citizens beyond the Mura River. It is interesting that the Romany people we spoke with also shared the opinion of the majority population. More than 70 percent of them believed that Prekmurje is the best place to live, at least in Slovenia. Furthermore, over 50 percent of the people in this region see themselves, first and foremost, as Prekmurjans and only then as Slovenes, Hungarians, Croats, etc. Therefore it is not surprising that for one third of this region's inhabitants, the border is not a state border but the border of their province.

Another main contributor to the establishment of multicultural coexistence is local solidarity. A good example was the referendum in the late 1970s, when the inhabitants of the region voted to finance jointly the basic medical care and kindergarten for the Roma settlement located just outside the province's capital.

One issue in providing this support, of course, was propelled by the ambition to keep the majority of Roma separate from other people living in the region. But most of the people who voted for the proposal were supporting the initiative for better housing and social care for the Roma. Nevertheless, in the 1960s and in the beginning of the 1970s, most Roma were still living in the suburban areas of Murska Sobota, the capital of the province, and in slightly removed hamlets on the village borders. And as in most Slovene regions, they were facing the problem of formal/legal regulation of their settlements. In the first place, this is an issue of ownership, since they have built their houses on land owned by the state or by the local farmers.

After the change

Three decades later the situation remained largely unchanged. The only things that changed were the attitude towards Roma living in the province's capital and the quality of housing. However, in Slovenia as a whole, things changed for the worse; even the president of Helsinki Monitor, Neva Miklavčič-Predan, identified discrimination against the Roma on the part of the state. In March 2000 she even spoke of "administrative ethnic cleansing" going on in Slovenia.

In her opinion, the Roma, who are the victims, face obliteration from the resident register.[13] On the other hand, there seems to be a great difference between the living conditions in Prekmurje and in all other Slovene regions. In the latter the situation is very much like the situation in Hungary, Romania or the Czech Republic. Children from Roma families who cannot speak Slovene are still segregated in schools, the unemployment rate among them is almost twice the average and there is almost no positive presence of them in the media.

Knowing all this, the Roma in Slovenia are more than ever aware that if they want to solve these and similar problems they should get better organised. They still see themselves as the most marginalized national community, either due to them being different and thus unaccepted by the wider social community, or due to their low self-esteem, self-respect and self-recognition.[14]

Communication between the representatives of the state and Roma communities outside Prekmurje lack common ground, or, to put it differently, one would like to see the message "get better organised" finally putting into practice the "best intentions of the government". As a matter of fact, in 1995 the Slovene government adopted a proposal put forward by an inter-departmental commission[15] which called for a programme of measures including suitable housing and regulated settlements, activities to provide employment and education, measures for the protection of children and families, improved possibilities for education and schooling of Roma children, cultivation of social awareness and information of the Roma, as well as assistance in self-organisation and participation in decision-making regarding the issues of their status within local communities and the state.[16] Yet Roma communities did not get much from these programmes. Therefore it is quite understandable that a year later (in 1996) a new report had to be prepared. And that in this revised document the authors had to acknowledge that a lot more had to be done in promoting co-operation between the state and local communities.[17]

And finally, the representatives of the state had to recognise that the results of various forms of training and employment of Roma have been scarce. Given the disparity in the communication of these two parties, one would prefer a little more than a simple pledge for more co-ordinated activities of the state and municipalities, and, of course, one would expect more opportunities for active

---

[13] Neva Miklavcic Predan, Report on Forms of Racial Discrimination of the Roma Population and other non-Slovenes in Slovenia, http://www.arnes.si/news/archive/soc.culture.slovenia/msg14141.html.

[14] Jožek Horvat: Položaj Romov v Sloveniji. In: V. Klopčič/M. Polzer (eds.), Poti za izboljšanje položaja Romov v srednji in vzhodni Evropi. Ljubljana 1999, p. 25.

[15] A special inter-department commission in which, apart from representatives of the Ministries and government services, representatives of municipalities and Roma associations also take part, was established by the Slovene government in the mid 1990s.

[16] Cf. Horvat, Položaj Romov v Sloveniji; Peter Winkler: Izkušnje Slovenije pri urejanju položaja Romov. In Klopčič/Polzer, Poti za izboljšanje, pp. 20-36.

[17] Simona Pilko: Sporen položaj Romov. *Dnevnik*, 12.10.2001, p. 25.

participation in the decision-making concerning their status in the Slovene society.[18]

This kind of situation, where the parties involved speak without hearing each other, will not help the situation; especially not now, when others speak more openly of Roma with racial prejudice. It would be too much to say that the old strategies of segregation of the Roma (generalisation and stereotyping) had turned into direct hate speech; they never in the last five decades faced open hatred – at least not in Prekmurje. It is also safe to say that what happened in Maline could have never happened in Prekmurje; not to speak of the beatings, killings, punitive police raids and house arrests that were typical for Meciar's Slovakia.[19]

On the other hand it is also clear that no one expects the "Roma problem" to be solved in the short run.

"The temptation to exist"[20]

The cultural changes in Slovenian Roma communities now are entering the phase which Ian Hancock would describe as *Sar laci and'ekh vadra* = "like-crabs-in-a-bucket"[21] – a situation in which not only educated Roma hinder instead of helping each other to get ahead. Indeed there is more than one representative speaking in the name of the Roma community of Prekmurje today. Two of the formal representatives are urban dwellers, one a member of the regional centre's city council, while almost every settlement has its own informal representative. It is needless to say that their stories differ in quite many ways. This was quite apparent at their latest appearance on POP-TV, the largest commercial television channel in Slovenia, in May 2003. Different representatives of the various Roma communities did not recognise the legitimacy of the others for representing their communities.[22]

On the other hand, this behaviour is to a great extent a consequence of the general attitude of the majority population to the Roma in Slovenia. Thus we hear increasingly the stereotypical opinion that since the Roma population cannot even agree among themselves, how are they going to reach agreement with others? Some still even speak of the need to civilise the Roma population. This latter point of view is fairly cynical, if not racist, considering the fact that sev-

---

[18] Winkler, Izkušnje Slovenije pri urejanju položaja Romov, p. 35.

[19] Steven Erlanger: The Gypsies of Slovakia: Depised and Despairing. *The New York Times*, 2.4.2000, p. A10.

[20] The subtitle is borrowed from Isabel Fonseca: Bury Me Standing. The Gypsies and Their Journey. New York 1995, pp. 278-305.

[21] Fonseca, Bury Me Standing, p. 304.

[22] Cf. the programme "Trenja", POP TV, 8.5.2003.

eral municipalities still refuse drinking water and other communal services to Roma communities. This is also reflected in the latest opinion poll – a featured part of the same television programme – according to which only 27 percent of Slovenes support the election of Roma representatives to the municipal councils in those municipalities that were designated "Roma municipalities" by the state.[23] The fact that the members of the National Assembly ten years ago passed a resolution, according to which these municipalities must also have a Roma councillor, while the local courts still tolerate the violation of that resolution, gives a clear picture of the actual treatment of the Roma community in Slovenia.

Of course there are a few shining exceptions and Prekmurje is among them.[24] People in Prekmurje have far less problems with the inclusion of Roma councillors in the municipal councils. This is in part also a consequence of the fact that the Prekmurje Roma were the first to found their own association, thereby forming the basis for later activity on a higher level. In addition, manipulation of the numbers of Roma citizens occurs less frequently in Prekmurje, and cynical remarks about how the Roma had never fought for the rights that are now given to them are far less frequent in Prekmurje than elsewhere in Slovenia. However it certainly has not yet happened in this province that the majority population would be ignorant of the Roma representatives from the EU, or that it would claim that the Roma do not need "false prophets".[25]

Going under cover

On the other hand, in the whole region enormous social changes have taken place, caused by changes in politics and the economy. The new situation, in which the Roma wanted to work, as there was no work to take on, forced them to (re)invent some new practices of "buying the sympathy of the majority". Their strategy is similar to the one used by the members of the Hungarian minority who emphasise tolerance[26], although they are more pragmatic in many

[23] These are the 20 municipalities that include Roma communities. Most of these are in Prekmurje and in the area south of Ljubljana.

[24] Roma settlements are usually established without legal permission, on both private and state lands. Since this repeatedly caused disputes between the owners and the settlers, the National Assembly passed a resolution in the 1990s dictating the legalisation of these settlements. Similarly to the resolution on Roma councillors, this resolution also met with great resistance and the status of the majority of these settlements has still not been resolved – cf. Horvat, Položaj Romov v Sloveniji, pp. 20-25.

[25] The remark about "false prophets" was made by an advocate of the position of the Nationalist Party of Slovenia during the above mentioned television programme "Trenja" on POP TV, 8.5.2003.

[26] According to interviews the Hungarians living in Slovenia are less opposed to mixed marriages than others. Their construction of relationship towards other groups is rather poetic ("love is

different ways. As they have done throughout their long history and whenever needed, they continue to change their names. In this way we can, in addition to the Roma who are hidden or invisible, differentiate an additional subgroup of Roma who decide to go "under cover". This is their "strategy" for establishing a connection with the core culture. Although this process involves a complicated procedure of changing personal documents, some Roma change their names several times during their lifetimes. It is not unusual for a person with the common Roma names "Šerkezi" or "Baranja" to alter their names to more typical Slovene ones. Even more common is to take the name of a minor local celebrity, someone who enjoys the respect of the "borrower" or who helped him or her in some way. Most new names are those of popular local officials, obstetricians, surgeons, other physicians from a local hospital. Another source of inspiration is the mediated popular culture, either names of fictional characters or famous performers. Among the names the Roma of Prekmurje have adopted are Doris (after the Croatian singer Doris Dragović), Manuela, Gloria or Mišel after characters from Brazilian, Columbian and Peruvian serials like "Esmeralda", "Vengeance is sweet", "After you will be mine" or "Undesirable".

Gender differences are unimportant and the "bricoleurs" imaginatively change the names of female and male celebrities for their own use. A male fan of Sophia Loren transformed Sophia to Slavko Loren. The names appropriated by the Roma population have varied over time, reflecting the changing celebrities produced by the global culture industry and locally distributed by the indigenous popular culture through which the stars´ images gain their symbolic meaning for the Roma "users".

The practice of renaming is connected with the relationship of the Roma to mainstream culture. While this practice may be influenced by traditional cosmology, it more likely arises from the historical genealogy of names in Roma culture. In the 17th century, when Roma in this region began using surnames, they borrowed most of them from surrounding objects or domesticated animals (*Kokaš* from *kokoš* = Chicken), and later from the region of their origin (*Baranja*, now in Croatia) or the ethnic groups among whom they lived (for example, the family name *Horvat*, i.e. Croat). In addition to names such as Baranja and Horvat, which are of "Croat origin", there are also surnames like *Cener* (*Zehner*, in German), which attest to Austrian or German origin. The assimilation practices of "urban" and "suburban" Roma, or "real" and "authentic" Roma, differ considerably. While the later, by using popular culture as the imaginative source, establish an imaginary relationship with the mainstream culture, the former use renaming as a means of individualisation. Contemporary urbanised Roma changed their names to stress their individuality. Adopting a new name enables them to re-identify, to emphasise a distinctive individ-

---

ignorant of borders", for example), and they use every opportunity to express their loyalty towards Slovenia.

ual identity different from collective Roma identity. Naming is a first step in the active construction of an identity of difference, and an example of both the resistance to marginalization within the generally welcoming "core" culture, and a manifestation of an entirely non-essentialist view of identity. Roma perspectives on identity are fluid. There is no "true" identity that would be fixed and persistent across time with an authentic source in "true" history.

On the other hand there are also some people who are considering changing their names back to their original ones. This is actually a very recent way of thinking more often found among the better educated and influential people. They hope that their roots will not be forgotten, showing in this way a high degree of emancipation on the one hand and a high degree of assimilation on the other; nevertheless, these so-called "White Gypsies" are relatively few. Even in multicultural Prekmurje, the partially invisible or hidden Romany people still dominate and although they have gained representation in city councils they now experience yet another form of exclusion. Sometimes it is the connection to the water supply, at other times something else that would be taken for granted by the majority population. In this regard we can still claim for the Prekmurje Roma that they daily experience their invisibility and therefore remain the best litmus test of civil society in the region. Generally, however, all of the examples enumerated once again simply confirm that the categorisation of otherness in this part of Europe has never been based merely on visible characteristics, but mostly on the search for the different within the same, the foreign within the domestic and the others among us.[27]

The opinion of the Slovene ombudsman Matjaž Hanžek is reliable in making an assessment of the situation in Slovenia: He maintains that the "Slovene character", essential for the majority of violations of human rights, can well be seen in attitudes towards the Roma. This is ignorance – and the keeping of the marginalized on the margins – meaning non-inclusion and "passive intolerance". I echo his call when he says that the state should have a "joint Roma policy for all of Slovenia" and that "responsibility should not be left to the local community". He is also correct in stating that in this way the state "incites conflict" and "only passes responsibility to the municipal organs". It is not enough just to find money for Roma projects; society must find means for their inclusion. However the great majority of Slovenes would rather not. They are indifferent to how the Roma live as long as it is not in their neighbourhood. They are prepared to give them a lot of money, "so long as they are alone, silent and out of the way". The Law on Romany Representatives is otherwise appropriate but still by far too small a "step towards the inclusion" of the Roma into Slovenian society.[28]

---

[27] Cf. Mirjam Milharčič-Hladnik: Sodobni evropski rasizem. *Ampak* 5 (2003), p. 50.

[28] All citations referring to the position of Matjaž Hanžek are taken from the interview "Ignoranca in prikrita nestrpnost = Ignorance and hidden intolerance" made by Jure Trampuž and published in the Slovenian Weekly: *Mladina* 63/20 (2003), pp. 34-37.

Bibliography:

BIBO, István/HUSZÀR, Tibor/SZŰCS, Jenő: Regije evropske povijesti. Zagreb 1995.

DIVJAK, Milan: Šola in človekove pravice: vzgoja in pouk za človekove pravice v osnovni šoli. Ljubljana 1998 (= Slovenija in Svet Evrope 4).

ERJAVEC, Karmen/HRVATIN, Sandra B./KELBL, Barbara: We About the Roma. Discriminatory Discourse in the Media in Slovenia. Ljubljana 2000.

ERLANGER, Steven: 'The Gypsies of Slovakia: Despised and Despairing', *The New York Times*, 3.4.2000, p. A10.

FONSECA, Isabel: Bury Me Standing. The Gypsies and their Journey. New York 1995.

GERLICH, Peter/GLASS, Krzysztof (eds.): Der schwierige Selbstfindungsprozess. Regionalismen, Nationalismen, Reidiologisierung. Vienna – Torun 1995.

GERLICH, Peter/GLASS, Krzysztof/KISS, Endre (eds.): Von der Mitte nach Europa und zurück. Vienna – Poznan 1997.

GLASS, Krzysztof/KRANJC, Janez/LUTHAR, Oto (eds.): Grenzlandidentitäten im Zeitalter der Eurointegration. Vienna – Poznan 1998.

GORDON, Avery F./NEWFIELD, Christopher (eds.): Mapping Multiculturalism. Minneapolis – London 1996.

HORVAT, Jožek: The Status of Roma in Slovenia. In: V. Klopčič/M. Polzer (eds.), Poti za izboljšanje položaja Romov v srednji in vzhodni Evropi, Ljubljana 1999, pp. 20-25.

JENKINS, Keith: Refiguring History. New thoughts on an old discipline. London – New York 2003.

JOHNSON, Lonnie R.: Central Europe. Enemies, Neighbours, Friends. New York – Oxford 1996.

JOHN, Michael/LUTHAR, Oto (eds.): Un-verständnis der Kulturen. Multikulturalismus in Mitteleuropa in historischer Perspektive. Klagenfurt/Celovec 1997.

KATUNARIĆ, Vjeran: Ohranjanje pluralne družbe v kulturnem pomenu. *Teorija in praksa* 30/7-8 (1993).

KLOPČIČ, Vera/POLZER, Miroslav (eds.): Poti za izboljšanje položaja Romov v srednji in vzhodni Evropi. Ljubljana 1999.

MILHARČIČ-HLADNIK, Mirjam: Sodobni evropski rasizem. *Ampak* 5 (2003), p. 50.

PILKO, Simona: Sporen položaj Romov. *Dnevnik*, 12.10.2001, p. 25.

MIKLAVČIČ-PREDAN, Neva: Report on Forms of Racial Discrimination of the Roma Population and other non-Slovenes in Slovenia, http://www.arnes.si/news/archive/soc.culture.slovenia/msg14141.html.

TANCER, Mladen: Vzgoja in izobraževanje Romov na Slovenskem. Maribor 1994.

TRAMPUŽ, Jure: Ignoranca in prikrita nestrpnost (Interview). *Mladina* 63/20 (2003), pp. 34-37.

WINKLER, Peter: Izkušnje Slovenije pri urejanju položaja Romov. In: V. Klopčič/M. Polzer (eds.), Poti za izboljšanje položaja Romov v srednji in vzhodni Evropi, Ljubljana 1999, pp. 20-36.

Language and Identity of the Serbs in Southern Slovenia[1]

Tanja Petrović

1. The Serbs of Bela Krajina as hidden minority

In the Southern Slovenian region of Bela Krajina, close to the border with Croatia, there are four villages – Bojanci, Milići, Marindol and Paunovići – inhabited by descendants of the *Uskoks*, renegade refugees from the Ottoman Empire. They settled down here in several waves of migration after 1526.[2] The three hundred inhabitants of these four villages represent the last remnants of a once much more numerous Orthodox population that came to this region, which in the 16th century formed part of the emerging Habsburg Military border against the Ottoman Empire. The overwhelming majority of the Uskok population in Bela Krajina have become Catholic Slovenes or Greek-Catholic Croats in the neighbouring region of Žumberak on the Croat side of the border.

In the above-mentioned four villages of Bela Krajina, however, the Serbian-speaking inhabitants have managed to preserve their native vernacular for more than five centuries, mainly because of very strict social rules inhibiting interaction with the surrounding Slovene-speaking, Catholic population. But the current situation indicates that a language shift[3] in its final phase is taking place: only the oldest generation of villagers has full competence in their native Serbian vernacular, the middle generation makes use of it occasionally, mainly in communication with their parents, while the youngest generation only has a passive knowledge of the Serbian language, i.e. the children in these villages understand their Serbian-speaking grandparents but almost always respond to them in Slovene. This type of language shift is usually termed *gradual language death* by linguists.[4] In a group of people speaking a different language from that one of the majority, the shift from the minority language to the ma-

---

[1] This chapter is part of the research project *Hidden Minorities between Central Europe and the Balkans (Versteckte Minderheiten zwischen Zentral- und Südosteuropa)*, funded by the Austrian Science Fund (FWF) (project No. P15080). It is based upon Tanja Petrović: Ne tu, ne tam: Srbi v Beli krajini in njihova jezikovna ideologija v procesu zamenjave jezika. Ljubljana 2006.

[2] Historical data on these migrations can be found in Josip Mal: Uskočke seobe i slovenske pokrajine. Ljubljana 1924 (= Srpski etnografski zbornik XXX).

[3] Language shift is usually defined as a gradual or a radical shift of an individual or group from one language to another – cf. David Crystal: Language death. Cambridge 2000, pp. 17, 23, 31.

[4] Lyle Campbell/Martha Muntzel: The Structural Consequences of Language Death. In: N. Dorian (ed.), Investigating Obsolescence. Studies in Language Contraction and Death. Cambridge 1989 (= Studies in the social and cultural foundation of language 7), pp. 184-185.

jority one usually happens within three generations.[5] In the case of Serbs in Bela Krajina, it is taking place right now, but it was preceded by almost five centuries of the native idiom's vitality. Reasons for the rapid decline of native language use have certainly to be sought in significant social changes in the wake of modernisation and industrialisation in the region in the period after the Second World War. They have led to relatively rapid changes in the way of life such as in increased mobility, inter-marriage and in several other phenomena. These changes, taken together, make Slovenian, from the viewpoint of the villagers, the language of prestige and a pre-requisite for progress and integration into the broader community of Bela Krajina on a regional and of Slovenia on a national level. The concurrent role of the native vernacular as a code of local solidarity was questioned, in particular with respect to the increasing number of mixed marriages (mainly with Slovene women) – the native vernacular lost its former privilege of being the only idiom spoken within the family.

The data presented in this paper results from fieldwork conducted in the period June 2001 – February 2002 in the four Orthodox villages through interviews, participant observation as well as in questionnaires. The main goal of the fieldwork was to obtain information about the social function of the Serbian vernacular and symbolic values attached to it as well as to observe language behaviour and strategies used by the inhabitants of the Orthodox villages concerned. I also investigated the status of the vernacular within a broader set of values and attitudes in the villages. Such a perspective can inform about the real nature of relations, values and processes resulting in language shift.[6] Combined with demographic and other "objective" data, information collected in the field provides a sound basis for determining the current sociolinguistic situation and future implications for this ethno-linguistic community.

2. The ethno-linguistic vitality of Serbs in Bela Krajina

The classic definition of *ethno-linguistic vitality* as determined by Giles, Bourhis & Taylor is "that which makes a group likely to behave as a distinctive

[5] Rudolf Filipović, Sociolingvistički uvjeti očuvanja konavaoskog dijalekta u Watsonvilleu (SAD). *Hrvatski dijalektološki zbornik* 7/1 (1985), p. 90; Marija Vučković: Govor Kajkavaca u Boki. Sociolingvistički aspekt. *Južnoslovenski filolog* 56/1-2 (2000), p. 263.

[6] The social anthropologist Robert G. Minnich, quoting Dell Hymes: Ethnography of Speaking. In: J.A. Fishman (ed.), Readings in the Sociology of Language. The Hague – Paris 1968, pp. 99-138, suggests that "language's role as a marker of collective self-ascriptions can be usefully investigated from the perspective of individual actors and the groups to which they belong. This drives attention to the context of communication" – Robert G. Minnich: Speaking Slovene – being Slovene. Verbal Codes and Collective Self-Images: Some Correlations between Kanalska dolina and Ziljska dolina. *Slovene Studies* 10/2 (1988), p. 126. This concept is being developed further within the theoretical framework of language ideology – cf. Kathryn A.Woolard/Bambi B. Schieffelin: Language Ideology. *Annual Review of Anthropology* 23 (1994), pp. 55-82.

and active collective identity in inter-group situations".[7] They name status, demography and institutional support as "the structural variables most likely to influence the vitality of ethno-linguistic groups". In the case of the Orthodox population in the above-mentioned four villages, these three factors are decisive for an assessment of the current sociolinguistic situation there. Apart from these "objective" parameters, it seems necessary to take into account the subjective perception of language vitality, i.e. how members of a given ethno-linguistic group perceive their situation, since "subjective assessment may be just as important in determining interethnic group behaviour".[8]

Patterns of language use in a multilingual setting and communicative strategies – such as code switching, code mixing and language accommodation based on collocutor and topic – are inevitably related to a broader frame of social relations and values; the description of the respective patterns and strategies can lead to an understanding of both linguistic and social processes that Serbs in Bela Krajina have undergone, both as individuals as well as a community.

2.1. Status

The inhabitants of the Orthodox villages in Bela Krajina claim that they were always treated equally by Slovene authorities and there were no differences between them and the Slovene population. Indeed, they do not differ from other local inhabitants in their economic and social status. This region has been among the poorest in Slovenia for decades, despite the Communist project of modernisation and industrialisation, which concentrated on the regional towns. This project, however peripheral it was in the Slovenian context, put its mark even on the Bela Krajina. The process of Communist modernisation resulted in a gradual shift away from agriculture as primary occupation and brought better living conditions, including the four Orthodox villages.

Traditional and immediate contacts of the inhabitants of Bela Krajina with the population of Croatia were strong. These contacts rested upon the fact that Bela Krajina had always been a traditional border region. Its Slovene population has always been in immediate contact with the population in neighbouring Croatia. These contacts also had a linguistic impact on the local Slovene dialect, which is characterised by a number of features borrowed from Serbo-Croatian dialects. Language differences in the region have never been a barrier for communication, and mutual intelligibility of all language varieties in Bela Krajina as

---

[7] Howard Giles/Richard Y. Bourhis/Donald M. Taylor: Towards a Theory of Language in Ethnic Group Relations, Language, Ethnicity and Inter-group Relations. London – New York – San Francisco 1977 (= European monographs in social psychology 13), pp. 307-348.

[8] Josiane Hamers/Michel Blanc: Bilinguality and Bilingualism. Cambridge – New York 1989, p. 163.

well as in the neighbouring Croatian regions eliminated any obstacle for everyday contacts. Such a multilingual context, on the other hand, makes linguistic resources available, which the inhabitants of Bela Krajina can consciously use to express values and attitudes; and this context is also decisive for the formation of the speakers' language ideology.

2.2. Demography

Demographic data obtained through census material can give a first insight into the process of how new identities among the Serbs in Bela Krajina were adopted, as well as the role language had in this process. Comparison of data obtained from censuses in the period 1880-1991[9] indicates that the only stable category was that of religion. Answers about spoken language and nationality vary significantly from census to census depending on social circumstances and power relations. That census data cannot be taken as a reliable indicator of colloquial language use may be illustrated by the fact that in the village of Bojanci, all 264 inhabitants declared themselves Orthodox in 1890, 258 of them stated that they spoke Serbian and 1 Slovenian. Ten years later all 220 inhabitants of the village were recorded as speakers of Slovenian, 219 of them as Orthodox and one as Catholic:

[9] Sources for the census data used in this article include: for the 1880 census – Spezial-Ortsrepertorium von Krain. Vienna 1884, p. 146; for the 1890 census – Spezial-Ortsrepertorium von Krain. 1890. Vienna 1894, pp. 140-141 (cited in Marija Hudelja: Etnološka topografija slovenskega etničnega ozemlja – 20. stoletje. Obkolpski del občine Črnomelj s poudarkom na interetničnih odnosih. Ljubljana 1982, manuscript); for the 1900 census – Gemeindelexicon von Krain. Bearbeitet auf Grund der Ergebnisse der Volkszählung vom 31. Dezember 1900. Vienna 1905; Popis žiteljstva od 31. prosinca 1900. Zagreb 1902; for the 1910 census – Spezial-Ortsrepertorium von Krain. Bearbeitet auf Grund der Volkszählung von 1910. Vienna 1919, p. 102; data for censuses in 1981 and 1991 were taken from Marko Terseglav: Uskoška pesemska dediščina Bele Krajine. Ljubljana 1996; data for the 2002 census were obtained from the official web site of the Statistical Office of the Republic of Slovenia: http://www.stat.si/popis2002/si/rezultati/. As for the last census, it was only possible to obtain the absolute number of inhabitants in the village since, according to a newly introduced Slovenian law, census data for categories such as language, religion and nationality can be provided only for municipalities – cf. Zakon o popisu prebivalstva, gospodinjstev i stanovanj v Republiki Sloveniji v letu 2002. *Uradni list Repbublike Slovenije* 66 (2000) and 26 (2001); Zakon o državni statistiki. *Uradni list Republike Slovenije* 45 (1995) and 09 (2001), as well as Zakon o varstvu osebnih podatkov. *Uradni list Republike Slovenije* (59) 1999.

Figure 1: Number of speakers of Serbian according to census data:

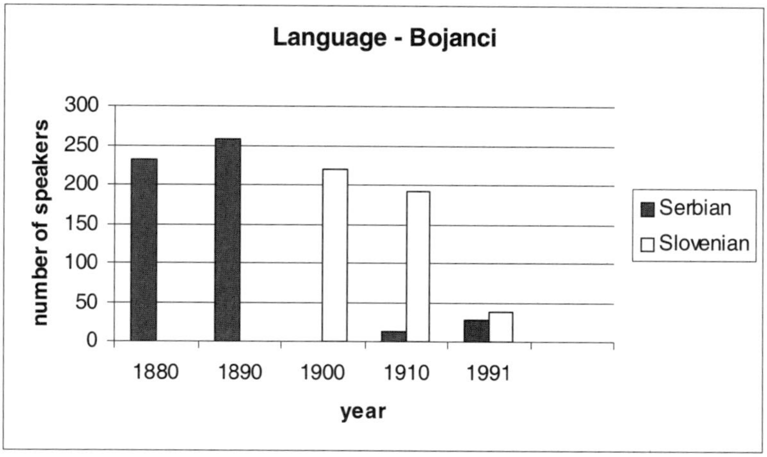

The fact that data obtained in censuses can vary so drastically within only ten years opens the essential question of their interpretation. With respect to similar phenomena, Nelde points out that "census statistics on individual linguistic behaviour demonstrate more about social identity then about the true language use of the informant".[10] The only statistical category that can be taken as true without reservation is the absolute number of inhabitants. In case of the four Serbian villages in Bela Krajina, this number decreases systematically:

Figure 2: Number of inhabitants according to census data:

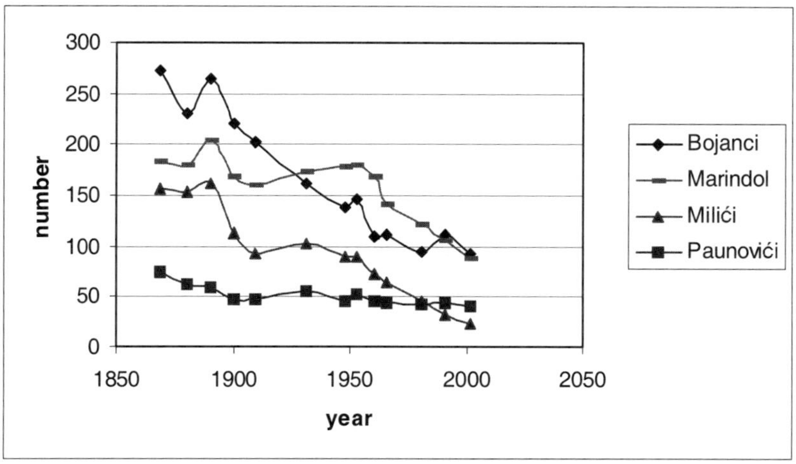

[10] Peter H. Nelde, Identity among Bilinguals: an Ecolinguistic Approach. *Estudios de Sociolingüística* 1/1 (2000), p. 43.

This incessant population decline has decisive effects on village identity. In conversation, in a more or less nostalgic way, they often stress the fact that there are more and more empty houses and less and less children in the villages. In such a context, they consider language shift as inevitable consequence of a general situation of depopulation concomitant with the adoption of new, modern ways of life, the abandonment of traditional customs and of the increasing disappearance of the village way of life.

2.2.1. Intermarriages

The Serbian community in Bela Krajina managed to retain its Orthodox identity for such a long time by not allowing intermarriages. They are situated close to Croatian regions settled by a mainly Orthodox population (Gorski Kotar, Lika) and marriage partners were found in these regions for centuries. This relationship was reinforced by the fact that the villages of Marindol, Milići and Paunovići were part of Croatia until the early 1950s. At that time however their inhabitants decided in a local referendum to join Slovenia. They deemed their economical gravitation towards Bela Krajina more important than their traditional contacts with the rest of Croatia from which they were separated by the river Kolpa, which was not spanned by bridges.

After the Second World War one could observe the increasing significance of the rather new phenomenon of Slovene-Serbian intermarriages. It seems that they occurred as an inevitable consequence of modernity and of Communist secularisation, which promoted civil marriage. With the industrialisation and de-agrarisation of the Bela Krajina during the first decades of Communist rule, an increasing mobility of the inhabitants of the four Serbian villages can be observed. This change occurred not only in the form of emigration, which was a constant of local demography since the beginning of the 20th century[11] but also in the form of urban labour migration. Today agriculture is no longer the main occupation of the middle generation anymore; its members are mainly commuters and work in nearby towns (Metlika, Črnomelj, Vinica), where they have intensive contacts with Slovenes and consequently use the Slovene language in everyday communication.

In the Orthodox villages, as in the surrounding Slovenian settlements, older people still remember the first mixed marriage, when a young man from Bojanci married a Slovenian girl from the neighbouring village of Tribuče. "It was a big sensation", to quote a Slovenian interviewee from the neighbouring village of Adlešiči. He also stressed that it was very strange in that time not be-

[11] A significant number of these villages' inhabitants emigrated to the United States in the first decades of the 20th century.

cause of bad relations between Slovenes and Serbs but “only because religions were different”.

Because of the social changes which took place in the second half of the 20th century, among the local Serbian population the common attitude towards Slovenian brides has changed: Marinka Dražumerič, who has researched the four villages, cites a teacher from Adlešiči – the neighbouring Slovenian village, where children from Marindol, Milići and Paunovići attend primary school – who mentioned that “pupils with non-Slovenian mothers have difficulties with the Slovenian language, especially with respect to grammar”.[12] Similarly, a woman from Paunovići told me: *When my* [Slovenian] *daughter-in-law checks the homework of her children written in Slovene, she always finds mistakes and says 'this is from the Paunovići way of speaking'.* In the current situation, therefore, having a Slovenian daughter-in-law is perceived as an advantage, while some decades ago, a son’s intention to take a Slovenian for a wife would have been met with strong opposition from his parents.

According to the musical ethnologist Marko Terseglav, only one of the 26 families in Bojanci can claim to be a “pure” Serbian family, in all other cases either a daughter- or a son-in-law is of Slovenian origin.[13] Data collected in the field shows that even in some Orthodox Church marriages in Marindol during the last decades the bride was Slovenian. In Bojanci the last church ritual was conducted immediately after the Second World War.

The emergence of intermarriages in the last fifty years is one of the most reliant indicators of the intensification of the peaceful absorption of the local Serbs by the surrounding Slovene majority. Along with Slovenian wives, the Slovene language made its way into the Serbian households of Bela Krajina. The native Serbian vernacular is about to lose its only domain of predominance, since Slovenian now is also becoming the means of communication among family members.

2.3. The Institutional Context

In Slovenia, Serbs are not officially recognised as a minority. According to the Slovenian constitution of 1991 (article 64), detailed rights are guaranteed to the autochthonous Italian and Hungarian minorities (and are envisaged for the autochthonous Roma population; article 65), regardless of the number of per-

[12] Marinka Dražumerič: Srbi v Beli krajini. In: I. Slavec-Gradišnik/T. Dolžan Eržen/B. Rogelj Škafar (eds.), Zgodovinske vzporednice slovenske in hrvaške etnologije 5. Ljubljana 1988 (= Knjižnica Glasnika Slovenskega etnološkega društva 18), p. 313.

[13] Cf. Terseglav, Uskoška pesemska tradicija, p. 29; Slovenian sons-in-law often live in the Orthodox villages together with the wife’s family in those cases when there is no male descendant in the family.

sons belonging to these minorities. These minorities also have the right of representation and participation (including a right to veto) both in local government bodies and in the parliament. These minorities also enjoy special rights in the field of education.[14]

The oldest inhabitants of the four villages were instructed in Serbian during primary school, since teachers were most often Serbs coming from Serbia speaking Ekavian.[15] But the local elementary schools of Bojanci and of Marindol were closed in 1954 and 1958 respectively because of the decreasing number of pupils and difficulties with finding Serbian teachers ready to come to this remote and poor area. Since that time, children have attended the Slovene primary schools in Vinica and Adlešići, where they at least had a reduced instruction in Serbo-Croatian; it was compulsory at all elementary schools in Slovenia within the Yugoslav context and lasted for one year. Instruction in Serbo-Croatian was abolished in 1992 with Slovenian independence, since this language lost all functions in public communication. New states and changes in borders usually imply the redistribution of social power and changes in the status relationships between languages in contact.[16] This was also the case in Bela Krajina. Today, Serbian children no longer have the opportunity to be instructed in Serbian; at home they only acquire the local dialect, mainly from their grandparents, not to speak of the Serbian standard language or the Cyrillic script.

In the course of the second half of the 20th century the Orthodox Church lost its integrative function due to Communist secularisation. Two Orthodox churches are still in use in the region – one is located in Bojanci, the other is to be found in Milići, while the villages of Marindol and Paunovići are affiliated to the parish of the latter. The Orthodox priests have not lived in the parishes for decades – the competent clergy are resident in neighbouring Croatia, in the monastery of Gomirje and in the village of Moravice some twenty kilometres away. These Serbian priests come only occasionally, i.e. for celebrating the most important religious holy days. The village of Bojanci still celebrates the local holiday of Đurđevdan (the day of St. George), while traditional family holy days celebrating the saint of a household (*slava*) have been widely abandoned.

---

[14] Zakon o posebnih pravicah italijanske in madžarske narodne skupnosti na področju vzgoje in izobraževanja. *Razprave in gradivo* 38/39 (2001), p. 399.

[15] Serbian and Croatian dialects are divided to Ekavian, Ijekavian and Ikavian according to reflex of the Old-Church-Slavonic (i.e. pre-Slavonic) vowel "jat" [ě]. Ekavian is mainly spoken in Serbia, Ijekavian is spoken in western Serbia, Montenegro, Bosnia, Herzegovina and part of Croatia, while the third variant, Ikavian, is predominantly spoken in the central and areas of the Croatian coast. The Serbs in Bela Krajina speak the Ijekavian variety of Serbo-Croatian – cf. Pavle Ivić: Iz srpskohrvatske dijalektologije. Izabrani ogledi III. Niš 1991, p. 270.

[16] Cf. Albina Nećak-Lük: Language Issues in Ethnic Studies. Research Approach in Some Slovenian Studies. In: O. Mišeska-Tomić/M. Radovanović (eds.), History and Perspectives of Language Study. Amsterdam – Philadelphia 2000 (= Amsterdam studies in the theory and history of linguistic science IV/186), p. 228.

Consequently, only few people attend the occasional church services; in Milići the attendance at church is slightly better.

The Serbian community in Bela Krajina can be considered a hidden minority in the sense that they want to remain "undercover" and try to avoid any exposure to public debates. As a matter of fact, they were a topic of intense discussion in the Slovenian public discourse in the late 1980s and early 1990s in reaction to a propaganda campaign by the Serbian press, which wanted to politicise their status in the aftermath of the Slovene declaration of independence.[17] But speakers of the four villages rejected a conciliatory initiative of Slovene institutions, which proposed to open a primary school with instruction in the Serbian language. An interviewee from Marindol, who otherwise insists on using the Serbian language within his family, explains the rejection of this initiative by saying: *If children were educated in Serbian, they would hardly find a job in Slovenia. That is why we decided to send them to a Slovenian school. The fact that my grandchildren have instruction in Slovene does not bother me, because they will learn Serbian at home.*

3. The "voice of the people": language vitality in the perception of the inhabitants of the four villages and their language ideology

As mentioned, status, demographic data and institutional support are "objective" parameters that help us to define the vitality of a locally used vernacular within linguistically different surroundings; this is valid in particular, if this vernacular forms an essential trait of a local ethno-linguistic community. In such cases it is, however, likewise important to take into account the subjective narrations and perceptions of the members of such a group, since – with respect to the "objective" parameters – "subjective assessment may be just as important in determining interethnic group behaviour".[18] It was the awareness of a possible rift between "objective" factors on the one hand, and subjective perceptions of speakers from an ethno-linguistic group on the other, that motivated linguists to introduce the concept of *perceived language vitality*.[19] The "objective" parameters, functioning as socio-structural factors, are translated in the individuals' cognitive representations, which on the group level may be in accordance or in variance with objective reality, thus it makes

[17] Cf. Christian Promitzer: "Gute Serben". Ethnologen und Politiker über die Identität der Serben in der slowenischen Bela krajina. In: U. Brunnbauer (ed.), Umstrittene Identitäten. Ethnizität und Nationalität in Südosteuropa. Frankfurt/M. et al. 2002, pp. 192-194.

[18] Hamers/Blanc, Bilinguality, p. 163.

[19] Cf. ibidem, p. 163.

sense to introduce the concept of *perceived* or *subjective vitality.*[20] This vitality determines individual and group speech behaviour and contributes to either maintenance of shift.[21]

The attention of the researching linguist is thus directed towards individual interpretations and attitudes of speakers of a given linguistic community. The narratives and perceptions of the autochthonous Serb population of Bela Krajina in my field research are an important source for identifying the status and destiny of the local idiom and the strategies of its speakers.

3.1. Language Attitudes and Linguistic Ideology

Linguistic anthropologists consider the evaluation of idioms and of concomitant attitudes towards the language of a given linguistic group, as well as its linguistic and ideological response to the language of the neighbouring linguistic groups, part of a larger concept which they describe as language ideology.[22] Such an approach focuses on "the ideas with which participants and observers frame their understanding of linguistic varieties and the differences among them, and map those understandings onto people, events, and activities that are significant to them".[23]

In the case of the Serbs of Bela Krajina the commonly shared attitude towards the native idiom can be formulated in the following way: *We speak that language, although it is not the real Serbian language, it is rather a mixture of Serbian and a dialect spoken in Croatia, in addition there are many Slovene words in our language...*

Such an attitude is often followed by a kind of self-deprecation[24], since in this case the Slovenian standard language is considered an ideal that can only be reached with difficulty. A Serbian interviewee explains: *My granddaughter says: "Children from Preloka and Zilje* [Slovene villages of Bela Krajina]

[20] Richard Y. Bourhis/Howard Giles/Doreen Rosenthal: Notes on the Construction of a "Subjective Vitality Questionnaire" for Ethnolinguistic Groups. *Journal of Multilingual and Multicultural Development* 2 (1981), pp. 145-155.

[21] Nećak-Lük, Language Issues, p. 224.

[22] Cf. Paul Kroskrity: Regimenting Languages: Language Ideological Perspectives. In: P. Kroskrity (ed.), Regimes of Language. Ideologies, Polities, and Identities. Santa Fe 2000, pp.1-34; Bambi B. Schieffelin/Kathryn A. Woolard/ Paul V. Kroskrity (eds.): Language Ideologies, Practice and Theory. New York – Oxford 1998; Stephanie Lindemann: Koreans, Chinese or Indians? Attitudes and Ideologies about Non-Native English Speakers in the United States. *Journal of Sociolinguistics* 7/3 (2003), pp. 348-364.

[23] Judith Irvine/Susan Gal: Language Ideology and Linguistic Differentiation. In: Kroskrity (ed.), Regimes of Language, p. 35.

[24] Cf. in general Lukas Tsitsipis: A Linguistic Anthropology of Praxis and Language Shift: Arvanítika (Albanian) and Greek in Contact. Oxford 1998.

speak the dialect of Bela Krajina, and those coming from Croatia speak Croatian, but I speak Slovene in the correct way". But I said to her that it is not easy at all to speak real Slovene.

Speaking "pure" or "correct" standard Slovene is perceived by all generations as one of the highest cultural values, and the correct use of this idiom is placed above all local language varieties. The native Serbian idiom is only perceived as a local means of communication and due to its spatially restricted use valued accordingly. In general, the inhabitants of the Orthodox villages in Bela Krajina call their native vernaculars simply "our way of speaking" (*po naše*), or after the village where it is spoken: "the Bojanci way of speaking", "the Milići way of speaking" (*po bojansko, po milićki*), etc. It is to be noted that such classifications of locally used native vernaculars are typical for the phenomenon of hidden minorities. In the same manner, emigrant Meglen Vlachs in Turkey, who originate from the Greek village of Nânti, designate their language as *nântineşti*. And those still living in Meglen (Greece) also name their language using the same model of local affiliation: *oşineşti* (Oşań/Archángelos), *umineşti* (Uma/Huma), *cupineşti* (Kupa/Cúpa), etc.[25] The social anthropologist Robert Gary Minnich notes for the Slovene speaking communities in Italian Val Canale, situated close to the borders of Slovenia and Austria, that "elderly residents of Ukve/Ugovizza [one of the Slovene speaking villages] consistently claim that the language they have learned at home is neither Slovenian, Austrian nor Italian, but 'our language' (*naše narečje*)".[26] These examples fortify the conclusion that locally and relatively grounded language variety nominations characteristic of small ethnic groups make direct reference to the fact that these varieties function within the local frames only and are valued accordingly; the language of the nation state, which is simultaneously a means of public communication, is the only language which "deserves" to be designated more universally – in the case of the Bela Krajina Serbs this is the Slovenian language.

Such a strong opposition between the idealised "pure" Slovene and "spoiled", "degenerated" native idiom as described by its speakers, differs sharply from the idealised image advanced by the Slovenian anthropologist Niko Županič (1876-1961), who was a strong supporter of the Yugoslav idea and took active political stance in the SHS Kingdom.[27] Since Slovenia as a whole seemed to lack "Balkan features" like the rest of Yugoslavia, Županič was very glad to have found some of these features in Bela Krajina: "[...] from an ethnographic point of view, Bela Krajina represents small Yugoslavia" and "the Western

---

[25] Cf. Thede Kahl: Zur Islamisierung der meglenitischen Vlachen (Meglenorumänen): Das Dorf Nânti (Nótia) und die "Nântinets" in der heutigen Türkei. *Zeitschrift für Balkanologie* 38/1-2 (2002), p. 33.
[26] Minnich, Speaking Slovene, p. 126.
[27] Christian Promitzer: Niko Županič kot slovenski etnolog. Njegovo ravnateljevanje v Etnografskem muzeju v Ljubljani (1923-1940). *Etnolog* 13 (2003), p. 146.

Balkans given in miniature".[28] Already in 1912, in a monograph dedicated to Serbs in Bela Krajina, Županič had written that "any inhabitant of Bela Krajina already on his threshold gets in touch with all South-Slavic tribes except the Bulgarians".[29] "People from Marindol and Bojanci", writes Županič in the same place, "are the only Carniolian Serbs who have preserved their beautiful old Ijekavian language, costumes, customs as well as Orthodox religion".[30] At the end of 1960s, the Serbian ethnographer Filipović could not share the same enraptured admiration for the purity of the language and the vitality of the Serbian people in Bela Krajina. He notes strong Slovenian influences in the vernaculars of the four villages and the traditional culture of the Bela Krajina Serbs, predicting that this small ethnic group will disappear within the next few decades.[31]

The lack of reverence for their native vernacular may have to do with the fact that no intellectual elite developed among the Serbs in Bela Krajina, which would have been in a position to act as an advocate and promoter of the Serbian language and of the traditional Orthodox belief. As can be seen in various other examples, in the course of the appearance of such advocates, ideally in the form of teachers or priests who are able to enjoy response among the local population, an ethno-linguistic group may manifest itself as a national minority vis-à-vis the national and linguistic community they are living among, all the more so if such a group has economically or ideologically significant contact with its respective nation of reference – in this case the Serbian one. With respect to the admittedly Serbian inhabitants of the four villages of Bela Krajina this has hardly been the case.[32]

The only potential national elite would have been the Orthodox priests from neighbouring Croatia who treated the population of the four villages as a kind of Serbian "Diaspora". But this clerical and in its intention maybe even national treatment of the existing population did not end in the formation of a cohesive and self-conscious Serbian community interested in the rights considered usual for the survival of a national minority. This may have been because the priests were not from this region, or because they were concerned primarily with the fate of the Serbian community in Croatia, which was likewise a "Diaspora". Finally, also the Yugoslav context between 1918 and 1991 and the exis-

---

[28] Niko Županič in an official report about his fieldwork in Bela Krajina on 2 April 1930 – cited in Promitzer, Niko Županič kot slovenski etnolog, p. 161.
[29] Niko Županić: Žumberčani i Marindolci. Prilog antropologiji i etnografiji Srba u Kranjskoj. Beograd 1912, p. 16.
[30] Ibidem, pp. 9–10.
[31] Cf. Milenko Filipović: Srpska naselja u Beloj krajini (u Sloveniji). In: *Radovi Akademije nauka i umjetnosti Bosne i Herzegovine* 35/*Odjeljenje društvenih nauka* 12 (1970), p. 148.
[32] Ethnologists like the Slovene Niko Županič and the Serb Milenko Filipović could not act in such a way; and the would-be advocates for Serbian autonomy in the late 1980s were certainly only pretending to be interested in the real issues of these four villages – cf. Promitzer, "Gute Serben", pp. 193-195.

tence of linguistic environment, which was likewise South Slavic, alleviated the need for such initiatives.

In the case of the Serbs of Bela Krajina we have to take into consideration the absence of a quantitative relevant critical mass of people necessary to form a cohesive national minority. Nevertheless, the existing population is large enough that we cannot ignore them simply as irrelevant fragments of nation building among Slovenes, Croats and Serbs, but have to treat them within the context of hidden minorities. On the other hand, as is the case with other hidden minorities, among the inhabitants of the four villages we can also observe the fact that the (Slovene) majority language is considered the exclusive code of power and progress and the highest values are attached to it.

3.2. Language Behaviour

The oldest generation of Serbs in Bela Krajina appears to be linguistically most adaptable; its members are equally competent in Serbian and Slovene dialects – with Slovenes they use the Slovene dialect of Bela Krajina; among themselves they use their native Serbian vernacular. With their sons and daughters they are used to speaking both Serbian and Slovene. In communication with the youngest generation, e.g. with their grandsons and granddaughters, they also speak both vernaculars, but they are always responded to in Slovene. Already Terseglav and Dražumerić identified this phenomenon, saying that "fieldwork research showed that Serbs in Bela Krajina are linguistically extraordinarily adaptive: with a Slovenian from their region they speak his Slovene dialect, with a Slovenian from Carniola they would speak a colloquial variety of Slovene, while with a Croat they would speak Croatian".[33]

The oldest Orthodox inhabitants of Bela Krajina are in fact the only ones who possess a full, native-like competence both in the Serbian idiom and the local Slovene dialect. The language behaviour of the older generation shows how deeply rooted the process of language shift in this ethno-linguistic community already is. Accommodation to collocutors and topics has left its mark on their language strategies, which are characterised by willingness to code-switch immediately: If a collocutor or even one person within a group of collocutors is Slovenian, they immediately switch from their native vernacular to Slovene. In such cases the first utterance is usually doubled – initially it is stated in Serbian, and then repeated in Slovene: *Vi zajedno radite?* <Serbian> *Delate skupaj?* <Slovene> [*Are you working together?*]; similarly, a sentence will be also repeated in Slovene in communication with grandchildren – in case the

[33] Marko Terseglav/Marinka Dražumerič: Prispevek k preučevanju Srbov v Beli krajini. *Traditiones* 16 (1987), p. 211.

latter did not clearly understand an utterance in Serbian: *To su vještice.* <Serbian> *Coprnice* <Slovene> [*These are witches*].

Code mixing even within one utterance, on the other hand, is a language strategy typical for inhabitants belonging to the middle generation: in utterances produced by them, one can find elements of one language transferred into the other – as a rule, they use Slovene elements when speaking Serbian: *stare vodnjake* <Slovene> *su* <Serbian> *iskali* <Slovene> [*They sought old wells*]; *nič* <Slovene> *mu ja ne pomažem, tu sam ga zaposlila* <Serbian> *da mora delati* <Slovene>. [*I for myself do not help him; I have employed him there, so that he must work*]

The youngest inhabitants speak Slovene even if spoken to in Serbian; they would answer in Serbian only if they are just encouraged to do so, or explicitly asked by the phrase: *What is the word for that in our language?* This shows that they still posses a passive knowledge of Serbian, but seldom use it in everyday communication.

The Slovenian language, being an official means of communication in the country and connected with administration, media (radio and television) and power relations, is connected symbolically with the progress and modernisation that have left their mark on the region in the last decades. The symbolic link between the Slovene language social change has also left its traces in language use: even the members of the old generation, despite their basic competence in Serbian, use Slovenian expressions for most phenomena outside the domain of traditional village life: *Onda je dala opština crkvu pod kulturnu dediščinu* <Slovene> [*Thereafter the community declared the church a cultural heritage*]; *Ona je socijalna delavka* <Slovene> *sa hiljadu đaka* [*She is a social worker with a thousand wards*]; *Mladi imadu avte* <Slovene> [*The young ones had cars*]; *dva študenta <Slovene> iz Maribora* [*two students from Maribor*]. Consequently, pensioner meetings in Bojanci are held in Slovenian, despite the fact that the majority of the attendees are not native in that language – Slovene, however, is perceived as an official means of communication and it is the idiom used in official situations. The increased mobility of the population after the Second World War and the enhanced everyday interactions with Slovenes have contributed to the general principle that different values are attributed to the native idiom and the Slovenian language. A growing number of Slovene words are incorporated into Serbian discourse. Since programmes broadcasted by the Serbian television are still available in Bela Krajina, the members of the local Serbian population could theoretically expand their local use of Serbian with modern vocabularies. But since the social relations in which communication about these expressions takes place are exclusively connected with the Slovenian context and the use of the Slovenian language, vocabularies imported from the standard Serbian language would simply appear unmotivated, artificial and unnecessary.

4. The linguistic identity of hidden minorities – research perspectives

The autochthonous Serbs of Bela Krajina are a small community without its own elite. Apart from priests form the Serbian Orthodox Church in neighbouring Croatia who provide religious services, but are little concerned with the survival of the community as such, there are no external (i.e. Serbian) factors available to them which would be interested in the survival of the cultural traits of these four villages. Since the Serbs of Bela Krajina did not develop an intellectual elite of their own, they can be considered a hidden minority. This is all the more so because they have no desire to be supported and "(re)discovered" by would-be advocates of their imagined "national issue". In the contrary, none of them would say that such an issue is on the agenda, even if the old generation mourns the loss of tradition.

The research of hidden minorities is closely linked with the perception of their linguistic extirpation. Historical processes such as assimilation with the majority population and language shift seem to be linear and always predictable. There are many factors, however, that must be taken into account when dealing with the issues of ethnic identity; hidden minorities are only one example. They can show us in an intensified way, how the opposition between the urbanising forces of modernity on the one hand and traditional economic factors and local identity strategies, be they ethnically and linguistically different or not, on the other, develops historically.

And the study of hidden minorities can furthermore teach us something about the use of sociolinguistic and ethno-linguistic approaches for the study of small ethnic groups insofar as they provide an essential contribution to the research of possible strategies for identity building since, as is stressed by Bickel, "language provides essential resources for acting-out life styles, it provides a crucial means for establishing social identities".[34]

Based on these considerations, several research maxims for future research can be formulated:

1. Discourse-oriented studies of the languages of small ethnic groups that consider patterns of language use and connect them with social structures and processes can open new perspectives in the study of language-related identity strategies, emphasising anthropological aspects of language shift and offering a key for the understanding of this process as seen from the intrinsic perspective of the speakers. The exploration of dialectic relations between social practice and forms of talk could also add new perspectives, if the focus is on multilin-

[34] Baltasar Bickel: Grammar and Social Practice: On the Role of Culture in Linguistic Relativity. Essen 1998 (= Working paper in preparation for the LAUD Symposium 425), p. 16.

gual communities or single ethnic groups undergoing language shifts. The nostalgia trap could thus be avoided.[35]

2. Such a criticism is also valid for the discourse of the *pastoral tradition* in which "a rhetorical convention prevails, which continually looks back, often nostalgically and for moral guidance, to a lost but supposedly more pristine, rural, homogeneous, and authentic past".[36] Here researchers looked for the "*best speakers*, who [would] provide evidence of the most 'unadulterated' form of the language"[37], while processes of innovation were only rarely noticed and usually seen as a degeneration of an authentic language.

3. In recent studies of idioms spoken by members of small ethnic groups, notable efforts have been made to go beyond description and to relate linguistic and cultural features of minorities with the identity strategies they adopt. There is an emerging consensus that "what people think or take for granted, about language and communication is a topic that rewards investigation".[38] Language ideology, which is broadly defined as "sets of beliefs about language articulated by users as a rationalization or justification of perceived language structure and use",[39] can serve as "a mediating link between social structures and forms of talk".[40]

Bibliography

BICKEL, Baltasar: Grammar and Social Practice: On the Role of Culture in Linguistic Relativity. Essen 1998 (= Working paper in preparation for the LAUD Symposium 425).

BOURHIS, Richard Y./GILES, Howard/ROSENTHAL, Doreen: Notes on the Construction of a "Subjective Vitality Questionnaire" for Ethnolinguistic Groups. *Journal of Multilingual and Multicultural Development* 2 (1981), pp. 145-155.

BUCHOLTZ, Mary: Sociolinguistic Nostalgia and the Authentication of Identity. *Journal of Sociolinguistics* 7/3 (2003), pp. 398-416.

[35] For more on nostalgia in sociolinguistics, anthropology and related disciplines cf. M. Bucholtz: Sociolinguistic Nostalgia and the Authentication of Identity. *Journal of Sociolinguistics* 7/3 (2003), pp. 398-416.

[36] Raymond Williams: The Country and the City. New York 1973.

[37] Nancy Dorian: Language and Death: The life cycle of a Scottish Gaelic dialect. Philadelphia 1981, p. 3.

[38] Woolard/Schieffelin, Language Ideology, p. 53.

[39] Michael Silvestrein: Language Structure and Linguistic Ideology. In: P. R. Clyne/W. Hanks/C. Hofbauer (eds.), The Elements: A Parasession on Linguistic Units and Levels. Chicago 1979, p. 193.

[40] Woolard and Schieffelin, Language Ideology, p. 53.

CAMPBELL, Lyle/MUNTZEL, Martha: The Structural Consequences of Language Death, In: N. Dorian (ed.), Investigating Obsolescence. Studies in Language Contraction and Death. Cambridge 1989 (= Studies in the social and cultural foundation of language 7), pp. 181-196.

CRYSTAL, David: Language death. Cambridge 2000.

DORIAN, Nancy: Language and Death: The life cycle of a Scottish Gaelic dialect. Philadelphia 1981.

DRAŽUMERIČ, Marinka: Srbi v Beli krajini. In: I. Slavec-Gradišnik/T. Dolžan Eržen/B. Rogelj Škafar (eds.), Zgodovinske vzporednice slovenske in hrvaške etnologije 5. Ljubljana 1988 (= Knjižnica Glasnika Slovenskega etnološkega društva 18), pp. 302-317.

FILIPOVIĆ, Milenko: Srpska naselja u Beloj krajini (u Sloveniji). In: *Radovi Akademije nauka i umjetnosti Bosne i Herzegovine* 35/*Odjeljenje društvenih nauka* 12 (1970), pp. 147-237.

FILIPOVIĆ, Rudolf: Sociolingvistički uvjeti očuvanja konavoskog dijalekta u Watsonvilleu (SAD). *Hrvatski dijalektološki zbornik* 7/1 (1985), pp. 89-97.

GEMEINDELEXKIKON VON KRAIN. Bearbeitet auf Grund der Ergebnisse der Volkszählung vom 31. Dezember 1900, Vienna 1905.

GILES, Howard/BOURHIS, Richard Y./TAYLOR, Donald M.: Towards a Theory of Language in Ethnic Group Relations. In: H. Giles (ed.), Language, Ethnicity and Inter-group Relations. London – New York – San Francisco 1977 (= European monographs in social psychology 13), pp. 307-348.

HAMERS, Josiane F./BLANC, Michel H. A.: Bilinguality and Bilingualism. Cambridge – New York 1989.

HUDELJA, Marija: Etnološka topografija slovenskega etničnega ozemlja – 20. stoletje. Obkolpski del občine Črnomelj s poudarkom na interetničnih odnosih. Ljubljana 1982 (manuscript).

HYMES, Dell: Ethnography of Speaking. In: J.A. Fishman (ed.), Readings in the Sociology of Language. The Hague – Paris 1968, pp. 99-138

IRVINE, Judith/GAL, Susan: Language Ideology and Linguistic Differentiation. In: P. V. Kroskrity (ed.), Regimes of Language: Ideologies, Politics, and Identities. Santa Fe 2000, pp. 35-83.

IVIĆ, Pavle: Iz srpskohrvatske dijalektologije. Izabrani ogledi III. Niš 1991.

KAHL, Thede: Zur Islamisierung der meglenitischen Vlachen (Meglenorumänen): Das Dorf Nânti (Nótia) und die "Nântinets" in der heutigen Türkei. *Zeitschrift für Balkanologie* 38/1-2 (2002), pp. 31-55.

KROSKRITY, Paul: Regimenting Languages: Language Ideological Perspectives. In: P. Kroskrity (ed.), Regimes of Language. Ideologies, Polities, and Identities. Santa Fe 2000, pp. 1-34.

LINDEMANN, Stephanie: Koreans, Chinese or Indians? Attitudes and Ideologies about Non-Native English Speakers in the United States, *Journal of Sociolinguistics* 7/3 (2003), pp. 348-364.

MAL, Josip: Uskočke seobe i slovenske pokrajine. Ljubljana 1924 (= Srpski etnografski zbornik 30/Naselja i poreklo stanovništva 18).

MINNICH, Robert G.: Speaking Slovene – being Slovene. Verbal Codes and Collective Self-Images: Some Correlations between Kanalska dolina and Ziljska dolina. *Slovene Studies* 10/2 (1988), pp. 125-147.

NEĆAK-LÜK, Albina: Language Issues in Ethnic Studies. Research Approach in Some Slovenian Studies. In: O. Mišeska-Tomić/M. Radovanović (eds.), History and Perspectives of Language Study. Amsterdam – Philadelphia 2000 (= Amsterdam studies in the theory and history of linguistic science IV/186), pp. 217-234.

NELDE, Peter H.: Identity among Bilinguals: an Ecolinguistic Approach. *Estudios de Sociolingüística* 1/1 (2000), pp. 41-46.

PETROVIĆ, Tanja: Ne tu, ne tam: Srbi v Beli krajini in njihova jezikovna ideologija v procesu zamenjave jezika. Ljubljana 2006.

POPIS žiteljstva od 31. prosinca 1900. Zagreb 1902.

PROMITZER, Christian: "Gute Serben". Ethnologen und Politiker über die Identität der Serben in der slowenischen Bela krajina. In: U. Brunnbauer (ed.), Umstrittene Identitäten. Ethnizität und Nationalität in Südosteuropa. Frankfurt/M. et al. 2002, pp. 173-199.

PROMITZER, Christian: Niko Županič kot slovenski etnolog. Njegovo ravnateljevanje v Etnografskem muzeju v Ljubljani (1923-1940). *Etnolog* 13 (2003), pp. 287-347.

SCHIEFFELIN, Bambi B./WOOLARD, Kathryn A./KROSKRITY, Paul V. (eds.): Language Ideologies: Practice and Theory. New York – Oxford 1998 (= Oxford Studies in Anthropological Linguistics 16).

SILVESTREIN, Michael: Language Structure and Linguistic Ideology. In: P. R. Clyne/W. Hanks/C. Hofbauer (eds.), The Elements: A Parasession on Linguistic Units and Levels. Chicago 1979, pp. 219-259.

SPEZIAL-ORTSREPERTORIUM VON KRAIN. Vienna 1884.

SPEZIAL-ORTSREPERTORIUM VON KRAIN. 1890. Vienna 1894.

SPEZIAL-ORTSREPERTORIUM VON KRAIN. Bearbeitet auf Grund der Volkszählung von 1910. Vienna 1919.

TERSEGLAV, Marko: Uskoška pesemska dediščina Bele Krajine. Ljubljana 1996.

TERSEGLAV, Marko/DRAŽUMERIĆ, Marinka: Prispevek k preučevanju Srbov v Beli krajini. *Traditiones* 16 (1987), pp. 205-246.

TSITSIPIS, Lukas: A Linguistic Anthropology of Praxis and Language Shift: Arvanítika (Albanian) and Greek in Contact. Oxford 1998.

VUČKOVIĆ, Marija: Govor Kajkavaca u Boki. Sociolingvistički aspect. *Južnoslovenski filolog* 56/1-2 (2000), pp. 261-271.

WILLIAMS, Raymond: The Country and the City. New York 1973.

WOOLARD, Kathryn A./Bambi B. SCHIEFFELIN: Language Ideology. *Annual Review of Anthropology* 23 (1994), pp. 55-82.

ZAKON O POSEBNIH PRAVICAH ITALIJANSKE IN MADŽARSKE NARODNE SKUPNOSTI NA PODROČJU VZGOJE IN IZOBRAŽEVANJA. *Razprave in gradivo* 38/39 (2001), pp. 399-402.

ŽUPANIĆ, Niko: Žumberčani i Marindolci. Prilog antropologiji i etnografiji Srba u Kranjskoj. Beograd 1912.

The Catholic Serbs – a "Hidden Minority" on the Adriatic Coast[1]

Ivica Šarac

The phenomenon of Catholic Serbs is considered in scientific discourse a deviation from the so-called "religious 'rule'".[2] The latter is associated with the assumption that religious affiliation was a decisive factor in the formation of the modern Croat and Serb nations: while the Croat nation is connected with Catholicism, the Serb nation is associated with Orthodoxy. To investigate the genesis and the contemporary existence of the *Catholic Serbs* in the area of Dubrovnik, where this atypical phenomenon – due to specific historical developments and the location of this city – is most pronounced, can contribute to a more thorough understanding of nation building among Croats and Serbs.

In order to understand the genesis of Catholic Serbs as a distinguishable group, it is necessary to give an introduction into the socio-political framework within which they came into being. Thereafter it will be possible to spotlight the main period of their socio-political engagement and their public activities. Finally, it will be necessary to deal with the present situation and the possible survival of such a unique confessional/national group.

The linguistic and confessional setting

The specific geographic position of Croats and Serbs in the Balkans, their provincial fragmentation, the overlapping of eastern and western religious, cultural and political influences, the reign of foreign rulers and often unfavourable economic development has with the time bred in both nations an aspiration to territorial integrity and to overcome provincial and spiritual fragmentation. Among the Croats such considerations can be traced back (among some influential individuals) as early as to the Renaissance.[3] However, only with the formation of intellectual circles, whose participants no longer came exclusively from the ranks of the clergy and who had been educated in Western European universities, integrative concepts of Western European origin were also dis-

[1]This paper is part of FWF-Project P 15080 "Hidden Minorities between Central Europe and the Balkans", financed by the Austrian Science Fundation FWF.

[2] Ivo Banac: Vjersko pravilo i dubrovačka iznimka: Geneza dubrovačkog kruga Srba katolika. *Dubrovnik* 1/1-2 (1990), p. 179.

[3] Cf. Ivo Banac: The national question in Yugoslavia. Origins, History, Politics. Fourth printing: Ithaca – London 1988, pp. 70-75.

cussed among South Slavic Catholics.[4] Under the influence of Herder's ideas[5], Pan-Slavism with its notions of Slavic interconnectedness and linguistic and ethnic unity spread. Integrative aspirations could be also found in the constitutional struggle fought by intellectuals of the Kingdom of Croatia against aggressive Hungarian hegemony in the 19th century.[6] These were manifested in the Illyrian Movement[7]; its antique and artificial name was intended to overcome Croatian provincial differences and contrasts and gather other South Slavs in a cultural unity. These plans, when put into political practice, had a double consequence: it accelerated Croatian national integration while at the same time cultivating the idea of the ethnic unity of South Slavs, especially of Croats and Serbs, an idea which was later pursued under the term Yugoslavism.[8]

The "religious rule" was at the time of the Illyrian Movement more or less neglected for the sake of linguistic unity, but it was just this confessional question, which was pushing the Serbs away from the Illyrian Movement[9], since a national consciousness was already beginning to take shape among the Orthodox population in Dalmatia on the basis of religion. According to Stjepan Ćosić[10], this weak response to the Illyrian Movement among Orthodox Christians became especially manifest in the city of Dubrovnik; the small local Orthodox community[11] feared that the Illyrian Movement might intend to unite

---

[4] On the formation of the intelligentsia in the South-Eastern Europe cf. Srećko M. Džaja: Intelligentsia und Südosteuropäischer Raum. In: E. v. Erdmann-Pandžić (ed.), Regiones paeninsulae balcanicae et proximi orientis. Festschrift für Basilius S. Pandžić. Bamberg 1988, pp. 132-174.

[5] Holm Sundhaussen: Der Einfluß der Herderschen Ideen auf die Nationsbildung bei den Völkern der Habsburger Monarchie. Munich 1973.

[6] Nikša Stančić: Hrvatska nacija i nacionalizam u 19. i 20. stoljeću. Zagreb 2002, pp. 157-196.

[7] For the Illyrian Movement cf. Jaroslav Šidak et al.: Hrvatski narodni preporod – ilirski pokret. Zagreb 1990; Wolf Dietrich Behschnitt: Nationalismus bei Serben und Kroaten 1830-1914. Analyse und Typologie der nationalen Ideologie. Munich 1980 (= Südosteuropäische Arbeiten 74), pp. 133-161.

[8] Petar Korunić: Jugoslavizam i federalizam u hrvatskom nacionalnom preporodu 1835-1875. Studije o političkoj teoriji i ideologiji. Zagreb 1989; for Dalmatia at the time of the Illyrian Movement cf. Konrad Clewing: Staatlichkeit und nationale Identitätsbildung: Dalmatien in Vormärz und Revolution. Munich 2001 (= Südosteuropäische Arbeiten 109).

[9] Cf. Ilija Mamuzić: Ilirizam i Srbi. *Rad JAZU*, 247, 1933, pp. 68-88.

[10] Stjepan Ćosić: Dubrovnik nakon pada Republike (1808-1848). Dubrovnik 1999, p. 325.

[11] The number of ethnic Serbs in the Republic of Dubrovnik was permanently small. The reason can be found in Dubrovnik's religious exclusivism – the citizens of Dubrovnik (Catholics) did not allow the settling of the Ortodox. In 1808, under the French rule, on the whole territory of the former republic the number of Ortodox citizens numbered 68 men and 40 women; cf. Banac, Vjersko pravilo, pp. 184-185, note 15. – With the fall of the Dubrovnik Republic, religious exclusivism disappeared as well Ortodox Serbs were given the opportunity to settle in the city undisturbed. In 1857, 1 percent of the population was Orthodox, by the end of the 20th century (1991) their number would rise to 7 percent – cf. Stjepan Krivošić: Stanovništvo Dubrovnika i demografske promjene u prošlosti. Dubrovnik 1990, p. 70; Popis stanovništva 1991. Narodnosni sastav stanovništva po naseljima. Zagreb 1992, p. 80; for the size of the Serbian population in Dalmatia in the 19th century cf. Vladimir Stipetić/Nenad Vekarić: Povijesna demografija

the two confessions by means of language. Since they lived in an almost exclusively Catholic city, which for centuries (until the end of the Republic of Dubrovnik in 1809) had been intolerant towards the Orthodox population, such a stance is understandable.

The language model, however, also contributed to the process of national integration among the Serbs. By choosing the Štokavian dialect[12] for the Serbian standard language, Vuk Stefanović Karadžić initiated a theory which implied a broader national integralism, which integrated a large part of the non-Serbian ethnic body and gradually became a political programme.[13] By identifying all speakers of Štokavian as Serbs, Karadžić laid the foundations for a modern political perception of who could be a Serb, since his concept abandoned confessional restrictions for the first time and was open towards religious pluralism.[14]

Reasons for the emergence of the Catholic Serbs

At that time, the linguistic and political situations in the territories that would later become Croatia were quite confusing and fragmented. The young Serbian state, which had just been created in a victorious uprising, supported actively the dissemination of Karadžić's ideas. Štokavian was spoken in Dubrovnik too and a local group of Catholic intellectuals accepted Karadžić's linguistic concept. It should be pointed out that Dubrovnik in many respects was a specific area compared to other parts of Croatia. It had a century old history as an independent city state; after the fall of the Republic, it was marginalised economically, which was quite a new situation for its residents, who were characterised by a distinctly anti-Austrian attitude.[15] The inhabitants of the surrounding regions, who felt themselves oppressed, undoubtedly admired the Principality of Serbia as it gradually freed himself from Ottoman rule and asserted itself more and more as factor in the Western Balkans. The example of Serbia and especially Karadžić's language model need thus to be considered principal influ-

---

Hrvatske. Zagreb – Dubrovnik 2004 (= HAZU: Posebna izdanja, serija: Prilozi povijesti stanovništva Dubrovnika i okolice 11), p. 94.

[12] The štokavian dialect receives its name through the interrogative pronoun "što" (what); it is spoken in the greater part of Croatia, through-out all of Bosna and Herzegovina, Montenegro and the greater part of Serbia. This dialect is spoken by Croatians, Serbians, Montenegrins and Bosniaks (Bosnian Muslims).

[13] This was not an original idea. Karadžić only adopted an incorrect opinion held by early Slavists (August Ludwig von Schlözer, Jernej Kopitar, Jan Kollár, Josef Dobrovsky, Pavel Josef Šafárik) who mantained that the štokavian dialect was exclusively Serbian – cf. Banac, The national question, pp. 80-81.

[14] For Karadžić's national ideology and reactions to it cf. Behschnitt, Nationalismus bei Serben und Kroaten, pp. 65-82.

[15] Cf. Ćosić, Dubrovnik nakon pada Republike.

ences in the formation of the Catholic Serb community of Dubrovnik. It should be emphasised, however, that only intellectual circles took over the concept of being Catholic Serbs. According to Ivo Banac, the impulse for the emergence of this phenomenon came from "outside"; it started asserting itself only when somebody from the Catholic intellectual circles in Dubrovnik (i.e. "inside") accepted and adopted the idea.[16] In this respect the genesis of the phenomenon could be characterised as a political construct of which every important detail can be reconstructed *a posteriori*.[17] The progenitors of this new political direction, Medo Pucić (Orsatto Pozza 1821-1882) and Matija Ban (1818-1903), elaborated their standpoints as early as in the 1840s, in their attempt to align their Catholic tradition in Dubrovnik with the Serbian national and political context which they believed to belong to. However, it must be emphasised that Pucić and Ban, despite their choice of Serbian nationality, did not reject the ideas of the Illyrian Movement and they were not completely opposed to the term Illyrian.[18] They differed from Karadžić, whose national ideology they otherwise accepted, in this sense. Both Pucić and Ban worked in their own distinctive ways[19] in promoting Slavic mutuality and Serbian-Croatian cooperation.

Visible resistance to Karadžić's thesis developed in the emerging Croatian political scene. It was dominated by Ante Starčević's Croatian national exclusivism.[20] In order to grasp the phenomenon of Catholic Serbs, it is further necessary to emphasise that in the Croatian case the various parts of the population entered the processes of national integration in different ways. In the political life of Dalmatia and Dubrovnik during the second half of the 19th century, a motley variety of understandings and definitions of the Croatian nation became manifest, and several different national ideologies, concepts and political programmes were formed. But in spite of different points of departure and of the many variants of the Croatian national ideology, their principle ob-

---

16 According to Banac, the first Orthodox parish priest in Dubrovnik, Đorđe (Georgije) Nikolajević (1807-1896), born in Jazak in the County of Srijem, belonged to the most zealous missionaries of Serb nationalism in Dubrovnik and Dalmatia – cf. Banac, Vjersko pravilo, pp. 184-185, note 15.

17 Cf. Banac, Vjersko pravilo, p. 180.

18 Stjepan Ćosić: Nacija u stranačkim ideologijama: primjer Dubrovnika krajem 19. stoljeća. In: H.G. Fleck/I. Graovac (eds.), Dijalog povjesničara-istoričara. Pečuj 12.-14. maja 2000. Zagreb 2001, p. 58.

19 For the activities of these two figures and their motives in adopting Serbian nationality cf. Banac, Vjersko pravilo, pp. 188-189; Banac describes Matija Ban, who worked as a Serbian agent, as an opportunist without considerable political accomplishments – cf. Banac, Vjersko pravilo, p. 189. Medo Pucić, a descendant of a noble family, is described as a devout Catholic and an adherent of Italian romantic nationalism with which he came in contact as a law student at the University of Padua. He became friend of Jan Kollár, who was in Venice at that time, and probably learnt about the ideas of Šafárik and maybe even of Karadžić on the linguistic relationship of the South Slavs – cf. Banac, 'Vjersko pravilo i dubrovačka iznimka', p. 188.

20 Cf. Behschnitt, Nationalismus bei Serben und Kroaten, pp. 172-186; Mirjana Gross: Izvorno pravaštvo. Ideologija, agitacija, pokret. Zagreb 2000.

jective was more or less common: national integration and emancipation. The political subordination of the underdeveloped civic society to national aims prevented, however, that during this process a so-called civic nation – based on a community of equal citizens – was created; the Croatian national ideology, however, was rather developing willy-nilly in the direction of ethno-nationalism, which imagines the nation primarily as an ethnic/linguistic collective.[21]

Culmination and aftermath

Two exclusivist national ideologies clashed in Dubrovnik; needless to say that in terms of numbers this was quite an unequal struggle. This was not only a consequence of the fact that the majority of the population in the town considered themselves Croats; Dubrovnik could not become Serbian since it had never belonged to a Serbian Orthodox cultural environment. An ethno-nationalist approach based on Vuk's linguistic Serbianism, could only win over a small number of followers who became Catholic Serbs. They would nevertheless play an important political role at the end of the 19th century at which time they would abandon their ideas of mutuality which until then had been an integral editorial element in their journal "Slovinac".[22] Instead, they would adopt overt anti-Croatism, accepting the Serbian national idea thoroughly. There are two main reasons for this complete turnaround in their way of thinking. The first was due to the Austrian-Hungarian occupation of Bosnia and Herzegovina.[23] The second was the split in the National Party, which until that time had rallied the Croats and Serbs of Dalmatia, but was now confronted with the establishment of the independent Serbian Party of Dalmatia (1879). With time, the intellectuals among the Serbian Catholics of Dubrovnik became members of this party. In coalition with the pro-Italian Party, the so-called Autonomists, they came to rule in Dubrovnik in 1890.[24] At the same time these

---

[21] Cf. Ćosić, Nacija u stranačkim ideologijama, p. 54.

[22] "Slovinac" was established in 1878 in Dubrovnik and promoted the building of good relations between Serbians and Croatians. The founders of the journal thought that a non-national name (Slovinac = Slavic), as opposed to national designations of Croatian or Serbian provenience, would most effectively contribute to harmony – cf. Ivo Perić: Dubrovačka periodika 1848-1918. Dubrovnik 1980, pp. 26-28.

[23] Cf. Banac, Vjersko pravilo, p. 210.

[24] This needs to be seen in the context of a struggle for power in Dubrovnik in 1890 between two political groups: the first consisted of Croatian-orientated politicians (The National Party) who were for the unification of all Croatian territories; the second was a coalition of a smaller groups of pro-Italian (Autonomists) and pro-Serbian politicians (The Serbian Party), which was against the unification of Croatian territories and generally against Croatian political influence in the region – cf. Trpimir Macan: Susreti s hrvatskom Kliom. Povijesne rasprave i članci. Zagreb 1991, p. 295.

intellectuals began to play an increasingly important role in the leadership of the Party.[25]

For nine years (1890-1899) the Catholic Serbs formed part of the government of the municipality of Dubrovnik.[26] But their coalition with the Autonomists was apparently interpreted as directed against South Slavic mutuality and contributed to a loss of credibility. They also became alienated from the national ideology and policy of the vast majority of Dalmatian Serbs as a result of their neglect of the religious component of Orthodoxy; for mainstream Serbians, ethno-national differentiation by way of the ethnic/confessional model became predominant in these years.[27] In the struggle for the leadership of the Serbian Party in Dalmatia, the Catholic Serbs of Dubrovnik were severely opposed by the Orthodox Church hierarchy, headed by the distinguished Dalmatian Orthodox bishop, Nikodim Milaš, who played a key role in the social and political life in Dalmatia. His suspicion might be explained through the fear of the Serbian Orthodox hierarchy in Dalmatia that the Catholic Serb movement might hide an aspiration for Uniatism or even proselytising intentions of the Vatican.[28]

Decisive for the political collapse of the Catholic Serbs of Dubrovnik in the 1899 municipal election and their withdrawal from the political scene were the activities of the Party-of-Right leader Frano Supilo.[29] He was editor of "Crvena Hrvatska" ("Red Croatia")[30], a political weekly which – free from Starčević's exclusivism and romanticism – propagated an appealing political programme for the realisation of a Croatian nation state. He was anxious to define "Croatian national consciousness" as a civic-based form of identity, but his concept nonetheless leaned upon the Croatian ethnicity of the general population of Dubrovnik, where a collective identity had already been defined to some extent. The national integration process in this region had already largely been determined by the confessional model, i.e. by the so-called "religious rule". With the exception of the intellectual group of Catholic Serbs, the major part of

---

[25] Cf. Vlaho Benković: Dubrovački Srbi-katolici i novi kurs u hrvatskoj politici 1903.-1905. *Dubrovnik* 1/1-2, 1990, p. 211 f.

[26] For the political and cultural activities of the Serb-Catholics of Dubrovnik at the end of the nineteenth century cf. Lidija Jelić: O jednom zanimljivom nalazu u biblioteci SANU ili Jedno moguće čitanje plakata. In: www.bib.sanu.ac.yu/ciril/Plakat.htm

[27] Cf. Ćosić, Nacija u stranačkim ideologijama, p. 55 ff.

[28] In his somewhat biased and oversimplified critique of Catholicism, Milaš maintained that it was impossible to co-operate with Catholics. Milaš cites Dubrovnik and its inhabitants as particular examples of Catholic intolerancy against Serbian Orthodox believers – cf. Nikodim Milaš: Pravoslavna Dalmacija. Novi Sad 1901, p. 212.

[29] On the political and cultural activities of Frano Supilo in Dubrovnik cf. Ivo Perić: Dubrovačko radzoblje političkog djelovanja Frana Supila. *Anali Zavoda za povijesne znanosti Istraživačkog centra JAZU u Dubrovniku* XVII (1979), pp. 503-659.

[30] The weekly journal "Crvena Hrvatska" (Red Croatia) first appeared on 7 February, 1891. The last issue went to print on the 25 June, 1914 – cf. Perić, Dubrovačka periodika, pp. 17-18; for more information on "Crvena Hrvatska" cf. Perić, Dubrovačko radzoblje, pp. 545-561.

the Catholic rural and urban population in the region of Dubrovnik was already deeply involved in the process of Croatian national integration.

The public activity of individual Catholic Serbs did not, of course, end with the loss of their political influence. On the contrary, in the further development of the Croat-Serb relations, i.e. with the strengthening and realisation of the idea of Yugoslavism and aspirations for a common state, they would find consolation for their failed attempt to establish themselves as a distinct group. It has not been examined sufficiently, if and in how far they were informally engaged politically in the period of the first Yugoslavia. There are some unverified indications that the Serb-Catholics of Dubrovnik occupied important political positions at that time – and maintained their anti-Croatian sentiments and the idea of a Greater Serbia.[31] There are some elderly people of Dubrovnik who maintain, on the contrary, that Catholic Serbs were much more religiously than politically involved in this period.[32] The lack of archival and other written sources makes it impossible to reconstruct the role and position of the Catholic Serbs since the unification of 1918. The only available written sources coming from their own ranks fail to give any relevant data on their positions and activities at that time; these focus on Croat-Serb-relations. In 1938 Lujo Bakotić, a Catholic Serb himself, makes only brief reference at the end of his work *Serb People in Dalmatia from the Fall of Venice to the Unification* to the existence of Catholic Serbs and the enumeration of distinguished (historical) individuals from this group. Bakotić writes:

The Serbs of Catholic faith are a specific Dalmatian phenomenon. There used to be and there still is a Catholic Serb in Bosnia and Herzegovina here and there, but they are rare. Here in Dalmatia they are fairly large in number. They are mostly intellectuals but there are also workers and peasants among them. They are everywhere in Dalmatia [...] but most of them are in Dubrovnik and its surroundings.[33]

All the authors who deal with the Catholic Serbs agree that they disappeared as a cohesive group in the interwar period.[34] After the radical anti-Serb period of the so-called "Independent State of Croatia", the second, Socialist Yugoslavia did not offer a favourable climate for such small ethnic groups either. In the case of the Catholic Serbs, neither their national nor their confessional identification was opportune. All in all, one gets the impression that the Catholic Serbs, as an ephemeral historical phenomenon, melted away together with

[31] Cf. Franko Mirošević: Srbo-katolici u Dubrovniku. *Časopis za suvremenu povijest* 24/1 (1992), pp. 203-212.
[32] According to information obtained in fieldwork carried out by the author.
[33] Lujo Bakotić: Srpski narod u Dalmaciji od pada Mletačke Republike do ujedinjenja. Beograd 1938, pp. 182-183.
[34] Cf. Banac, Vjersko pravilo, p. 210; according to authors like Stipetić and Vekarić this idea completely disappeared during the reign of the first Yugoslavia, especially after the murder of Stjepan Radić (1928) and the sixth of January dictatorship (1929) – cf. Stipetić/Vekarić, Povijesna demografija Hrvatske, p. 96.

Yugoslavist mergers and Croat-Serb divisions. The phenomenon generally continued to exist only in scientific and pseudoscientific discourses, which were basically reduced to the analysis of the genesis and of the political activities of the Catholic Serbs at the turn of the 20th century. Polemic debates on this group, if they were conducted at all, mostly concerned its total number or formed part of over politicised and ideologised Croat-Serb historical disputes on the national affiliation of Dubrovnik.[35]

Experiences from fieldwork

Initial fieldwork in Dubrovnik seemed to show that the phenomenon of Catholic Serbs was only a transient historical episode, more unknown than known by informants; they are no longer present in the memory of the middle and younger generations; it was even unknown that they had once formed an integral part of the history of the city. Needless to say, that conducting fieldwork implied all kinds of embarrassment, since after the war of 1991-1995, people have become suspicious of enquiries that may question the Croat origin of the local population. My wish to meet descendants of formerly distinguished Catholic-Serb families was met with seemingly insurmountable obstacles. Many families were extinct or had moved away long ago; the descendants of some families who remained unanimously left the impression of amazement at my questions.

I found myself quite accidentally in the hinterland of Dubrovnik, in a rural area called Župa Dubrovačka when during conversation with elderly individuals from the local area, discrete hints were made, which clearly supported the conclusion that traces of a marginalised "hidden minority" of Catholic Serbs still existed. Contacts with representatives of this group were made possible only by way of a promise of full discretion. The data obtained has been restricted to some general assessments.

According to these individuals, it is true that a few Catholic families with suppressed "Serbian" identities exist in the hinterland of Dubrovnik. Those who meet these criteria belong to the middle and older generation. Even though the Dubrovnik intellectual circles did not propagate the idea of Serbianism among Catholics in the hinterland of Dubrovnik in the 19th century, being primarily

[35] This subject entered, first indirectly and later directly, rather ideological disputes initiated by some Serbian authors with the intention of proving the "Dubrovnik Serbianity" through denial of the Croatian character of the literary and historical heritage of Dubrovnik. This biased approach has recently been supported by Kosta Milutinović: O pokretu Srba katolika u Dalmaciji, Dubrovniku i Boki kotorskoj 1848-1914. In: Zbornik o Srbima u Hrvatskoj. Beograd 1989, pp. 33-90; Nikola Tolja: Dubrovački časopis Srđ 1902-1908. In: *Dubrovnik* 29/5-6 (1989), pp. 131-144; and most recently Svetozar Borak: Srbi katolici. Novi Sad 1998.

interested in the youth of Dubrovnik, remnants of the Serbian Catholic political identity may be found among the people in the surrounding area of Dubrovnik. Since members of these families are not intellectuals – they are mechanics, waiters and cooks –, one must pose the question of how they came to adopt such an identity. The answer seems to lie in the fact that the nobles and intellectuals from the city of Dubrovnik owned properties in the hinterland. It is possible that those who worked on these properties or even had family ties with the owners came into contact with their ideas, which, once adopted, were consequently passed down through family tradition from one generation to another. More than likely it is this internal family circle that is responsible for preserving this almost unknown and marginal identity.

This identity manifested today in hidden codes: in the elections after 1990 they have not voted for parties, which stressed Croatdom. Only rarely were they actively involved in the recent war, taking sides with one of the warring parties; those joined Montenegrin and Serb military units.[36] Today they are not on excessively bad terms with their Croat neighbours, but some of them think it convenient to stress their Croatian identity; under these circumstances it is not surprising that the changing of names into more Croatian sounding ones was practised.

I was also told of an incident – during the census-taking in 1990 – in which a person declared himself a Catholic Serb. The census taker, who was not personally familiar with this phenomenon, took it for some kind of humorous political provocation. From the point of view of the older Croatian population in the region of Dubrovnik, such individuals would today be regarded as descendants of traitors and opportunists, ready to play the part of a Trojan horse in a possible Croat-Serb conflict.[37]

Epilogue

A distinguished historian from Dubrovnik warned me that my thesis about the existence of a "hidden minority" of Catholic Serbs in Dubrovnik would be an exaggeration since we are dealing here with a barely perceptible group of people who are active neither socially or politically. His warning was intended more as a reference to the fact that being a Catholic Serb would be more a matter of a subjective or psychological attitude, a kind of unarticulated and

[36] Local inhabitants reported similarly that during the Second World War two members from such families joined the Chetniks.

[37] An elderly woman from Dubrovnik whispered to me in the City Cafe: "You know there are Catholics in the City who breathe Serbian." Both breathing and whispering are, of course, indicative of a social reality, which does not only include the recent tragedy of war, but also the identity practices of the families and persons concerned.

undefined individual feeling than a collective identity. He was correct in the sense that Catholic Serbs are an extremely atypical and marginal phenomenon in the nation building of Croats and Serbs, but the genesis of the Catholic Serbs can be clearly traced back to the early 19th century; and can be characterised as a product of the ideo-political orientation of a certain group of intellectuals of that period.

The question is, whether a politically motivated orientation, an act, which is certainly of a subjective nature and a conscious decision, can create a separate identity. The history of the Catholic Serbs seems to be connected with the idea of Yugoslavism; there are many similarities between these two phenomena. Both are atypical for the process of Croatian-Serbian national differentiation. Both phenomena negate the mainstream of Serbian or Croatian perceptions of collective (national) identities as "eternal" categories. Both phenomena emerged in specific socio-political contexts as a product of personal choice and/or the thinking of a particular political and intellectual group. Both are marked by instability and weakness of identity due to their lack of a firm "material base" (for example they are "not very rooted in any solid ethnicity").[38]

It seems to me, however unimportant it might be, that there is however a difference between the phenomena of "Catholic Serbs" and later "Yugoslavs". The first group, no matter how small it is today, emerged in the very process of the formation of modern Croat and Serb nations. Although this group is primarily composed of a specific, intellectual social stratum, it *existed* as a definite identity (from the 19th century until the beginning of 20th century),

---

[38] The example of Cvijeto Job, one of Tito's diplomats, whose ancestors came to Dubrovnik from Udine, Italy and pronounced themselves as Roman Catholic Serbs from Dubrovnik can illustrate this argument. The family tradition of these intellectuals cultivated sympathy for Serbian national history. The diversity of social-political frameworks of the twentieth century negatively affected the identity of Serb-Catholicism and manifested its lack of firm base. While Cvijeto Job's father Nikola declared himself a Serb-Catholic to the Ustashe during the Second World War, later, in a different socio-political context in Zagreb, he considered himself a Croatian. Toward the end of his life he experienced complete "disillusionment and disgust with the whole nationality thing" and declared himself "a 'Tanganyikan'". Cvijeto speaks of his own experince: "I had spent my childhood in Belgrade, steeped in the family's strong tradition of Yugoslav patriotism mixed with empathy of the Serbs and Serbian history. Subsequently, after having lived for some years in Dalmatia, and returning to Šibenik and coming to Zagreb after my almost three-year stretch in Tito's Partisan Army, fighting mostly along the Adriatic coast – I, a nineteen-year-old war veteran, denoted myself as a Croat. Why? Trying now to reconstruct the clarities and fogs of those *tempi passati*, I think I thought that, first, my family's early Roman Catholic Serbian allegiance, while an inspired choice, was not very much rooted in any solid ethnicity. Then, spending my most formative political and guerilla years in Dalmatia, I felt it would be somehow more logical to consider myself a Croat. Anyway, it was not a very big deal then. We were all brothers, you see. Finally, I settled on the following definition or description of my personal 'ethnic' identity: a Dalmatian from Dubrovnik, a Belgrader, a Croat – and therefore a Yugoslav. But such a personal stance increasingly flew in the face of stark and hostile new realities, especially in the 1990s, after Yugoslavia's hate-filled collapse" – Cvijeto Job: Yugoslavia's Ruin. The Bloody Lessons of Nationalism, A Patriot's Warning. Lanham et al. 2002, pp. 4-5.

while Yugoslavism[39], although historically colossal in its realisation, remained a political idea in the minds of its addressees.

Bibliography

BAKOTIĆ, Lujo: Srpski narod u Dalmaciji od pada Mletačke Republike do ujedinjenja. Beograd 1938.

BANAC, Ivo: The national question in Yugoslavia. Origins, History, Politics. Fourth printing: Ithaca – London 1988.

BANAC, Ivo: Vjersko pravilo i dubrovačka iznimka: Geneza dubrovačkog kruga Srba katolika. *Dubrovnik* 1/1-2 (1990), pp. 179-210.

BEHSCHNITT, Wolf Dietrich: Nationalismus bei Serben und Kroaten 1830-1914. Analyse und Typologie der nationalen Ideologie. Munich 1980 (= Südosteuropaische Arbeiten 74), pp. 133-161.

BENKOVIĆ, Vlaho: Dubrovački Srbi-katolici i novi kurs u hrvatskoj politici 1903.-1905. *Dubrovnik* 1/1-2, 1990, pp. 211-232.

BORAK, Svetozar: Srbi katolici. Novi Sad 1998.

CLEWING, Konrad: Staatlichkeit und nationale Identitätsbildung: Dalmatien in Vormärz und Revolution. Munich 2001 (= Südosteuropäische Arbeiten 109).

ĆOSIĆ, Stjepan: Dubrovnik nakon pada Republike (1808-1848). Dubrovnik 1999.

ĆOSIĆ, Stjepan: Nacija u stranačkim ideologijama: primjer Dubrovnika krajem 19. stoljeća. In: H.G. Fleck/I. Graovac (ed.), Dijalog povjesničara-istoričara. Pečuj 12.-14. maja 2000. Zagreb 2001, pp. 51-66.

DŽAJA M., Srećko: Intelligentsia und Südosteuropäischer Raum. In: E. v. Erdmann-Pandžić (ed.), Regiones paeninsulae balcanicae et proximi orientis. Festschrift für Basilius S. Pandžić. Bamberg 1988, pp. 132-174.

GROSS, Mirjana: Izvorno pravaštvo. Ideologija, agitacija, pokret. Zagreb 2000.

JELIĆ, Lidija: O jednom zanimljivom nalazu u biblioteci SANU ili Jedno moguće čitanje plakata. In: www.bib.sanu.ac.yu/ciril/Plakat.htm.

JOB, Cvijeto: Yugoslavia's Ruin. The Bloody Lessons of Nationalism, A Patriot's Warning. Lanham-Boulder-New York-Oxford 2002.

[39]According to Konrad Clewing, Yugoslavism, which had its beginnings in the Illyrian Movement, lost much of its popularity already in the wake of the 1848 revolutions. Clewing asserts that "in terms of linguistic consciousness and more generally on the level of pre-national ethnic identity, there existed [...] no positive predisposition toward South Slavic nation building" – Clewing, Staatlichkeit und nationale Identitätsbildung, p. 364.

KORUNIĆ, Petar: Jugoslavizam i federalizam u hrvatskom nacionalnom preporodu 1835-1875. Studije o političkoj teoriji i ideologiji. Zagreb 1989.

KRIVOŠIĆ, Stjepan: Stanovništvo Dubrovnika i demografske promjene u prošlosti. Dubrovnik 1990.

MACAN, Trpimir: Susreti s hrvatskom Kliom. Povijesne rasprave i članci. Zagreb 1991.

MAMUZIĆ, Ilija: Ilirizam i Srbi. *Rad JAZU*, 247, 1933, pp. 68-88.

MILAŠ, Nikodim: Pravoslavna Dalmacija. Novi Sad 1901.

MILUTINOVIĆ, Kosta: O pokretu Srba katolika u Dalmaciji, Dubrovniku i Boki kotorskoj 1848-1914. In: Zbornik o Srbima u Hrvatskoj. Beograd 1989, pp. 33-90.

MIROŠEVIĆ, Franko: Srbo-katolici u Dubrovniku. *Časopis za suvremenu povijest* 24/1, (1992), pp. 203-212.

PERIĆ, Ivo: Dubrovačka periodika 1848-1918. Dubrovnik 1980, pp. 17-28.

PERIĆ, Ivo: Dubrovačko radzoblje političkog djelovanja Frana Supila. *Anali Zavoda za povijesne znanosti Istraživačkog centra JAZU u Dubrovniku* XVII (1979), pp. 503-659.

POPIS stanovništva 1991. Narodnosni sastav stanovništva po naseljima. Zagreb 1992.

ŠIDAK, Jaroslav et al.: Hrvatski narodni preporod – ilirski pokret. Zagreb 1990.

STANČIĆ, Nikša: Hrvatska nacija i nacionalizam u 19. i 20. stoljeću. Zagreb 2002.

STIPETIĆ, Vladimir/VEKARIĆ, Nenad: Povijesna demografija Hrvatske. Zagreb-Dubrovnik 2004 (HAZU: Posebna izdanja, serija: Prilozi povijesti stanovništva Dubrovnika i okolice 11).

SUNDHAUSSEN, Holm: Der Einfluß der Herderschen Ideen auf die Nationsbildung bei den Völkern der Habsburger Monarchie. Munich 1973.

TOLJA, Nikola: Dubrovački časopis Srđ 1902-1908. *Dubrovnik* 5-6 (1989), pp. 131-144.

Being "Hidden" within a Minority. The Adoption of Bulgarians into the Ethnic Group of Serbs in Hungary[1]

Biljana Sikimić

Serbs in Hungary

The majority of Serbs in Hungary live scattered in the south, in the region of Baranya, in the south-east, around the river Moris[2] and in the environs of Budapest. Historians estimate that the migrations of Serbs to the territory of today's Hungary occurred in the period from the beginning of the 15th until the end of the 17th century[3]. The majority of Serbs left Hungary after the First World War to return to Yugoslavia.[4] This advanced interdisciplinary research is based on the dialectological description of Serbian vernaculars by the dialectologist Pedrag Stepanović, which is also available in English[5], and several smaller dialectological studies and questionnaires of the Common Slavic Linguistic Atlas ("Opšteslovenski lingvistički atlas") from the villages of Lovra (Lórév), Medina (Medina) and Tukulja (Tököl). Access to the questionnaires is restricted at the Serbian Academy of Sciences and Arts in Belgrade. Further impressive anthropological data on the Hungarian Serbs have been collected within a series of scientific publications and journals[6] as well as in local newspapers such as the weekly "Srpske narodne novine" published in Budapest.

---

[1] This paper is a part of scientific project No. 2167, supported by the Ministry of Science, Technology and Development of Serbia.

[2] Serbian transcriptions are used for Hungarian terms.

[3] Cf. E.g. Predrag Stepanović: O govorima Srba u Mađarskoj. In: N. Čobeljić et al (eds.), *Društvene nauke o Srbima u Mađarskoj,* Budapest 2003, p. 223.

[4] According to recent estimates, 14,000-17,500 persons were repatriated from Hungary, cf. N. L. Gaćeša: Optanti iz Mađarske u kraljevini SHS posle Prvog svetskog rata. In: N. Čobeljić et al (eds.), *Društvene nauke o Srbima u Mađarskoj.* Budapest 2003, pp. 33-44.

[5] Predrag Stepanović: Govori Srba i Hrvata u Mađarskoj. Gornji Milanovac – Beograd – Novi Sad 1994; idem: A Taxonomic description of the Dialects of Serbs and Croats in Hungary: the Štokavian dialect. Budapest 1986.

[6] The most important is the Budapest collection *Etnografija Južnih Slovena u Mađarskoj,* ("Ethnography of South Slavs in Hungary"), which was divided at the beginning of the 1990s into *Etnografija Hrvata u Mađarskoj* ("Ethnography of Croats in Hungary") and *Etnografija Srba u Mađarskoj* ("Ethnography of Serbs in Hungary"). The Belgrade Academy of Sciences and Arts has published three volumes of *Sentandrejski zbornik* ("Sent-Endre rniscellany"). Useful scientific data can be found on the internet page www.rastko.org.yu/rastko-hu.
See also the anthropological study by Mladena Prelić: Srbi u selu Lovri u Mađarskoj tokom dvadesetog veka. Budapest 1995.

Serbs on the Csepel Island

This paper is based on ethno-linguistic field research among Serbs and Bulgarians living on the Csepel Island. The research was completed in September 2001 in two neighbouring villages: the village of Lovra (Lórév) and Čip (Szigetcsép).[7] The main goal of the research team was to acquire insights into lexicon and discourse of traditional Serbian culture. Interest for the Bulgarians arose spontaneously during the fieldwork. Applied linguistic and anthropological methodology enabled the collection of both dialectological and sociolinguistic data and, at the same time, the gaining of valuable insights into the contemporary anthropological situation and traditional culture.

In the village of Čip, approximately one hundred Serbs are living together with Hungarians and Germans. The majority of the Serbian population moved from this village to Yugoslavia in 1924 to settle in the village of Bački Brestovac. The village of Lovra, with three hundred inhabitants, is generally considered a unique, pure Serbian village in Hungary. Not far to the north the Croat settlement of Tukulja (Tököl) is to be found.[8] A tradition of mutual weddings between these two geographically close villages existed as well as strong connections with Serbs from the villages of Medina in the South, three villages north of Budapest – Kalaz (Budakalász), Pomaz (Pomáz) and Čobanac (Csobánka) – and the small town of Sent Endre (Szentendre). Serbs once also used to live in the small town of Kovin (Ráckeve), but today, only several immigrant Serbian families can be found there. South of Budapest, very close to the island of Csepel, three Serbian groups lived in the urban communities of

---

[7] This fieldwork was supported by the Serbian self-government in Hungary. Members of the research team were: Marija Ilić, Marija Vučković and Biljana Sikimić. The fieldwork report was published by Marija Ilić: Terenski rad u Mađarskoj. *Lingvističke aktuelnosti* 10, www.main.amu.edu.pl/~sipkadan/la.htm. At the time of writing two scientific papers based on the fieldwork were in print: Biljana Sikimić: Srbi na Čepelskoj adi, etnolingvistički pogled. *Etnografija Srba u Mađarskoj* 4. (2003 [2004]), pp. 34-48 and Marija Ilić: Čipska svadba u kazivanju Jelene Ljube Nikolić. *Etnografija Srba u Mađarskoj* 4 (2003 [2004]), pp. 49-78.

[8] Serbs from Čip consider "Ijekavian"-speaking Roman Catholics from Tukulja ethnically as *Raci;* the plural form is *Tukuljci,* the female archaic form *Tukuljača.* There is no evidence of mixed marriages with Orthodox Serbs. Inhabitants of the village of Tukulja consider themselves "Catholic Ratz", "Bunyevatz" and "Schokatz". They number around 1,000, have their own folklore group and club, a bilingual nursery and four years of elementary schooling in their mother tongue since 1984/85 (Cf. Prelić, Srbi, p. 64). According to the previously mentioned anthropological research done in Lovra at the beginning of the 1990s, Serbs maintained the greatest ethnic distance toward the Roma; later the ethnic distance toward Croats increased, especially since Belgrade TV was available via satellite. In the middle of the 1990s, the majority of Serbs from Lovra declared that they would not like to marry Croats or live with them in the same neighbourhood. Answers to questions asked previous to the collapse of Yugoslavia were quite different. This ethnic distance was maintained mainly vis-à-vis the abstract concept of "Croat", not the Croats living in the neighbouring village (e.g. "With the people from Tukulja we always had good relations, we have friends [...]", Prelić, Srbi, p. 136).

Aljmaš (Rácalmás), Pantelija (Dunaújvaros) and Bata (Száshalombatta). The Serbian communities of Aljmaš and Pantelija are practically extinct today.[9] Some of the remaining Serbian families in the settlement of Pantelija are considered "Tzintzars" and therefore of Aromanian origin. This situation has yet to be studied.[10]

Thanks to contemporary anthropologists, the linguistic identity of Serbs in Hungary is a seriously researched topic.[11] The attitude towards Serbs coming from Serbia was described as ambiguous, because the standard Serbian language was in part not understandable for the Hungarian Serbs ("You do speak correctly, we do not speak the Serbian language correctly "). But differences in mentality existed as well.[12] These can be compared with the results of sociolinguistic research on Croats in Hungary[13], where stagnation in language development, diglossy, early bilingualism, transformation of symmetric bilingualism into an asymmetric one favouring the Hungarian language and latent conflicts between the Croat dialect and standard language are considered important. But considering the difference between the Croat dialect spoken in Hungary and standard Croat, comparison with the sociolinguistic data on Serbian dialects spoken in Hungary is only of limited value, because the Hungarian Serbian dialects are much closer to the Serbian standard language. Even the influences within the local Serbian speeches favour the major dialect group ("šumadijsko-vojvođanski") and the small enclave of another dialect ("kosovsko-resavski") in Čobanac has changed completely today.[14]

All Serbs participating in the study in both Serbian villages of Csepel were bilingual. According to the census data of 1900, 75% of the Serbs in Lovra also spoke Hungarian. This high percentage is questionable, since knowledge of Hungarian appears only to have existed on an elementary level at the time, particularly among women. From the transcriptions of the conversations presented in the appendix, it is evident that elder Serbs remember their parents speaking Hungarian very poorly. The figures of the census of 1941 are even higher (95.1%), but the quality of the spoken Hungarian is also controversial.

---

[9] In the village of Aljmaš, which has to date not been studied, there are only two or three Serbian houses. Some traces of the Pantelija vernacular were described by Predrag Stepanović: Ijekavski elementi u ekavskim govorima Srba u Mađarskoj. *Južnoslovenski filolog* LVI/3-4 (2000), pp. 1103-1109, here 1106.

[10] For more details about the Aromanians adopted within the Serbian ethnic group in Hungary cf. Dinko Davidov: Kult sv. Nauma u Budimskoj eparhiji. *Balcanica* XI (1980), pp. 85-106 and Dušan Drljača: 'Tzintzars among the Serbs in Hungary', *Glasnik Etnografskog instituta SANU* 42 (1993), pp. 61-72.

[11] Cf. Mladena Prelić: Neki aspekti etničkog identiteta Srba u Mađarskoj, *Društvene nauke o Srbima u Mađarskoj*. Budimpešta 2003, pp. 81-87.

[12] Prelić, Srbi, p. 135.

[13] See in detail Jadranka Grbić: Obrazovni jezik – materinski jezik. *VII Folklór és tradíció*. Budapest 1994, pp. 262-268, here p. 264 and idem, Mother tongue and ethnic identity. Kultúrák találkozása – kultúrák konfliktusai. Békéscsaba – Budapest 1995, pp. 117-121, here p. 119.

[14] Pavle Ivić: O kosovsko-resavskom govoru Čobanca blizu Sentandreje. *Sentandrejski zbornik* 3 (1997), pp. 226-237, p. 232; Stepanović, Ijekavski elementi, p. 1105.

The results of recent anthropological research in Lovra in the 1990s show several levels of Serbian-Hungarian bilingualism. According to these data, the people from Lovra estimate their own language competence as follows: "We speak neither Serbian nor Hungarian correctly."

Traditionally it was considered shameful to speak Hungarian in the local church, at home and the graveyard. The attitude was different during a local annual feast called *bučura* – even in the last century friends were invited from neighbouring villages.[15] From a linguistic point of view, this "openness" of the village annual feast to non-Serbs is underlined by the use of the Hungarian term *bučura* instead of the Slavic *seoska slava*, or *zavetina*.

In the lexicon of both Lovra and Čip, a significant number of Hungarian and German loanwords appeared. Collected examples of linguistic calques based on the Hungarian language as a model are of the same type as described in the linguistic literature and are typical for all the Serbian vernaculars in Hungary. The establishing of linguistic micro-differentiation between the two Csepel villages, Lovra and Čip,[16] was also one of the goals of the research.

A great deal of data on traditional wedding and funeral customs and calendar feasts were collected. Serbs in both villages confirmed that the custom of the maypole, which is unknown among Serbs in Serbia, is still in use today. A summary overview of Serbian traditional customs in Hungary, given by the Belgrade ethnologist Dušan Drljača, does not mention the maypole, although it stresses the recent penetration by Hungarian traditional culture.[17] In comparison with the actual image of demons in the traditional spiritual culture in the Vojvodina, a region appropriate for the comparison with the Serbs in Hungary, a reduced demonic system was evidenced in the villages of Čip and Lovra: only the *bosorka* and *tatoš* (both words are of Hungarian origin, the image of these demons as well) can be mentioned. The complete Slavic demonic corpus is missing, not to mention the widespread and still present belief in the existence of *vampires*. Such a reduced repertoire could be the result of the strong influence of the local Orthodox Church, but for the definite explanation of this phenomenon more serious historical research – above all in the archives of the local Orthodox churches – is needed.

Hungarian influence was very strong in the practice of several forms of handicrafts and trades such as the raising of pigeons, and the relevant terminology is based completely on the Hungarian. The heritage of Serbs in Hungary differs in

---

[15] Prelić, Srbi, pp. 145-146.

[16] In these two Serbian villages on the Csepel Island there was no exclusive specialization, there were only differences caused by different soil. In the village of Čip the soil has a lot of sand which forms the base for the vineyards there, while the inhabitants often had to buy cereals on the market – cf. Prelić, Srbi, p. 82.

[17] Dušan Drljača: Neke odlike narodnih običaja Srba u Mađarskoj. In: N. Čobeljić et al. (eds.), *Društvene nauke o Srbima u Mađarskoj,* Budapest 2003, pp. 89-100, this paper is based mainly on earlier published data.

several inessential details from the actual, but slightly less endangered tradition among Serbs in Serbia.

Bulgarian gardeners on Csepel Island

Before 1989, Bulgarians in Hungary were officially non-existent. The Hungarian Act on the Rights of National and Ethnic Minorities requires for the recognition of a "national or ethnic minority" at least one century of presence in Hungary. Today the Bulgarians are considered an official minority group, although they do not demand the right to use their language and culture. Their dispersion makes it impossible to define a geographical area or region where their language is used; Bulgarian is considered a "non-territorial" language.[18]

The minority data of the 1980 and 1990 Hungarian censuses show a significant number of Bulgarians. Based on mother tongue, 3,426 (1980) and 2,953 (1990) Serbs and 1,370 (1990) Bulgarians were registered; based on nationality, 2,805 (1980) and 2,905 (1990) Serbs lived in Hungary. No data for Bulgarians was collected. Hungary-based minority organisations estimated the number of Serbs at 5,000 and the number of Bulgarians at between 3,000 and 3,500 in 1990.[19] According to the unofficial summary data from the 2001 census, Serbian is spoken as a mother tongue by 3,388 persons and Bulgarian by 1,299; 3,816 persons declared that they belong to the Serbian minority and 1,358 persons declared that they belong to the Bulgarian minority. 5,279 persons had ties with Serbian cultural values and traditions (Bulgarian: 1693) and 4,186 persons spoke Serbian in the family and with friends (Bulgarian: 1118).[20]

The largest part of the Bulgarian minority lives in and around Budapest. Collected field data and available ethnographic literature also revealed the presence of Orthodox Bulgarian gardeners in both Serbian villages on Csepel Island. In 1905 the Orthodox priest of Lovra stated: "At Lovra there are 5 foreigners, 651 are Orthodox Serbs. In this number I have included 22 Bulgarians,

[18] "HAEMUS", a social and cultural periodical and "Bulgarski Vesztnik", are monthly reviews published by the Bulgarian National Self-Government since 1995, see: Tania Gosselin: Minority Media in Hungary and Slovenia. A Comparative Assessment (2002), http://pdc.ceu.hu/archive/00001048/01/1.pdf. On the Bulgarian minority in Hungary see also Ljubomir Mikov: Bălgarinăt ot Sazhalombata. *Bălgarski folklor* XX/1 (1994), pp. 90-95; Natalija Raškova: Prăsnati sme bălgarite – edni naljavo, drugi nadjasno. *Bălgarski folklor* XX/1 (1994), pp. 96–101.

[19] Toso Doncsev: Investigating national and ethnic minorities in Hungary. In: N. Čobeljić et al. (eds.), *Društvene nauke o Srbima u Mađarskoj*. Budapest 2003, pp. 213-220.

[20] Bulgarian Minority Self-Governments were set up in Budapest (9), and in several other counties. „It is true for the Bulgarians, the Greeks, the Poles and especially the Armenians that their cultural affinity tends to be stronger than regarding themselves to a specific minority, at the same time the knowledge and use oft he minority language is less general among them", www.meh.hufnekh

they have their gardens close to Budapest, but they are married here, they have their permanent domicile, they speak good Serbian, and have the same family saint cult (*slava*) as we do."[21] This Bulgarian group is now considered assimilated by marriage to Serbian women. The first Bulgarian-Serbian mixed marriage was attested in 1881, the last one in 1922. Another group of Bulgarian gardeners was assimilated among the Serbs from Bata (Százhalombata) – an urban settlement on the other side of the Danube.[22] The first generation of Bulgarian gardeners spoke Bulgarian among themselves but they quickly learned Serbian. This assimilation process involved negative ethnic stereotypical terms such as "nasty", "black", "unfaithful" for Bulgarians when talking about newcomers. Contrary to these common negative stereotypes, attitudes such as "They are the same as we, those who live among us do not differ at all" can be found in the anthropological literature on Lovra.[23] The Bulgarians were sometimes considered "unreliable" and responsible for discord in the village; nevertheless, the current president of the village council, elected by secret ballot, is a descendant of Bulgarian immigrants.[24]

Only poor Serbian girls without dowry used to marry Bulgarians. The "pure" Serbs did not like to marry even the second generation of Bulgarians as they were considered of "lower" class. Before 1930 they were not accepted in the church community as equal members, and some Serbian priests changed Bulgarian names into Serbian.[25] With the exception of three persons today, the descendants of the Bulgarians consider themselves Serbs; the other residents of Lovra are of the same opinion. The descendants of the Bulgarian gardeners in Lovra and Čip are completely integrated into the community, their mother tongue is Serbian, but, on the other hand, they do not deny their Bulgarian origin. In Lovra we heard the story of one Bulgarian descendant, who even travelled to Bulgaria to search for his relatives, but did not succeed in finding them. No traces of Bulgarian traditional folk culture can be found in Lovra with the exception of one traditional dance, but it is not performed anymore. This can be explained by the dominantly male population of the Bulgarian gardeners.

Bulgarian language competence was not studied and we had no conversation in or recorded data of the Bulgarian language on Csepel Island. It is evident that the belonging to the South Slavic dialectological continuum eased a Serbian-Bulgarian communication and supported the process of assimilation. A statement from Čip is typical: "I was in Bulgaria. Bulgarians were at my place. This

---

[21] Dinko Davidov: Sveštenički opisi Srba u selima Lovri i Pomazu 1905. godine. *Sentandrejski zbornik 2,* (1992), pp. 237-241, here p. 238.

[22] For details about Bulgarian gardeners in Lovra see at Prelić, Srbi, pp. 77-78 where a list of local Bulgarian families with the names of their family saints is presented. See also Marija Kiš: Godišnji praznici kod Srba u Bati. *Etnografija Srba u Mađarskoj* 1 (1997), pp. 13-23, here p. 19.

[23] Mladena Prelić: Serbs in the village Lovra-Lórév near Budapest and their ethnic stereotypes. In: Kultúrák találkozása – kultúrák konfliktusai. Békéscsaba – Budapest 1995, p. 328.

[24] Prelić, Srbi, p. 329.

[25] The list of these new Serbian names is given in: Prelić, Srbi, p. 107.

is, one can say, spoiled Serbian. But, they speak more rudely than we. I can't understand."

Due to these possibilities of restricted communication, the Bulgarians were probably initially considered as unable to learn Serbian and dialectological differences are still mentioned (e.g. the word *Bulgarian* pronounced in a Serbian – *bugarski* – and Bulgarian variant – *b'lgarski*) as a conversation with two elderly men at Čip demonstrates: "They are of Bulgarian origin, what to add. This Ivan was from Bulgaria. He was here for one hundred years, but he didn't learn Serbian, he knew only *Bugarski*, *b'lgarski*. – Mixed. – This and that. I don't even know whether he spoke Hungarian well."

Today, people of Bulgarian origin express a positive attitude towards Serbs and Serbia: *"Did your parents speak Bulgarian?"* – "Me too, I do speak, why not. I do speak. But I like Serbian very much. And Belgrade is my favourite town. I have been a lot of time in Belgrade." On the other hand, some local Serbs now argue the "percentage" of neighbours with Bulgarian origin: "We had here one godfather, also Bulgarian. I am Bulgarian. He used to play the violin". – "To what percentage are you Bulgarian?" – "What a question – how much?" – "Half? Mother's side?" – "Well, more. I am sorry, my grandfather was, what do you mean?" – "Your father was Bulgarian, I know." – "I am seventy-five percent Bulgarian. Half of this village is Bulgarian."

"Tradition" and multilingualism at the local level

Retrospective questions reveal that "multilingualism" in the village of Čip is rather complex. Knowledge of the contact languages was restricted to local dialects and probably one-dimensional. In the first half of the 20th century, the knowledge of the contact German dialect was more important than official Hungarian. One elderly man from Čip stated: "Bulgarian and Hungarian, and Swabian. I do not speak German, I do speak Swabian. Here were mostly Swabians. We did not speak much Hungarian, and Serbian women spoke Swabian. They went to the store and asked in Swabian. But the Serbs were more clever than the Swabians, because they all knew Swabian, but the Swabians did not know Serbian, it was very rarely that Swabians spoke Serbian." On the contrary, the few Hungarian families in Serbian Lovra used to speak Serbian: "There were only three Hungarian families and they spoke Serbian, they attended our schools, some Hungarians didn't even speak Hungarian". This statement, like the others, has to be considered from the point of view of perceptual sociolinguistics. All the informers reconstruct the past and speak about an undefined, very vague period of the past.

In the transcriptions in the appendix the members of the small Serbian group in Hungary stress the importance of belonging to the same Christian Orthodox church; in some extreme cases the Roman Catholics and other Christians are even considered “non-believers”. It is possible that the Aromanians, who are not native speakers of Slavic languages, according to the example of the Bulgarians, passed through the same procedure of ethnic adoption within the ethnic group of Serbs easily and quickly, because they belonged to the Christian Orthodox religion.

Serbian anthropologists point out that the Serbian population in Hungary has not been “regenerated” by new immigrants from Serbia, pointing to the fact that the number of Serbs in Hungary is progressively decreasing by 1% a year. They use the terms “depopulated, marginalized, unable, rural minority group” or “dispersed dwarfish ethnic community" to describe this condition. They also describe the situation among the Serbs in Hungary as similar to the fragmented Jewish communities in today’s Serbia, which consist to a high degree of persons with non-Jewish origins as secondary keepers of tradition.[26]

In conclusion we can state that the concept of ‘hidden minorities’ is appropriate for the description of those Bulgarian gardeners and Aromanian tradesmen that were adopted by the Serbs in Hungary during the 19th and 20th century.[27]

Appendix:

1. Conversation in Čip with two older men, **S1** and **S2** (born in 1930 and 1929), on 18 September 2001; questions are reproduced in brackets.

S1: Bugarski i mađarski, a švapski. Ja ne nemački znam, ja švapski. Tu su bili Švabi ponajviše. Tu mađarski se nije zdravo razgovaralo, i srpske žene su švapski, pošle u dućan i tamo su iskale švapski. A Srbi su mudriji bili neg Švabi, jer Srbi su svi znali švapski, a Švabo nije znao, retko je znao Švabo srpski. – *Bulgarian and Hungarian, and Swabian. I do not speak German, I do speak Swabian. Here were mostly Swabians. We did not speak much Hungarian, and Serbian women spoke Swabian, they went to the store and asked in Swabian. But the Serbs were cleverer than the Swabians, because the Serbs all knew Swabian, but the Swabians did not, it was very rare that Swabians spoke Serbian.*

[Gde ste bugarski naučili? – *Where did you learn Bulgarian?*]

S1: Bio sam u Bugarskoj. Bugari bili kod mene. Ma to je, kažu, pokvareno srpski. Samo oni još oštrije govore neg mi. Ne mogu ja razumeti. – *I was in Bulgaria. Bulgarians were at my place. This is, one can say, spoiled Serbian. But, they speak more rudely than we. I can't understand.*

[Ima li u susedenim selima Bugara? – *Are there Bulgarians in the neighbouring villages?*]

---

[26] Drljača, Neke odlike, p. 98.

[27] Although based on a small selected sample (50 Bulgarian families) the individual and group ethnic identification of members of Bulgarian minority in Hungary has been studied by Maria Homisinova: “The research of the ethnic processes in the minority communities living in Hungary”, www.saske.sk/cas/4-2001/homisinova.html

S1: Ima i tu Bugara, dve-tri kuće bile Bugara ovde. U Čipu. Sad ih nema, svi pomrli. Sad zaparložilo. – *Bulgarians live also here, there were two or three houses here. In Čip. By now they are not existing any more now, all of them died. Everything is deserted now.*

[Kako ste sa njima ziveli? – *How were relations with them?*]

S1: Pa dobro. – *Well, good.*

S2: Oni su bugarskog porekla, šta ja znam. Onaj Ivan je bio iz Bugarske. – *They are of Bulgarian origin, what to add. This Ivan was from Bulgaria.*

S1: Tu je bio sto godina al nije naučio srpski, znao samo bugarski, blgarski. – *He was here for a hundred years, but he didn't learn Serbian, he knew only Bulgarian, B'lgarski.*

S2: Mešano. – *Mixed.*

S1: I ovo i ono. I mađarski ne znam da je znao zdravo. Mađarski jezik težak. – *This and that. I even don't know whether he spoke Hungarian well. The Hungarian language is difficult.*

S2: Prije žene stare nisu znale mađarski. – *At that time older women didn't speak Hungarian.*

S1: Ne, kad moja majka bila. – *They didn't, when my mother lived.*

S2: Moja mama nije znala zdravo mađarski da govori. – *My mother couldn't speak Hungarian well.*

S1: Tu je valda tri frtale bilo Švaba, a par kuća bilo Mađara. Par kuća. Ovde Srbi od krsta, ovamo to su sve Srbi bili. Sad je pomrlo. I Mađarice žene. – *I suppose that three quarters were Swabians here, and few Hungarian houses. Few houses. Here lived Serbians from the cross on, here were only Serbs. But now all of them died out. And the wives are Hungarians.*

[Kako su vaše majke govorile? – *What language did your mothers speak?*]

S1: Srpski. Samo srpski. – *Serbian, only Serbian.*

S2: Pa nije bilo mađarski. Moja žena bila iz Kalaza. I tamo bili Srbi. I tamo bili Švaba i Totova. – *There was no Hungarian language. My wife was from Kalaz. Serbs lived there also. There were Swabians and Slovaks, too.*

2. Transcript of a conversation with three women over sixty years of age on 21 September 2001 in Lovra, Hungary. **S1** was born in Lovra, **S2** was born in Kalaz and **B** is of Bulgarian origin, born in Lovra. Omitted parts of the conversation are indicated. All the women in this transcript speak the local dialect except B, whose speech is closer to standard Serbian.

B: A tu nam je bio jedan kum, isto Bugarin. Ja sam Bugarka. On je sviro u cigulku. – *We had here one godfather, also Bulgarian. I am Bulgarian. He used to play the violin.*

S1: Koliko procenata si Bugarka? – *How many percent are you Bulgarian?*

B: Pa kako – koliko? – *What a question – how much?*

S1: Pola? Mamina strana? – *Half? Mother's side?*

B: Pa više. Izvini, i deda mi je bio, pa nego šta! – *Well, more. Excuse me, even my grandfather was, what's the difference?*

S1: Otac ti bio Bugarin, znam. – *Your father was Bulgarian, I know.*

B: Sedamdeset pet procenata sam ja Bugarka. Tu je pola sela bugarsko. – *I am seventy-five percent Bulgarian. Half of this village is Bulgarian.*

[...]

B: Moja mama nikad nije imala vremena da izađe ovako, da priča, mi smo bili baštovani i kod nas su uvek ljudi radili i ona je uvek trebala da kuva, lebac peče, da šije. Ni se to nekad gotovo uzimalo. Ona sve šila, od košulje, od belog veša, do gornjeg, sve sama. I nije imala vremena. Nije imala vremena ovako da sedne da divani. Bio praznik, bio svakidan, ona je uvek jadna radila, tako da ja ne znam ove stvari. – *My mother never had time just to go out and to talk. We were gardeners, we had workers and she had to cook, to bake bread, to sew. In those times one could not find it ready made. She used to sew everything, shirts, underwear, clothes, everything alone. She never had time. She didn't have time to sit like this and to talk. On holidays, working days, poor woman, she was always working, so I don't know these things.*

[Da li su vaši stari govorili bugarski? – *Did your parents speak Bulgarian?*]

B: Govorim i ja, kako da ne. Govorim, govorim. Samo ja srpski jezik jako volim. I Beograd, omiljen mi je grad, tako da sam puno bila tamo u Beogradu. Imam jednu porodicu u Rakovici, oni su isto tries druge godine izašli odavde, njiovi stari. – *Me too, I do speak, why not. I do speak. But I like very much the Serbian language. And Belgrade is my favourite town, I have been a lot of times there in Belgrade. I know a family in Rakovica, they also came here in the 1932, their parents.*

[Koji se jezik govorio kod vas u porodici? – *Which language was in use in your family?*]

B: Ne, nažalost ne. Sin mi je Mađaricu uzo, i on se razveo, imao je prvo Srpkinju, a sad je Mađaricu uzo, ali govorimo i srpski i mađarski. – *No, its a pity, but no. My son took a Hungarian wife, he got divorced, first he had Serbian, now he took a Hungarian, but we talk both in Serbian and Hungarian.*

[A kad ste vi bili dete? – *And during your childhood?*]

B: Onda smo govorili srpski, i sa ocom sam bugarski govorila. – *In that time we spoke Serbian, and with my father I spoke Bulgarian.*

[On je govorio dobro bugarski? – *He used to speak Bulgarian well?*]

B: Jeste, jeste. – *Yes he did, he did.*

[On je bio odavde? – *He was born here?*]

B: Ne, on je došo iz Bugarske, iz Trojana. I on, i stric, brat mu, da. – *No, he came from Bulgaria, from Troyan. He, his uncle, his brother, yes.*

[Kada su Bugari došli ovde? – *When did the Bulgarians come here?*]

B: Moj otac je došo hiljadu devetsto osamnajste godine. – *My father came 1918.*

[Da li ih bilo i ranije? – *Were they here even before that time?*]

B: Kako da ne. Oni su izdržavali. Pa ovde su se ženili Bugari sa Srpkinjama. – *Of course, yes. They made a living. And here the Bulgarians married Serbian women.*

S1: Bogati. Što za crkvu dalo, na primer, zvona, zvono najveće. – *The rich ones. They donated the bells for the church, for example, the biggest bell.*

B: Sve to. Puno su Bugari, jer tu su bašte bile, na Čepelskem ostrvu su bile bašte. Bugari – oni su izdržavali Budimpestu. To sama bašta je. Pa i ovde su bile bašte. – *All this. They did a lot, here there were gardens, on Csepel Island were gardens. The Bulgarians – they sustained Budapest. It is all gardens. And here were gardens, too.*

[...]

S2: Kalaz sad je vec varoš. – *By now Kalaz has become a town.*

B: I tamo i je malo bilo [Mađara]. Ovo je nekad selo samo, mislim, Srbi i Bugari. – *There also lived few [Hungarians]. This village was once only one of Serbs and Bulgarians, I suppose.*

S2: Ovo je mala Jugoslavija. Šta da vam kažem, tu nema ništa, hatur. – *This is a small Yugoslavia. What to say, there is nothing here at all.*

B: Ako je bilo tri porodice mađarske, i oni su srpski govorili, oni su išli u naše škole, pa bili su koji nisu ni znali mađarski, Mađari. Sad se mešaju brakovi, to nekad nije bilo da se smelo, recimo druga vera da se venča u našoj veri. – *There were only three Hungarian families, even they spoke Serbian, they attended our schools, some Hungarians even didn't speak Hungarian. Now we have these mixed marriages; this was not allowed in old times that, for example an other faith marries with our faith.*

[...]

Bibliography

DAVIDOV, Dinko: 'Kult sv. Nauma u Budimskoj eparhiji'. In: *Balcanica* XI, (1980), pp. 85-106.

DAVIDOV, Dinko: Sveštenički opisi Srba u selima Lovri i Pomazu 1905. godine. In: *Sentandrejski zbornik* 2. (Belgrade 1992), pp. 237-241.

DONCSEV, Toso: Investigating national and ethnic minorities in Hungary'. In: N. Čobeljić et al. (eds.), Društvene nauke o Srbima u Mađarskoj. Budapest 2003, pp. 213-220.

DRLJAČA, Dušan: Tzintzars among the Serbs in Hungary. *Glasnik Etnografskog instituta SANU* 42 (1993), pp. 61-72.

DRLJAČA, Dušan: Neke odlike narodnih običaja Srba u Mađarskoj. In: N. Čobeljić et al. (eds.), Društvene nauke o Srbima u Mađarskoj. Budapest 2003, pp. 89-100.

ETNOGRAFIJA JUŽNIH SLOVENA U MAĐARSKOJ. Budapest 1 (1975) – 10 (1993).

GAĆEŠA, Nikola L.: Optanti iz Mađarske u kraljevini SHS posle Prvog svetskog rata. Budapest 2003.

GOSSELIN, Tania: Minority Media in Hungary and Slovenia. A Comparative Assessment (2002), http://pdc.ceu.hu/archive/00001048/01/1.pdf.

GRBIĆ, Jadranka: Obrazovni jezik – materinski jezik. In: VII Folklór és tradíció. Budapest 1994, pp. 262-268.

GRBIĆ, Jadranka: Mother tongue and ethnic identity. In: Kultúrák találkozása – kultúrák konfliktusai. Békéscsaba – Budapest 1995, pp. 117-121.

HOMISINOVA, Maria: The research of the ethnic processes in the minority communities living in Hungary, www.saske.sk/cas/4-2001/homisinova.html.

ILIĆ, Marija: Terenski rad u Mađarskoj. *Lingvističke aktuelnosti* 10, www.main.amu.edu.pl/~sipkadan/la.htm.

ILIĆ, Marija: Čipska svadba u kazivanju Jelene Ljube Nikolić. *Etnografija Srba u Mađarskoj* 4. (2003 [2004]), pp. 49-78.

IVIĆ, Pavle: O kosovsko-resavskom govoru Čobanca blizu Sentandreje. In: *Sentandrejski zbornik* 3 (Belgrade 1997), pp. 226-237.

KIŠ, Marija: Godišnji praznici kod Srba u Bati. *Etnografija Srba u Mađarskoj* 1 (1997), pp. 13-23.

MIKOV, Ljubomir: Bălgarinăt ot Sazhalombata. *Bălgarski folklor* XX/1 (1994), pp. 90-95.

PRELIĆ, Mladena: Srbi u selu Lovri u Mađarskoj tokom dvadesetog veka. Budapest 1995.

PRELIĆ, Mladena: Neki aspekti etničkog identiteta Srba u Mađarskoj. In: N. Čobeljić et al. (eds.), Društvene nauke o Srbima u Mađarskoj. Budapest 2003, pp. 81-87.

PRELIĆ, Mladena: Serbs in the village Lovra-Lórév near Budapest and their ethnic stereotypes. In: Kultúrák találkozása – kultúrák konfliktusai. Békéscsaba/Budapest 1995, pp. 326-339.

RAŠKOVA, Natalija: Prăsnati sme bălgarite – edni naljavo, drugi nadjasno. *Bălgarski folklor* XX/1 (1994), pp. 96–101.

SIKIMIĆ, Biljana: Srbi na Čepelskoj adi, etnolingvistički pogled. *Etnografija Srba u Mađarskoj* 4 (2003 [2004]), pp. 34-48.

STEPANOVIĆ, Predrag: Govori Srba i Hrvata u Mađarskoj. Gornji Milanovac/Belgrade/Novi Sad 1994.

STEPANOVIĆ, Predrag: O govorima Srba u Mađarskoj. Budapest 2003.

STEPANOVIĆ, Predrag: Ijekavski elementi u ekavskim govorima Srba u Mađarskoj. *Južnoslovenski filolog* LVI/3-4 (2000), pp. 1103-1109.

From a Majority to a Hidden Minority. The German-Speaking Population of the Abstall/Apače Basin (19th and Early 20th Centuries)[1]

Eduard G. Staudinger

The geographical setting

The term Abstaller Feld/Apaško polje – or Abstaller Becken/Apaško kotlina (Apače Basin), as it is often called in the primary sources and the literature – is an area up to four kilometres wide, south of the Mur River and north of the Windische Bühel/Slovenske gorice in the north-eastern corner of the Republic of Slovenia.[2] From the Austrian side, the area can be accessed across the Mur via bridges in the towns of Mureck in the west and Bad Radkersburg in the east. Four ferries crossed the Mur until 1918, connecting the Apače Basin to the railroad between Spielfeld and Bad Radkersburg and markets for local agricultural production. The area, populated since the late middle ages by a primarily German-speaking population belonged to the principality of Styria until the end of the First World War.[3] With the constitution of the political districts in 1868, the area became part of the district of Bad Radkersburg; in terms of judicial districts, the area was divided between Radkersburg and Mureck. The Peace Treaty of St. Germain, signed by Austria on 10 September 1919 stipulated in Part II, Art. 27 the new Austrian borders, including those with Yugoslavia as following the Mur River[4] in the border sections IV and V. The Apače Basin fell to Yugoslavia as part of the district of Ljutomer/Luttenberg.

New parish delineations were not regulated in peace treaties following the First World War. The Parish of Abstall/Apače was mentioned for the first time in 1420 as an offshoot of the Parish of Radkersburg, although with the exception of the Parish church, no additional church existed in the Parish until 1693. The borders of the Parish shifted repeatedly with the founding of new parishes but

---

[1] This is the slightly revised version of the paper "Von der Mehrheit zur Minderheit. Die deutschsprachige Bevölkerung des Abstaller Feldes im 19. und frühen 20. Jahrhundert", published for the first time in: H. Heppner (ed.), Deutsche und Slowenen im gemeinsamen Raum. Neue Forschungen zu einem komplexen Thema. Munich 2002 (= Buchreihe der Südostdeutschen Historischen Kommission 38), pp. 111-124. Andreas Hemming translated the text into English.

[2] The term "Abstaller Becken" is the local name for the region – cf. Mirko Križman: Reste der deutschen Minderheit im slowenischen Grenzgebiet der Mur. In: R. Hinderling/L. M. Eichinger (eds.), Handbuch der mitteleuropäischen Sprachminderheiten. Tübingen 1996, pp. 185-198, here p. 186. In the following I will use the term Apače Basin.

[3] Cf. Arnold Suppan: Jugoslawien und Österreich 1918-1938. Bilaterale Außenpolitik im europäischen Umfeld. Vienna 1996, pp. 663-664.

[4] Cf. Staatsvertrag von St. Germain-en-Laye. *Staatsgesetzblatt für die Republik Österreich* 90/303 (1920).

belonged continuously to the Deaconry of Radkersburg and the Diocese of Seckau.[5] Although after the erection of the new international border, the Parish of Abstall/Apače came to be administered from Maribor/Marburg, the formal modification of the diocese borders to those of the state was only undertaken in 1964. These official modifications made to match the diocese borders to the state borders were undertaken by the Consistorial Congregation in Rome at the request of the Bishops of Maribor, Szombathely, Gurk and Graz-Seckau. Those areas already administered informally by Maribor were officially added to that Diocese. These were the Parishes of Hl. Geist/Sveti Duh na Ostrem vrhu, Kappel/Kapla and Abstall/Apače.[6]

Apače, the central village in the Basin, was not only home to the parish church, it also had a school. A teacher was first mentioned in 1734, although the first one-room school was only built at the beginning of the 19th century. Lessons were taught initially in the house of the sexton until the school acquired its own building in 1836. It was extended to include a second class in 1870. The school, in which German was spoken, was visited not only by children from Apače but from villages in the entire area and it was until 1918 a centre of both German language and cultural education.

There also existed a private girl's school run by German nuns. This latter school initially continued operation after 1918. After the creation of the Yugoslav state, state primary schools were established in Apače and in Stogovci/Miethsdorf. Teaching was generally done in Slovenian and Slovenian language education was compulsory. In accordance with the laws on minority schooling, a section in which German was the language of instruction was established for the lower grades, although Slovenian language education remained compulsory. The schools in the Apače Basin belonged to the School District of Gornja Radgona/Oberradkersburg.[7]

---

[5] Cf. Josef A. Janisch (ed.): Topographisch-statistisches Lexikon von Steiermark mit historischen Notizen und Anmerkungen, vol. 1. Graz 1878, p. 1.

[6] Cf. Karl Amon/Maximilian Liebmann (eds.): Kirchengeschichte der Steiermark. Graz 1993, p. 422; France M. Dolinar: Cerkvena uprava in Slovenci. In: V. Melik/S. Granda/V. Rajšp (eds.), Slovenija 1848-1998: Iskanje lastne poti. Maribor 1998, pp. 198-215, here p. 213. The protestant parish in the Apače Basin belonged until 1919 to the parish of Radkersburg. Thereafter it was governed from Murska Sobota, the seat of the protestant bishop, as a sub-parish in which Zoltan Kertschmer served as deacon and religion teacher.

[7] On the development of German language education in Slovenia after 1918 cf. Andrej Vovko: Nemško manjšinsko šolstvo na Slovenskem v obdobju stare Jugoslavije. *Zgodovinski časopis* 40/3 (1986), pp. 311-321. German was initially taken completely from the curriculum after the Second World War; it was reintroduced in Apače in the 1950s.

Germans and Slovenes up to 1918

According to the census of 1910, Apače had 480 residents of which 444 were, based on their everyday language use, German-speaking and 13 Slovenian-speaking. The remaining 23 people were classified as "foreigners". Distilling exact information on linguistic orientation in the Basin based on this census data is difficult and dependent above all on to what degree the residents of the northern slopes of the Windische Bühel are included. According to Mirko Križman, whose estimates are based on the census of 1910, 6,197 residents of the 19 communities of the Basin spoke German in their day-to-day lives and 717 spoke Slovenian, although the proportion of Slovenian speakers had increased slightly since the end of the 19th century as a result of migrations and was centred in particular villages in the Basin. These Slovenian-speaking immigrants from the Prekmurje were left unconsidered in the census of 1910 since they came from Hungary and were thus classified as "foreigners".[8] Arnold Suppan on the other hand, writes that in 1910 the Apače Basin merely included 13 communities, of which 11 proved to have a 90 percent German-speaking majority. To simplify his calculations he nevertheless added all 22 communities of the judicial district of Radkersburg (7 communities) and Mureck (15 communities) south of the Mur together. The Apače Basin had, accordingly, 9232 residents of which 6000 were German and 2818 were Slovenian.[9] Independent of the exact figures and how they were come by, the German-speaking population in the Apače Basin was a compact local majority with a well anchored German ethno-cultural identity.

A contested border

Although the Peace of St. Germain designated the Mur River the official international border between Austria and Yugoslavia, who would have sovereignty over the Apače Basin remained an issue for some time. An agreement reached between representatives of the governments of Styria and Slovenia between 9 and 13 February 1919 in Maribor/Marburg and ratified later by the respective governments in the wake of violent clashes in the area of Radkersburg at the beginning of the same month, defined a demarcation line and declared the Apače Basin to a neutral zone. The demarcation line followed, like the border later, the course of the Mur and around the southern edge of the Apače Basin.

[8] Cf. Križman, Reste der deutschen Minderheit, pp. 190-191.

[9] Arnold Suppan: Slowenen und Deutsche in Krain, der Untersteiermark und in Slowenien in den Volkszählungen von 1880, 1910, 1921 und 1931. In: H. Rumpler/A. Suppan (eds.), Geschichte der Deutschen im Bereich des heutigen Slowenien 1848-1941. Vienna 1988 (= Schriftenreihe des österreichischen Ost- und Südosteuropa-Instituts, Bd. XIII), pp. 311-318, here 316-317.

The same was decided for the customs boundary, which was of vital importance for trade. The Peace of St. Germain, which was signed by the Austrian side on 10 September 1919, conferred the Apače Basin to the Kingdom of Serbs, Croats, and Slovenes. The Styrian government in Graz as well as the "Central Office on Provinces" (*Länder-Zentralbüro*), established in February 1920 to support the activities of the Central Border Commission, developed in the course of several proposals a plan on how the final fixing of the new border was to be implemented locally and above all how deviations from the stipulations of the peace agreement were to be realised. The Apače Basin and the area around Radkersburg were of particular interest here, especially since the town of Radkersburg itself spanned the Mur and risked losing its southern Untergries quarter to Yugoslavia. The latter town was also a major market for the agrarian production of the Apače Basin.[10]

Plans were made in various directions to ensure that the Apače Basin remained part of Austrian Styria, including several territorial exchange models. The respective authorities in Vienna became involved as of February 1920 and the German-speaking population of the Apače Basin also demonstrated clearly their desire to join the Austrian Republic. A marked highpoint was a demonstration on 25 August 1920, at which time the Allied Border Commission were staying in Apače on their way from Mureck to Radkersburg. On 21 January 1921, the representatives of eight communities in the basin, including Abstall/Apače, Sögersdorf/Segovci, Seibersdorf/Žiberci, Proskersdorf/Drobtinci, Leitersdorf/Lutverci, Schöpfendorf/Žepovci, Frattendorf/Vratja vas and Schirmdorf/Črnci, petitioned the Austrian government to begin negotiations with Yugoslavia to allow these communities to join Austria. They suggested as compensation the surrender of the Slovenian-speaking communities of Windisch-Goritz/Slovenska Gorica, Dedenitz/Dedonci, Sicheldorf/Žetinci, Zelting/Zenkovci and part of Laafeld/Potrna as well as permission to use the rail line between Spielfeld and Radkersburg for Yugoslav transports. This same appeal was made to the Yugoslav government on 11 September 1920, much to the chagrin of the Styrian authorities.[11] These initiatives can be traced back to the summer of 1919 at which time 15 local communities protested against the planned allotment of the area to Yugoslavia (i.e. the Kingdom of Serbs, Croats,

---

[10] Cf. Hermann Kurahs: Die Abtrennung des Untergries 1919/20. *Jahresbericht BORG Bad Radkersburg* 16 (1984/85), pp. 10-17; Hermann Kurahs et al.: Bad Radkersburg. Naturraum und Bevölkerung, Geschichte, Stadtanlage, Architektur. Bad Radkersburg 1997, pp. 112-120.

[11] Styrian State Archive/Steiermärkisches Landesarchiv (= StLA), Statth. Länder-Zentralbüro Graz, A5b-101/1920, Akt Nr. A5b-339/1920. The community representatives pointed explicitly to the northerly economic and transportation ties in the Apače Basin and the limited possibilities the Basin provide for developing these towards the south over the Windische Bühel towards Maribor/Marburg. They also considered any decision to give the region Yugoslavia without consulting the local population as illegal; the communities with Slovenian-speaking majorities, such as Windisch-Goritz, Dedenitz, Sicheldorf, Zelting and Laafeld felt the same about their being granted to Austria.

and Slovenes) in the form of a petition to the Austrian delegation in St. Germain.

These and other initiatives, activities and plans had little effect on the Apače Basin being allotted to Yugoslavia. They nevertheless reveal a history parallel to official events and provide insights into the thought processes and perceptions of local actors and those people affected directly by events in a period of intensive and far-reaching change. Furthermore, they demonstrate how developments in a relatively small region may be dictated by and are dependent upon supra-regional and international considerations. Finally, they are exemplary of a further aspect of political borders and border areas, which on the one hand informs a decades old field of research with changing foci and perspectives, on the other hand has drawn particular interdisciplinary attention in the last few years.[12]

Until the final ratification of the Peace of St. Germain on 16 July 1920, the Styrian state government and the "Central Office" were only prepared to consider territorial compensation as a last resort. Instead, the compensation they were prepared to offer for sovereignty over the Apače Basin in the spring and early summer of 1920 were transportation oriented, including Yugoslav use rights to the rail line between Spielfeld and Radkersburg and the eventual financing of the extension of this line to Murska Sobota. This proposal could count on Yugoslav interest, above all because north-eastern Slovenia was only difficult to access from Maribor via the Windische Bühel and that the military occupation of this region, including Spielfeld and Radkersburg, by Yugoslavian troops since December 1918 was dependant to a great degree on control of this rail line.

In terms of potential territorial compensation, in the first half of 1920, the area south of Radkersburg was being considered. This decision was based, as mentioned, on the fact that several villages in this area had Slovenian-speaking majorities.

The leadership of the "Südmark" Association in Graz, which had shown particular interest in how the border issue was developing, mentioned, in passages marked "secret" in its reports to the "Central Office", areas south of Arnfels and Leutschach on the borders of the districts of Leibnitz and Maribor as potential exchange candidates should this be the only way to secure Austrian sovereignty to the Apače Basin.[13]

This intensive occupation with the future of the Apače Basin in the spring and summer of 1920 was the direct result of the order of the Ambassador's Conference in Paris for Yugoslavia to evacuate the town of Radkersburg. This order,

---

[12] Wilfried Heller: Grenzen und ihre Erforschung. Gegenstände, Fragestellungen, Zielsetzungen. In: I. Diekmann/P. Krüger/J. H. Schoeps (eds.), Geopolitik. Grenzgänge im Zeitgeist, vol. 1/1: 1890 bis 1945. Potsdam 2000, pp. 325-350.

[13] StLA, Statth. Länder-Zentralbüro Graz, A5b-115/1920.

pushed through by the Austrian side, meant on the other hand that from this point on the Mur River would form the new state and customs border, as stipulated in the Peace of St. Germain.

The domestic Austrian debate was joined not only by the Styrian government and the "Central Office" in Graz but also the Foreign Ministry and the Central Border Commission in Vienna and the Austrian representatives in Paris, Belgrade and Ljubljana, and they each had their own clear position. The Styrian instances considered the Apače Basin and the areas north of the Mur as a single geographic, economic and linguistic-cultural region and that the Mur was at best an artificial border. This position was supported by the fact that several farmers had land both north and south of the Mur. Economic aspects such as the significance of the markets in Radkersburg and Mureck for the agrarian production from the region and its importance in supplying Styrian industrial centres with foodstuffs found particular attention here. The role these economic arguments played can be seen in the fact that after their arguments for a territorial integrity failed, they tried as a last resort to implement a customs union for the Apače Basin with Austria.[14]

These Styrian diplomats pushed to enter into direct negotiations with the representatives of the Entente powers in Paris. Johann Eichhoff, the Austrian emissary in the Ambassador's Conference in Paris, did not consider it opportune to demand a partial revision of the border at a time when the peace agreement had already been ratified by Italy and was about to be passed by France and Great Britain. Additionally, so Eichhoff, the peace agreement stipulated that potential territorial revisions were to be dealt with directly by the affected parties. Furthermore, if the Austrians were to initiate a protest against the planned new borders in Paris at all, he suggested they should concentrate on South Tyrol. Second place on this list of priorities was in his opinion the Czechoslovakian border to the north of Lower Austria.[15]

After these first attempts to win the Apače Basin for Austria failed and the peace agreement was ratified internationally – on 16 July 1920 – exertions on this issue were shifted to the allied Border Commission. This commission made up of representatives from Great Britain, France, Italy, Japan, Yugoslavia and Austria had its seat in Maribor and was mandated to negotiate the detailed course of the border. They were authorised by the Ambassador's Conference in Paris in a decision from 23 October 1920 to revise the "course of the natural

---

[14] Stefan Karner: Grenzziehungsfragen der Republik Österreich nach den beiden Weltkriegen in ihrer ökonomisch-politischen Relevanz. In: E. Zöllner (ed.), Österreichs Erste und Zweite Republik. Kontinuität und Wandel ihrer Strukturen und Probleme. Vienna 1985 (= Schriften des Instituts für Österreichkunde 47), pp. 17-42.

[15] Eduard G. Staudinger: Zum Plan eines Gebietstausches zwischen Österreich, Jugoslawien und Ungarn aus dem Jahr 1921. *Veröffentlichungen des Verbands Österreichischer Geschichtsvereine* 26 (1989), pp. 97-101, here p. 98; Hanns Haas/Peter Mähner: Verfeindete Brüder an der Grenze: Südböhmen/Südmähren/Waldviertel/Weinviertel. Die Zerstörung der Lebenseinheit. "Grenze" 1938 bis 1945. Forschungsbericht. Horn 1998, pp. 350-391.

border" if this was agreed to by the affected parties and confirmed unanimously by the Commission. These stipulations were not met in the case of the Apače Basin and the Mur became the international border on 10 December 1920.

Compensation plans

This meant that any changes in the territorial association of the Apače Basin was only to be realised in direct negotiations between Austria and Yugoslavia and that possible compensation needed to be considered. These included, beside economic and financial considerations, several possibilities for territorial exchanges. The latter eventually became central to planning since this seemed the only way to raise Yugoslav interest. The Yugoslav position in general and the Slovenian position in particular hardened. This was in the first place the result of the severe setback the government in Ljubljana suffered in the plebiscite in Carinthia on 10 October 1920 and the Rapallo Agreement with its decision on the course of the Italian-Slovenian border. This naturally affected their position on the question of the Apače Basin. The government in Graz was aware of this fact and that gaining sovereignty to the Basin would only be possible, if at all, if adequate territorial compensation was made. Combined with concessions in the area of transportation, such as in an agreement that would allow the use of the rail line between Spielfeld and Radkersburg by the Yugoslavs, the Slovenian-speaking villages south-east of Radkersburg were put on the table. Beginning in the spring of 1921, further projects entered into the discussion reaching beyond the borders of Styria itself. First discrete advances were made in Carinthia, if areas there with Slovenian-speaking majorities in the southern parts of the juridical districts of Eisenkappel/Železna Kapla might be seceded to Slovenia. In exchange, Carinthia was to receive undefined areas of Styria near the Soboth or in the vicinity of St. Lambrecht. The Carinthian government proved to be unwilling to cooperate, itself being intent on avoiding opening so quickly any discussion about an area the future of which was decided in the plebiscite only a few months past.[16]

The head of the Styrian government, Anton Rintelen, proposed another plan at the end of March 1921, on the occasion of a visit by Chancellor Michael Mayr in Graz.[17] Rintelen proposed a three-way territorial exchange between Austria, Yugoslavia and Hungary. Yugoslavia was to relinquish the Apače Basin to Austria in return for areas south of the Raab River near Szentgotthard in Hungary. The latter would be compensated by Austria with areas in the southern

[16] StLA, Statth. Länder-Zentralbüro Graz, A5b-207/1921.

[17] On Chancellor Michael Mayr cf. Hermann J.W. Kuprian: Zwischen Wissenschaft und Politik: Die politische Entwicklung Michael Mayrs von 1907 bis 1922. Innsbruck 1985 (unpublished doctoral dissertation).

Burgenland. This proposal was based on Yugoslav interests in the Slovenian-speaking villages south of Szentgotthard. Chancellor Mayr forwarded this proposal to the Central Border Commission, the chairman of which was at the time also dealing with the agenda of the Burgenland administration office in the Home and Education Ministry. Both the Central Border Commission and the Burgenland administration office turned Rintelen's proposal down. The latter even formulated a letter of protest, vehemently rejecting this encroachment on the territorial integrity of the Burgenland, which, after all, had been granted the status of an independent and equal state in the constitution.[18]

The "Central Office" in Graz was reservedly optimistic about the chances this plan had for success. On 19 April 1921 the chairman of the district school board of Gornja Radgona, Dr. Vaupotič, asked the Radkersburg district school board to send the files of the public and girl's schools in Apače to his office, since his board would be responsible for them in the future. The latter board sent the letter to the state school board, which in turn asked the "Central Office" to clarify the situation. In its answer dated 13 July 1921 the "Central Office" reported that the area belonged, according to the peace agreement and the current legal situation, to Yugoslavia but added "for internal use only" that "chances are good that an agreeable solution to the Apače Basin question may be found."[19] Anton Rintelen, namely, had asked the new chancellor Johannes Schober at the end of July 1921 to support his exchange project. The "Central Office" had in the meantime also approached President Michael Hainisch about the issue. The Central Border Commission for its part remained against the proposal.

The inner Austrian discussion on the Apače Basin acquired a new dimension in autumn, 1921, when the Foreign Ministry brought up the issue of a multilateral territorial transfer to the Yugoslavian government. The Austrian government also endeavoured to raise the issue of the Apače Basin at the Conference of Venice on 13 October 1921 chaired by Italy, where the actual issue on the table was the status of the Burgenland. This attempt was nevertheless met with disapproval since no Yugoslav representative was present. This was one of the major difficulties with the exchange project, namely that the plan as conceived by Rintelen required a trilateral agreement. Even if Austria managed to come to terms with each of its neighbours individually, its Hungaro-Yugoslav aspect remained unresolved.[20]

A second major difficulty was the territorial compensation offered Hungary. Rintelen modified his plan in the course of 1921 in that he began to concentrate his efforts on the area of Sopron/Ödenburg. The Conference of Venice con-

[18] Austrian National Archives/Österreichisches Staatsarchiv (= ÖSTA), NPA, Liasse Österreich 9/III, Zl. 3143-1 B/1921; Burgenländisches Landesmuseum (ed.): Burgenland 1921. Anfänge, Übergänge, Aufbau. Eisenstadt 1996 (= Wissenschaftliche Arbeiten aus dem Burgenland 95).
[19] StLA, Landesschulrat, C42A, 3243/1921.
[20] Cf. Staudinger, Zum Plan eines Gebietstausches, p. 100.

cluded by calling a plebiscite to decide who would gain sovereignty over this area. Rintelen and the "Central Office" took up this thought and claimed Hungary should be encouraged to relinquish its claims to regions in which it was interested in exchange for this concession. Austria could then, in turn, realise its claims to the Apače Basin. The Austrian Foreign Ministry rejected this proposal, stating that a plebiscite decided upon in Venice on the future of the Ödenburg area could not be tied to Hungarian territorial concessions after the fact, much less to a state not represented at the conference.[21]

Anton Rintelen, who demonstrated his ambitions for a regional foreign policy repeatedly in the early years of his administration in Graz, and various other Styrian authorities, continued their endeavours despite their initial failures. Various interest groups from the Styrian border areas were also active and went so far as to put the issue directly to Chancellor Schober. In parliament, members of the Großdeutsche Volkspartei raised the issue of the status of the exchange project. Rintelen himself raised the issue of Ödenburg in a letter to Schober dated 21 December 1921. The plebiscite, which had taken place in the middle of December, had resulted in a majority for Hungary. Rintelen proposed that this fact could convince Hungary to secede territory to Yugoslavia with the concomitant Yugoslav secession of the Apače Basin in turn. But Schober continued to see the tying of the Ödenburg question to the discussion on the Apače Basin as unrealisable since Yugoslavia had not been involved in the decision making process on the Austro-Hungarian border question. The Chancellor, who was at the same Foreign Minister, was moreover of the opinion that the Yugoslav government had first to voice its position on the matter.[22] But the position that had come to dominate there was that all border and sovereignty issues vis-à-vis Austria were at the time to be considered closed. As for the position of Hungary on this trilateral exchange, the losses suffered in the Peace of Trianon played a central role. This shock left Hungary unwilling to discuss further territorial secessions, even those where it would be compensated. To what degree the regional foreign policy adventurer Anton Rintelen was aware of these facts and ignored them, or if he simply failed to assess what was realistically possible as a result of his single minded focus on winning back the Apače Basin, is a matter for speculation.

Changing demography after 1919

After the establishment of the new international borders in 1919, the demographic relations in the Apače Basin shifted in favour of the Slovenian residents. On the basis of the census of 1921, which, among other things, asked for

[21] ÖSTA, NPA, Liasse Österreich 9/III, Zl. 6245-1 B/1921.

[22] ÖSTA, NPA, Liasse Österreich 9/III, Zl. 7569-1 B/1921.

the respondents' mother tongue and included the immigrants from the Prekmurje, 7,835 people resided in the Apače Basin of which, according to M. Klemenčič, 4,775 were listed as German and 2,690 Slovenian. The analogous data as presented by Arnold Suppan show 9,241 residents of which 4,847 were German and 4,331 were Slovenian.[23] These changes were in the first place the result of emigration by Germans and the immigration of Slovenes from Prekmurje.[24] This nevertheless had little effect on the rural nature of the area. Agriculture, animal husbandry and orchard and viniculture remained the economic staple of the population, although the concentration of land in German hands played an increasingly important role. Like the farmers in the region of Kočevje/Gottschee and to a lesser degree in the Drau Valley, the Apače Basin was an area in which compact rural German settlements could be found. Other Germans in Slovenia after 1918 belonged for the most part to the middle and upper classes in the cities and market centres.[25] But the Apače Basin had become a peripheral north-eastern area with little access to Slovenske gorice in the south and severed traditional economic and communication ties to the north, the result of the new international border. Yugoslav sovereignty, the demographic shift and transformation into a regional backwater were three marked changes with which the German-speaking population of the Basin saw themselves confronted after 1919. Additionally, many of their associations and clubs had been dissolved and their property confiscated. The changes in the school system have already been discussed.

These significant changes did not result in a rupture in an ethno-cultural identity among the German-speaking population. It received support from official authorities and associations in the Styrian capital, where emigrants from the arean acted as a pressure group. In the communal elections of 1927/28, the Germans in Apače gained the absolute majority.[26] Their economic dominance continued well into the 1930s; in 1935 ca. 80 percent of the landed property was still in German hands. At auctions, rich buyers from Austria were sought to block Slovenes from acquiring land. This activity acquired a political note in the 1930s as well. According to an official Slovenian report from Ljubljana to the Cabinet Presidium in Belgrade on the economic situation of the northern border of Yugoslavia, dated 21 September 1934, these Austrian financiers were

---

[23] Cf. Matjaž Klemenčič: Die Slowenen und Deutschen im Lichte der sprachlichen Statistik in der Südsteiermark und in der Untersteiermark 1830-1991. In: C. Stenner (ed.), Slowenische Steiermark. Verdrängte Minderheit in Österreichs Südosten. Vienna – Cologne – Weimar 1997 (= Zur Kunde Südosteuropas II/23), pp. 68-105, here p. 103; Suppan, Slowenen und Deutsche in Krain, p. 316.

[24] On the issue of Slovene immigration cf. Franjo Baš: Prispevki k zgodovini severovzhodne Slovenije. Maribor 1989, p. 100.

[25] Cf. Suppan, Jugoslawien und Österreich, pp. 692-693; Stefan Karner: Die deutschsprachige Volksgruppe in Slowenien. Aspekte ihrer Entwicklung 1939-1997. Klagenfurt – Ljubljana – Vienna 1998.

[26] Cf. Dušan Nećak: Die "Deutschen" in Slowenien (1918-1955). Kurzer Abriss / "Nemci" na Slovenskem (1918-1955). Kratek oris. Ljubljana 1998, p. 12.

for the most part National Socialists.[27] In March 1939 after Hitler's march into Czechoslovakia, "Anschluss" propaganda began to be spread by the "Swabian Cultural Union" in the Apače Basin, part of the Union's official policy.[28] In the period of the National Socialist dictatorship, beginning on 6/7 April 1941, a Germanisation and deportation policy was initiated against the Slovenian population with the support of the "Styrian Homeland Union", which also affected the Apače Basin.[29] But the National Socialist dictatorship and the Second World War were, in the end, also catastrophic for the German-speaking population. Expulsion, internment and liquidation by the new Yugoslav state and mass exodus after 1945 led to a near complete destruction of the autochthonous German-speaking population in the Apače Basin. Several of them returned to their homes in 1948 after their release from internment camps. They found refuge among the Slovenian farmers and earned their living in agriculture. A return to their own houses and fields as owners was nevertheless no longer possible. 453 properties were confiscated in the Basin. In the course of the agrarian reform and inner colonisation as of 1946, 720 families were settled in the 46 villages of the Basin and the bordering slopes of the Slovenske gorice. These came primarily from Carniola, namely from the regions of Dolenjska, Notranjska, and Bela krajina. They were moved to the Basin, among other things, to further fundamentally shift the ethnic balance there. But the unfavourable conditions in the Apače Basin convinced many of these colonists to quickly return to their homes. Several families that had been resettled in the Vojvodina returned to the Apače Basin in 1947/48.[30] If the Slovenian population had in the past represented the largest part of the agricultural labourer population, after 1945 these were joined by the remaining and returning Germans. The latter became, after 1945, a very small "hidden" minority. After their marginalisation in the course of events in 1919 – which nonetheless had little effect on their compact and dominant position locally – their local marginalisation followed in 1945. Intensified assimilation processes were also effective in this respect. But nevertheless, as the linguistic studies of Mirko Križman have shown, elements of the German-speaking population remain. In

[27] Cf. Suppan, Jugoslawien und Österreich, p. 694.

[28] Cf. Nećak, Die "Deutschen" in Slowenien, p. 15. NS-Propaganda on the "Anschluss" of Slovenian Styria to the German Reich reached its peak after French capitulation in June 1940. From this point on, national-socialist oriented Germans began to prepare for an invasion by the Wehrmacht and their eventual "Anschluss".

[29] Cf. Tone Ferenc: Quellen zur nationalsozialistischen Entnationalisierungspolitik in Slowenien 1941-1945/Viri o nacistični raznarodovalni politiki v Sloveniji 1941-1945. Maribor 1980, pp. 250-252, 612.

[30] Cf. Zdenko Čepič: Problematika kolonizacije Apaškega polja pri izvajanju agrarne reforme po drugi svetovni vojni, in: *Časopis za zgodovino in narodopisje* 65/1 (1994), pp. 137-149.

the course of the Slovenian census 1991, 25 people in 11 communities identified their mother tongue as German.[31]

Bibliography:

AMON, Karl/LIEBMANN, Maximilian Liebmann (eds.): Kirchengeschichte der Steiermark. Graz 1993.

BAŠ, Franjo: Prispevki k zgodovini severovzhodne Slovenije. Maribor 1989.

BURGENLÄNDISCHES LANDESMUSEUM (ed.): Burgenland 1921. Anfänge, Übergänge, Aufbau. Eisenstadt 1996 (= Wissenschaftliche Arbeiten aus dem Burgenland 95).

ČEPIČ, Zdenko: Problematika kolonizacije Apaškega polja pri izvajanju agrarne reforme po drugi svetovni vojni, in: *Časopis za zgodovino in narodopisje* 65/1 (1994), pp. 137-149.

DOLINAR, France M.: Cerkvena uprava in Slovenci. In: V. Melik/S. Granda/V. Rajšp (eds.), Slovenija 1848-1998: Iskanje lastne poti. Maribor 1998, pp. 198-215.

FERENC, Tone: Quellen zur nationalsozialistischen Entnationalisierungspolitik in Slowenien 1941-1945 / Viri o nacistični raznarodovalni politiki v Sloveniji 1941-1945. Maribor 1980.

HAAS, Hanns/MÄHNER, Peter: Verfeindete Brüder an der Grenze: Südböhmen / Südmähren / Waldviertel / Weinviertel. Die Zerstörung der Lebenseinheit. „Grenze“ 1938 bis 1945. Forschungsbericht. Horn 1998.

HELLER, Wilfried: Grenzen und ihre Erforschung. Gegenstände, Fragestellungen, Zielsetzungen. In: I. Diekmann/P. Krüger/J. H. Schoeps (eds.), Geopolitik. Grenzgänge im Zeitgeist, vol. 1/1: 1890 bis 1945. Potsdam 2000, pp. 325-350.

JANISCH Josef A.(ed.): Topographisch-statistisches Lexikon von Steiermark mit historischen Notizen und Anmerkungen, vol. 1. Graz 1878.

KARNER, Stefan: Grenzziehungsfragen der Republik Österreich nach den beiden Weltkriegen in ihrer ökonomisch-politischen Relevanz. In: E. Zöllner (ed.), Österreichs Erste und Zweite Republik. Kontinuität und Wandel ihrer Strukturen und Probleme. Vienna 1985 (= Schriften des Instituts für Österreichkunde 47), pp. 17-42.

KARNER, Stefan: Die deutschsprachige Volksgruppe in Slowenien. Aspekte ihrer Entwicklung 1939-1997. Klagenfurt – Ljubljana – Vienna 1998.

KLEMENČIČ, Matjaž: Die Slowenen und Deutschen im Lichte der sprachlichen Statistik in der Südsteiermark und in der Untersteiermark 1830-1991. In: C. Stenner (ed.), Slowenische Steiermark. Verdrängte Min-

[31] Cf. Mirko Križman: Das Deutsch als pragmatische und kulturelle Überlieferung bei Resten der deutschen Minderheit im Grenzgebiet der Mur. *Uporabno jezikoslovje/Applied Linguistics* 1 (1993), pp. 158-174; ibidem: Jezikovna razmerja. Jezik pragmatike in estetike v obmejnih predelih ob Muri. Maribor 1997; Nećak, Die “Deutschen” in Slowenien, p. 54.

derheit in Österreichs Südosten. Vienna – Cologne – Weimar 1997 (= Zur Kunde Südosteuropas II/23), pp. 68-105.

KRIŽMAN, Mirko: Das Deutsch als pragmatische und kulturelle Überlieferung bei Resten der deutschen Minderheit im Grenzgebiet der Mur. *Uporabno jezikoslovje/Applied Linguistics* 1 (1993), pp. 158-174.

KRIŽMAN, Mirko: Reste der deutschen Minderheit im slowenischen Grenzgebiet der Mur. In: R. Hinderling/L. M. Eichinger (eds.), Handbuch der mitteleuropäischen Sprachminderheiten. Tübingen 1996, pp. 185-198.

KRIŽMAN, Mirko: Jezikovna razmerja. Jezik pragmatike in estetike v obmejnih predelih ob Muri. Maribor 1997.

KUPRIAN, Hermann J.W.: Zwischen Wissenschaft und Politik: Die politische Entwicklung Michael Mayrs von 1907 bis 1922. Innsbruck 1985 (unpublished doctoral dissertation).

KURAHS, Hermann: Die Abtrennung des Untergries 1919/20. *Jahresbericht BORG Bad Radkersburg* 16 (1984/85), pp. 10-17.

KURAHS, Hermann et al.: Bad Radkersburg. Naturraum und Bevölkerung, Geschichte, Stadtanlage, Architektur. Bad Radkersburg 1997.

NEĆAK, Dušan: Die "Deutschen" in Slowenien (1918-1955). Kurzer Abriss / "Nemci" na Slovenskem (1918-1955). Kratek oris. Ljubljana 1998.

STAUDINGER, Eduard G.: Zum Plan eines Gebietstausches zwischen Österreich, Jugoslawien und Ungarn aus dem Jahr 1921. *Veröffentlichungen des Verbands Österreichischer Geschichtsvereine* 26 (1989), pp. 97-101.

STAUDINGER, Eduard G.: Von der Mehrheit zur Minderheit. Die deutschsprachige Bevölkerung des Abstaller Feldes im 19. und frühen 20. Jahrhundert. In: H. Heppner (ed.): Deutsche und Slowenen im gemeinsamen Raum. Neue Forschungen zu einem komplexen Thema. Munich 2002 (= Buchreihe der Südostdeutschen Historischen Kommission 38), pp. 111-124.

SUPPAN, Arnold: Slowenen und Deutsche in Krain, der Untersteiermark und in Slowenien in den Volkszählungen von 1880, 1910, 1921 und 1931. In: H. Rumpler/A. Suppan (eds.), Geschichte der Deutschen im Bereich des heutigen Slowenien 1848-1941. Vienna 1988 (= Schriftenreihe des österreichischen Ost- und Südosteuropa-Instituts, Bd. XIII), pp. 311-318.

SUPPAN, Arnold: Jugoslawien und Österreich 1918-1938. Bilaterale Außenpolitik im europäischen Umfeld. Vienna 1996.

VOVKO, Andrej: Nemško manjšinsko šolstvo na Slovenskem v obdobju stare Jugoslavije. *Zgodovinski časopis* 40/3 (1986), pp. 311-321.

Part III.

Crossing borders – Living with Borders

The Kolpa River as Linguistic and / or Political Border Line between Slovenia and Croatia

Duška Knežević-Hočevar

Introduction

After the fall of the Berlin Wall, the establishment of the new border regime between Slovenia and Croatia gained central attention in the daily political arena. Soon after the proclamation of independence of both states in 1991, the experts on the Slovenian-Croat border commission determined the so-called points of disagreement along the borderline. The Upper Kolpa River, which divides two border regions on the Slovenian-Croat international border, was determined to be an unproblematic, clear political line. However, the borderlanders in the Upper Kolpa Valley did not quite agree. Their understandings of the new border situation did not fit the commonsensical notion that was so often employed in the political rhetoric, holding that the Kolpa River is the linguistic border between Slovenes and Croats 'from time immemorial'.

The article discusses precisely such "scientifically" reinforced political views as highly problematic and oversimplified. Endavours of the linguists since the mid- nineteenth century, who sought to confirm the linguistic division line on the Kolpa River are reviewed and compared with the local perceptions of the distribution of linguistic repertoires and boundaries of spoken and written languages. Analysed in the wider context of local national self-ascriptions, these understandings proved much more complex than the state-building politics and science assumed. On the one hand they defy the official categorical notions of national membership, on the other, such official categories are built into the locals' everyday identity repertoire. This seeming contradiction will be addressed in some detail.

My research on the Slovene-Croat border has focused on the identity of the people of the Upper Kolpa Valley. I have carried out two separate field studies, the first in 1993; the second in 1996. In both instances it was hypothesised that the establishment of the state border on the Kolpa River in 1991 represented the crucial event that has substantially recast the local population's self-perception in terms of their national identity. However, the research perspective was significantly different in the two studies. While the second study was indeed the continuation of the first, the differently organised observation not only gathered a distinct set of data, it also added significantly to the case built in the first study.

My research interest in the Upper Kolpa Valley border region grew out of the work of Slovenian anthropologist, Stane Južnič. In the *Prolegomena* to his textbook *Linguistic Anthropology* (1983), he built into the argument his own experience as a native of the Upper Kolpa Valley. Because of this spatial determinant, he found himself "faced with linguistic dilemmas, torn between competing linguistic usages and knowledges, traditions and assurances. On this border, [...] two linguistic communities touch and intertwine in a strange divisiveness."[1]

The official linguistic border, which was gradually consolidated through the elementary school education in the second half of the nineteenth century, divides the uniform spoken language of the locals on both sides of the river. Južnič insists that it was precisely this institution that introduced the chasm into the mother tongue, denoting it as a lower dialect vis-à-vis Standard Slovenian and Croat. The two standards were increasingly seen as the proper codes for "serious linguistic communication".[2] School education also insisted that the uniform local spoken language was actually divided into Slovenian (*Kostelsko*)[3] and Croat (*Kajkavština*[4]of Gorski Kotar) dialects. Južnič writes: "After that we indeed believed that on the Slovenian side we speak Kostelsko and on the Croat side Goransko."[5] In his endeavour to elucidate the linguistic dilemma of the border locality, Južnič concludes that in terms of ethnicity, the Kolpa River connected rather than divided the people living on either side. He goes on to explain why the differences in spoken language in the valley are more longitudinal, i.e. running along the river rather than latitudinal or cutting across it.[6]

This description of the linguistic situation in the Upper Kolpa Valley proved to be particularly topical with the imposition of the international state border on the Kolpa in 1991. The media created an image of an unproblematic – in the sense of "correct" and "just" – delimitation between Slovenes and Croats. Appropriately, the joint Slovenian-Croat state border commission corroborated their statements to create such an impression. The commission took the cadastral record as the key criterion for drawing the demarcation line between the two sovereign states and found it clearly defined in the Upper Kolpa Valley. No area along the Kolpa River was recognised as a point of dissension between the two states. Yet, the borderlanders themselves did not share this point of

---

[1] Stane Južnič: Lingvistična antropologija. Ljubljana 1983, p. 9.

[2] Ibidem.

[3] The term *kostelsko* refers to a border region of Kostel in the southern part of the Upper Kolpa Valley. This region has had the status of a border county since 1998.

[4] The three types of spoken Croat as determined by linguists of the nineteenth century are *Štokavština*, *Čakavština* and *Kajkavština* after the word for 'what' (*što*; *ća*; *kaj* respectively). As Central European nation-building processes relied heavily on linguistic arguments, early speculation held that this triple systematisation is the delineator among Serbs, Croats and Slovenes. The spoken language of the entire area of Gorski Kotar was, and is, largely a variant of the so-called *Kajkavština*, a type of speech very similar to spoken languages in the territory of present Slovenia.

[5] Južnič, Lingvistična antropologija, p. 10. In the local naming *Goransko* is a term for a local dialect of *Gorski Kotar*.

[6] Ibidem, p. 197.

view. Since the establishment of the new international border in 1991, and even some years earlier, they have seen the side-effects of the border imposition as seriously inconveniencing in their everyday lives, despite the fact that they have, as have their predecessors, lived with a kind of border for centuries. In my research, I decided to investigate the situation as it developed along the Upper Kolpa River after the imposition of the international border, emphasising in the process the views of the borderlanders themselves. I presumed that their understanding of the new border situation was markedly distinct from the one that the state and its promulgators imagined to be proper for the ideal borderlander. While the nationalist position of the state is formed predominantly through the ideologically and legally defined categories of membership, the understanding of the borderlanders themselves proved much more complex.

The Kolpa River as a linguistic border

Figure 1: Map of research area

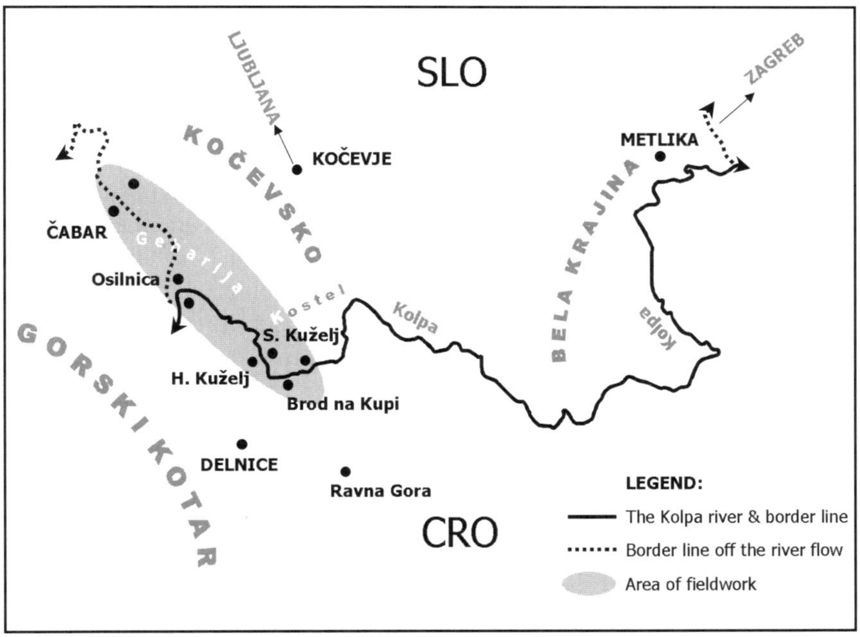

The Upper Kolpa Valley divides the regions of Gorski Kotar on the Croat and of Kočevsko on Slovenian side. The valley itself was the location of a variety of forms of political delineations at least since the fifteenth century, at first between diverse feudal estates and later between different statehoods. The border between the Austrian and Hungarian parts of the Empire, i.e. between the imperial province of Carniola and the Kingdom of Croatia-Slavonia, was fixed here.[7] It seems that the locally preferred usage of "national" denominations Croat/Carniolian instead of Croat/Slovenian demonstrates the memory of those times as firmly embedded among the locals.

Academic linguistic, historical, folklorist and geographical debates of the nineteenth and early twentieth centuries discerned the geographical characteristics of the valley as explanatory of the "natural" isolation of its inhabitants. Such a view has its merits. While the locals were not completely cut off, it is certain that throughout the last five hundred years, for various reasons, none of the representatives of the various powers that gained sovereignty over the locality founded an important urban centre in the valley that could bind the settlements. Additionally, the river was not a suitable large scale transportation avenue[8], the few roads were of poor quality and the large impassable forests proved to be real barriers for the inhabitants in their communication with the hinterland. Such environmental conditions indeed created a closed social universe in which the river functioned as primary communication channel.

These geographical characteristics of the Kolpa Valley have often been incorporated into other scientific contexts. Most questionable but quite typical for the various scholars of the early twentieth century were "scientific" arguments that the Kolpa River was not only a geographic border, but also a "natural" dividing line between the two nations, Croats and Slovenes, and that from time immemorial. An important field for proving such "theories" was linguistics.

Slovenian and Croat linguists usually did not deny the obvious similarities of various dialects on both riverbanks. The differences in interpretations pertain mostly to their attempts to reconstruct the spoken languages and their origins in the area of Gorski Kotar (Croatia) in the fifteenth century, i.e. in time of the "Turk invasions" of Gorski Kotar and Kočevsko. The linguists of the day interpreted their way right through a host of unpalatable facts in order to fabricate a clear distinction between the local Croats and Slovenes in their nation-building project that viewed nationality as a permanent and immutable social sign with an equally clear-cut history. Such judgements were retroactively nationalist and mirrored the ahistorical ideology of the time.

For instance, the distinguished Slovenian linguist Fran Ramovš, rooted as he was in the historiography of the day, thought that early differentiation between Slovenian (west) and Serbian-Croat (east) dialect groups arose when Southern Slavs had already lived in the new homeland (that is, in the Balkans) for some generations. He did not hesitate to assert that Standard Slovenian and the *kajkavian* and *ćakavian* dialects of Standard Serbian-Croat had developed jointly over "more than a thousand years".[9] In a similar vein, he ascribed the

---

[7] Ibidem, p. 287.

[8] Anton Melik: Posavska Slovenija. Geografski opis. Opis slovenskih pokrajin. Ljubljana 1959, p. 472.

[9] Fran. Ramovš: Karta slovenskih narečij v priročni izdaji. Ljubljana 1957, p. 6.

reasons for the total emancipation of the Slovenian language from other Slav languages to two external factors: firstly, to the early socio-political border that separated the Alpine foothills from the Lake Balaton along the Sotla River, over the Gorjanci hills to Gorski Kotar, and secondly, to the so-called "particular structure of the Alpine-Slovenian country".[10] He further explained the loosening of the ties between the Slovenian language and the Balkan Slav language and the beginning of linguistic particularism. How he imagined the dialectal development of Bela Krajina, the broader region around the Kolpa River, is noteworthy:

> The dialects of Bela Krajina are mixed Slovenian-Serbian-Croat dialects in the strict sense of the word. [...] the Slovenian population of Bela Krajina arrived to this region along the Kolpa River from the south, from what is now the Croat side. [...] Accordingly, we might think that the original development of the dialects of Bela Krajina was the same as that of the Croat dialects across the Kolpa River up to the thirteenth century.[11]

He also noted that: "All this was not essential for the existence of the present dialects of Bela krajina; only the events since the fifteenth century mattered significantly for dialectal formation in Bela krajina."[12]

One of his contemporaries, the Croat linguist Rudolf Strohal, also believed that the events of the fifteenth century were of primary importance for the formation of modern dialects of Gorski Kotar. He sought to explain the extraordinary similarities of spoken languages on both sides of the river with rather far-fetched arguments. The Croats had been a *ćakavian* speaking population until the sixteenth century, when two rejuvenations of the Croat language occurred. Firstly, at the beginning of the sixteenth century, when the use of *štokavština* (i.e. Uskoki)[13] from the southern regions of the Balkans spread to the present-day Croatia, and by the end of the sixteenth century, when the use of *kajkavština* spread southwards from the northern regions of the present Slovenia.[14] According to the historian Simonič, it was precisely the "Turk invasions" of the Kočevsko in the years 1522, 1528 and 1530 that caused the extensive emigration and depopulation of the Kolpa River Valley and its hinterland.[15] However, Strohal believed that at that time, the once exclusively *ćakavian* speaking Croat refugees became, through their decade long exile in Carniolia, *kajkavian* speaking, which, in effect, he purported to be a "slovenisation" of the Croat language. Returning to their homeland in Croatia, the descendants of these migrants not only brought the *kajkavian* dialect to the region, but they

---

[10] Ibidem, p. 8.

[11] Fran. Ramovš: Karta slovenskih narečij v priročni izdaji. Ljubljana 1935, p.135.

[12] Ibidem.

[13] *Uskoki* were medieval migrants from the inner Balkans, mostly Orthodox and nomadic people. They were hired by the Austrian authorities to defend the Empire against the advancing Ottoman army. The majority of them were *štokavian* speaking.

[14] Cf. Josip Lisac: Geneza kajkavštine u obradi Rudolfa Strohala. *Radovi 28/18 (1988/89)*, pp. 61-68, here p. 63.

[15] Ivan Simonič: Zgodovina kočevskega ozemlja. In J. Mačkovšek (ed.), Kočevski zbornik. Razprave o Kočevski in njenih ljudeh. Ljubljana 1939, pp. 45-130, here p. 83.

were also able to consolidate it as the only local spoken language. Strohal's linguistics therefore implied the "biological" purity of the speakers who thus, despite their changed language, remained thoroughly Croats.[16]

Employing such a complicated re-migration theory in the academic fashion of his time, Strohal strove to prove two things: the origin of *kajkavština* of Gorski Kotar and "the pureness" of the Croat *kajkavci* in that region.[17] It was important to insist that the very similarities between the tongues somehow developed independently. However, some scholars of the use of *kajkavština* in Gorski Kotar disclaimed Strohal's viewpoint. In his attempt to discover the origin of the spoken language of the inhabitants of the border town of Čabar and its environs, the Croat historian Laszowski went back to the seventeenth century. At that time, the duke of the Croat lands, Petar Zrinski, found the iron deposits in Čabar and its immediate vicinity. In 1651, he built an iron foundry, and populated the region with miners and mining experts from the then well known mining areas of Upper Carniola (present day north-west Slovenia), Idrija (a mining town in present day west Slovenia), Carinthia, Tyrol and Bavaria. In order to supply the miners with food, Zrinski also brought peasant families from the nearby villages of Gorski Kotar and Carniola. According to Laszowski, this colonisation of the Čabar region in the second half of the seventeenth century was crucial for the extant *kajkavština* in the border region. He wrote: "The dialect displays Slovenian origin, and it is quite reminiscent of that from Idrija. But schooling indeed transformed this dialect into Croatian only."[18]

Another of Strohal's contemporaries, the Croat linguist Majnarić, offered a similar explanation. Studying the colonisation of the settlements around Delnice, and particularly the nearest town Ravna Gora, he discussed some of Strohal's arguments about the two rejuvenations of the Croat language. Majnarić insisted that the colonisation that accompanied the construction of the *Karolina* road in 1732 significantly determined the spoken languages in this border region. In 1727, the Austrian Emperor Charles VI instigated the building of a road to connect the border area with the Adriatic coast. Due to insufficient labour available from among the locals, the contractors brought to the region masons from Primorje (the Austrian coast of the eighteenth century), and *rovtarji*[19] from Upper Carniola, who were to clear the forests for the road.

---

[16] Cf. Južnič, Lingvistična antropologija, p. 107; Josip Lisac: Goransko predmigracijsko dialektalno stanje i podrijetlo suvremenih organskih idioma u Gorskom Kotaru. *Dometi* 24/6-7 (1991), pp. 381-387.

[17] Lisac, Geneza kajkavštine, p. 63.

[18] Emilij Laszowski: Gorski Kotar i Vinodol. Dio državine knezova Frankopana i Zrinskih. Zagreb 1923, p. 43.

[19] *Rovtarji* are people who settled a secluded and especially hilly area in present day central Slovenia. *Rovte* is a landscape between Škofja Loka (app. twenty kilometres north of Ljubljana) to Logatec (app. twenty kilometres west of Ljubljana) and Tolmin (the town close to the Slovenian-Italian border).

In accord with this assumption and his own linguistic observations, Majnarić concluded that

> the dialect of Ravna Gora is rovtarsko. This implies that great grandfathers of the major part of present day population of Ravna Gora had arrived from Upper Carniolia, mostly from the areas around Cerkno, Idrija, Črni Vrh over Idrija and Poljane [...]. If that was the case, then Strohal's assertion that "onetime ancient inhabitants – the Croat refugees from Carniolia" – brought the dialects to Ravna Gora, fails.[20]

Certainly, 'Croatness' and 'Sloveneness' were never contested in the valley in such a way that the locals would seek to be something completely other than Croats or Slovenes. Being Slovenes or Croats was determined largely along the delineation lines of the imperial Hungarian state and its Croat provinces on the one hand and the Austrian state on the other rather than on the basis of formerly extant dialects, either the Croat (goranska) *kajkavština*, or a Slovenian dialect.[21] The constructions of dialectal 'origins' on the part of the linguists cited above should not be confused with the continued implementation of two written standards, the Slovenian and Croat, a process that begun in the second half of the nineteenth century. It is also true, however, that the so-called national consciousness at the political border between the onetime Austrian (Carniolia) and the Hungarian (Croatia) estates were consolidated separately, much as it was the case with the language. As Južnič put it: "The cultural pressure of the hinterland did not stop at the political border but set up cultural tensions there. Thus the people on the one side of the Kolpa were in fact becoming Croats and, on the other side, Slovenes."[22]

Two 'national' riverbanks

In the 1993 research, I did not take particular interest in the historical memory of the locals or in how the political authorities of the twentieth century affected the lives of the borderlanders through the written word. Nevertheless, the preliminary research did show that the Slovenian/Croat differentiation was activated in a rather unexpected way immediately after the establishment of the international border. Although the locals on both riverbanks were highly sympathetic vis-à-vis the creation of the two nation states, they opposed the establishment of the new state border. They expressed the latter sentiment mainly through the reiterated complaint that "before 1991, we were as one, and now we are divided." However, the alleged, strongly emphasised former "unity" was itself soon exposed as highly problematic: various forms of recognition of differences between the people on respective riverbanks are historical and well

---

[20] Nikola Majnarić: Jedno Rovtarsko narečje v Gorskom Kotaru. *Južnoslovenski filolog* XVII (1938/39), pp. 135-149, here 149.

[21] Južnič, Lingvistična antropologija, p. 287.

[22] Ibid., p. 10.

established in the region, notably that between Slovenes/Kranjci and Croats/Gorani.[23] As stated before, there has been a political border on the Kolpa River of one type or another throughout the past five hundred years. In the 1993 research, I focused on the question, what the nature of the new border was, given that the locals only now seem to perceive it as a dividing line.

The main goal of the 1993 study was to unveil such contrasts by means of quantitative analysis carried out in a defined research area. In accord with the expressed feelings of national dichotomisation and national unity, I took the political border to be the prime separator of the two populations. The research included sixty residents of the valley, thirty from the Croat and thirty from the Slovenian side. They were selected from among the four pairs of cross-river villages[24] on the basis of certain 'independent' variables – age, gender, professed nationality and the population of the villages.

First I tested the local understandings of the two "nations" through statistical estimations of intensity and frequency of the various kinds of contacts (that of kin, business, labour, festive, shopping, entertainment, mutual solidarity and sport) maintained by the inhabitants of the respective settlements both before and after the establishment of the new border. The results showed that only formal contacts dropped perceivably while informal contacts among kin and friends remained stable.

The analysis further showed that the differing perceptions of the new border situation were not uncomplicated. There were no clear categorisations of Slovenes and Croats. Only half of the respondents identified themselves first and foremost with one of the national denominators (Slovenes/Croats), while the other half chose the name of their settlement. Nearly all (fifty-six out of sixty) saw their cross-river neighbours as more similar to themselves than the other members of their "nation" outside the valley. Similar results prevailed regarding questions pertaining to language. Fifty respondents out of sixty recognised their everyday spoken language as the shared, cross-border local dialect rather than either Slovenian or Croat. However, a further specification of the question, "Which dialect are you speaking daily", obtained answers of a very wide spectrum, usually in accord with the name of the respondents' respective settlement of residence. A majority (forty-three out of sixty) also emphasised that the locals on both sides of the river shared their everyday language, with such minimal differences that a newcomer would be unable to perceive them. They themselves said that,

> "When we speak our local language there are no differences between cross-river dialects; otherwise we do use more Slovenian or Croat words"; "When we speak our home language, the difference between our own and their dialect is insignificant"; "Us locals, we speak the same way while immigrants speak differently"; "Differences are bigger along the border than across it"; "Once we spoke in the same way. But now, the school and the border prevent that."

---

[23] Kranjci and Gorani are local terms for Slovenian and Croat.

[24] For more on my first study see Knežević 1998.

Needless to say, the inhabitants of the Upper Kolpa Valley developed a specific system of self-naming and naming of their more or less distant neighbours along and across the river. This system is recognisable in many local terms denoting either a specific settlement location (upper or lower river-bank) or the particular style of dress of the villagers in question. In view of language division, the locals use the term *geberji* or *gebarji*. I was told that the term itself has a humorous and sometimes even pejorative connotation: "Up to here (Mirtoviči) there live the speakers of our spoken language, from here on (towards Osilnica and Čabar) live *gebarji* in their own territory – *gebarija*." The interviewees were not sure about the etymology of the word *gebarji*. Some of them believed that the meaning of the word was connected somewhat with the Slovenian word *gobarji* – gatherers of mushrooms. The others were certain that the word *gebarji* referred to the particular way the women traditionally wore their clothes – peasant women used to fold (*spodgibile*) long skirts lest they hinder them in performing their chores. Another explanation has it that the term refers to the folds (*gube*) that appear in women's long garments while walking. A minority of the informants stressed the German origin of the word though they were not familiar with its meaning. The use of the term itself is not limited to the Kolpa Valley; it is well known up to Kočevje. Some respondents told me that people from Kočevje designate all inhabitants from the Upper Kolpa Valley as *gebarji*. Therefore, the cognitive map of numerous *gebarije* point to the peoples' affiliations with the various everyday spoken languages. This map gives evidence of the wide scope of social contacts in the Kolpa border region and on the social relations between the people from the *gebarija* in the valley and those who live in the nearby towns out of the valley.

One of the most significant findings was the apparent inconsistency in the statements of the respondents. On the one hand, the often-voiced complaint, "Before we were as one, and now we are divided" seemed in accord with the locals' negative attitude towards the new border regime. The majority of interviewees (forty-eight out of sixty) stressed only the disadvantages of the new border, while two of them believed that the new border regime brought only advantages. Eight respondents mentioned both, the advantages and disadvantages of the new border, while two of them noticed neither disadvantages nor advantages. Yet there were sporadic differences conveyed in the form of negative stereotypes: "Slovenes/Croats have always been [...]" Moreover, such observations seemed in accord with rarely, but clearly expressed positive attitudes towards the new border:

"Because of the difference in currency, we (on the Slovenian side) can afford much more"; "Now, order is restored regarding smuggling by gypsies and thieves"; "The advantage is symbolical: to let it be known where Slovenia is"; "There is more safety now from the 'southern attack' (migration)"; "It is good that the Croats are not here anymore; before, they shopped incessantly, went to local inns, etc."; "The border brought cheaper goods on the Slovenian side"; "Finally, there is no more intertwining and mixing among the locals"; "Here (on the Croat side), we are becoming more connected along the river compared to former connections across the river"; "The territory to which I belong is finally confirmed."

I could not find in 1993 a significant drop in intensity in those contacts among cross-river neighbours that represented essential and functional relations, particularly among kin. However, one could also see that the process of deepening of the locally defined differences between the two 'nations' on respective riverbanks was already underway. This observation instigated the study in 1996, which in turn was carried out after a significant reorganisation of the research perspective.

Boundaries among the members of an extended cross-river family

In 1996 I shifted the research perspective from an assumed 'national' dichotomy (two "national" riverbanks) to the repertoire of self-perceptions of the members of an extended "nationally-mixed" cross-river family.[25] I focused on the relative significance of the 1991 event in the context of self-perception of the locals and their biographies. I sought to obtain evidence on the impact of the establishment of the state border in 1991 in comparison to other possible "milestone events" that, in the views of my informants, were important in the differentiation of the borderlanders in the past.

I chose a "nationally-mixed" family in Slovenski Kuželj, the only settlement in the valley that has an immediate counterpart across the river, Hrvatski Kuželj. It is a case of a unified settlement that was divided administratively earlier in history, and since 1991, legally constituted as two separate villages in two different states.

The Brelih family[26] met the study requirements the best of all families in the respective villages: individual members of the family were married cross-river and were more or less permanent residents of the valley. The Brelihs are offspring of a couple born at the beginning of the twentieth century. The entire first generation (six in all), three sons and three daughters had declared themselves as having been born Slovenian but had adopted Croat citizenship when they chose to live across the river. Their own parents were also "nationally-mixed". In 1996, they were already deceased.

---

[25] For more on the shifting research perspective in 1996, see Knežević-Hočevar 1999, pp. 12-16.

[26] Brelih is a pseudonym.

Figure 2: the Brelih family

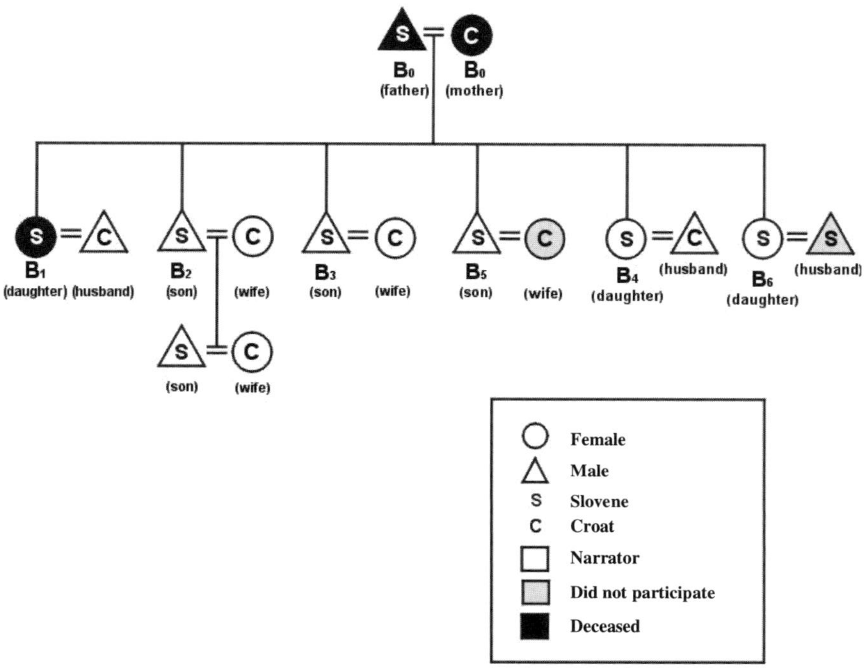

I found all six descendants to be well-suited informants for biographic research since they were all, with the exception of the youngest daughter (B_6), married cross-river. From among the second generation, I selected only the son of the oldest first-generation male offspring B_2 and his wife, who lived in a joint household with his parents in Slovenski Kuželj. His siblings did not live in the valley by then, because they had moved away early in their lives. Of the other family members that met the research criteria, the oldest first-generation daughter B_1 was deceased. The husband of the youngest first-generation daughter B_6 and the wife of the youngest first-generation brother B_5 never resided in the Upper Kolpa Valley or its immediate vicinity during their adult lives. In this research I did not verify the linguistic situation in the valley in general. Instead, I anticipated it eventually crystallising out of the gathered biographies themselves.

The valley life from "time immemorial" to "new pragmatism"

The local understanding of the events that had a crucial impact on valley life "from time immemorial" were elicited through interviews, both with members of the Brelih family as well as their neighbours from both sides of the river. According to the more elderly interviewees, in the period from the beginning of the century to the end of the Second World War, the locals shared the same way of life. They were poor, cut off from the world outside, married cross-river and made a living mainly by raising cattle, along with cultivation of the scarce fertile soil and seasonal employment in the forest. In the winter, men worked in sawmills or peddled either in the vicinity of the valley or deeper into the Austro-Hungarian provinces. Meanwhile, the women were responsible for quite large extended families, often consisting of the couples' parents, their unmarried sisters or brothers and frequently five to ten children. Most of them also worked as day-labourers in larger nearby farms. Peasant women also made a living by selling seasonal vegetables, fruits, diary products and eggs on the market place in Delnice, or, when necessary, by selling their own home produce from house to house around the valley. According to the eldest villager (92), the misery of this border region was well known even to the Austro-Hungarian Empress Maria Theresa: "Once visiting her border-estates, she found the greatest poverty precisely in the settlement Srobotnik, near Kuželj. There were eight houses, two goats, some sheep and no cows. Since then, the villagers of Srobotnik have been exempt from state taxation."

Many locals immigrated to the United States and others to various European countries, especially during the 1920s, due to the economic situation in the valley. Once abroad, some maintained contact with their relatives or neighbours in the valley. Usually they would help by sending packages of clothes, food or other goods. Such aid was of particular importance especially during the Second World War, when many families were left without adult male labour. At that time, the Kolpa River was the border between Mussolini's Italy and the fascist Independent State of Croatia (NDH). Barbed wire separated the villagers across the river, although the border regime itself did not prevent daily contacts between neighbours. As one informant explained:

> Here (on the Slovenian side of the bridge) was the Italian guard; on the other side the Croat home guard set up a sort of a hut. Sometimes soldiers allowed us to go to the other side, sometimes they did not. But when I really wished to go, I did not mind. I simply forded the river.

Despite the first harsh measures of the Italian occupation – the internment of all adult males from the Slovenian riverbank in the labour camp on the Croat island of Rab – the interviewees stressed that those who lived under Italian rule had a sufficient food supply. The "Italians" delivered provisions to the locals once a month. The system of distributing the provisions was commensurate to one's economic status, which gave some families a fair subsistence, while others, especially big families, were left in a more difficult situation. It occurred that some villagers had "enough macaroni to feed even their pigs", while the majority with relatives across the river, or those who were known to help the resistance partisans, lived in rather dire circumstances. Yet all the informants agreed that the border regime during the Second World War did not substantially impede cross-river contacts.

In the period from the World War II to the establishment of the international border on the Kolpa River in 1991, they still shared the same way of life. The only new development was an increase in non-agricultural employment. As before, they shared common social institutions: the church in Hrvatski Kuželj, the local inns, the grocery stores, some common places of leisure activity on both riverbanks along the Kolpa, and the bridge, the meeting point of many locals. An illustrative description of its importance was given by an informant, who was born in 1944 in Slovenski Kuželj and had married to Hrvatski Kuželj:

> As I told you, we (the children from cross-river villages) had a wonderful childhood, played on the bridge and under the bridge. Down there, we had a beach for us all. Also the adults. As young people, we kept each other company on the bridge. Some old villagers, especially men, brought chairs and would chat. It was really a bridge of meetings.

After 1991, however, it seems that the only thing the borderlanders still shared was a form of "new pragmatism". It is expressed by the descriptions of various strategies to ease their everyday lives. As they say themselves: "This is easier done here/there"; "The police, customs officers and officials in general make more difficulties here/there"; "It is easier to earn money here/there"; "Here/there one can buy supplies cheaper".

The villagers from both Kuželj and the nearby settlements also worried about life in the valley in the future. They complained that the valley was almost completely depopulated; that the young people were few, although they knew why: "Why should they stay in the valley when they can barely make a living here." They are all gravely concerned about increasing unemployment and the lack of "secure jobs" in the valley and its immediate vicinity. Moreover, those rare enterprises in the valley and its surroundings often pay their wages very irregularly. Even when pay is regular, the currency differences cause more and more dissatisfaction among the locals. Finally, the bridge has lost its previous importance. In many cases, police controls prevented the people using the local bridge to cross the river, sending them kilometres down the river to cross the international border. Sometimes it was the mere presence of the police that made people reluctant to go across the bridge.

On the basis of these preliminary narratives, I extracted four major themes for the collection of biographies of the selected members of the Brelih family: preferred relatives; recollections of the past ways of life; assessment of local space and places in the valley for social interaction; and the assessment of the valley's prospects for the future.

Preferred relatives

Regarding the first general topic, all eleven narrators singled out only those relatives who have been important to them in the context of the life in the valley. All of them mentioned parents, brothers, sisters, brothers and sisters in law, occasionally grandparents, rarely uncles and aunts and never cousins, nephews or nieces. When they sought to explain the origin of their ancestors, they just mentioned from which river bank the person in question had come from or had gone to live. They would frequently tell me the proper name of a settlement or village from which someone originated or has moved to without any explicit statement as to whether the persons in concern declared themselves Slovenes or Croats. They would use denominators Slovenian/Croat only when asked about a person's official national self-declaration.

Past ways of life

Assessing the past way of life in the valley, the majority of the Brelihs emphasised the poverty of villages and settlements in the border region and its surroundings in general. Consequently, before World War II, the region witnessed frequent emigration to America, France and Germany. Moreover, until the Second World War, it was almost a rule to leave the valley after the harvest; men traditionally peddled from house to house throughout Austrian, Hungarian and Czech lands. They also laboured seasonally in the forests in both hinterlands of the Kolpa Valley as forest workers and finally they were occasionally employed as farm hands in the remote region of Baranja. After World War II, they also occasionally worked on the better-off farms downstream, up to the town of Metlika. Irrespective of the riverbank, the borderlanders sought to find additional work whenever the occasion presented itself. Differentiation among the locals appeared only along the line rich-poor, which, according to the interviewees, was not linked to one or the other specific riverbank.

Local space for social interaction

Local inns and taverns on both river banks had many functions in the past: they were social places where the population were able to relax after the hard working day playing cards, not for money but for fun, or for discussing lively; they were the only public entertainment facility. Nearly all of the Brelihs agreed that at times, the inn in Slovenski Kuželj was about the "only fun" in the valley. Today the inns function as an arena for daily internal delineation. In words of the son of B_2: "When we drink a little, we then tease each other about Slovenian-Croat daily policy." His aunt, B_4, observed the same:

One man from Gladloka (a village adjacent to Slovenski Kuželj) frequents a pub here in Grbajel (a village adjacent to Hrvatski Kuželj). Men in our pub often tease him, "What do you Slovenes really want?" When he had a few drinks, he would take such teasing to heart, and then there is a major fuss. Moreover, if the media report about a political incident between Slovenia and Croatia, a sort of tension is presented even within our family, let alone among the people around here.

During my fieldwork, the Slovenian media reported on a local incident in the Upper Kolpa Valley. Locals from the Croat riverbank were to build a concrete wall on the shore to prevent the river from washing the soft soil away. This very act was interpreted as an attempt to redirect the Kolpa in favour of the Croatian territory. Talking about daily discussions in the local inns, I asked B_4 whether she was informed about the recent incident in the settlements ten kilometres up the Kolpa. B_4 replied: "We know nothing about it. There is gebarija. We do not know anything about what is going on there." Her husband added: "I do not know. Croats spare words in such cases while Slovenes make a noise for nothing." B_4:

Now, we (Croats) are facing much more serious problems here in Croatia, while Slovenes are dealing with daily trivialities. Besides, the Croat settlements Zagolik, Kočičin and Suhor are border-settlements with gebarija. There is a wall between us locals. Horrible. A real wall without a wall.

Husband of B_4: "And up there, there they have a completely different language." B_4: "They speak differently, and are doing things in a different way."

This sequence of comments clearly points to the approval of the afore-mentioned locally determined linguistic line between gebarji and non-gebarji. Yet, mentioning media reporting on the building of the concrete wall, immediately provoked the couple from the Croat riverside to comment, "Slovenes emphasise every pettiness while Croats deal with more serious problems (such as the war)."

Similarly, some sequences of the Brelihs' stories indicate that after the establishment of the border in 1991, different, and much more controversial, interpretations about the Catholic Church in Hrvatski Kuželj developed. Most explicit was B_5, who complained that after the establishment of the border, "Slovenes wish they could have everything for themselves; they set up the new crucifix in Slovenski Kuželj only so that they need no longer visit the church in Hrvatski Kuželj." His younger sister, B_6, admitted that it was only after the new border that she became conscious that she, as a Slovenian, attended the Mass in the church in Hrvatski Kuželj in Standard Croat. It never bothered her before; now she was taken aback.

The valley's prospects for the future

The most salient comments I could extract from the members of the Brelih family were on the subject of their explicit estimations of the new Slovenian-

Croat state border in terms of the fourth topic under consideration – the assessment of the valley's prospects for the future. In the words of the husband of B_4:

Before the establishment of the border, nobody in the valley felt the need to name the cross-river neighbour according to his official national status. But now, we are using those we-you distinctions even within our family. When we discuss daily political events, the question of who is who among us suddenly becomes very important.

B_4 and her husband explicitly mentioned the husband of B_6, "a Slovenian", who in such debates inevitably lets them know that on the one bank of the border river there live the Slovenes and on the other, Croats. To confirm "the absurdity" of such and similar designations, B_4 emphatically reminded me of the fact that all brothers and sisters, except the youngest one, have married cross-river. At the same time, she did not herself refrain from employing a stereotype when she related:

I have gotten used to live as a Croat. I enjoy the company, and I prefer to be gallant. Slovenes are different. They are stingy and they do not enjoy being around a cheerful company. What a nation! Croats in general are not as irritable as Slovenes are.

Informant B_5, from the Croat side, shared her opinion. He noted that especially from the time of Slovenian independence, his brother in law, the husband of B_6, has been very intrigued by the question of "who is who in the Brelih family". Occasionally, the husband of B_6 even warned him that, being a Slovenian, he (B_5) should speak only Slovenian with him:

He (a brother in law from Slovenia) does well, and don't get me wrong, I wouldn't say a word against Slovenes! However, I live in Croatia. Everything I have, everything, is Croatian. And why should I always speak in Slovenian with him only because I was born in Slovenia? Now, we are in Croatia. I told him, let us speak Croatian. When I am in Slovenia, I will speak Slovenian with you.

Quite the opposite view was voiced by the oldest of the Brelihs, the husband of B_1. He restricted himself to pointing out only the good characteristics of his Slovenian brother in law, saying, "Nobody among the Slovenes is as good as the husband of B_6." Moreover, he stated that the "youngest daughter of the Brelihs (B_6) made a good match marrying him." Finally, the husband of B_1 is held in high regard with B_6; in her narration, she stressed many times that in her childhood it was precisely he who regularly visited them (the Brelihs) in Slovenski Kuželj. She will never forget that, he being a salesman doing business mostly in Slovenia, he always brought gifts for her family, which was at that time very poor. Comparing the two "Croat" brothers in law, she admitted that she still prefers the older one, the husband of B_1, while with the younger one, the husband of B_4, she had just recently quarrelled a lot about politics, because "I hold I am a Slovenian and he holds he is a Croat".

The Brelihs' estimations of the impact of the new border regime sometimes produced "allied interlocutors" within the family when there were two or more relatives present. The "allies" in the debate did not always form according to the riverbank of their origin, or along the lines of marriage. Rather, the shifts in forming the alliances depended on the number of persons present and the topic under discussion. However, national stereotypes were (re)produced as a matter of rule. For instance, once the Brelihs from the B_2 family developed a discussion on the legitimacy of the Slovenian/Croat official interpretation of the maritime boundary between the states. The daughter in law of B_2 was at first the most opinionated, speaking in favour of the solutions offered by the Croat border commission. B_2 agreed that in this case, Croats were right. His son opposed that and reminded them that Croats had recently illegally cut the trees in Slovenian woods. The daughter in law of B_2 remarked that the politicians on both sides were scoundrels while B_2 insisted that only Slovenes were good-for-nothings. Although B_2 and his daughter in law both criticised Slovenian politics, she kept her father in law at a distance denoting him as "always exaggerating", or opposed his expressed views even when they agreed with hers. All along, the wife of B_2 quietly nodded to her daughter in law; they both married into the Brelih family in Slovenski Kuželj and had come from the Croat side.

In another debate among the relatives, the husband of B_4 initially commented on the border regime:

> Everything would be fine on the Kuželjski bridge (the local crossing point) if the Slovenian police did not check every local that wants to cross. I am disturbed when they stop me and make notes on me as if I were a thief or drug addict. Before, I visited the relatives and neighbours on the other side at least twice a day. Now, I simply would not go there anymore.

B_4 heard her husband's comment and added:

> Oh, this border gets on my nerves. Once, the Slovenian policeman wouldn't allow me to cross the bridge. I told him that I was born in Slovenski Kuželj and that I was headed to my mother's grave. He couldn't be bothered. He simply ordered me to go back home for documents. I don't like such an attitude. I would like to go there many times but for this reason I don't go anymore.

Meanwhile, her brother, B_5, entered the room, and said:

> You may feel a certain chauvinism among Slovenes. On the bridge they would ask me: "Do you have the national label on your car? Show me!" They would tell you "show me" three times a day if necessary. Croats are not like them. Croats would know you. They would only wave to you. I know that both states want to have everything on their own. But Slovenes exaggerate.

Despite the increased presence of the border after 1991, the Brelihs still maintain close contact. The older they get, the closer they seem to become. They all emphasised that despite their different views regarding the Sloveneness or Croatness they still eagerly and regularly visit each other. The only thing they explicitly regretted was the lack of good prospects in the valley. Or to conclude with B_5: "Actually I do not care about politics and their borders. The only matter I really care about is how to bring more life into the valley."

Conclusion

The authors from the beginning of the twentieth century who investigated the historical processes in the Kolpa Valley often attached particular importance to the "natural" characteristics of this border region. Aside from geographical characteristics, they often invoked the 'ethnographic attributes' of the locals to justify the 'naturalness' of the political line.[27] Accordingly, particular significance was attached to the linguistic border, which caused a specific misunderstanding in this literature. The linguists of that time interpreted the political border on the Kolpa River as the border between two written languages, the Slovenian and Croatian. Yet, at the same time, they focused their attention to dialect characteristics, which did not conform to the officially recognised political and linguistic lines of division. To put it in Melik's terms:

> The feudal border between the Alpine countries and Hungarian Croatia determined the emergence of the national border between Slovenes and Croats. Actually, this border denotes the use of literary languages, Slovenian and Croatian, while it does not reflect the substantial difference in people's spoken language. Dialects across the border share so many characteristics that their common linguistic basis is more than obvious.[28]

In short, the linguistic interpretations from the beginning of the past century pointed more to the series of various manipulations in explaining the differences and similarities between the dialects as natural languages, and the written Standards as political means for the homogenisation of spoken languages.[29] It is this nationalist scholarly reinterpretation of the dynamic situation on the ground that serves as the confirmation of the "natural" border between two nations from "time immemorial".

According to the research presented above, the locals in the border region at the time of research still insisted that their spoken language was similar or uniform on both sides of the river. Before the 1991 border, the valley itself presented a firmly united social space, maintained through the persistent kin, economic and other functional bonds among the people. One may even speculate that the population in the Upper Kolpa Valley presented a uniform "ethnic mass" defined by common spoken language, territory and origin or, according to Benedict Anderson, an 'un-imagined community'.[30] Finally, the people on both riverbanks were closely connected because of their relative isolation from the valley's hinterlands, which rendered possible the function of the Kolpa as a link between the borderlanders rather than an obstacle.

It seems, however, that the establishment of the international border in 1991 called forth a specific misunderstanding between the local and the state dis-

---

[27] Cf. Ante Cividini: Gorski Kotar vol. 1/1. Zagreb 1934, p. 41.
[28] Anton Melik: Slovenija. Geografski opis 1: splošni del. Ljubljana 1963 (1937), p. 325.
[29] Južnič, Lingvistična antropologija, p. 174-176; ibidem: Identiteta. Ljubljana 1993, p. 6.
[30] Benedict Anderson: Imagined Communities: Reflections on the Origin and Spread of Nationalism. London 1983.

course. In their interpretation of the border situation, the state-builders have relied on the already strengthened juxtaposition of both written standards on the Kolpa River and automatically saw the local population as "naturally" divided into two distinct political entities. Consequently, they created the "appropriate image" of the borderlander, implying the unambiguous national affiliations. The borderlanders' perception, however, of a "uniform ethnicity" across the river was conveyed simultaneously and equally strongly with their expressed loyalty to both newly created nation states. For the locals, the division between the literary languages and the anticipated action did not play a crucial role in their everyday lives, although it seems the opposite when national stereotypes emerged among them after 1991. The case of the Brelih family proved that in certain social contexts, the relatives include explicit national denominators into the creation of local stereotypes. These situational contexts have also demonstrated that such differentiation did not happen only after the establishment of the border. Some parts of the Brelihs' life histories indicated such persistent self-presentations that implied the existence of the locally perceived categorical delineations even before the establishment of the border in 1991. Yet local perceptions of such differentiation differ from the official ones. If the state-builders register the shifting of the "pure" national identities at the border, mostly defined by the official language, the locals rather apply nationalist terminology to the more complex local differentiations. The presented material showed that the borderlanders' situational use of nationalist arguments, mostly in the form of national stereotypes, should not be mistaken for the shifting of their national identities.

Bibliography:

ANDERSON, Benedict: Imagined Communities: Reflections on the Origin and Spread of Nationalism. London 1983.

CIVIDINI, Ante: Gorski Kotar vol 1/1. Zagreb 1934.

JUŽNIČ, Stane: Lingvistična antropologija. Ljubljana 1983.

JUŽNIČ, Stane: *Identiteta (Identity).* Ljubljana 1993.

KNEŽEVIĆ, Duška: State vs. locality: the new Slovene–Croat state border in the Upper Kolpa valley. In: S. Abram / J. Waldren (eds.), Anthropological Perspectives on Local Development. London – New York 1998, pp. 55-74.

KNEŽEVIĆ-HOČEVAR, Duška: Družbena razmejevanja v dolini zgornje Kolpe. Domačinska zamišljanja nacije in lokalitete. Ljubljana 1999.

LASZOWSKI, Emilij: Gorski Kotar i Vinodol. Dio državine knezova Frankopana i Zrinskih. Zagreb 1923.

LISAC, Josip: Geneza kajkavštine u obradi Rudolfa Strohala. *Radovi* 28/18 (1988/89), pp. 61-68.

LISAC, Josip: Goransko predmigracijsko dialektalno stanje i podrijetlo suvremenih organskih idioma u Gorskom Kotaru. *Dometi* 24/6-7 (1991), pp. 381-387.

MAJNARIĆ, Nikola: Jedno Rovtarsko narečje v Gorskom Kotaru. *Južnoslovenski filolog* XVII (1938/39), pp. 135-149.

MELIK, Anton: Posavska Slovenija. Geografski opis. Opis slovenskih pokrajin. Ljubljana 1959.

MELIK, Anton: Slovenija. Geografski opis 1: splošni del. Ljubljana 1963 (1937).

RAMOVŠ, Fran: Historična gramatika slovenskega jezika, VII, Dialekti. Ljubljana 1935.

RAMOVŠ, Fran: Karta slovenskih narečij v priročni izdaji. Ljubljana 1957 (1935).

SIMONIČ, Ivan: Zgodovina kočevskega ozemlja. In: J. Mačkovšek (ed.), Kočevski zbornik. Razprave o Kočevski in njenih ljudeh.. Ljubljana 1939, pp. 45-130.

Family and Identity among Migrants from Slovene Istria

Mojca Ravnik

Introduction

After the First World War, new borders were drawn between Italy and the new states of Austria, Hungary and the Kingdom of the Serbs, Croats and Slovenes (Yugoslavia). These borders – with the exception of that with Italy, which was shifted after the Second World War – would become the present borders of the Republic of Slovenia. The last Slovenian border to come into being was that with Croatia in 1991, although it is still subject of bilateral negotiations. These borders have strongly affected and shaped the political, economic and cultural orientations of the regions through which they pass; what is more, they have also strongly influenced the whole of Slovenia, which, because of its relatively small size, can be defined a borderland state. Ethnological research in Slovenia can reveal the influences – be they direct or indirect – of borders on all regions and on all walks of life in the course of the 20th century.

The new borders divided many once flourishing Slovene-populated regions after the First World War, and old, previously vital economic, cultural and social communication routes were cut off. Towns such as Monošter (Szentgotthárd), Gradec (Graz), Celovec (Klagenfurt), Beljak (Villach), Čedad (Cividale), Gorica (Gorizia), and Trst (Trieste) now lay beyond the borders; extensive Slovenian hinterlands were cut off from their traditional centres of gravitation. The Slovene border regions near Hungary, Austria and Italy suddenly became closed-off backwaters, suffocated territories with bleak prospects; in Austrian Carinthia and in the Hungarian region of Porabje (i.e. the valley of the river Raba)[1] the indigenous Slovene populations became national minorities. Similarly, the Slovenes living in the territory that was annexed to Italy after the Second World War also became national minorities. The same is true for the Slovene populations of Slavia Friulana[2] and Val Canale.[3] For the latter two regions minority rights were granted in 2001.

---

[1] Before the First World War, Slovenian Prekmurje and Hungarian Porabje were a common region, populated by Slovenes, within the Hungarian part of the Austro-Hungarian Empire. In 1920 Prekmurje and Porabje were separated by the new border between Hungary and the Kingdom of Serbs, Croats and Slovenes.

[2] Slovene populated *Venetian Slavia* (Beneška Slovenija) was a part of the Republic of Venice until the latters disintegration in 1797. During the Napoleonic wars the region found itself initially under Austrian and then under French rule. From 1814 until 1866 it belonged to Austria, therafter it came to Italy. The current border between Venetian Slavia and Slovenia is the old Austro-Hungarian-Italian border, established in 1866.

In the case of the Istrian peninsula and the region of Primorska, developments differed. After the First World War the border between Italy and Yugoslavia cut both regions off from the Slovene hinterland, while links with Trieste as their principal centre of gravitation remained. After the Second World War the border between Italy and Yugoslavia was shifted towards the west; in 1947 a "Free Territory of Trieste" with two zones under the respective control of Italy and Yugoslavia was created. In 1954 the new border followed the demarcation line between the two zones and resulted in Istria and Primorska being integrated into Yugoslavia (or the Republic of Slovenia and, with respect to the southern part of Istria, of the Republic of Croatia). Since then both regions have shared the fate of being separated by an international border from their centre of gravitation, Trieste. A large Slovene minority remained in Italy.

For decades the borders delimited opposing political, social and economic orders. While the borders with Italy and Austria separated East and West, communism and capitalism, the border with Hungary separated two opposing communist orders, the Warsaw Pact on one side and "block free" Yugoslavia on the other.

In 1988, a long-term project titled "*Family and Kinship in Bordering Regions*" was initiated at the Institute of Slovene Ethnology at the Scientific Research Centre of the Slovenian Academy of Sciences and Arts in Ljubljana. Its objective was to acquire detailed insight into family and kinship relations in regions which during the 20th century were affected by the new state borders. Although the establishment of new borders was the common denominator for research, the respective political situation and the economic and cultural conditions of the various regions were not the same. The project investigated features of family structures and kinship relations specific for the given regions in its initial phase. In a second phase the consequences of the establishment of the borders on these features were examined.

Field work started in Prekmurje (Slovenia) and Porabje (Szlovénvidék, Hungary) and was continued in Istria[4] in the area of Kambreško (between the valley of Soča/Isonzo and Idrija), in Beneška Slovenija (Slavia Friulana, Italy), and in Kanalska dolina (Val Canale, Italy). In the early 1990s a wider and more thorough study of family and kinship relations was completed in Slovene Istria.[5]

---

[3] Before the First World War the *Canal Valley* was part of the Austro-Hungarian Empire. It belonged to Carinthia and was also connected culturally, socially and economically with neighbouring Carniola. Its inhabitants had intensive contacts with the Slovene population in the surrounding areas. After the First World War the region was assigned to Italy. Massive Friulian and Italian immigration would change the old ethnic structure, which was until that time mainly Slovene and German.

[4] Cf. Mojca Ravnik: Družina in sorodstvo v slovenskem Porabju, v Prekmurju in slovenski Istri. *Traditiones* 28/1 (1999), pp. 331-342.

[5] Cf. Mojca Ravnik: Bratje, sestre, strniči, zermani. Družina in sorodstvo v vaseh v Slovenski Istri. Ljubljana 1996.

This paper focuses on Slovene Istria and on specific features of its rural hinterland, the characteristics of family structure, inheritance customs, community kinship structures, settlement development and decay, the role that Trieste played in everyday life and the process of migration from the interior of Istria to the coastal towns, above all to Trieste. In three case studies (a family in the Istrian hinterland, the family of a woman of Istrian origin in Trieste and an Istrian family in Prekmurje) I will evaluate the role of family history and the impact of traditional settlement, family and kinship structures on migration. I will illustrate further, how kinship has spread across space and international borders. Finally I will discuss cultural continuity or discontinuity in family history within the context of language and identity. This will develop a better understanding of why an individual feels, chooses, expresses and shows or hides their identity or identities.

1. Family, settlement and community in Slovene Istria: Staying on and migrating

1.1. Two micro-regions

Research in Slovene Istria was based on life stories and memories related by local residents. The oldest informants could recall at least three generations of their family history or lineage; oral tradition went back to the first half of the 19th century. Istria witnessed various political administrations and upheavals since that time, Austrian rule, the First World War, Italian rule, the Second World War, the Free Territory of Trieste and its division into Zones A and B, the Yugoslav Republics of Slovenia and Croatia and finally, since 1991, the two independent states Slovenia and Croatia. The changes in national authority brought about changes in the organisation of municipalities, parishes, schools, official languages and political systems as well.

During the 20th century, the Slovene part of Istria (*Slovenska Istra*) as well as the entire Istrian region underwent acute demographic changes. Population decline, emigration from and immigration into the area resulted in the formation of two very different worlds: a densely populated, nationally diverse, built-up area along the coast and an increasingly under-populated and economically underdeveloped interior. These opposing developments were accompanied by an extremely uneven population distribution. In the interior, the rate of population growth decreased and the population grew older while the towns and settlements along the coast became overpopulated.

Initially, research focused on the villages of Abitanti and Zanigrad situated in two different micro-regions in the interior of Istria. Abitanti lies in the deep hinterland, while Zanigrad is located on the edge of the Karst region. Research spread from here across a larger area, in time including villages on the Croatian side of the border and areas closer to the coastal towns of Koper and Trieste.[6]

Figure 1: The villages of Abitanti, Zanigrad and other places in which interviews with locals took place. Bold lines demarcate the borders with Croatia and Italy.

The above-mentioned two cultural micro-regions represent two different areas of colonisation with regard to settlement types and linguistic characteristics. The people living in these two areas speak different Slovene dialects, their school systems developed differently and the standard languages used at school

[6] Cf. the map of the villages of Abitanti, Zanigrad and other places in which interviews with locals took place at the end of this article.

and in church are different.[7] Both regions belong to those areas with the highest population decline.

The aim of my research was the analysis of the local histories of the villages, houses and settlements, the evaluation of family relations, inheritance patterns, division of property, relations between children and siblings, family and community kinship structures, the integration of incomplete families, relatives who replace family members, non-relatives in the family, adoption and people without families, the role of children and the impact of relatives and neighbours in general. Additional information on subsistence farming and division of labour and settlement structure was also collected. The question if cultural micro regions were endogamous was examined as well as the impact of war and the period after the Second World War, new construction of houses and the disappearance of settlements. Finally, it was necessary to pursue Istrians who left their home villages and settled in Trieste, in other coastal towns or elsewhere.

1.2. Family, kinship, houses, settlements, community

The division of property and the principle of virilocality were the most prominent characteristics of these Istrian communities. Virilocality is a social norm that prescribes that daughters move away from their natal family upon marriage; post-marital residence is with the husband's family. It was usual for the father to determine the division of his possessions among his sons in his will; if there was no will, the sons would reach an agreement among themselves. Groups of brothers came to different solutions, some split the land and lived separately, others remained together, even after their parents had died. When a property had undergone too many divisions and several brothers were forced to share a single, overcrowded house and a meagre patch of land, it became impossible to continue land division and they had to remain together. Such extended families existed until the first years after the Second World War. The

[7] The villages below the rim of the Karst mountains were among the first to acquire public schools in the second half of the 19th and the beginning of the 20th centuries; instruction was in Slovene. In Pregara, however, the chaplain started to teach children in Croatian in 1910. With the Fascist reform of the Italian school system of 1923 Slovene was replaced by Italian as language of instruction. After the Second World War, lessons were first conducted in Slovene, from 1947 until 1956 in Croatian and since 1956 again in Slovene. Church services in the parish of Pregara were held in Croatian before it was annexed to the Diocese of Koper in 1973 – cf. Valerij Novak: Razvoj šolstva. In: S. Žitko (ed.), Kraški rob in Bržanija. Koper 1990, pp. 101-104; Andrej Vovko: Doneski k zgodovini istrskega osnovnega šolstva. *Kronika*, 3, 26, 1978, pp. 166-175; France Ostanek: Slovensko-hrvatska jezikovna meja v Istri. Gradivo za obdobje od leta 1860 do 1956. *Annales*, 1, 1991, pp. 213-221 and *Annales*, 2, 1992, pp. 245-254.

contradiction between the principle of equal division and the desire to preserve the farm was a constant source of distress for Istrian families.[8]

There were regional differences, of course. These were related to the proximity of Trieste and the coast as well as to the opportunities of earning an additional income or of moving into or closer to the city. The closer to Trieste the more frequent were divisions within a person's lifetime; divisions further in the interior occurred at greater intervals. Co-habitation was a temporary solution that merely postponed land division for a generation or two. Even if they divided land and lived in separate dwellings, the members of large groups of relatives lived in closely knit communities, the houses of the younger generations were added to those of their forefathers and were built either in a straight line or grouped around a central courtyard.[9]

A section of a family tree from a small family settlement named *Stara Mandrija* in the village of Abitanti is based on the story narrated by Matija, born in 1912.[10] His great-grandfather Jure moved from the old village located on the top of the hill above the present-day village and built the first house at the foot of the hill. Matija was born into a large joint family (i.e. a family unit formed through the decision of married brothers to live together) made up of the families of his father and his uncle; it formally split in 1927, but had practically broken apart already in 1920. A further division took place in 1949, at which time two of his three brothers were already married; each got a very small part, which compelled two of them to leave the village and move to coastal towns. His sister had already gone to Trieste. At the beginning of the 1990s only Matija, together with his nephew, his wife, and their son's family were living in the settlement. It had only taken four generations from the time, when the first house had been built by Matija's great-grandfather for the settlement to begin to empty. Since the beginning of the 20th century, every generation had a relative living in Trieste. Matija's grandfather's sister married into a village in Croatia. Other descendants wound up in other Istrian villages in Slovenia and Croatia, as well as in or near the Slovene coastal towns of Koper and Izola.

---

[8] This was also observed by Martine Segalen in Pays bigouden in France, where the egalitarian division of property prevailed, as she wrote: "Le système égalitaire porte en germe son autodestruction. A chaque génération se repose le conflit entre idéologie, pratique et reproduction sociale." – Martine Segalen: Quinze générations de Bas-Bretons. Parenté et société dans le pays bigouden Sud 1720-1980. Paris 1985, p. 83.

[9] The histories of Istrian families are closely connected with the histories of their houses and villages. The original founder, the great-grandfather or grandfather built the first, and the oldest, house. Each new division of the family resulted in additions to the original house, construction of new houses and different use of the existing ones. The relatives and descendants on the male side always lived near each other. This led to the development of rows of houses and neighbourhoods composed of relatives. Istrian stone is ideal for house improvements and alterations because it is easy to work, changes in family structure are reflected in house exteriors. The less durable the construction material was, the clearer was the link between the family and their house.

[10] Cf. the family tree of Matija at the end of this article.

Figure 2: Family settlement in the hinterland (family of Matija). Black circles and triangles denote individuals, who remained in the village the longest.

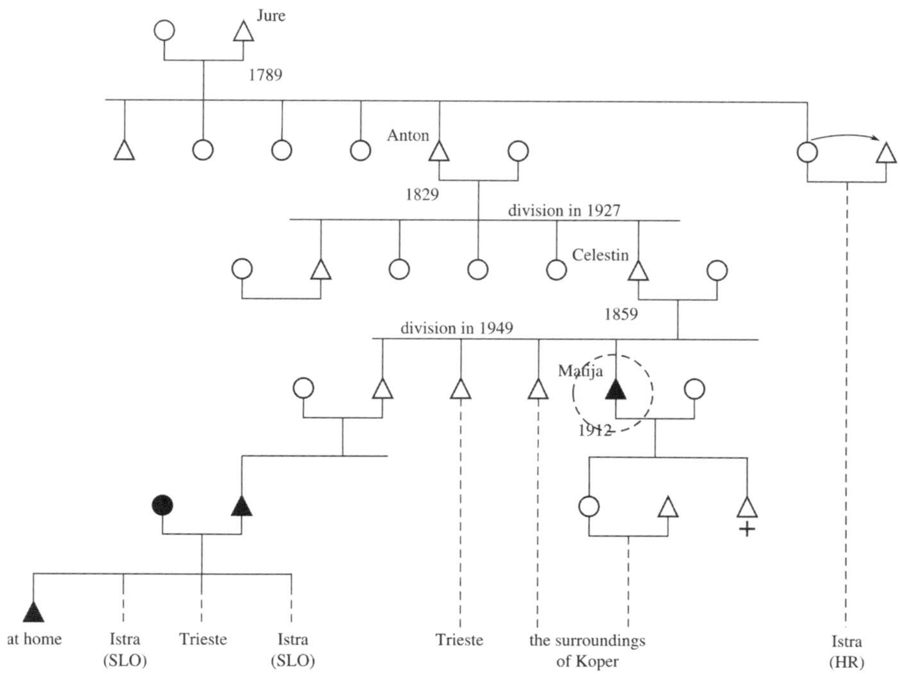

It is surprising, how close the relation between family history and the past of a house connected with that family in Istria can be. The history of the family and of the settlement coincides as well. As we see in Matija's case, the story begins with his ancestors settling in the area, and it ends with the moving away of their descendants. The short life span of settlements is related to the system of equality and equal division of property, which has led to cyclical overcrowding and forced people to migrate, regardless of whether they were able to postpone division for a shorter or longer period of time by co-habiting in complex family households.

1.3. Istria and Trieste, Istrians in Trieste and in other towns and countries

Trieste was by far the most important centre of gravitation for the whole of Istria. Principal activities in the villages in the interior were agriculture and animal husbandry. People also supplemented their income by various commercial activities linked to the coastal towns, mainly to Trieste. Daily, weekly, seasonal and permanent migrations from the hilly areas toward the coast, and from the entire rural hinterland towards Trieste were common.[11]

Numerous Istrians – mostly unmarried men and women – also found permanent jobs in Trieste and were thus able to secure their future. First they either lived at home and walked to work every day, or they sought overnight accommodation in the city. Later they set up permanent quarters in Trieste. Relatives generally tended to help each other; a sister might help another sister, a cousin would help another cousin, but by far the most common link for newcomers from Istria to Trieste seemed to be their aunts and uncles, who already lived and worked there. They helped their nephews and nieces from Istria to find employment and an apartment in the city. For Istrians, Trieste was, so to say, a part of their extended home.

There was little emigration overseas until the end of the Second World War. The reason has to be sought in the unique self-sufficiency and self-reliance of the villages of the Istrian hinterland and Trieste; it was more than just an ordinary relationship between the town and its surrounding rural area. It has already been mentioned that economic survival in Istria depended upon additional sources of income, which could only be found in Trieste. Since the houses in the villages became overcrowded within short intervals, people were again and again forced to leave for the town to find work and quarters there.

Istrians, furthermore, were not compelled to emigrate, since they could work in Trieste even without leaving home. What is more, the economic links between the city and the interior corresponded to the egalitarian system of inheritance, combined with the principle of division of property. Such an egalitarian system keeps people at home (living either in large joint families or in divided families on a small patch of land), encouraging them to be mobile within the region if there is a possibility of additional income.[12] Istrians found this income primarily in Trieste.

The Second World War left the Istrian hinterland devastated. People saw no possibility of staying at home and were uncertain of the political future. The previously united region was divided by a new international border, access to Trieste was obstructed and many had to change their plans to settle there. Young people, who saw no future in their impoverished and burnt villages, viewed Trieste as their only salvation. They fled across the border en masse. Once in Trieste, they stayed there with relatives and neighbours who already lived there. But many migrated onwards, often to Australia.

For many years the border was impassable for the majority of the population living in this area. In the mid-1950s, however, following an agreement between

---

[11] Cf. Julij Titl: Socialnogeografski problemi na koprskem podeželju. Koper 1965.

[12] This was also observed by Martine Segalen in *pays bigouden*; the system preferred that the local population remained in the region, it discouraged emigration and favoured intra-regional mobility – cf. Segalen, Quinze générations de Bas-Bretons, p. 112.

Italy and Yugoslavia, the local population was able to acquire special visas for local cross-border traffic, if they lived within twenty kilometres from the border. Contacts began to reach across the border again. Relatives who had moved away now returned on Sundays and on holidays, and many Istrians were able to work in Trieste again. Without a doubt, the border profoundly affected the lives of the people living in these areas, but it seems that the private aspects of family life have been successful in bridging the divide.

The second example describes a section of a family tree based on the story recounted by Marija, an Istrian woman from Trieste.[13] She was born in Zanigrad in 1918. An old uncle of hers, her grandfather's cousin and an aunt, her father's sister, were living in Trieste during her youth. As a young girl she worked in the city; together with her sister she walked daily from her village to Trieste. In 1939 she married a man from the city. They had two sons who both married and had children. Until old age she was selling flowers at the entrance to the Trieste cemetery. One of her brothers, who had married a woman from his home village, emigrated to Australia. Her other brothers and sisters live in villages in Istria, in the nearby rural region of Brkini and in the town of Izola. Their contacts are warm, especially those between Marija and the sister living in a village close to the border, who often exchanges letters with the brother in Australia. Marija's sons never go to Slovenia and do not understand their mother's native tongue.[14]

This case illustrates a typical biography of an Istrian migrant to Trieste. Marija was one of many young women from Istria who worked in Trieste (either washing laundry or working as maids, selling milk, bread or produce), but lived in their home village until they acquired better-paid work or until they married and went to live for good in Trieste. They were accustomed to the fact that in Trieste, the Italian language prevailed. When working together with other women from Istria they spoke their Slovene Istrian dialect, but in contact with their customers they used Italian. Under the Fascist regime the Slovenian language was oppressed and stigmatised; it became more and more difficult and dangerous to use it, so that people who had always spoken both languages simply stopped using the one that could cause difficulties. It is therefore not surprising that many villagers from Istria who had moved to Trieste do not speak Slovene in public and did not teach their children their mother tongue. Yet they continue to speak it with their kin and neighbours when they visit their home village.

---

[13] Cf. her family tree at the end of this article.

[14] The interview was conducted in 1994. Since that time the situation has changed. Some relatives who had not known each other as children have grown closer because of a marriage or a death in the family. A new dynamic can also be observed in Istrian villages; people who have moved away or were born in coastal towns are returning to their home villages to renovate their houses.

Figure 3: The family of an Istrian woman (Marija) in Trieste

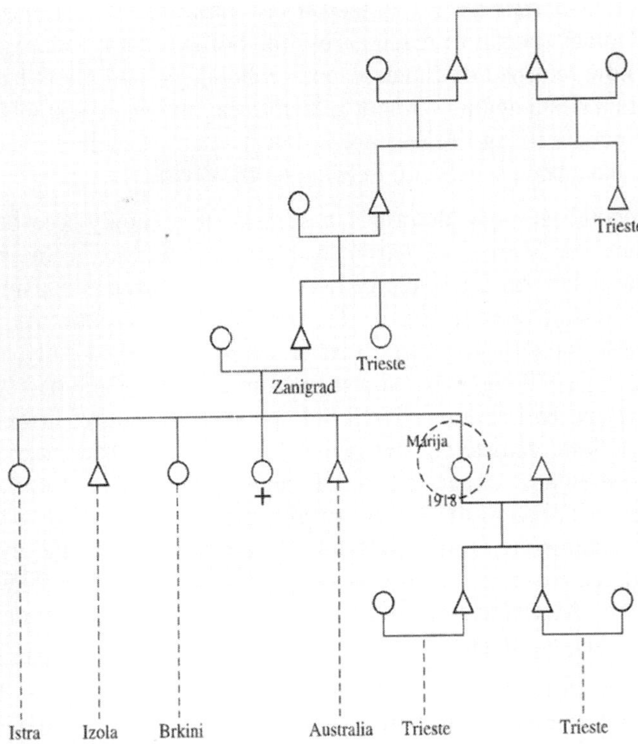

It is of significance that most of the migrants from Istria were women; virilocality prevailed, sisters left their home, leaving their married brothers with their families behind. The young women often left their villages without having previously secured a residence in Trieste. After marriage they adjusted to their Italian husband's way of life; their children did not develop any attachment to their mother's village of origin.

Istrians from the interior were accustomed to moving to Trieste, where they already had generations of relatives. The emigration to Italy that took place after the Second World War was thus a continuation of the centuries-long movement from the interior; it was only intensified due to the harsh living conditions in the Istrian villages. However, never before had the move to Trieste denoted emigration; this was a condition of the new border.

The following family tree is based on the story recounted by Justina.[15] She was born in 1903 in a village in Istria which is now in Croatia; her husband was from the neighbouring village. In 1929 they emigrated to Yugoslavia and after

[15] Cf. her family tree at the end of this article.

having lived for a brief time with a friendly Istrian family in Maribor, they settled in Prekmurje.[16]

Figure 4: Istrian family (Justina's family) in Prekmurje

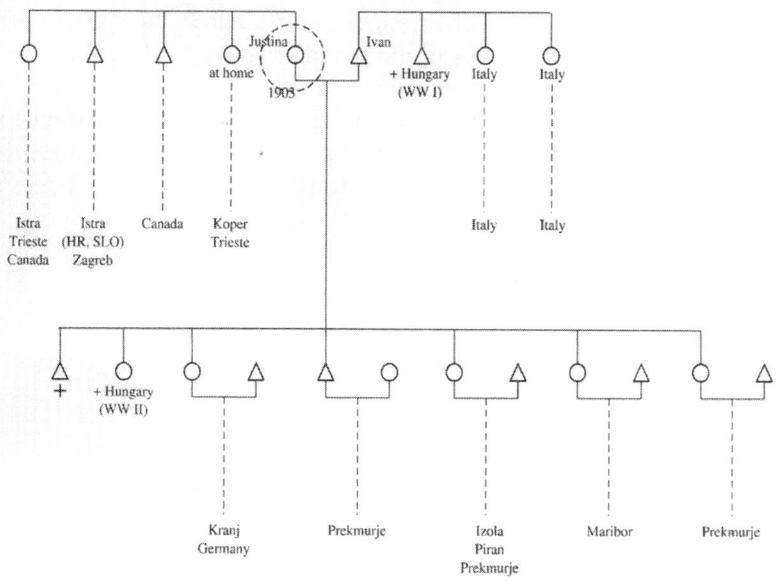

While colonists in some parts of Yugoslavia only received a piece of land for cultivation, in the village of Kamovci the family also received a house. It nevertheless took some time for the fields to yield crops. Initially the colonists had nothing to work with, neither tools nor cattle. When Hungary annexed Prekmurje in 1941, the Hungarian authorities deported them to the concentration camp in Sárvár. The children were saved by Serbian orthodox priests and taken to the Vojvodina, where they lived with peasant families until the end of the Second World War. When Justina's family returned to Prekmurje, they found their house occupied by a Hungarian family that soon left. The old house in the colony is empty now. Justina lives with her daughter's family; her children and

[16] During the First World War and after, refugees, first those from the regions, where the fighting took place by Isonzo/Soča and followed by those who lived in regions that were annexed to Italy after the war, settled in Styria and in Prekmurje. From 1921 until 1934, numerous colonies were founded in Prekmurje close to the border with Hungary built on the former land of wealthy Hungarian landowners, who had been expropriated in the agrarian reform. The approximately 140 colonist families (ca. 600 individuals) colonists were mainly refugees from Primorska and Istria. Cf. Jože Vidič: Kolonizacija ob meji v Prekmurju od 1921 do 1934 leta. Ljubljana 1964 (unpublished).

grandchildren are scattered in Prekmurje, Maribor, Slovene Istria, Kranj and Germany.

One of Justina's brothers stayed in the home village, married and had children. His descendants now live in Koper and in Trieste. The old house in Istria is empty now. Justina's second brother had emigrated to Canada after the First World War; the third brother married into a nearby village and his descendants now live in Slovene and Croatian Istria and in Zagreb. Justina's sister went to Trieste after the First World War and got married there. Her descendants live in Slovene Istria, in Trieste and in Canada. Justina's husband had a brother who died in Hungary during the First World War, his two sisters went to Trieste; their descendants now live in Italy. In the course of their lifetime Justina and her husband have lived in Austria-Hungary, Italy, Hungary, Yugoslavia and Slovenia; their brothers, sisters, nephews and nieces now live in four different states (Slovenia, Croatia, Italy and Canada).

2. Cultural continuity or discontinuity? – Language and identity

I have summarised and interpreted the stories of three individuals together with their family histories and kin networks. The interviewees were born in Istria at the beginning of the 20th century. In all three narratives, individual members from different generations had moved away from their home villages. Close relatives (parents, children, grandparents, grandchildren, brothers, sisters, aunts, uncles, nephews, nieces and cousins) now live scattered over vast distances, in different countries and even on different continents. Not all of those who live in foreign countries are migrants, neither did all of them move abroad; some of them simply found themselves living abroad after new international borders had abruptly made them residents of other states. Such radical changes naturally affected contacts between relatives: Brothers, sisters and cousins often maintained contact even across long distances; their descendants, however, less and less. When they meet, relatives from different countries are no longer able to communicate in the common language of their ancestors, who – only a few generations ago – had co-habited in large families and in close neighbourhoods.

Families not only from Istria, but also from Prekmurje, Porabje, Kambreško, Beneška Slovenija and Kanalska dolina have in common that they are determined by the borders in their vicinity and by the fact that their villages are affected by emigration; some of them (those in Beneška Slovenija, Porabje and in Kanalska dolina) can or could be also treated as minorities.

Among the methods used for the analysis of field material and written sources, the analysis of family histories yielded the best results because it embraces a wide range of questions concerning individuals, family and kinship, spatial mobility, social stratification, language and identity, cultural continuity and change. The basis for an analysis of family history is the concept of continuity/discontinuity and of uninterrupted/interrupted cultural development. An uninterrupted cultural development would unfold ideally in the form of several successive generations living in the same house, speaking the same language and belonging to the same state; family property and tradition would be transmitted from generation to generation, the house would be in a settlement, which had remained in the same state for generations, under the same civil and religious authority, with the same official language and with the same economic, social and cultural centre of gravitation for several generations. In this social and cultural environment, one generation succeeds another and every individual absorbs the tradition, knowledge and experience of his or her ancestors from birth.

The three selected cases reveal quite the opposite. If we asked each family member where they were born, in which house, village or town, in which houses they lived, what language they spoke at home, with close and distant relatives, at school, in church or at work, we would hear of numerous changes, interruptions and differences. Among "hidden minorities" or "hidden identities", we would come to similar results, if we applied the methods of family history with its synchronic and diachronic perspectives. When dealing with a hidden identity, the focus should be on the criteria (in different generations) that define it as "hidden" (spoken and written language, the language spoken at home, in the neighbourhood, at school, in church and at work, annual and life cycle traditions, marriage strategies etc.). The objective of such an analysis would be to find out whether the identity of a group of persons in question had always been "hidden" and if previous generations hid their identity as well. This dynamic is essential for the understanding not only of "hidden minorities" but of minorities in general. It may namely be said for different Slovene minorities that the developments of the 20th century led to both extremes – from overt to covert minorities and vice versa. When we ask why and how this happened, we have to concentrate upon the role and function of the family as a vehicle of cultural continuity and transmission through generations. We may then find an answer to the question of why grandparents and grandchildren no longer speak the same language.

The relation between language and identity is determined by many economic, social, political and other factors and circumstances, which cannot be generalised easily. When we speak of "hidden minorities" of Slovene descent, however, it can be said that the relation between language[17] and identity generally

[17] The Slovene language is especially vulnerable in this respect, since there are considerable differences between dialects and the standard language. At home, children would only learn the

depends on three different sets of circumstances: the transmission of the knowledge of the mother tongue within the family through generations, the availability of schooling in this language and the general political atmosphere. Since these preconditions were never met for most of the members of the second generation of migrants in Trieste they have remained a potential "hidden minority".

Bibliography:

NOVAK, Valerij: Razvoj šolstva. In: S. Žitko (ed.), Kraški rob in Bržanija. Koper 1990, pp. 101-104.

OSTANEK, France: Slovensko-hrvatska jezikovna meja v Istri. Gradivo za obdobje od leta 1860 do 1956. *Annales* 1 (1991), pp. 213-221 and *Annales* 2 (1992), pp. 245-254.

PIRY, Ivo: Demografska gibanja na Slovenski obali. Ljubljana 1983 (unpublished).

RAVNIK, Mojca: Bratje, sestre, strniči, zermani. Družina in sorodstvo v vaseh v Slovenski Istri. Ljubljana 1996.

RAVNIK, Mojca: Družina in sorodstvo v slovenskem Porabju, v Prekmurju in slovenski Istri. *Traditiones* 28/1 (1999), pp. 331-342.

SEGALEN, Martine: Quinze générations de Bas-Bretons. Parenté et société dans le pays bigouden Sud 1720-1980. Paris 1985.

TITL, Julij: Socialnogeografski problemi na koprskem podeželju. Koper 1965.

VIDIČ, Jože: Kolonizacija ob meji v Prekmurju od 1921 do 1934 leta. Ljubljana 1964 (unpublished).

VOVKO, Andrej: Doneski k zgodovini istrskega osnovnega šolstva. *Kronika* 3/26 (1978), pp. 166-175.

---

dialect. As long as they do not get instruction in school, they cannot speak the literary language. The vocabulary of the different Slovene dialects is primarily related to their agricultural surroundings. In order to express other things, it is necessary to use the literary language. That means that a person who speaks only his or her dialect will soon run out of words to communicate outside the immediate family. Dialects could therefore be used as a means of proving different theories that claim that Slovene minorities have nothing in common with the Slovenes living in Slovenia.

Part IV.

Languages and Language Contacts in Medieval Times

The Gospel of Nicodemus: A New Source for the History of German-Slavic Language Contact in the High Middle Ages?

Giorgio Ziffer

The importance of the Alpine-Adriatic region for the study of language contact and mixed languages has been acknowledged since the publication of the classical work by the great German linguist Hugo Schuchardt, *Slawo-deutsches und Slawo-italienisches* (Graz 1884).[1] It is evident, however, that the possibility of reconstructing the history of language contacts in this region is seriously limited by the nature and extent of the sources at our disposal; sources, which can only yield a fragmentary picture of the linguistic reality of more or less distant times. Nonetheless, through the use of an inductive method, we can trace the origins of this process back to the High Middle Ages in general, and to the formative stages of the Church Slavonic tradition in particular. It has to be stressed, moreover, that for historical reasons our research should also include testimonies that might have emerged in the territory of Moravia and Pannonia.

The existing documentation on which our analysis should be based simply does not permit us, however, to assign individual linguistic features or even entire texts with absolute certainty to one particular area of the wide transitional zone between the German and the Slavic world. Therefore we first have to deal with the nature of the existing textual documentation relating to German-Slavic language contact in the High Middle Ages. Its core is represented by a number of texts written either in Church Slavonic, that is, the first literary language of the Slavs, created by the Byzantine missionaries Constantine and Methodius between 960 and 970, or in a different language (which we may call Proto-Slovenian) but with indisputable elements of Church Slavonic origin, as is the case for the *Freising Fragments*. It is important to emphasise that – apart from new sources that have been added in recent years such as the new and still unedited *Sinaitic Missal,* the relevant documentation consists of texts, like, for example, the *Kiev Leaflets* or parts of the *Euchologium sinaiticum*, the existence of which has long been known to us.[2] Like the *Freising Fragments,* all these texts reveal some degree of Western (i.e. both Latin and German) influence. Indeed, a long-lasting critical tradition has accustomed us to see in Old Church Slavonic a language modelled above all, if not exclusively, on the Greek, whereas

[1] See also the important reprint, Hugo Schuchardt: Slawo-deutsches und Slawo-italienisches. Mit Schuchardts übrigen Arbeiten zur Slawistik und mit neuen Registern, Hrsg. u. eingel. v. Dietrich Gerhardt. Munich 1971.

[2] For an overall introduction to and a broad critical bibliography on these texts belonging to the earliest era of the Church Slavonic literary tradition, see Jos Schaeken/Henrik Birnbaum: Die altkirchenslavische Schriftkultur. Altkirchenslavische Studien II. Munich 1999.

Western elements have often been considered only of minor importance, even more in 20th- than in 19th-century scholarship. But if the influence of Old High German on Old Church Slavonic has really been more extensive and fundamental than is generally assumed, uncovering new facts concerning the German-Slavic language contact in Church Slavonic texts may shed some light on the beginnings of the Church Slavonic tradition.

In this regard, on the basis of various historical sources such as the *Conversio Bagoariorum et Carantanorum* and the Church Slavonic *Lives* of Constantine and Methodius, which contain valuable information for the period from the 8th to the second half of the 9th century, we are able to conclude that the Alpine-Adriatic region and the bordering zones were distinguished by a firmly-rooted Slavo-German bilingualism.[3] Yet whereas the *Lives* of Constantine and Methodius are sparse in concrete details, the *Conversio* constitutes a document rich in names and places and provides us with a living image of the area of Carantania and Pannonia. It is of note that while the linguistic facts suggest a deep influence of Old High German on Slavic, the influence of the latter on the former was quite limited; this conclusion coincides with historical data, which demonstrate that the Slavonic populations of Carantania and Pannonia were politically and culturally subordinated to the Bavarians and the Franks.[4]

Thus, we can study individual lexical elements of German origin that are to be found in many ancient Church Slavonic texts or we can examine entire Church Slavonic texts (e.g., the *Freising Fragments* and the *Kievan Leaflets*) and certain portions of the *Euchologium Sinaiticum*, which are undoubtedly of Western provenance. The following lexemes are indicative of the paramount importance of the lexicon involved, inasmuch as the specific Christian terminology plays a decisive role: *milosru`die* (mercy), *oplatu`* (host), *vu`so^du`* (communion), *zakoni`niku`* (priest). However, in addition to investigating individual linguistic features, it is obviously important to try to reconstruct – to the greatest possible extent – the concrete situation of bilingualism that made possible the language contact in question. As Roberto Gusmani put it a decade ago:

It is especially desirable that the theme of contacts in the High Middle Ages between the two great linguistic and cultural areas of Central Europe – that is, the Germanic and Slavonic areas –

---

[3] Herwig Wolfram: Conversio Bagoariorum et Carantonorum. Das Weißbuch der Salzburger Kirche über die erfolgreiche Mission in Karantanien und Pannonien. Vienna et al. 1979; Zwischen Rom und Byzanz. Leben und Wirken der Slavenapostel Kyrillos und Methodios nach den Pannonischen Legenden und der Klemensvita. Übersetzt, eingeleitet und erklärt von Josef Bujnoch. Graz et al. 1972 (see for example the well-known passage taken from prince Rostislav's embassy to emperor Michael the Third, quoted in the *Life* of Methodius, ch. 5, p. 114: "Durch die Gnade Gottes sind wir gerettet, und es sind viele christliche Lehrer aus Welschland, Griechenland und von den Deutschen zu uns gekommen, die uns verschieden gelehrt haben." This Western context of the origins of the Church Slavonic literary tradition is highlighted by Franz Zagiba: Das Geistesleben der Slaven im frühen Mittelalter. Vienna et al. 1971.

[4] B. Peters: Deutsch-slawischer Lehnwortaustausch. In: W. Mitzka (ed.), Wortgeographie und Gesellschaft. Festgabe für Ludwig Erich Schmitt zum 60. Geburtstag. Berlin 1968, pp. 624-643, here pp. 629-636.

is studied more deeply in all its complexities, without limiting ourselves to the examination of individual effects and contacts but trying above all to reconstruct the conditions of bilingualism the represented the very underpinnings of these effects and contacts. It is precisely because bilingualism was in this period a widespread and productive phenomenon that it does not make much sense to allow our perspectives to be conditioned by the boundaries that separate individual academic disciplines. The collaboration among Germanists and Slavists working in diverse areas of expertise can provide a crucial contribution to the reconstruction of a stage of undoubtedly primary importance in the process of linguistic osmosis that for centuries has characterised this part of Europe.[5]

There exists a further Church Slavonic text which has long been known but whose significance – it seems to me – has not yet been sufficiently grasped in all its linguistic and historical magnitude: the Church Slavonic translation of the *Gospel of Nicodemus* or *Acts of Pilate*, a 'best-seller' of European medieval literature, written between the 4th and 6th century and subsequently translated into many Eastern and Western languages.[6] At issue here, in fact, is a text translated not from Greek – as is the case with the majority of Church Slavonic versions of every period – but from Latin. This fact allows us to link this translation to the *Kievan Leaflets* and to consider it a Church Slavonic work connected with other works of Western origin sensu lato. Yet it is the language of the translation that captures our attention, with a series of very rare and even absolutely unique equivalences between Latin and Old Church Slavonic (OCS) which clearly reflect an Old High German (OHG) influence (e.g. *discipulus* – OCS *jun'i* as OHG *jungiro*; *sed*, *nisi* – OCS *razv´* as OHG *suntar*; *sacerdos* – OCS *zakoni`niku`* as OHG *êwarto*; *inferus* – OCS *pi`ku`lu`* as OHG *peh*, and so forth).[7] The important fact here is that no translation of the *Gospel of Nicodemus* is documented in Old High German (the first translation will be made later, in Middle High German) and the translator thus was compelled to base his translation on the Latin text. At first glance we could think that we are dealing here not only with a bilingual translator, but even with a trilingual one, given that – in addition to Latin, from which he was translating, and Church Slavonic, the target language of his translation – he seems to have had (at least indirectly) a good knowledge of Old High German. Indeed, his Church Sla-

---

[5] Roberto Gusmani: L'influsso tedesco nella formazione della terminologia religiosa slava. In: Lingue e culture in contatto nel mondo antico e altomedievale. In: Atti dell'VIII Convegno internazionale di linguisti tenuto a Milano nei giorni 10-13 settembre 1992. Brescia 1993, pp. 63-76, here on p. 76.

[6] The first two parts, relating Jesus' trial (ch. 1-11) and the adventures of Joseph of Arimathea (ch. 12-16), were composed in Greek before the last quarter of the 4th century, whereas the third part (ch. 17-27), which recounts Christ's Descent into Hell, might have been originally written in Latin during the 6th century; see L'Évangile de Nicodème ou Les Acts faits sous Ponce Pilate. Introduction et notes par R. Gounelle et Z. Izydorczyk. Traduction par R. Gounelle, à partir d'un texte mis au point par Z. Izydorczyk. Turnhout 1997, pp. 101-119. See also the impressive bibliography of more than 1000 titles gathered by the same two authors: Thematic Bibliography of the Acts of Pilate. In: Z. Izydorczyk (ed.), The Medieval Gospel of Nicodemus. Texts, Intertexts, and Contexts in Western Europe. Tempe, Arizona 1997, pp. 419-519; and Thematic Bibliography of the Acts of Pilate: Addenda and Corrigenda. *Apocrypha* 11 (2000), pp. 259-292.

[7] Some Germanisms (but by far not all of them) have been pointed out by Alain Vaillant: L'Évangile de Nicodème. Texte slave et texte latin. Genève – Paris 1968, pp. XIX and XII.

vonic reveals a profound German influence, which is manifested above all in the high frequency of semantic calques (Lehnbedeutungen). And precisely the fact that the number of calques (and not loan words) is so considerable presupposes a highly bilingual German-Slavic milieu.

We are faced here with two possible explanations as to the origin of the unique language blend of this translation. The simpler one is of a kind of 'scribal dialect' specifically invented for this translation by the translator himself. However, taking into account the relative length of the text and the importance of an apocryphal work quite often considered a quasi-canonical text in the Middle Ages, it seems more realistic to imagine that the translator used a type of Church Slavonic influenced by a particular Slavic dialect, which in its turn had undergone a strong German influence, so that his translation in the end might have been comprehensible to the 'audience' of readers familiar with this dialect. This second thesis could be confirmed through the detection of traces of spoken language in the translation itself,[8] but this analysis, part of the thorough investigation of all aspects of the language of the translation, is a task still to be fulfilled.

Directly relevant to the geographical frame of this volume is another problem that was quite frequently discussed in the secondary literature: the problem of where the Church Slavonic *Gospel of Nicodemus* was translated. Some scholars have placed the translation of our 'Gospel' in Bohemia, other scholars have proposed Croatian origins, and still other scholars have hypothesised a Slovenian provenance. I have no particular theory or hypothesis (either new or old) to put forward here, but would rather like to insist on the fact that the translator operated in a zone of strong Slavonic-German bilingualism. As to the question of dating, a translation such as this one already presupposes the creation of Old Church Slavonic on the part of Constantine and Methodius, and it certainly cannot be attributed to a period prior to their arrival (in 863). But it cannot be much later considering the very archaic Church Slavonic language used by the translator; in fact, most Slavists agree with a dating to the 10th century.[9]

While for the moment it does not seem possible to situate the translation in space and time exactly, the possibility cannot be totally excluded that something more precise might be said on this topic in the future thanks to a more comprehensive and careful study of the language used by the translator. At any rate, it seems difficult to think about a place very distant from the Alpine-Adriatic region or rather Carantania (in its medieval extension), where the contact between the German and Slavic population was particularly close in those times. Finally, if the hypothesis that the Church Slavonic *Gospel of Nicodemus*

---

[8] See Vaillant, L'Évangile, p. XVIII, where in connection with one particular construct (adverb plus verb) the French Slavist speaks of the influence exerted by a Romance language or by German on the (translator's) spoken language.

[9] See, for example, the opinion of Vaillant, L'Évangile, p. IX: "La traduction slave sur le latin doit être du Xe siècle, et elle restitute donc un manuscrit qui par sa date n'est pas sans intérêt."

really reflects some particular Slavic dialect of this period should be proven correct, we would then be in a position to speak about the existence of a kind of "hidden minority" (a particular group of Slavic speakers, which has not been considered in research until now and for which of course we would have no other written testimony except this one text). Multilingualism, as well as multiethnicity, can be regarded as the proper context for favouring the appearance of such a rarity like the Church Slavonic *Gospel of Nicodemus*, which has preserved for us a concrete situation of German-Slavic bilingualism and which seems indeed to offer some new insights in the history of German-Slavic language contact in the High Middle Ages.

Bibliography

L'ÉVANGILE DE NICODEME OU LES ACTS FAITS SOUS PONCE PILATE. Introduction et notes par R. Gounelle et Z. Izydorczyk. Traduction par R. Gounelle, à partir d'un texte mis au point par Z. Izydorczyk. Turnhout 1997, pp. 101-119.

GOUNELLE, Rémi/IZYDORCZYK, Zbigniew: Thematic Bibliography of the Acts of Pilate. In: Z. Izydorczyk (ed.), The Medieval Gospel of Nicodemus. Texts, Intertexts, and Contexts in Western Europe. Tempe, Arizona 1997, pp. 419-519.

GOUNELLE, Rémi/IZYDORCZYK, Zbigniew: Thematic Bibliography of the Acts of Pilate: Addenda and Corrigenda. *Apocrypha* 11 (2000), pp. 259-292.

GUSMANI, Roberto: L'influsso tedesco nella formazione della terminologia religiosa slava. In: Lingue e culture in contatto nel mondo antico e altomedievale. In: Atti dell'VIII Convegno internazionale di linguisti tenuto a Milano nei giorni 10-13 settembre 1992. Brescia 1993, pp. 63-76.

PETERS, Bernhard: Deutsch-slawischer Lehnwortaustausch. In: W. Mitzka (ed.), Wortgeographie und Gesellschaft. Festgabe für Ludwig Erich Schmitt zum 60. Geburtstag, Berlin 1968, pp. 624-643.

SCHAEKEN, Jos /BIRNBAUM, Henrik: Die altkirchenslavische Schriftkultur. Altkirchenslavische Studien II. Munich 1999.

SCHUCHARDT, Hugo: Slawo-deutsches und Slawo-italienisches. Mit Schuchardts übrigen Arbeiten zur Slawistik und mit neuen Registern, ed. by D. Gerhardt. Munich 1971.

VAILLANT, Alain: L'Évangile de Nicodème. Texte slave et texte latin. Genève – Paris 1968.

WOLFRAM, Herwig: Conversio Bagoariorum et Carantonorum. Das Weißbuch der Salzburger Kirche über die erfolgreiche Mission in Karantanien und Pannonien. Vienna et al. 1979.

ZAGIBA, Franz: Das Geistesleben der Slaven im frühen Mittelalter. Vienna et al. 1971.

ZWISCHEN ROM UND BYZANZ. Leben und Wirken der Slavenapostel Kyrillos und Methodios nach den Pannonischen Legenden und der Klemensvita. Translated by J. Bujnoch. Graz et al. 1972.

List of Contributors

Dr. Klaus-Jürgen Hermanik is collaborator at the Institute for History at the University of Graz; his current research project on "Identity Management of the Germans and Hungarians in South-East Central Europe" is funded by the FWF Austrian Science Fund. Hermanik studied German Philology and Ethnology/Cultural Anthropology in Graz. From 2001-2004 he was collaborator in the project "Hidden minorities between Central Europe and the Balkans", funded by the FWF Austrian Science Fund. His main interests are: the small ethnic groups of Slovene descent in the Austrian Federal Province of Styria and the ethnomanagement of the German and Hungarian speaking ethnic groups on the Western Balkans, in Hungary and Romania. Hermanik co-edited the memoirs of Anton Šantel on the ethnic situation of Southern Styria in the 19th century.

Marijana Jakimova MA was born in Silistra/Bulgaria and works in Graz. She received her MA as cultural scientist at the University Kliment Ohridski in Sofija and likewise as historian at the University of Graz. During the last years Jakimova investigated the history of the Bulgarian gardeners and of other South-East European migrants in Austria. She was also collaborator of the project "Hidden minorities between Central Europe and the Balkans." Now she prepares her doctoral dissertation on "Immigration from South-East Europe to Austria in the interwar period."

Dr. Marija Jurić Pahor is higher scientific collaborator the Institute for Ethnic Studies in Ljubljana She studied pedagogy and sociology at the Universities of Klagenfurt and Ljubljana. She lives and works mainly in Trieste. Her research fields are interculturalism; minorities (especially the Slovenes in Carinthia and Italy); gender, nationalism, and ethnicity; fascism and Nazism in the generation transfer. She wrote the monograph "Narod, identiteta, spol" (Nation, Identity, Gender) and co-edited the books "Zweisprachigkeit und Identität," (1988) and "Auf der Suche nach hybriden Lebensgeschichten." (2005)

Dr. Duška Knežević-Hočevar, sociologist and anthropologist, is head of the Sociomedical Institute at the Scientific Research Centre in Ljubljana; she is Assistant Professor, and Module Coordinator for *Anthropology of Ethnicity, Nationalism and Boundaries* at the Institutum Studiorum Humanitatis (ISH) – Ljubljana Graduate School of the Humanities. Her research interest, among other, concentrate on anthropology of ethnicity and nationalism, anthropology of international borders and demographical anthropology. She published the book, actually her doctoral thesis, "Družbena razmejevanja v dolini zgornje Kolpe" (Social boundaries in the upper Kolpa Valley).

Dr. Oto Luthar is director of the Scientific Research Centre in Ljubljana and Professor at the Institute for Cultural Studies at the University of Nova Gorica.

He has authored and edited books on the theory of history and historiography ("Masters and Muses", "Between Chronology and Fiction"), history of ideas ("Don't Send a Word of Sorrow") and textbooks for civic education ("Liberal Democracy, Citizenship & Education", "Restless Hearts"). He has been a Fulbright Scholar at Yale University.

Dr. Tanja Petrović, sociolinguist, is Assistant Professor and head of the Institute for Cultural Studies at the University of Nova Gorica. In 2006 she published her doctoral dissertation on "Not here – not there: The Serbs in Bela krajina and their language ideology in the process of linguistic exchange" in Ljubljana and the book "The Ritual Toast of the Balkan Slavs" at the Serbian Academy of Sciences and Arts. She has published several articles on anthropological linguistics, language contacts, linguistic identity and language ideology of small ethnic and refugee groups.

Dr. Mirjam Polzer-Srienz studied jurisprudence at the University of Graz. Her doctoral dissertation was on "the Representation of Ethnic Groups in Forming the Volition of State: Austria and Slovenia in Juridical Comparison." From 1998-2000 she was collaborator of a research project on the issue of Kosovo, and from 2000-2003 she was funded by the Hertha Firnberg Program for highly qualified women at the Institute for Political Studies in Innsbruck. 2005-2007 she was holder of the Marie-Curie Fellow Intra-European Fellowship "Conflict prevention through integration: The participation of ethnic minorities in political decision-making processes – The case of Roma in South-East Europe". Since 2004 she is director of the community of interests of the Green Party in the provincial diet of Carinthia. Her focus is on policy and public law in South-East Europe, minority and Human Rights, and comparative jurisprudence.

Dr. Christian Promitzer is Assistant Professor at the Department for South-East European History of the University of Graz. He wrote his dissertation on a former Slovene community of the Austrian Federal Province of Styria and was the leader of the project "Hidden minorities between Central Europe and the Balkans." Promitzer published on the South Slavs in the Austrian imagination, the concept of "Hidden Minorities", and on the social history of medicine in South-East Europe.

Dr. Mojca Ravnik is Senior Research Fellow at the Institute of Slovenian Ethnology at the Scientific Research Centre in Ljubljana. She is ethnologist, but has also a MA in art history. She is author of two monographs – "Galjevica", which is on urban ethnology, and "Bratje, sestre, strniči, zermani. Družina in sorodstvo v vaseh v Slovenski Istri" (Brothers, Sisters, Cousins. Kinship and family in villages of Slovene Istria). Ravnik's research focus is on urban ethnology, architectural heritage, emigration and immigration, and on family and kinship relations in border regions.

Dr. Ivica Šarac is Assistant Professor at the Department of History of Philosophical Faculty/University of Mostar. He received his doctorate of Church History and Ecumenism at the University of Graz with a dissertaton on the Catholic Church in Croatia during the Second World War. His scientific fields of interest are national and religious identities in South-East Europe, concentrating on deviating confessional groups in Dalmatia (Catholic Serbs) and in Western Herzegovina (Muslims).

Dr. Biljana Sikimić is Senior Research Fellow at the Institute for Balkan Studies of the Serbian Academy of Sciences and Arts, Belgrade. 2002-2005 she was head of the project "Ethnolinguistic and sociolinguistic research of refugees and multiethnic societies on the Balkans." In 2004 Sikimić edited a volume on "Skrivene manjine na Balkanu/Hidden Minorities in the Balkans." Her research interests are on anthropological linguistics, language of folklore, Diaspora, and multilingualism.

Dr. Eduard G. Staudinger is Assistant Professor at the Dempartment for Contemporary History of the University of Graz. He has been mentor and collaborator in the project "Hidden minorities between Central Europe and the Balkans." His research concentrates on central topics of Austrian and Styrian history during the 19th and 20th centuries; among these are the British occupation zone in Austria from 1945 to 1955 and a special focus on aspects of living with and at state borders between Slovenia and Austria.

Dr. Giorgio Ziffer is Professor of Slavonic philology and head of the Department of Languages and Cultures of Eastern and Central Europe at the University of Udine. His main scientific interests concentrate on the Cyrillo-Methodian literature, the literature of Kievan Rus', the textual philology of Church Slavonic literature, the history of the Church Slavonic language, and translations from Italian into Slavonic languages up to 1800.

Index